T0224285

Domain-Driven Laravel

Learn to Implement Domain-Driven Design Using Laravel

Jesse Griffin

Apress®

Domain-Driven Laravel: Learn to Implement Domain-Driven Design Using Laravel

Jesse Griffin
Spring Valley, CA, USA

ISBN-13 (pbk): 978-1-4842-6022-7   ISBN-13 (electronic): 978-1-4842-6023-4
https://doi.org/10.1007/978-1-4842-6023-4

Managing Director, Apress Media LLC: Welmoed Spahr
Acquisitions Editor: Louise Corrigan
Development Editor: James Markham
Coordinating Editor: Nancy Chen

Cover designed by eStudioCalamar

Cover image designed by Freepik (www.freepik.com)

Distributed to the book trade worldwide by Springer Science+Business Media New York, 1 New York Plaza, New York, NY 10004. Phone 1-800-SPRINGER, fax (201) 348-4505, e-mail orders-ny@springer-sbm.com, or visit www.springeronline.com. Apress Media, LLC is a California LLC and the sole member (owner) is Springer Science + Business Media Finance Inc (SSBM Finance Inc). SSBM Finance Inc is a **Delaware** corporation.

For information on translations, please e-mail booktranslations@springernature.com; for reprint, paperback, or audio rights, please e-mail bookpermissions@springernature.com.

Apress titles may be purchased in bulk for academic, corporate, or promotional use. eBook versions and licenses are also available for most titles. For more information, reference our Print and eBook Bulk Sales web page at http://www.apress.com/bulk-sales.

Any source code or other supplementary material referenced by the author in this book is available to readers on GitHub via the book's product page, located at www.apress.com/9781484260227. For more detailed information, please visit http://www.apress.com/source-code.

Printed on acid-free paper

I want to dedicate this book to my parents, Lori and Wayne. Dad, I know you would be proud of me if you were still here, and I think about you every day. Mom, I don't know where I'd be in life without you, and I could never pay you back for all the help and guidance you've given me over the years.

To my family, I love you guys—thanks for the support. Big shout-out also to Jim and Brenda, who have put up with me for many years, and continue to do so.

I want to thank my editor and reviewers, James and Nancy. Couldn't have done it without you guys. Also, I want to mention Gracie, who kept me motivated throughout the course of writing this book (even though we've gone our separate ways). Thank you.

Table of Contents

About the Author

Jesse Griffin is a seasoned Laravel and Symfony developer who specializes in building e-commerce systems as well as add-ons for a variety of purposes and platforms related to shipping, packaging, warehouse management, inventory control, barcode systems, asset management/tracking, customer tracking, as well as statistics and reporting. He has more than 10 years of professional web application development experience and holds a bachelor's degree in computer science, although he's been programming since he was 9 years old.

About the Technical Reviewer

Zeeshan Chawdhary is an avid technologist, with 14 years of experience in the industry. Having started his career with mobile development with J2ME, he soon ventured into web development, creating robust and scalable web applications. As a chief technology officer, he has led teams to build web and mobile apps for companies such as Nokia, Motorola, Mercedes, GM, American Airlines, and Marriott. He is currently the head of technology for an international team, serving clients with technologies such as Drupal, React, React Native, GraphQL, WordPress, WooCommerce, Laravel, NodeJS, Google Puppeteer, and occasionally .NET. He has also authored books on iOS, Windows Phone, and iBooks, writing his fourth one titled *Practical Laravel* for Apress.

PART I

An Odd Combination

CHAPTER 1

Laying the Foundation

Domain-driven design (DDD) has been around for almost two decades. During this time, it has seen a sharp increase in interest because of its clear guidelines and tactical strategies and approaches to the problems that you might face when developing applications in any industry, particularly complex ones. It is immensely practical in the real world and has provided solutions for what used to be a lack of any standards or practices suggesting how to best go about solving the underlying business's domain-specific problems...the kind you *don't* see in everyday programming and wouldn't even write if it weren't in the context of the domain that your business operates in to achieve a goal (which is probably to make a profit, but may be to service customers, support users, market products, tracking metrics, etc.).

How This Book Is Designed

There is a lot of material to be covered when studying *either* of the two central topics in this book. Laravel and domain-driven design each has its own respective anthologies of blog posts, white papers, books, tutorials, and, of course, practical examples. We will go over some basics of Laravel, but I highly recommend you find some introductory tutorials on the Web so you can get a feel for how the framework's components fit together. A good resource for this is Laracasts.com. I highly recommend checking out at least the starting episodes; or, if you prefer to read rather than watch/listen, you can always do a quick "glerch" (that's a "Google search") for *Intro to Laravel Tutorial*.

However it is that you become familiar with the framework on the level that you will need to apply a domain-driven Laravel application is acceptable. It's from this foundational information that we will develop a practical, real-world example later in the book, which will be set up in a controlled environment using DDD as the backbone of our decision-making. Along the way, I'll give you practical advice and potential patterns to look for when attempting to implement a domain-driven Laravel application.

© Jesse Griffin 2021
J. Griffin, *Domain-Driven Laravel*, https://doi.org/10.1007/978-1-4842-6023-4_1

My hope is that you will find the material digestible as well as useful in a real-life environment and team.

What I don't expect you to be fully knowledgeable in (or even heard of before) is domain-driven design. I take ample page space in this book to describe and define DDD and lay out the concepts in terms of their application to developing web applications. If you are already familiar with DDD's concepts, that's great! That will flatten the learning curve a bit, but it is not a requirement. I will describe some of the *modification*s that had to be made to the original version of DDD to be applicable as a practical approach to developing modern-day web applications (using Laravel as the *means* of implementation), with a core focus being on designing, modeling, and refining the domain layer.

I will show you a variety of best practices throughout the book that are either widely accepted standards regarding software development or my own practices and shortcuts that have taken me a decade or so of working as a professional web developer and more than twice that long researching curiosity-inspired topics (with the help of somewhere in the ballpark of 150 IT and software engineering books I've read so far) to discern this information. Oftentimes, I will demonstrate these concepts in code so you can get a clear understanding of what they are and also give you some context borrowed from SOLID principles. I will provide examples to what would otherwise be a bunch of random suggestions that you probably won't remember, and almost certainly never use in your own projects.

There is a section in this chapter that goes over all the basic tools of the trade and some basic concepts and definitions of important terms that are relevant to the demos and examples given to support all the theory I dish out. On a higher level, however, what I'd like for you to take away from this chapter is an appetite for *construction* (pun intended!). Along with giving you some basic fundamentals on web development so as to empower you to follow along in the theoretical examples we walk through later in the book, it is also my aim to instill within you the desire to learn domain-driven design principles and ideally spark an interest in learning advanced usage and customization of Laravel to make it as flexible as you need it to be for your application.

I will be jumping around a little in this chapter to give you a good sense of what we are attempting to learn here: what is DDD is and how does it relate to the quality of our software? To answer this question, I will introduce you to some important concepts, patterns, and practices that you will need to be successful at modeling real-world domains in software.

Domain-Driven What?

DDD is itself built using a variety of best practices and reliable design patterns, and it has origins stemming from both extreme programming (XP) and agile development. I will introduce to you a few of the more fundamental aspects of DDD, including the software horror that can become reality if these best practices and SOLID patterns are ignored because of either developer ignorance or a poorly managed development effort.

The simplest way I can think of describing DDD is this: it is a series of practical and useful concepts, processes, and techniques that aid in modeling complex software systems in a systematic and structured way by focusing on the core aspects of the underlying business rules in order to manufacture a domain model that truly describes and represents that business in terms of software and then letting that knowledge and insight from repeated discussions and group meetings with the respective domain experts guide the development and construction of the software that is ultimately being built to serve that business's customers or front-end users. DDD basically arose from a gap in the software industry relating to answering the question of how to properly design and develop software that best suits that business's needs. There was no magical manual that gave any sort of standard or basic approaches to constructing applications that are focused on the domain of the application (domain-centric), nor were there any published approaches to learning the ins and outs of a business's core processes enough to construct software that represents it.

Programmers have had design *patterns* in our code toolboxes for many years, although they were never documented as such until 1994 when the Gang of Four published the holy grail of design pattern books, *Design Patterns: Elements of Reusable Object-Oriented Software*. Design patterns serve as an important, core set of practical and repeatable solutions to the common problems that you are likely to face when constructing computer programs. They are well thought out and thoroughly tested ways to tackle the most common aspects of problem scopes you're likely to encounter in virtually any program, in any programming language. One such pattern, the famous *strategy pattern*, is useful when you need to give objects additional behaviors at runtime by encapsulating changes into families of behaviors. Another is the *adapter pattern*, which is used to integrate two unlike interfaces (such as those running on different systems or programmed in different programming languages entirely). If you needed your objects to have dynamic behaviors that could be added or removed at runtime and that follow a similar suite that allowed for aggregation calculations to be placed on said group of objects, you could employ a *decorator pattern*.

5

What we needed was that very same thing for developing solutions—in terms of code—to the ever-growing and vast set of business problems that arose in response to the increase in demand of software development In other words, we needed some sort of approach to developing the *domain layer* of an application so that we could express any such domain (business) model in terms of software. The nature of business problems is that they tend to be very specific, and their respective solutions were products of many years of designing, developing, testing, and refining business processes that are unique to each business, or industry. As such, it was and sill is difficult to establish any sort of standards or best practices to facilitate the development of the most critical aspect of any software project: the domain layer. In contrast, there are mountains of references, toolkits, and frameworks that help in designing the other layers (which may indeed *talk to* and *know about* the domain layer), but they don't encapsulate it. Rather, they surround it. The infrastructure layer is basically the liaison between the application layer and the domain model. It facilitates all the moving parts that are operating on, managing, and otherwise handling the domain objects directly.

What we needed were tactics on how to go about seeking out sources of truth in the companies in which we worked in order to properly model them in software, and tools to help us implement that model in a domain-driven way. The business information isn't always direct or easy to derive, especially in the context of a complex business process spread across multiple components (at least we would hope they are separated into some component structure, but this is not always a reality). In a case where the code in the application is so "stepped on," or beaten up, by the slew of developers over the years forcing its behavior to bend in ways in which it was not intended or designed, implementing a domain-driven approach becomes more difficult. But it is possible to still avoid an entire rewrite of the application (which is almost always a terrible idea). We will explore how to do this later in the book, but the short answer is to use an *anti-corruption layer* to section off portions of the app and then keep replacing legacy code with the smaller sectioned-off ones until the layer absorbs the old code, until no legacy code remains at all.

Architecture

The architecture of a system embellishes the complete structure of the system's domain model including its domain objects, modules, bounded contexts, and the various interactions between them. Architecture is one of the most important things in an application, as it is the foundational fabric in the software and acts as the "support beams" for the rest of the application to be built upon.

What tends to happen in the real world is that these business processes and models are constructed without best practices or proper structure and are used in production because they "work." Don't get me wrong, developers work with what we have and can usually "hack" together something that will indeed "work." However, when we neglect to refactor this code after we've made refinements to the processes themselves or fail to fine-tune any unclear or blurred definitions we may have clarified or to reflect gained insight into the business models and how those insights affect business operations and its software, we are most likely headed toward a "big ball of mud" (or what I call it a big ball of sh...potato pottåto).

A **big ball of mud** is a:

"haphazardly structured, sprawling, sloppy, duct-tape-and-baling-wire, spaghetti-code jungle. These systems show unmistakable signs of unregulated growth, and repeated, expedient repair..."

—Brian Foote

More often than not, these mud balls are built as *monolithic architectures*, ones that lack the notion of a complete separation of concerns on a "platform level" (physical level). Monolithic architectures are self-contained and include within them all concerns of the application (infrastructure, database, application-level, and presentation concerns). We will discuss the architectural layers of software systems later in the chapter.

The opposite of a monolithic application is a microservice. *Microservices* are tiny applications distributed across a variety of different components that together make up a complete, usable system. The setup involved in a microservice architecture is much more dramatic than simply using directory names (which is really all that physically separates the various structures into groups of related ones). The components themselves oftentimes exist on separate platforms, usually on separate machines in the cloud, and implement a variety of strategies aimed at facilitating their usage and enabling communication between themselves and the client (the calling code).

Enter Laravel

One of the core features of DDD is that it is an agnostic approach to designing system architectures. This means it makes no assumptions what framework you are using, what database you decide on, or whether you even use data persistence at all for that matter (if you're a web dev, of course, you most likely do). It is meant to be more of a general approach to designing scalable enterprise systems. So why, then, would I suggest not only the concept of a framework, but a specific *flavor* of one (i.e., Laravel) combined with the concepts and strategies offered in DDD?

This question can be answered with an old expression that proves truer every day: necessity is the mother of invention. I noticed a real-world need for a set of guidelines of how to go about developing complex web systems and some strategies for how to implement a domain-driven application in a *real-world scenario*, without reinventing the wheel and while using some of the more popular tools of the web development trade such as Laravel and Eloquent—allowing them to do what they do best so that we may focus on modeling the business itself and building out a rich domain layer, *one that reflects the needs and requirements of the business it was built to manage.* We will accomplish all this with the tools and concepts that come with DDD, yet tuned for use in a web development project, along with the implementations of those concepts within a Laravel application.

Only lately have the two concepts (domain-driven design and frameworks) come close enough to each other to actually generate enough traction that would suggest it would be useful to have a domain-driven approach to developing web- and Internet-based applications. I made the realization, finally, that Laravel could be used as a medium in which to build out a domain-driven design.

However, because of the way DDD was created and also because of the basic structure of a web application, it doesn't quite mesh well with the idea of using a framework of any type. We will go over many examples of where the clouded area lies in relation to the DDD guidelines. We almost need a sort of custom DDD implementation to be able to work with it on the level that we would need to in order to build web applications using it as a backbone of the domain's design. If we take into consideration that working within a web development context is related to the contextual boundaries within a system that need to operate directly and primarily across the wire. If we look at the categories of knowledge contained within the Technical Strategies pillar of DDD, it is quite obvious that they could exist alongside a Laravel application (i.e., repositories, DTOs, factories, jobs, etc.)... we can actually see that most of DDD's suggested approaches coincide quite well with Laravel's components and inner workings. In this regard, DDD is well suited to shape a web system or Internet application.

The idea of implementing a domain-driven design using the Laravel framework seemed very feasible to me. If I could bend a few of the rules in the strategies and guidelines, I could make the two technologies work well together. Because of this, I will say right off the bat that this is not a true implementation of DDD and all of its different facets, patterns, approaches, and guidelines. DDD requires a lot of work up front, but pays off big time when you have things situated. That being said, I realized that this is not always desirable, especially if you are a startup or are working for a startup. Costs can make or break a startup, and it's not always possible to allocate such a large amount of resources, time, and money into putting into place all the tools, procedures, and architectural structures that will be the product of a deep exploratory analysis of not only the code (if you are already working in a codebase) but of the business's core functions as well.

So, you should be extremely careful with your decision to build an application using the guidelines of DDD: most domains are not complex enough to require the level of complexity that DDD attempts to manage succinctly. Laravel, on the other hand, offers a bite-size approach to crafting an implementation of some domain from a business model. My interest in writing this book lies in the utilization of using the two in combination with each other within the context of a real-world project. However, the decision to go with a DDD-based design must come only after carefully examining the requirements of the domain model and how complex the underlying business model is going to be to represent as software.

Selective Content

What I aim to do, then, is to provide you with the main essentials, tools, and tactics of DDD so you can gain *real* value out of implementing it in your own projects. This is possible because we initially forgo the usual large chunk of information and overhead that is part of traditional DDD—allowing us to focus on the core aspects and tactics needed to get started quickly—and return to these topics later in the book when we do a "deep dive" into both DDD and Laravel.

I also must mention that this is slightly risky when you attempt an implementation of a half-learned DDD implementation. If you start applying all the techniques and technical patterns of DDD willy-nilly, you will end up building things without knowing fully what they do or, worse, will apply a particular technique or pattern in an incorrect context, eventually forcing a big refactor or a complete rewrite. The reason for this is because of the pure size of DDD; there are so many concepts and ideas in the subject itself that it can be relatively easy to misconstrue things or mix up definitions. However, as long as you go about it in a *domain-driven* way, that is, by letting your business requirements and ubiquitous language steer development, the likelihood of this happening is minimal.

Avoiding the Pitfalls

The way I'm going to avoid such a disaster is by discussing the solid foundation of basics that you will need in order to comprehend *why* things are done a certain way or why it is best to implement some architectural component in a particular context. By inculcating the importance of a well-researched and refined ubiquitous language, along with some approaches on *how* to properly build one and how to then begin using it as the basis for which to construct the actual application, I have full confidence that you will have a well-rounded knowledge of domain-driven techniques and will not misuse or abuse them. Believe me, a poor implementation of DDD sometimes equates to *not* having an application at all because you end up having to rewrite the whole damned thing due to one or more of the following:

- Business terms were misrepresented and mixed up in the application due to a lack of any type of "source of truth" as to what a given *business term* really means, or the context in which it is applied.

- Domain experts were not involved when initially creating the system (or its processes), so concepts are applied either incorrectly or not at all—oftentimes causing a cascading domino effect of design issues within the domain layer (and the things that *touch* it) down the road when adding more complex logic to an incorrect business model.

- Due also to a lack of communication with domain experts, many assumptions are made as to what certain business processes do and get implemented wrongly as whatever the developer *thinks they should do*.

- Developers choose *not* to invest in the knowledge discovery or the refinement phase when initially mapping out the domain model and, as a result, build components and modules that solve the wrong problem.

I intend to arm you with the essentials of DDD in terms of its *practical* application in the real world. I will give you advice that I have myself cultivated after 10 years in the industry, and I teach you what "best practices" are and what you get in return for following them. We will learn the foundations of DDD and how to go about implementing a domain-driven model in a practical and feasible way. However, it is not a road easily traveled, and it's not all that difficult to get lost in the vast amount of information and distilled knowledge that the DDD *subject matter* contains.

Going About a Domain-Driven Design

We will go about building our domain models in an organized and thought-out manner that will give structure and form of basis for us to expand on and refine as we learn more and more about the business operations we are trying to model. Additionally, we will develop a ubiquitous language that are core definitions to business terms agreed upon by the entire company. However, a well-built ubiquitous language does not come cheap. It takes many conversations with various department heads, domain experts, developers, and stakeholders to establish clear definitions and boundaries encapsulating the various domain-level components and their interactions that together comprise the meat and potatoes of the business system.

There is a *little* overhead, of course, as with any adoption of any sort of standards, practices, and paradigms that weren't in place prior. After this initial dive into the heart of what DDD really is and how we will go about using it in a real-world scenario, we will implement what we have assimilated from all the various conversations, meetings, and exploratory research using Laravel. We will crunch all the knowledge we've gained in the beginning into a set of documented components and data mappings (i.e., creating an ubiquitous language) and then carve out how we are actually going to lay out the components that will make up an entire working distributed system with a model-driven design, well-documented policies and definitions, and well-tested code, and that will be built using tried and tested best practices that you can use in a real-world project.

That overhead comes in the form of learning and understanding the basic tools of the trade. I will briefly mention any tools or services I use on a daily basis and provide recommendations for alternatives so you get a good idea of what it's like to code in the real business world. Also, I hope to give you some ideas on how to increase your own productivity and quality of your work.

We will also be going over various best practices that could be implemented and what ends up happening to the codebase and the project when you ignore them.

The first few sections will get you up to speed on some of the more basic pieces we will need to actually put this machine into practice (in a real-world scenario) and get out of it an application with a model that has been developed using DDD's procedures and techniques and that is based on well-thought-out and implemented strategies and core best practices that will ensure it can handle any changes or updates that the business might need to make later.

An Interesting Combination

A key to success in adopting a domain-driven approach in a web development application is to not reinvent the wheel. We will start out focusing on strategies and tactics involved in creating a ubiquitous language specifically tuned to a specific business model so that we may use it to drive the development of the entities, value objects, and domain-level components, which we later implement surrounding services and infrastructure around—all while maintaining a clear separation of concerns and, most importantly, allowing our business rules and core processes to not only guide our development efforts but also create structure and give substance to code.

If you think about it, web frameworks—or frameworks in general—all aim to reduce the amount of time required to build applications by providing facilities to help manage the *flow* of the application that, in our case, is the request/response lifecycle. There are also a number of components that help manage the various aspects typical of a web development project: validation, authentication, database models, etc. All of this functionality is there so that you *don't have to* reinvent the wheel. What this allows us to do is focus almost entirely on the domain layer, which is important.

Eloquent ORM

One significant component that is included in a data definition language (DDL) goes against the practices and values inside DDD. The inclusion of the Eloquent ORM (allowed only by slightly bending the DDD suggestion of not having one) will allow us to do many neat things.

- Hooking up our domain events with the Eloquent lifecycle, allowing our models to emit specific domain events automatically or when something happens that we care about

- Creating relationships between models easily, enabling us to create and manage our domain models and query our database using an expressive syntax that makes interactions between them straightforward

- Setting up our entities and models for cascading updates (any *relational* models that have been modified during the update of a given model also get updated)

- Extending Eloquent's `Model` class, allowing us to inherit a bunch of cool features that are shipped with Eloquent

  - Mass assignment

  - Query scopes

  - Eager loading

  - Collections

  - Model events

  - Model observers

- A validation component that will make sure our models are in a valid, consistent state and have the proper restrictions in place to prevent erroneous usage

One of the most important tools for developing a domain-driven design in Laravel (on the "code side" of things) is Eloquent. Eloquent is an active record–based ORM that offers a whole slew of cool features and tools that are baked in (and indeed come for free in Laravel). These are some key things that we very much need to pursue our goal of a DDL application.

In modern-day programming, the tendency has grown toward devising a split of an object's *data* and its *behaviors.* The way this is achieved is by separating the raw *data* an object contains into a specialized class called a *domain transfer object* (DTO). Although we go over DTOs in extensive detail later in the book, for now understand that it's a basic object with getter and setter methods for every property that exists on the object that needs to be either retrieved or stored. It holds only data and not behavior.

I know this is going to sound odd and may indeed go against everything your inner programmer says is correct, but, in Eloquent, entities and their DTO counterparts are more or less mixed in a practical fashion and come for free inside any PHP object extending Eloquent's Model class. Now, that's not to say you *can't* have an independent DTO layer between your persistence layer and the ORM, but it really would be a pointless effort because all you would be doing is rewriting features that already exist in Eloquent's abstract Model class. If you ever wanted a model's raw database representation, you'd simply access whichever field it is directly from the model. If, however, you wanted a list of all the properties that exist on a Model object and their corresponding raw values that have not been modified by that class's accessors (similar to what you would find in a DTO), you could just use Eloquent's toArray() method.

Eloquent Model Example

Note   We're going to look past the fact that the design of the model in this example is flawed and could have been approached in a more methodical manner than I depict here, but it serves as a good demonstration for the current context.

Let's say you have a Customer model (and a corresponding customer table in the database, which has a phone field (containing the customer's phone number) and a phone_type field, containing either a 1 to indicate a home phone, a 2 to indicate a cell phone, or a 3 for a work phone. Using Eloquent, we could implement the class shown in Listing 1-1 to represent a Customer object.

Listing 1-1. Sample Customer Class Implementation

```php
<?php
namespace App\Models;
use Illuminate\Database\Eloquent\Model;
class Customer extends Model
{
    public $table = 'customers';
    protected $fillable = ['name', 'phone', 'phone_type'];
    }
```

Basically, here we have a public $table property that tells Eloquent the corresponding table in MySQL in which an object of this class would represent a single database table row. The $fillable property is a list of fields on that table that you want to enable a feature called *mass assignment*, which we cover more extensively in later chapters.

Table 1-1 provides a few sample records in the database.

Table 1-1. *Sample Records from Table customers*

id	name	phone	phone_type
1	Jesse Griffin	6197779125	1
2	Eric Evans	9998887777	2
3	Taylor Otwell	777888999	3

Listing 1-2 provides a quick demo of how the Customer model would be used by client code.

Listing 1-2. Sample Code Retrieving a Customer Record from the Database and Acting on It

```php
<?php

use App\Models\Customer;

$customer = Customer::first(); //gets the first in the db
                              //(with the lowest id)
echo $customer->phone;
//returns "6197779125"

echo $customer->phone_type;
//returns "1"
```

Note Eloquent's abstract Model class has numerous convenience methods on it such as first(), load(), intersect(), makeHidden(), only(), and many more. We'll explore these features in Chapter 14, but for a list of such methods available to you, check out http://laravel.com/docs/6.x/eloquent-collections#available-methods.

Now, let's say that we want to make a customer's phone type return value be returned dynamically. For instance, we may want to show a nice, pretty English representation of the phone type when displaying it in a template somewhere (most likely on the user's profile configuration page). There will be other times, however, that we want to use the raw *database value* that is stored inside that corresponding field in the table, say, for a comparison or precheck before executing additional logic on it.

There are multiple ways to approach this problem *without Eloquent*. Usually this entails defining some type of DTO that will basically act as a *transient object* that represents a given customer row in the database. These DTOs are said to be *transient* because they are *passed* around the application in a particular form, such as the one described earlier. Most often, they are used for transforming data objects into responses that get sent to the user or for custom-tuning API responses. That could be an adequate solution that would maintain a clear separation between the data layer and the application layer, but you would be basically separating two *forms* of the *same* object, which is generally considered bad practice.

For example, when designing a database schema, you would not want the fields `customer_type_name` *and* `customer_type_id` to both exist within the *same table*. That would be duplicating data in a redundant manner that isn't desirable.

Note   Use this as a hint to what should be refactored in the example I'm giving you regarding the `Customer` model.

All that aside, you would still be left with the need to implement *how* it does the *transforming part*, which is typically accomplished by a transformer.

Note   A *transformer* is a class dedicated to changing the values of properties of a specific object class so as to represent them in different ways.

Think about it, what do we really *need* the model to be able to do? In short, we need it to change what a particular property's return value is; we need a different *form* of the property. In the previous example, we want one form to be an English-readable word and the other to be a straight raw database value. The thing to realize is this: we are dealing with different *forms* of the same database object. The only difference is the way they are presented to clients that utilize them; they represent the same database entity. If that is the case, I don't see a reason to separate these behaviors.

As an added bonus, let's say we also want the name value to be returned with the first letter capitalized so we can display it properly on a web page without any additional formatting logic. Luckily for us, Eloquent provides an all-purpose solution for all of the concerns described using some built-in features of Eloquent: mutators and accessors. See Listing 1-3.

Listing 1-3. The Eloquentized Customers Class

```php
<?php

namespace App\Models;

use Illuminate\Database\Eloquent\Model;

class Customer extends Model
{
    public $table = 'customers';
    protected $fillable = ['name','phone','phone_type'];

    /**
    * Accessor returning the name with capital first letter
    */
    public function getNameAttribute($name)
    {
        return ucfirst($name);
    }

    /**
     * Accessor returning English version of phone_type
    */
    public function getPhoneTypeAttribute($phone_type)
    {
        switch ($phone_type) {
            case 1:
                return "home phone";
                break;
```

```
        case 2:
            return "cell phone";
            break;
        case 3:
            return "work phone";
            break;
        default:
            throw new Exception("dang!");
        }
    }
}
```

In Listing 1-3, we've added two new methods: getNameAttribute() and getPhoneTypeAttribute(). These are both referred to as *accessors*. They allow us to reference the given property on the model and automatically call the corresponding accessor (if any) defined on the model to return a specific *form* of that property. Listing 1-4 shows an example of using this model.

Listing 1-4. The Client Code for the New Eloquentized Customer Class

```php
<?php

use App\Models\Customer;

$customer = Customer::find(2); //retrieve customer Eric Evans
echo $customer->phone_type;
//displays "cell phone"

echo $customer->getAttribute('phone_type');
//displays the raw database value, "2"
```

As you can see, we have successfully added a level of dynamicity to our model by specifying accessors on the model class and writing the logic needed to transform the original value, which gets called immediately upon requesting the given property's value on the model via a *direct attribute* (i.e., $customer->{field_name}).

We were also able to keep the original database value intact and maintain the integrity of our data, *without even trying*, thanks to the abstract model's internal attributes array.

Note   Under the hood, this is made possible by the `Customer` model's internal `$attributes` array. This array holds the actual values *as they exist in the database*. The values can be saved in a similar fashion as accessors, only by modifying the value before it enters the database, using what's called a *mutator*.

This also indicates that we always have the database values, in their raw form, saved to this internal `$attributes` array, and we can access these values by using `$this->attributes['property_name']`.

I've found that using this approach dispels the need to implement separate DTO objects for each of your models (and the transformers that go with them), *unless* of course you were dealing with an overly complex domain that could have many different transformations of the object's data across a variety of contexts. In that instance, a full DTO and transformer implementation may be a viable solution.

The only drawback (if you'd even consider it one) is that Eloquent, by nature, mixes the infrastructure layer and parts of the domain layer to provide an all-encompassing solution that almost blurs the lines between the layers themselves. However, because of the straight power, expressive syntax, and easy-to-understand features in Laravel, it is worth blurring a few boundary lines between our application's layers. This is another example of how Laravel is more or less not fully compatible with the approaches of domain-driven design.

The key point to always keep in mind here is that *we are letting the domain lead the architectural and application decisions that ultimately drive the development effort and contribute to its realization of a rich and elegant domain model* that truly captures the needs and requirements of the business they represent.

Customizing DDD for Web Development

It is important to note in a "pure" DDD implementation is that the domain layer (and the models within it) are *dumb to the outside world that uses them.* The issue here is that in Web Development, we are going to have to rely on other code to handle the basic functionality and foundational operations involved in a web application. The notion in DDD regarding dependencies is to avoid them as much as possible... We need a way to better express this notion in terms that can be useful from a web development standpoint.

In the approach that I take in this book, this is not *exactly* the case. Instead, I bend the rules a little bit to make way for the Eloquent ORM. This component is important enough that it merits the adjustment that I have to make to the way DDD approaches the system's design. On an architectural level, the key difference is that domain models in Eloquent come with a database abstraction layer (DBAL) that can be used for (more or less) manually writing custom SQL queries *and* an active record implementation that facilitates the management of the model on an object level. What's more, you get an expressive syntax that allows you to elegantly work with entity relationships, perform inline mutations and attribute casting, set up eager loading, hook into Eloquent lifecycle events, and construct seamless filters using global and local scopes as constraints against all the objects residing in the underlying model's corresponding table in the database (denoted by its protected `$table` property).

Although I may have whetted your appetite for Eloquent with this example scenario, we won't be diving headfirst into Eloquent until later in the book. The one downside of the decision to use Eloquent as a means of expressing domain-driven models is that it violates the self-encompassing domain standards of DDD. This is just one example of things that I had to modify to fit into the context of developing domain-driven web applications. The violation is most certainly justified, as you will see, because the DDD that is implemented with Laravel and Eloquent work well together as a practical solution for developing web applications (as you have just witnessed, which was the tip of the iceberg).

Customizing Laravel for DDD

Domain-driven design, in the regular sense of the art, suggests that the groundwork of an application's lower-level components (the ones that, for example, govern the connection and configuration required to connect to a data store) be built around the domain layer (in that case, the infrastructure layer). That means we must also hand-build the plumbing code that facilitates these models on a persistence level, an application level, and a domain level—basically from the ground up. When you break down all the various structures involved in doing such a thing, you are left with the requirement to develop various driver implementations, DTO-level objects, ORM-type components such as entity managers, repositories, and a slew of other low-level objects that would otherwise be necessary to build to allow the models able to talk to services and persist captures data.

What we need, then, is a method of developing cloud-based solutions in a scalable and dynamic way that truly provides solutions to core business processes for which it was intended to do. It would be nice to have a clear-cut process and vision of a roadmap that could be followed when building custom applications in an enterprise-level architecture—one that uses best practices and allows the underlying business logic (i.e., the domain model/domain layer) to drive the development and refinement of a rich and powerful domain. A core necessity in defining a ubiquitous language (a prerequisite to a domain-driven design) is to have a solid grasp on the domain information yourself by constantly referring to the business's domain experts in your field/business/organization in order to get clear definitions of the business objects that the rest of the application may use to carry out whatever services and operations that it needs in respect to the domain layer.

That being said, it would only make sense to make use of the most popular and modern tools available that make web development easier, faster, and better. Enter Laravel. Laravel provides various implementations of the most common components that you will need to build when developing any web-based application. It is built using best practices and is completely open source, making its internals easy and quick to modify to change the behavior of the framework. It comes also with a code generator that can be invoked by a simple command to build complete controllers, API resources, models, jobs, and a whole bunch of other stuff we may use at our will.

The Problem with Laravel's Stock Installation

There is one important aspect of Laravel that does not mesh well with the domain-driven design mantra, and that would be its directory and namespace structure. Laravel is initially set up to be what is known as a monolithic application—all components of it are loosely coupled and promote best practices, but within a monolithic structure. This is a problem, because DDD is meant to be used to create *distributed* systems in which the various components may not even know about each other. This is the central goal and concern of the microservice architecture.

In the default Laravel installation, for instance, you will find that it, too, has a monolithic structure with directory names (and namespaces because of PSR-4) relative to the concerns of the *application* and not necessarily the *domain*. Figure 1-1 provides a look at a common Laravel directory structure out of the box (with descriptions).

├── **app** *main namespace in the application where most of the custom logic is held*

│ ├── **Console**   *console commands ran using the **artisan** program*

│ ├── **Exceptions**   *any context-specific exceptions*

│ ├── **Http** *houses http-transport classes*

│ │ ├── **Controllers**   *controller classes - routes point here*

│ │ │ └── **Auth**   *auth-specific controllers (login/logout, change password, etc)*

│ │ └── **Middleware**   *application wide middleware layer (session management logging and other per-request specific logic)*

│ └── **Providers**   *holds service container specifics for the package*

├── **bootstrap**   *compiled files required on framework bootstrap*

│ └── **cache**   *a cache of all classes in the app combined into one file*

├── **config**   *configuration and environment specific settings stored here*

├── **database**   *classes interacting with or relating to the database*

│ ├── **factories**   *provides testing*

│ ├── **migrations**   *houses complete database-specific schematics for the app's schema*

│ └── **seeds**   *records to populate the database to use for testing applications*

├── public   *the root web folder (contains index.php)*

├── resources

│ ├── js

Figure 1-1. *Default Laravel structure*

```
|  |    └── components    holds VueJS files (optional frontend framework)

|  ├── lang    language specific files (translation files)

|  └── views    blade template files - frontend template engine that comes w/
                Laravel

├── routes    application's routing files

├── storage    cache files, logs, minified laravel class files

|  ├── framework    internal laravel files

|  |    ├── cache    framework cache

|  |    ├── sessions    stored session files (if using the filesystem driver for
                        sessions)

|  └── logs    production and development log files

└── tests    application tests

    ├── Feature    feature, or integration tests

    └── Unit    unit tests
```

Figure 1-1. *(continued)*

A core aspect of Laravel that I had to modify is the directory and namespace structure. Because it's an all-encompassing framework (one that aims at implementing *all* concerns of the application in a single, monolithic structure), Laravel is broken down into application-specific boundaries—sectioned-off groups of classes that are related to corresponding application concerns, such as logging, making API requests, or managing authentication and access control.

Database layer concerns also should be separated from any logic that uses it or relies on it to perform their own duties. The separation of concerns help to solidify this way of thinking and serves as one of the more important guidelines of development. Ignoring the separation of concerns rule can end up costing a lot more than just messy, tangled code, with functionality being stuffed into a plethora of services spanning across several architectural boundaries and departments is a common scenario that occurs due to a lack of separation. Such projects may or may not be separated at all by domain and may be clumped into an all-encompassing, monolithic structure that is difficult to work with and maintain.

When the core business logic of the application is stored primarily inside the service layer, it is known as an *anemic service layer*. On a higher level, this correlates to the age-old mantra "Fat Controller, Skinny Model." For the purposes of our discussion, think of an anemic service layer as taking a "Fat Service, Skinny Model" approach—which turns out to be equally as counterproductive. Instead, what we will focus on in this book is how to approach modeling the domain in more of a "Fat Model, Skinny Controller" or "Fat Model, Skinny Controller" manner. When we place our domain logic within the confines of a service, we leave the door open for future development errors because developers (or anyone else for that matter) may forget one of the steps in the service when similar functionality within that service is needed elsewhere in the application. Long story short, it is better to place most business logic within the models themselves. This is my opinion, and we will be discussing this notion in more detail later in the book.

When to Use DDD on Your Project

Domain-driven design works best for complex applications involving 30 or more use cases, while a monolithic architecture is better suited for simpler and smaller projects. In fact, using DDD for such a simple application may be overkill and may result in a lot of wasted effort building all the plumbing and supporting structures required for a domain-driven design.

There are numerous reasons why this design and also reasons why this setup is desirable for developing web applications, such as simplicity, ease of deployment, fast time to market, and rapid application development.

A monolithic structure is simple. All classes, events, interactions, and processes are self-contained, living inside the same server, same filesystem, and even the same root directory and namespace. It is simple to work on because you don't have to worry about things like inner-object communication across a network or have to split up the access to various services into separate API calls—or even separate clients for every domain-specific service you need to hit or utilize to accomplish some task. In the context of web development, that implies that all we have to do to use any such service is either import it directly or use a static method (or *facade*—another design pattern) to access it. While simplicity is great when whatever you are developing is itself simple, any project requiring a more robust solution that is larger in size (more than 30 or so use cases) may outgrow the flat architecture that Laravel comes stock with, in which case a *distributed system* may be more appropriate (DDD would be ideal in a situation like that).

Ease of Deployment

Due to the flat structure of the monolithic architecture, all packages, classes, and domain services reside in the same root folder and have their dependencies existing in a different folder under the project root directory. This makes deploying web applications simple. Laravel itself can actually be installed completely from scratch with just a few commands, as shown in Listing 1-5.

Listing 1-5. Sample Laravel Installation via Command Line

```
curl -Ss getcomposer.org/installer | php
php composer.phar global require laravel/installer
laravel new blog
php artisan key:generate
php artisan serve
```

With these five commands, we have successfully downloaded the Laravel framework, installed all its required dependencies, configured a secure application key in base64, and spun up an instant web server using the `artisan serve` command (which just calls PHP's built-in web server to serve the files from a web root that is located inside the `public/` folder), all without breaking a sweat (shout-out to Skrillex).

The deployment process is made even easier when you have separate environments that run your source code. For example, you may have an environment configured to use a test database that you may do your development work on (and probably exists so that if you completely blow it up, you can easily re-create it without affecting anyone else's work or the production site). Development servers typically have a specific configuration that may disable caching, enable displaying on-screen errors, disable public access to or constrict outside IP addresses, and have other development-specific settings that allow programmers to do their actual development work on.

Then, of course, everyone has their functioning, public-facing (or company-facing) production environment that serves your real-world users. Configuration for a production environment most likely will have the production database connected, not show any errors by default and instead write to log files or throw exceptions, and may have caching to maintain a great user experience. Additionally, there could exist additional applications on the company's intranet that our application must have access to that have their own environment settings for production and development.

These situations are common, so Laravel has adopted the dotenv standard to define its configuration parameters, allowing each environment to have its own corresponding configuration that is specified in separate files residing in the root directory of the project and suffixed with the name `.env`. You can create multiple `.env` files for each environment you have: `.env.testing`, `.env.development`, `.env.staging`, etc.

Fast Time to Market

If you are working in the development industry or the IT industry in general, you may or may not have had the chance to work at a startup company. Startups are different from enterprise organizations in that they are much more concerned about costs, the time it takes to get an idea to the market, and the speed of the software development lifecycle. Many times, this means skipping the normal best practices and standards for the sake of time. Startups have needs that are met either as soon as possible or not at all because they operate in a "make it or break it" fashion.

Building even a complex application for such a company may scream to you that a distributed system is going to be the best approach, but given the time, money, and effort it takes to correctly establish a distributed system (and much more to actually achieve a domain-driven design), it is often an impossibility...at least at first. In this instance, it would be better to use a monolithic structure so that you can get the product out there to the clients and end users so that it starts making money. Once that happens, you will be in a much better position to try to convince upper management to do things the right way.

I can't tell you how many times I've walked into (or inherited, rather) a poorly constructed monolithic application with very little documentation that has been running the same outdated technologies, frameworks, and practices for the last ten years and desperately needs to be rewritten and redesigned. The only problem is that, by then, the code is so weighted down and littered with hacks, quick fixes, and work-arounds that a complete rewrite may seem to be a better solution (although this is still most likely not the case). Because the application was never nurtured and its inner structure never refined beyond the initial "get it out now" version, the company usually ends up being in a pretty bad position to do much about it when necessary (like, for example, when modern-day browsers lose support for the very technology that the company's foundational software is based on).

In a worst-case scenario like this, a complete rewrite is actually *required.* Don't get to this point! Refactor and refine the code, making sure it is written with high standards and can withstand changes and refactorings as they are made whenever additional insight into the domain model is learned. How? Keep reading this book for starters.

Rapid Application Development

Internally, Laravel provides out-of-the-box solutions for such concerns as logging, event broadcasting, job and queue facilities, caching, routing, views and templates (via blades), authentication, and authorization. It comes complete with a scaffolding system that makes rapid application development and proof of concepts easy and fast to create. It also comes with a whole bunch of general, all-purpose contracts that provide a set of interfaces that may be implemented to achieve various sorts functionality in a cohesive and loosely coupled manner. There are a bunch of built-in tools to manage API creation including API resources, REST development, request (input) validation, and authentication.

Supporting components like these aid in rapid application development because they are following one of the oldest best practices ever realized: *don't reinvent the wheel.* In doing this, we have cleared the path for us to focus on what really matters to the business: software that adequately meets the needs of the company paying for its creation. Whether it be internal or public-facing, monolithic or distributed, or anything else really, development effort toward a domain-driven design can be made easier and faster by utilizing these premade, "drop-in," plug-and-play solutions offered by frameworks such as Laravel.

Conclusion

In this chapter, we took a look at the various concepts that we will focus on throughout this book. We also went over the aspects of using the Laravel framework as a means of realizing a domain-driven design, including the few rules I had to "bend" to achieve the combination of these two technologies. We took a quick peek at Eloquent ORM and went over its importance in the journey toward domain-driven Laravel.

I may have jumped around a little in this chapter, but that was intentional in order to whet your appetite and, I hope, instill in you a desire to learn more about crafting domain-driven design using Laravel. We went over basic architectures and contrasted the differences between the microservice and monolithic architectures, as well as went over the impact that Laravel has on the ease of deployment of a web application. We briefly discussed DTOs as well as Eloquent and how Eloquent basically comes without the need to provide separate DTOs (unless desired, of course).

CHAPTER 2

Foundational Bootcamp

In this chapter, you will learn some core tools and terminology along with enough conceptual material to get you through the book and be able to comprehend the more difficult and technical chapters that come later in the book. I will also introduce some other key concepts that are not themselves the core principles and standards we will be learning about, but more of the surrounding "plumbing," if you will, that will help you get started in a real-world setting. Some of this chapter will be the theory that I have deemed worthy enough to mention.

We will also learn a bit about the history of web development frameworks and how it is we have arrived at using Laravel as the basis of our application (alongside DDD, of course). We will take a step back and look at things from a wider perspective.

Note Even if you are *not* reading this book to learn new concepts regarding Laravel or DDD, you will still benefit from reading this chapter. It is based on generalities that are true of the software industry.

What Does Being a Developer Mean?

It takes a lot to be a web developer, and a lot more to be a successful one. Over the last few decades, the definition of a web developer hasn't changed much regarding the type of work we do; however, the *way* in which we develop our applications has changed at an increasingly rapid pace, as have the available tools, packages, and frameworks available for building software, and it is showing no signs of slowing down in the future. (It is worth noting that most of today's software follows some type of design pattern or principle, all of which have been around since the early days of programming and were officially recognized as such around 1994 with the Gang of Four's object pattern book.)

© Jesse Griffin 2021
J. Griffin, *Domain-Driven Laravel*, https://doi.org/10.1007/978-1-4842-6023-4_2

These advances have changed the way we think about, build, scale, and track software systems and have ushered in a new era of programming and development. They can be thought of as being part of one of the following categories: software development tooling, software design paradigms and coding standards, and/or general programming best practices. Being a developer means utilizing such tools not because they're the latest and greatest things at the time, but because they add value, speed, and quality to our code and thus the end product. DDD itself was born from a need in the development industry that gave adequate guidance for crafting software specific to a particular domain but was general enough to actually apply to any domain we are trying to model.

Software Development Tooling

Software development tooling (more specifically, web tooling) is third-party software or services you might incorporate into your software development lifecycle—like those used to facilitate the creation of a web-based system. Collectively, the tooling has been a catalyst for the universal realization of the importance of creating high-quality code, successfully changing the programming landscape. The industry itself has made and is making leaps and bounds in the quality of code that gets put into production—so much so that it has helped increase the lifetime of applications because they are built to make the creation of code in a more maintainable manner, allowing them to be easier (or at least less difficult) to extend and collaborate on.

By software tooling, I'm referring to any third-party development tools such as IDEs, online services like Google Cloud and AWS, software versioning systems like Git (which come in proprietary flavors like Bitbucket and GitHub), and various other solutions offered by other companies to enhance some aspect of the development lifecycle (whether they be proprietary/open source, free or paid) and to make developing custom software and web applications more streamlined and reliable and that, most of the time, just so happens to be a naturally repeatable process.

From a developer's perspective, it is more enjoyable to work with modern tools and emerging technologies that keep my attention and offer new and improved breakthroughs and experiences than it is to work with Notepad++ as an IDE. This implies in the bigger picture that being a developer means being efficient in such technologies that add value to the code (which adds value to the business) and helping to facilitate a collaborative effort on a software development project in which multiple developers are working together. Each developer is working with the same codebase but different versions of it, and each is updating their own copy with their portions of changes, usually occurring frequently (multiple times a day is by no means strange), while making sure that they are working with everyone else's most recent code changes so as not to introduce any unforeseen bugs or merge issues when all the updates are incorporated into its final form.

PHP MVC Frameworks and Open Source

The Model-View-Controller (MVC) architecture has been around since the 1970s, where it was first introduced into "official" web applications within the last decade and a half. The open source world has seen some major advances in such MVC frameworks that they are now rolled out as de facto standards when implementing almost any web-based system.

The original frameworks that "changed the game" so to speak were the Zend Framework and Symfony framework (version 1) that were released around 2005. Since then, the PHP MVC playing field has exploded with dozens of different frameworks, the most popular today being the Laravel framework (which uses various Symfony and Zend components).

The majority of MVC PHP frameworks that are popular today are made from building blocks originally released by Symfony's Fabian Pontecier, who created them as loosely coupled, independent, reusable components representing an HTTP request and HTTP response with the intention of encapsulating an object to facilitate entry to the application (request) and an answer to that request (response), which encapsulate and mimic the various HTTP-level attributes, headers, and other metadata present in a typical client-server request/response cycle from the browser (obviously intended for use across the wire).

Integrated Development Environments

When I mention integrated development environments (IDEs), I don't mean things like TextPad, Notepad++, or Sublime. Those are all great programs, but they are not IDEs. They are text editors. Some of them have little plugins available that extend what the text editor can do, but they all just aim at making the editor function like an IDE with such extensions as syntax highlighting, LINT-ing capabilities, code formatters, etc.—basically all the things that a good IDE supports right out of the box.

Currently the two most common IDEs that I have seen used in the web development (PHP development) world are PhpStorm by JetBrains and VSCode by Microsoft. Personally, I use PhpStorm because it has almost everything I need to program in PHP included that will allow me to be a faster, cleaner, and better developer. Plus, the available extensions for Laravel, Symfony, and other commonly used components in the PHP ecosystem make it so I barely have to leave the IDE at all, and they allow me to focus on developing the domain model of the project (more on that later).

Both IDEs come with autocompletion (although PHP uses a more native approach to autocompletion and the handling of different file types). Also, there are a ton of color themes to choose from in both IDEs, which is important when spot-checking for bugs and which makes reading code much easier and more fun (again, maybe I'm just weird, but hey). There are other IDEs, of course; I'm just sharing the ones I've seen most for web development using PHP. The main point is that it increases the speed and correctness of the code by providing quick and easy low-level shortcuts to the IDE's high-level features. One such feature is providing autocomplete functionality for the almost labyrinth-like sea of vendor package namespaces. If you have ever used Composer to manage your dependencies, you know how much of a time-saver autocomplete can really be.

Version Control Systems

Although software versioning has been around forever, the notion of checking in code and pulling changes to the code in a manageable and logical way that accommodates an entire team working on the same project at the same time has never been as easy and straightforward as with the creation of the two main players in the code repositories industry: GitHub and Bitbucket. Both offer similar features, although Bitbucket is free and is not as pretty or feature packed (but does integrate nicely into Atlassian's task management software, Jira). GitHub offers a great interface along with various insights and statistics available on both its users and its projects, along with a beautiful profile page, commonly used to display or show off contributions to open-sourced projects. The Git version control system has become the standard for web development teams and software engineers to track their code.

Advancements in PHP

The languages we use to develop web applications has changed a lot in the past 15 to 20 years. Take, for example, PHP, which started out a scripting language meant to (pre) process hypertext markup and add logic to a logic-less HTML language that is used by browsers to render online content. It didn't support objects, classes, or inheritance until PHP version 4 and didn't really start offering true OOP support until version 5—namespacing didn't even exist until version 5.3! With its release of version 7, we now have such cool built-in features like return type declarations, the null coalescing operator (??), and the spaceship operator (<=>), not to mention a huge increase in performance from its previous versions. In fact, PHP7 has had the largest performance gain than I've ever seen in any new version of any other programming language. PHP has gained enormous popularity and is used today to run the majority of the Web. Here are some companies that utilize PHP for their own applications:

- Slack

- Etsy

- Cloudflare

- Tesla

- Wikipedia

- WordPress

- Tumblr

Frameworks that are built using PHP have become popular enough to be considered de facto standards in creating modern web applications and distributed systems (although the tendency these days is gravitating away from PHP toward such server-side languages as NodeJS, which utilizes JavaScript as its primary language, yet re-engineered for server-side programming). Even though PHP has been seeing a decline in overall usage recently, based on its hold on the Internet as a foundational language and the fact that 80 percent of it runs on PHP, I don't see it going away anytime soon. There will always be a need to support (and eventually convert) legacy systems, so PHP is never a bad thing to become proficient with.

Speaking of JavaScript, front-end development has come far in just the last few years. ECMAScript 6 has been the talk of the town for the last few years; so has the introduction of such groundbreaking technologies as React, Material, VueJS, and Angular, along with such conceptual advancements as the redux pattern and other state management concerns that bring a more sophisticated approach to front-end web development that has made it more like backend development.

Dependency Management Systems

Package management systems have been around for a long time, but the focus was on sharing libraries of code that had to be specially used and lacked any overall platform or means of acquiring. Nowadays, there are two such systems that drive the development of web applications for all PHP frameworks and that are standard approaches to managing dependencies in web applications, both on the front end and the backend. They are known as Composer (a PHP dependency manager) and Node Package Manager (NPM). Composer is most often used to pull in backend dependencies (and is almost always a first step when installing any kind of third-party dependencies for your application to use, including frameworks such as Laravel).

The popular command forming the basis of virtually all installations of any modern MVC framework looks like this:

```
composer install
```

These two words are powerful enough to download all required dependencies listed in the `composer.json` file at their specified versions (known as *version locking*, which is saved inside a `composer.lock` file) and create an all-encompassing autoloader that requires one simple line of code to import every single third-party dependency defined in your `composer.json` file (Listing 2-1).

Listing 2-1. Example Use of Installed Composer Dependencies

```
<?php
require_once('vendor/autoload.php');
//good to go! use your installed dependencies freely
```

NPM is used in combination with Webpack to provide front-end assets that are downloaded, installed, minified, and run in a similar fashion as Composer, using a single command: `npm install`. Webpack is used to configure the various options available with all the high-tech, new-aged libraries and packages currently dominating the front-end world (such as React and Angular). There is no more going to a web page, manually finding the download link, and then having to manually install and configure it before it gets used in your software. All this is done by NPM and Webpack. Although using these tools does require a little bit of overhead knowledge (even more experience should be required when deploying things on a production/operational system used by others), they add sanity to what was otherwise sometimes referred to as *dependency hell*.

In one fell swoop (and basically two commands), you can have virtually all third-party code required by your application for the front end and backend installed and ready for action immediately. This also gives an overall structure to front-end assets in terms of practices revolving around modern technologies in a streamlined and fluid way.

Overall, advancements made from these and other products, libraries, and platforms have made life easier and more interesting for us developers. We are no longer tasked with the often tedious requirement of managing our own dependencies and hooking those dependencies into a usable set of includes. We can just issue a Composer command or use NPM to pull in front-end packages.. With such products as PhpStorm, VSCode, and versioning systems like Bitbucket and GitHub, we as an industry have evolved web development practices on a global level. These advancements have a direct impact on the bottom line of any business that chooses to implement them, as well as a profound impact on developer happiness and contentment, both of which are recipes for success.

Coding Standards and Practices

Because of the nature of programming (and the web development industry specifically), there existed a global need for some sort of standardization among web applications and programs intended for use across the wire from a browser. Thanks to such initiatives as PHP-FIG (which is like RFC for web development), we now have a standard set of suggestions for such things as logging, structuring code so it is easier to read. Also available to developers are things like interfaces to handle basic request/response and specifications regarding streaming web responses, and autoloading concerns as well. Web programming was often not much more than a few extremely large files (usually in the form of "spaghetti code") with all the presentation, business logic, and page styling globbed into a single monolithic structure spread across two or three files that were difficult to read, modify, and maintain. Ignoring such practices as having a clear separation of concerns (on an architectural level and a domain level) made developers responsible for maintaining the code cringe at the very thought of looking through miles of poorly constructed and hacked together logic with equally as poor readability due to a complete disregard for basic indenting and code styling.

The other important thing to note here is that the presentation of the code not only affects the next guy working on it but, over time, can become a valid example of something known as the *broken window theory*. In urban areas, when a building has just a single broken window that doesn't get fixed in a timely manner, there is a natural existing tendency that additional windows will proceed to be broken, which in turn opens the door (or more precisely, window) for additional ones that get broken and stay unrepaired, further perpetuating the cycle and eventually leading to an inevitable windowless building...all starting from not fixing the very first one.

It is the same thing in software. Failure to fix the first issue or problem that pops up in an application just makes it all the more possible, if not probable, that additional issues will occur and, at this point, will seem to be "buggy anyway," so who cares if there is another little tiny bug as long as the thing still works? That's a poor mentality to have because, at some point, those small insignificant bastard bugs will add up to be a system-crashing slew of what are now critical errors causing serious downtime affecting the rest of the company—potentially to both employees and customers. If the first bug was instead fixed right away, any other bugs introduced to it would seem to be a larger issue. Think about it: what developer wants to be the one to introduce a bug into an otherwise bugless system? (Realistically there may or may not be such a thing as a "bugless" system, but you get the point.)

Best practices are tried and tested ways of developing software that are directly aimed at preventing this type of disaster. There are methods that, when put into effect properly, will help add structure, depth, and meaning to the source code and will be ultimately leveraged to create a working piece of quality software that ensures its maintainability and extensibility throughout its life.

The key is to develop software systems that can scale at any rate and that can withstand any changes to the system without messing with that system's integrity. Also important is to develop software components that have high cohesion, yet are expressed with loosely coupled components, so that we can reuse our code elsewhere in the application. Using best practices means creating a reliable, dependable, and repeatable continuous iteration/continuous development (CI/CD) flow. It means committing and pushing to the repository frequently, with bite-sized changes that are in small enough sections that they can be easily tested, managed, and deployed. Let's discuss what cohesion is within the context of development and also how this can be used in conjunction with low coupling to create reusable software components that can withstand change.

What Is Cohesion?

DDD offers a way to organize applications so that they work independently as separate processes but have a high level of cohesion when they operate in unison. *Cohesion* is an important concept in software development, along with *coupling*. The term *cohesion* as it relates to software development was coined by Larry Constantine in the late 1960s as a means to express the idea that a module (or group of classes) should be more or less aimed at a uniform solution. On a modular level, classes should be separated enough to be usable and extendable without too much overhead and should usually focus on a single aspect of the problem at hand. Each module should relate to one another in such a way as to make them as a group functionally cohesive—meaning that all elements in the module should contribute to a single, well-defined task.

Do take note of the various practices and try to recognize that there are two main principles in play here, albeit low-level ones. Once you can identify the single responsibility principle and separation of concerns, you will find that the two naturally complement one another. Once you maintain that a class focuses on solving only one particular problem (granularity aside), it is easy to simultaneously adhere to the separation of concerns by ensuring that the members of it are soundly grouped together in a way that is most natural and best-fitting of the company's business domain, almost always directly in accordance with the terms defined in the ubiquitous language.

- *Cohesion (noun)*: When the members of a group or society are united

- *Cohesive (adjective)*: United and working together effectively

At the same time, the classes need to actually "bind" together in the end to produce the desired solution to the problem at hand in such a way that it is testable, reusable, and segmented with clear boundaries between key system components, in respect to its functionality and core business logic.

Listing 2-2 provides an example of a class that is not so cohesive. Please keep in mind that the example has no validation or preconditions/postconditions and should not be used in a production environment but is strictly a learning exercise.

Listing 2-2. Example of Low Cohesion Within a Class

```php
<?php
namespace App\Registration;

use App\User;
class RegisterUser
{
    protected $name;
    protected $username;
    protected $isAdmin = false;
    protected $isPremierMember = false;
    public function setName($name) {
        $this->name = $name;
    }
    public function setUsername($username) {
        $this->username = $username;
    }
    public function makeAdmin() {
        $this->isAdmin = true;
    }
    public function getUserAttributes() {
        return [
            'name' => ucfirst($this->name),
            'username' => $this->username,
            'isAdmin' => $this->isAdmin == false ? "NO" : "YES",
            'isPremierMember' => $this->isPremierMember == false ?
                    "NO" : "YES"
        ];
    }
    public function registerUser() {
    $user = new User($this->name, $this->username,
$this->isAdmin, $this->isPremierMember);
        return $user;
    }
}
```

There are a few things you can probably spot immediately that are issues with the class's *design* and lack of semantics. For example, usually a class that's doing some high-level user registration process would most likely have checks for a duplicate username and certain criteria for the username to even be considered valid. For now, I want to just focus on the many cases of inner-referencing of member functions inside other member functions in the example and how it seems to pass *its own members* around the class for really no reason. What's more, a lot of work is left up to the client in order to use it. Listing 2-3 is an example client for the class in Listing 2-2.

Listing 2-3. Example of Client Code for Low-Cohesive Class RegisterUser

```php
<?php

use App\Registration\RegisterUser;

//... collect user attributes--most likely via a form request
$params = [`name` => `Jesse`, `username` => `debdubstep`];

$userRegister = new RegisterUser();
$userRegister->setName($params[`name`]);
$userRegister->setUsername($params[`username`]);
$user = $userRegister->registerUser();
//now we have an unsaved $user...
```

In general, this is a bad design. Leaving specific methods or routines up to the client code creates the possibility that they may not get called. Couple this with the fact that in the `registerUser()` method, it creates the user with the given parameters but doesn't persist it to the database. This can be a problem if the developer was expecting the returned user to be a record that was saved successfully to the database. Of course, we'd have no way of knowing from the app because of the lack of error messages or exceptions, until we started noticing that users were not being persisted to the database (or people started complaining, which is a more probable situation).

There are no checks to ensure that all the required data and methods have been placed on the class before it persists the user object. We could, of course, write the logic that will check if the local $username and $name parameters have been set on the object before we make and persist the new user. The thing about doing that, however, is that we have to then consider how to notify the user that these properties must be set first (by hand). Would we throw an exception?

We could, but I don't think a full-on error that stops the execution of the software is merited from the issue that parameters have not been set on the object, but maybe you are in a context in which it would. On a web form, for example, when you are signing up for a new account to some site, you get immediate feedback (usually via JavaScript) that you have missed a field or that the field is not in a valid format. Once you hit Submit, the request is handled by the app, and you are taken (usually) to some type of profile page. You don't know or want to know the internal processes that ran to create your user account; all you want to know is that you have access to the site and a login.

In a similar fashion, the code that actually registers a new user should be encapsulated into a separate class (probably in the application layer as a service that utilizes domain-layer objects) and should be relied upon as the single point of entry for creating a new user in the system. The client code should initialize an object of this class as needed to carry out the request and then "hit Submit." Obviously, there is no submit button that you click, but methods such as run(), execute(), and handle() would basically act as such, firing a job or initializing some type of registration service that would handle the various aspects of creating a new user as well as containing the logic to ensure the prerequisites of handling the task have been met.

Additionally, using technical analysis would lead us to conclude that the concept of registering a user should be broken down into its various concerns, making sure to keep the domain model intact. We could, for example, introduce a repository that would alleviate the class from the burden of handling the persisting of the User object, making the Registration class cleaner and lighter. We could also implement a UserFactory class that would encapsulate the knowledge and logic involved in registering a new user.

While all that is certainly the case with this example, we are getting ahead of ourselves. Let's focus on the more obvious concerns with this class as we described in the previous few paragraphs.

Listing 2-4 shows a better (but not best) solution.

Listing 2-4. A Refactored Version of RegisterUser with Higher Cohesion

```php
<?php
namespace App\Registration;

use App\User;

class RegisterUser
{
    protected $safeAttributes;

    protected $user;
    public function __construct(array $params) {
        $attributes = User::fillableFromArray($params);
        $this->safeAttributes = $attributes;
        $this->user = new User();
    }
    public function makeAdmin() {
        $this->user->admin = true;
    }
    public function makePremiumMember() {
        $this->user->premiumMember = true;
    }
    public function getUser() {
        return $this->user;
    }
    public function registerUser() {
        $this->user->fill($this->safeAttributes);
        $this->user->save();
    }
}
```

In this example, we've gotten rid of all the individual setter methods and instead
have made the attributes come in via the constructor (*constructor injection*), a type
of dependency injection technique. As you can see, the fields are validated by using
a handy Eloquent method called `fillableFromArray()`. This method is an Eloquent
function that takes an array and returns another array with the values inside it being
valid attribute names existing in the model. When I say "valid," I mean that the attributes

are considered by the User class to be "fillable." Also please note that I omitted any checks to ensure that the parameters were not blank (or that the incoming $params variable was not an empty array—for the sake of brevity).

I've left the two make() methods there in case the client needs to be able to set these up before the user gets saved, but I could have just as easily included these two additional parameters in the constructor as well as set their default values in the method signature. It is beneficial to use what is called a *fluent interface* (more on this later). When it's all said and done, the getUser() method would simply return the user that we've built up after calling registerUser(). From a client's perspective, the simplicity of using the class keeps the client simple, with fewer methods to call to achieve some result.

What Changed?

The internal referencing of attributes or the "passing around" of internal parameters too often can leave a class as a noncohesive mess that is difficult to test, maintain, and reuse elsewhere. It is good to strive for a clean separation of concerns. In the previous RegisterUser class, there is a high level of cohesion between it and the User object. The User object's attributes are specified by the RegisterUser class, but the persisting of it is handled inside the User class (User is meant to be an Eloquent model). A level of cohesion exists within this small section of an application such that the individual parts work together to achieve an ultimate outcome, and the section adheres to a clean separation of concerns within the objects that facilitate it.

Another factor at play here is the flexibility in which we provide the client, particularly through the methods getUser(), makeAdmin(), and makePremiumMember(). These methods provide additional "ad hoc" options that the client is responsible for calling. Again, we could have instead implemented these as additional constructor arguments and set then to a default of null. After the registerUser() method is called, we can use getUser to retrieve the now persisted new User object.

This design is far from perfect. In fact, we will go over a much better way to handle such functionality in the form of Laravel jobs and queues, but it works well as an introductory example.

Low Cohesion

Methods are not in any way linked to one another nor is there any utilization of shared resources among the procedures in the class. They all act on a single member variable separately, and there is nothing going on here that is interesting at all. Although this class can and may achieve a separation of concerns, it most likely has one with the wrong things separated out. Where we draw the line between the conceptual boundaries in the domain layer has profound consequences on the way our objects interact (or don't interact) with each to produce a desired outcome. Figure 2-1 shows an example of a class with low cohesion.

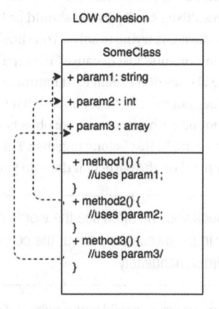

Figure 2-1. *Class with low cohesion*

Code that is considered to have a high level of cohesion usually exists as individual pieces that all contribute to and work toward a single defined goal or task. What we have in the SomeClass in Figure 2-1 is a class whose structure depends on its properties. Each function is separated, and they each only use their corresponding parameter defined in the class—which is fine if the structure was based on a particular business problem that warranted its use.

Generally speaking, classes such as these are not reusable or easy to extend. Maybe I shouldn't say "easy" but really "pointless" to extend because the child class is going to be using this structure and is usually only useful as a stand-alone object. There is no cohesion in this class because each method in it relates to only a single parameter defined in the class. The methods resemble some form of (and oftentimes unneeded) getter and setter methods. Eloquent has a more elaborate solution to getting and setting data (which we will dive into later in the book), namely, through its mutators (setters) and attributes (setters) but also via its magic methods.

Gotta Keep 'em Separated (Concerns, That Is...)

No, I'm not referring to the awesome old-school song by the Offspring, I'm talking about concerns existing within an application or piece of software. When actually "separating concerns," the resultisng configuration should be indicative of a specific business problem that the software is trying to solve. You should not separate things out into different classes and components "just because." If a separation between different classes or parameters inside classes don't seem to fit naturally with the overall tune of the domain, it most likely does not need to be separated that way or at all. By contrast, if two objects or properties found within two separate objects seem too intimately connected to be separate, they might just belong together. This is hard to get right and will of course completely depend on the particular domain you are working in.

Note   Throughout this book you will often see the words *namespace*, *folder structure*, and *directories* in my discussions about the code structure. Just know that I mean to use them interchangeably.

Oftentimes, this separation occurs as a rigid namespace and directory structure with the classes separated by what they are, not what they do. This just so happens to be the case with most, if not all, modern-day frameworks and is basically how Laravel's default namespace structure and directories are set up. Controllers are all inside a single `App\Http\Controller` folder. There may be subfolders set up under them, but still they all stem from this single directory under the main `App\` namespace, separated by what they *are* (Figure 2-2).

App\

> Http\
>
> Requests\
>
> Controllers\
>
> Responses\
>
> Repositories\
>
> Policies\
>
> Providers\
>
> Models\
>
> Exceptions\
>
> Listeners\
>
> Jobs\

Figure 2-2. *Sample directory structure from an in-progress Laravel application*

This type of structure relates to what each piece is; a repository would go in the App\Repositories namespace, and a controller would go in App\Http\Controllers namespace. This will all seem fine for a while, but as time goes on and additional features and business requirements get added to the system (virtually indefinitely), it will be difficult to manage all the controllers in a single namespace (or even a modularized one). Any true meaning of the domain isn't clear in a structure like this—it isn't specific to the domain.

Before we start using Laravel, I will give you a way to properly structure your application into individual silos. Each silo will have its own namespace, and inside each silo will be only the components and code required to make that silo function. By the way, I use *silo* and *module* to basically mean the same thing. Once you start breaking apart the single monolithic structure of applications in accordance with the importance each specific module has to the domain, you will find it easier to manage and test because all the modules are segregated from each other—yet all work together in synchronous harmony to produce the resulting application.

Prerequisites to Separation

There is some prerequisite work to do in order to implement the correct structure (with "correct" being whatever is agreed as "correct" for your business). The main thing to keep in mind is to be aware of where possible conceptual boundaries may be located within the core of the business. If we've strived to keep a model-driven design, the next step of turning those boundaries into actual code constructs will be easier depending on the quality and correctness of the things described inside the ubiquitous language.

Some things will be difficult to separate and if, for whatever reason, it seems like it is too complex or difficult to draw a proper separation between two components, the solution may be to make the boundary line thinner than one of a bounded context. This can be done using a *module* implementation of each component and carefully (and explicitly) abstracting out the communications needed between the two into separate classes or as part of a service or job's responsibility (that could then be set up behind a RESTful interface and used throughout multiple bounded contexts). Modules offer a less formal (but still explicit) mechanism for separating out the various components that your business (and thus your application) relies on.

Modules also offer another means of grouping similar concepts in an application and can (and should) be a representation of how the underlying business is *actually* structured. We should be able to look at a diagram of an application's modules and get a pretty good general sense of what is going on in them and how the modules fit together to form a whole working application.

We will study some different approaches for building modules when we discuss bounded contexts, but for now here is an example of a module structure in which we can derive a clear understanding of what it does and the various components involved in its operation.

Refactoring Legacy Systems

If after attempting to move that particular concept or class set into their individual modules or contexts they still don't seem to fit naturally with the rest of the application or the violate the definitions and relations defined in the ubiquitous language, consider the possibility that they might actually not need to be separated. This could be due to a lack of complete knowledge of the business rules that govern said concepts and processes or a mistake inside the inner workings of the ubiquitous language. Oftentimes

I see this as a result of an nu-enthused (or misinformed/misinterpreted, etc.) off-shore team that ends up leaving a big ball of mud for an application, and it just happened to be that they managed to make the thousands of little hacks they did to get to an MVP to all sync up and produce some form of a system that, without doing a whole lot more, works.

If this describes you, and you've inherited a bunch of crappy, off-shore code and have to step through the legacy application line by line to figure out what they were trying to do (because there is for sure no documentation that is there to help you), I feel for you! I've been there multiple times in my career. Most of the time (and for good reason), rewriting the legacy app from scratch will not be an option.

The best way to move forward is to implement any new features using best practices and standards as best you can and then (probably in a planned-out sprint) create what's called an *anti-corruption layer*. This layer is basically a sectioned-off area of a specific piece of the application; usually this piece is as big as an entire job or process would be to implement without it. Once you have established parameters around the legacy code and your new AntiCorLay (yes, it's a weird way to say anti-corruption layer, but ACL is already taken), build out an entire feature inside it, making only mandatory connections and points of integration with the old code, and build anything inside the new code with best practices. Eventually, what will happen is the legacy system basically absorbs this anti-corruption layer and treats it as if it weren't actually there at all—as if it was just another group of classes and objects that the legacy code imports or references.

After that, take a break and have a beer, because that's a great accomplishment and is considerably harder to do on complex systems! Once you get back to work, repeat the process, only with a different existing feature or even a new one. Build out another anti-corruption layer that acts as a more or less "drop-in" replacement or addition that the legacy app can inherently talk, make requests, and delegate to (this is usually best done via an API, event system, or queue) in order to process a user's request. In this case, the user and the legacy application should not be able to tell the difference. We've skillfully and tactically created a near invisible to the outside legacy app boundary encapsulating a dynamic feature using best practices and that comes complete with unit tests and documentation. Now that you have the process down pat, keep updating small portions of the legacy app and implementing bite-sized features inside their own respective anti-corruption layers until there is no more legacy code.

This is a surefire way to build out anything new using best practices and high-quality code while at the same time making the legacy application better and better until it disappears from the codebase entirely. There is, of course, more to it than that, but you get the point. Before we get any deeper into these concepts, I want to clarify what I mean when I say "domain layer" or "model layer." The definition is key to understanding the rest of the book's concepts and ideas.

Layered (Onion) Architecture

So, what is the domain layer? I'm glad you asked! In the sense of DDD, the domain (or model) layer is the core driving force behind a software's architecture and involves objects and processes indicative of the real-world business problems and requirements for which it was designed to solve (see Figure 2-3). Members of the domain layer are usually core objects or business processes that are expressed as first-class citizens to the overall business and the application.

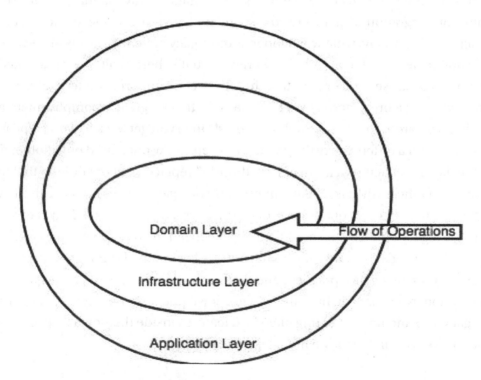

Figure 2-3. *The layers of the application. Sometimes referred to as an "onion"*

In essence, the model layer encapsulates all that exists in the context of what the business actually does. It is the heart of the application. All other code, policies, procedures, and infrastructure exist only to facilitate objects and components found in the model layer.

It is key, then, to be able to "section off" these business rules and classes that represent actual business entities into their own layer. This is the model layer. By focusing on the core business rules and foundational domain knowledge, we will build a powerful and rich domain model that is a true representation of the business itself. The various modules comprise multiple models into subsections—all geared toward achieving a (desirably) separation of concerns in which each module corresponds to one objective, or segment of the overall business's model-level concerns.

This may come in the form of a clear distinction between the various departments of the enterprise, where each module encapsulates an entire department's concerns or may exist on a more granular level, with modules instead representing various resources or product-specific focuses.

Where Do the Other Layers Fit In?

In Figure 2-3, notice how the domain layer is at the core of the application. The figure depicts the "flow" of operations (corresponding to the clients of each particular layer) and how each layer is generally pointed toward the layer below it, such that each layer can only depend on (and call) the layers below it.

Basically, the domain layer, at the heart of the application, exists as its own entity and thus should rely (or depend) on other members or components in this layer. The layer above it, the infrastructure layer, is used to facilitate the reading and writing of these domain-layer objects (and thus have to "know" about them directly). The final outside circle is the application layer. The application accesses the domain layer via the infrastructure layer but, in Laravel, can access the domain model directly.

Application Layer

The application layer is the layer whose clients are generally outside requests (via some input sources like an HTTP hit, an API call, or a SOAP-implemented operation). Clients of this layer are usually users of the application. When something needs to happen with regard to the business rules or business objects, the application layer does not deal with them directly.

Instead, it deals with the infrastructure layer, who knows best how to handle the various ins and outs of working with objects in the domain layer (or model layer). Here are a few clarifications of components that exist in each layer:

- Application services live in the application layer but are devoid of any domain logic.

- They control persistence transactions and security.

- They can send event-based notifications to other systems.

- They compose email messages to users.

- They can subscribe to events that are emitted from the domain layer.

- Application services inside this layer are the direct clients of the domain model.

Infrastructure Layer

The infrastructure layer contains the following:

- Houses repositories that get implemented in the infrastructure layer for an interface defined in the domain

- Can be turned "upside down" if used in conjunction with dependency injection, giving the infrastructure layer the ability to implement any interface in the layers below it

- Factories can exist in this layer (or the domain layer)

- Persistence mechanisms

Model Layer (Domain Layer)

The model layer contains the business-specific rules and entities that the company that built them uses in order to function. Remember, the code is the business. Treat it as such.

- Domain services handle specific processes and tasks related to the domain.

- This layer publishes domain events for the rest of the application to react to.

- Clients of this model usually exist in the application layer.

- Bounded contexts and separation of business components are key.

It is important to note a few things about the model layer.

- The model layer is the most important layer in any application.

- The other layers that exist in an application are there only to support the objects in the model layer.

- Constant iteration, reformation, clarification, and refinement of the model layer is important in a DDD distributed application.

- The model layer (domain layer) is the central point of focus in domain-driven design.

- Improvements to the model are typically made only after long discussions of how the business operates and functions, usually between a developer and a domain expert of some kind.

Service Layers

There is also an explicit distinction of service layers (or just layers) that almost every application has some notion of. These service layers are almost directly related to their "architectural layer" counterparts. For example, an application service is one that lives inside the application layer but performs operations against objects in the domain layer (usually through the infrastructure layer). Similarly, business processes that span multiple domain objects and are involved directly with the core business rules of the system will live inside the domain layer and be acted upon by objects or components in the infrastructure layer.

Application Services

These are pretty much the same as the application layers described earlier in the chapter, yet they are more granular in that they represent services themselves, which primarily focus on a specific action or process of the business rather than the whole "layer" of the application. Example services can be things like SendNotificationEmails, SubscribeToNewsfeed, ExportAccountingStatement, etc.

First on the list are application services. Services in this layer basically act as an intermediary between the outside clients (requests) and domain logic. This layer can (and usually does) exist as components other than services—an example being controllers. They are of course the "C" in an MVC architecture. Controllers dispatch particular services and jobs and also hold any listeners, subscribers, or other receivers to respond to those jobs and service calls. Requests and responses are also contained inside this layer.

Applications sometimes use controllers as a means of holding and running domain-layer procedures. By coding them inline with the controller, they reduce code reusability dramatically as well as make any sort of test on just the domain logic more difficult because the process is not isolated. The key to unit testing is being able to test things in isolation of each other (in "units").

No Fat Controllers

It is not good practice to have fat controllers; this should be avoided by explicitly defining services or other domain layer classes and components that encapsulate the specific domain knowledge of such processes that are then called on from within a controller, which hands the process off and returns a response. Unless the process is extremely simple that a separate class would be overkill, it is essential that the core business logic gets separated out into its own piece of the application's domain layer—either as a model, domain service, event listener, or whatever best fits its purpose. Name objects inside the domain layer according to the ubiquitous language.

The outside clients (requests) are the direct clients of objects in the application layer. The application layer then acts on that request, usually involving interacting with objects in the domain layer.

Where to Draw the Lines?

That is the question that this book hopes to help answer. We need an approach to developing web applications and system-wide architectures in the context of the Web. This is where DDD is going to come into play.

I want to touch on it briefly because it is crucial—not optional, but crucial—to cultivating a powerful and well-defined ubiquitous language that will be used to model the application's core structure as well as determine the granularity of its modules. This only comes after some digging and probing of the currently held "accepted" standards of the company (usually by drilling down into the finer points of how they work and what they actually do). A lot of times what you end up finding is more or less *assumed* knowledge of the business or fuzzy boundaries, namely, an unclear separation of departments or core processes, oftentimes appearing to span several services or having multiple primary concerns.

There is a good portion of Eric Evan's book *DDD: Tackling Complexity in the Heart of Software* regarding conceptual boundaries around the various aspects of the system and where to draw them. Oftentimes, correct placement of these boundaries inside our application is not always clear and direct as we'd like. Most likely, the sectioning off of components in the domain model requires many thorough talks between developers and domain experts in a process known as *knowledge gathering* or *information gathering*.

In the end, the products of these contextual boundaries mark off the different groups of functionality that exist normally and naturally within the context of the business itself. This is made even more robust when based on the concepts and definitions in the ubiquitous language. Less formal separation mechanisms include modules, domains, subdomains, or generic subdomains. In a broader sense, the bounded contexts as separation mechanisms also contribute to the refinement of the business-wide ubiquitous language—especially when set up as a *published language* that is implemented using a REST interface (we will get to that later).

Now, when you couple the strategies and tools offered by DDD and combine them with the cutting-edge Laravel framework, you are able to satisfy the needs of pretty much any architecture or business domain specification in a repeatable and streamlined process. The framework provides the implementation of the various components that were discovered through the strategic layer of domain-driven design (which highlights the drawing of conceptual boundaries around the variously decoupled structures in the domain you are building in). We will use a variety of techniques to better facilitate the process—things like relying on domain experts for the all-truth definitions of business concepts as well as implementing that attained knowledge in the form of business software that can be served across the Web on an enterprise scale. That will give us a clear path to implement what we need to on the code side of the application and basically utilize Laravel and PHP to implement the concepts and processes we've acquired.

What We Get from DDL/DDD

In the end we get a fully functional piece of software that is easy to deploy and built on best practices, with various structures and namespaces that actually correlate to the business-level entities and structures. The software is completely scalable because we've wisely decided to roll out our applications and infrastructure on the cloud, and they can be modified with ease due to the clear separation of concerns we've defined. We also have a clear roadmap for the modules that will need to be built to properly handle the core-level business processes it has been elected to facilitate.

As we progress from initial decomposition of domain concerns to a refined domain model reflecting the true needs and requirements of the business, we start to see things lining up in an organic way. Concepts and ideals seem to interconnect effortlessly, and there starts being far less overhead when implementing new features or changes to existing features because the underlying structure of the application is crafted in a way that is tightly coupled with (and represents) its domain model, making all of it easier to understand, extend, and test. We can use specific unit tests as quick and easy proofs of concept while developing. We'll discuss more about this in the later chapters.

Conclusion

In this chapter, we took a look at how Laravel is structured and contrasted that with the guidelines suggested by DDD so as to point out some noticeable differences. We discussed how monolithic applications are structured and how and why they are less desirable than a more separated approach (such as microservices). The decision to add this level of complexity must come directly from decisions made with regard to the domain, which should be separated according to the same logic that exists within the standard business processes that the application is built on top of.

We also covered some examples of an Eloquent model and went over some code that facilitated adding a new user to the database and why it is better to place domain-centric code within the confines of a model versus a controller or service. Services should be created only when the use of an entity or value object does not fit the context of the problem you are trying to solve.

Now that we know the shortcomings of Laravel in regard to building an architecture using DDD as a guideline, we can go over the various changes we will need to make the structure of a default Laravel installation actually feasible. I hope I also made you curious as to the other components offered by Laravel by whetting your appetite to learn more, which we will do in the coming chapters.

CHAPTER 3

Domain-Driven What?

In the previous chapter, I gave you a little taste of some of the things we go on to explore in this and other chapters in regard to the ideas and concepts that DDD is built on. Along the way, I hoped to have whet your appetite for learning domain-driven design in Laravel. We will continue to explore the strategies and approaches offered by DDD and then discuss ways we can implement these ideas using Laravel.

In this chapter, we will focus more on core definitions and strategies offered by DDD and also give some high-level overviews of domain-driven design and how its content is broken down. My intention is to give you enough knowledge and arm you with the basic core practices and procedures you will need to build a DDD-based project in the real world. I'll provide you with example problems you may face when building software in any domain, and I'll provide you with a variety of solutions that will highlight some of the various components as well as illustrate the various concepts and contexts that they define.

The Nature of Software

Software is rarely self-actualizing. Rather, it is a means to an end...a way to do something. Code is rarely written for the sake of *coding*. You will most likely not encounter too many situations where the end product was the code itself, unless perhaps you are writing code for a book or perhaps highlighting a section of source code in a blog post or even writing an open-sourced library. More often than not, your software is aimed at doing something that is unrelated to the software that that something is built from.

For example, a marketing company that has an email campaign wants to track the statistics of how many users opened the email, how many clicked the ad inside the email, how many of those actually purchased the product, etc. There is a lot of business

© Jesse Griffin 2021
J. Griffin, *Domain-Driven Laravel*, https://doi.org/10.1007/978-1-4842-6023-4_3

value in these reports that help drive business decisions and verify that the marketing campaign as a whole is meeting some tracking goal. The CEO and other executives often use this data to make important decisions that impact the company's health and focus.

For the stakeholders and the CEO of the company, all they want to see is their reports. They are most likely not going to care too much about how those reports are being built but that the reports are visible to them and that they are accurate. To them, and to the rest of the business, the code is just a means of collecting the data, calculating the figures, and generating the reports. They do not usually care about things like unit tests, security (unfortunately), architecture, coding style, programming language, or any other such technical aspect of the system...they just want their pretty report.

The split between the development and business goals is so intense that, most of the time, there is a separate language spoken among the departments to describe the same business concepts. In extreme cases, the departments themselves that surround a software system get so segregated that each of them has a version of the language that started as a single definition but grew to include several contextually biased definitions. Each definition corresponds to the central focus or aspect of the department in which they were conceived, in such a way as to create pseudo-concepts that mean *almost* the same thing as their ancestors but vary slightly enough for the concept not to valid across the organization.

What the business executives/stakeholders *are* going to care about are things like report accuracy, UI design, site usability, performance, and the general user experience because that's what the user sees. There most certainly is, and most likely always will be, some friction among these two fundamental aspects of any tech-related business or software endeavor: the requirements of the business and the quality of its software. When quality is compensated for the sake of time, the things that I discussed in Chapter 1 start becoming a reality, and you will eventually end up with unhappy developers, longer than usual turnaround times, unexpected fires, and a whole slew of other bad things that will eventually end up becoming a great ball of mud.

The Golden Triangle

Figure 3-1 represents a popular diagram used to convey the trade-offs between the three main aspects of a software development effort.

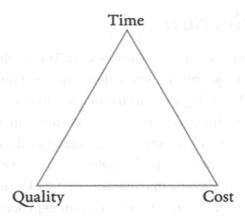

Figure 3-1. *The golden triangle of software development*

In Figure 3-1, you can have only two of the three desirable outcomes of a given software project: the speed it is developed (time), the quality of its source code (quality), and the cost (cost). We can determine the outcome possibilities based on Table 3-1.

Table 3-1. *Possible Outcomes of the Golden Triangle Combinations*

Selection #1	Selection #2	Outcome	Real-World Example
Quality	Time	A high-quality product that is quick to build is not going to be cheap.	Rapid application development
Time	Cost	A fast, cheap product is going to have poor quality.	Startup's flagship app
Cost	Quality	A cheap product that is high quality is going to take time to build.	Open source software
Quality	Quality	A super high-quality product is going to be timely and expensive.	Enterprise software
Time	Time	A super-fast product is going to be expensive and lack quality.	Any Microsoft software
Cost	Cost	A super-cheap product is going to be low quality and take time.	Outsourced overseas development

The What and the How

Software is both a thing of concretion and abstraction. The result of software development effort is the most obvious way to determine whether the project was a success. In the case of web development, a custom page in a web application—including its calculations, appearance, interactions, and conditions—can be judged by gauging correctness and completion using a browser to interact with the application. The user experience is almost always a priority for the higher-ups and executives, and how a page behaves is the means of proving that the work that took a dozen or more hours to complete was actually done. Therefore, there is this concept of concretion in this regard: the result of developing a modal for a web page should be finished when you can see a modal on the screen, and its behavior is exactly how the requirements dictated it to be. This area can be thought of as the *what.*

How software behaves on the outside (i.e., how it looks and functions from the perspective of the end user) does not necessarily indicate the quality or structure of the code shaping it on the inside. The code that makes up the user experience could potentially be extremely bad and poorly written (like, for example, if standard security measures were tossed aside for the sake of time or the practice of validation was not implemented in an HTML form), but the outside may or may not actually reflect this fact, because there is a conceptual difference in the code itself from the elements, frames, and functionality that exists as a result of that code. This inside area of an application can be considered the *how.*

The how is usually if not always the hardest thing to test in a system. This is because it isn't always clear how well the code is written until we start having bugs and weird issues that seem to have been solved many times over but are still presenting themselves within the application. The how includes all the actual code and is the source of truth for the answer to the question regarding the quality of the code itself, which isn't always what it appears to be inside the browser. You can't simply look at a form and conclude that CSRF protection wasn't used to prevent XSS attacks. You have to inspect the document and look at the form's code for some type of CSRF token or encoded string.

Problems can arise when the how and the what drift too far away from each other. While product managers and executives are usually much more concerned with the what of the application, the development team and engineering folk are (or should be) concerned with the how. If, for example, that modal we built looks and works great, the product manager signs off on it, and it is, as far as they are concerned, good to go.

Now let's say that, during the process of development, we left a huge security hold somewhere in our code that appeared only under a certain condition. Take this code as an example:

```php
<?php

if ($request->parameter == 3) {
    //to remove!
    exec('cat .env');
}
```

Let's say there is a form or input on the modal that we built, and on this form there was an input box with a drop-down for selecting and setting a form element. While developing this model, we put in the previous check because we were interested in seeing (for whatever reason) the result of issuing a cat command on the .env file (the .env file is what holds all your private configuration values for your application and is not part of the repository), but only if the form variable named parameter was equal to 3. Yes, I'm fully aware how atrocious the code in this example is, but it just serves as an example; don't look too much into it.

This is a bad security flaw that basically displays the entire .env file with all of our database passwords and other secret data that our application needs in order to run. We would never want to reveal this information to any user, so this is a pretty big problem. It is similar to the issues causing the Chernobyl nuclear accident. The safety measures and practices that would have prevented such a catastrophe were turned off to "test" the system. When the problem actually presented itself, it was in the form of a huge explosion that sent a huge amount of toxic, nuclear radioactive material emitted from the reactor core. Obviously, our problem is *much* less disastrous, but you get the point.

It could easily go unnoticed by the product manager, who thinks that everything "looked" all right because it did. Behind the scenes, however, was a deep-seated problem that started out as a simple test for the sake of development and was not properly removed after they shipped out the resulting software. The responsibility for preventing said situation completely rests on the shoulders of the development team. In this instance, the what of the application (which was the modal containing some form that worked as expected) was verified to be in good order, but the how was never properly reviewed by another developer, which leads us to question the standards and practices that either were not put into place in the beginning or were completely ignored during the development of this software.

> **Note**   As an additional reflection on this security issue, consider the reality of the situation: the code lacked all forms of a *code review*; if it hadn't, the error would have been caught. What else could have been done to prevent this flaw? Unit testing. If the feature had sufficient unit tests that covered this part of the modal logic (which it by all means should), a simple automated test conducted before merging into the master branch would have pointed to the issue, in a rather obvious manner (in this case, displaying the contents of the `.env` file)!

How software is built to realize *what* it actually does is the area that I refer to as the *abstract* side of development. The reason I became a programmer is because I had an interest in the *way* problems were solved. I was always fascinated by the decisions that had to be made and how to use the tools and functionality of a programming language as a means of solving complex problems. There is a certain art to this science. Regardless of your resulting paradigms and implementation of best practices, you should take care to write ample unit tests so that every portion of code in the application ideally would be covered by a corresponding test. These tests get run as part of an automated suite that is triggered upon every merge of the pull request into the master branch. A good CI/CD system is invaluable to a software development team.

Developing software requires a balance in thinking, learning, and coding. Code is not the only means of solving problems, and many problems can (and should) be solved *without* resorting to code.

> **Note**   Code as a last resort. If there are any other viable solutions *besides* writing more code, don't write more code. Every line of code is another line that must be maintained and refactored, and whenever we write code, we run the risk of introducing new bugs into the system.

Breakdown of DDD Concepts

The topics covered in DDD are intricate and deep subjects that are discussed in extreme detail in both the Red Book and the Blue Book. My goal is to give you an idea of what we will be focusing on in this book as well as get you familiar with the different areas of DDD that we need to cover in order to get a useful system built using DDL.

Take note that the diagram in Figure 3-2 leaves out the entire portion of DDD known as *distillation*. Concepts within this portion consist of refactoring strategies and how to implement certain patterns to phase out legacy software, as well as additional ways to refine your domain model and arrive at a more accurate model that expresses the business in proper terminology stated in the ubiquitous language.

In Figure 3-2, we have three points of a triangle (which have no relation to the golden triangle, just so you know) that have the interactions between them described by lines and a brief description of their relationship. However, notice that all of them seem to be intimately related (connected) to the ubiquitous language bubble. That's because they *all should be derived from or directly use items inside the ubiquitous language.*

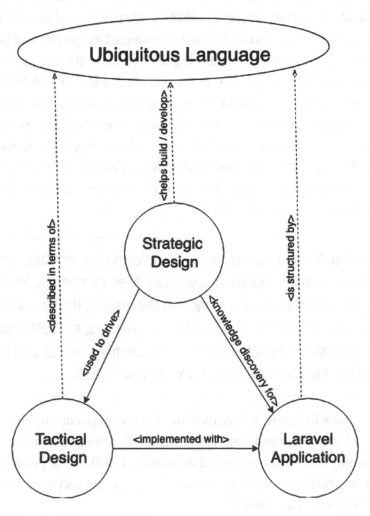

Figure 3-2. *Conceptual map of DDL*

Strategic design will consist of the strategies to accomplish a domain-driven design, as well as include best practices and high-level architectural discussions. It also contains processes and ways to go about designing your domain model (like keeping a domain expert close by to clarify any shortcomings or complex areas of logic that may not be fully comprehensible to a new hire entering the company). The knowledge we gain in the strategic design portion of DDD will be used to craft and refine a correct ubiquitous language that will be spoken by the entire company in order to convey various meanings as they exist within the actual business model. This knowledge will also be used to drive development of our application (in our case, using the Laravel framework to build these concepts and processes).

Tactical design is all the technical structures and considerations that we need in order to establish all the various objects, policies, and structures that we have realized by means of the tools and recipes located in the Strategic Design pillar of DDD. They will be what we use as a means of transitioning the objects in the ubiquitous language and the business processes that act on these objects into the actual code that will allow them to run in a web application. Tactical design is often expressed as UML diagrams or other OOP-type diagrams and visuals to help illustrate the complex concepts involved in creating a domain-driven design...and DDL as well. The components in tactical design will correspond directly to the code that it helps model, within our Laravel application. In the end, our Laravel application will be the implementation of these objects and processes we've built using tactical design.

Note   The tactical design process can be completed only *after* the initial knowledge discovery/rough modeling phase has been carried out. You can only start modeling the domain in terms of tactical design (i.e., the use of actual code *structures* like repositories, factories, entities, aggregates, etc.) after you have at least a partial understanding of the real-world system you are attempting to re-create in code. The book's contents will work in this fashion.

In the third bubble in Figure 3-1 we have our Laravel application. This application will be the result of many discussions, meetings, and planning sessions regarding the core functionality and requirements of the system. It will be the product of a collaboration of several (if not all) departments that have any sort of contact with the component or system we are building.

The Process of Domain Modeling

It is often said that domain modeling is more of an art than a science. That of course stems from software's unique fluid-like state of being. Its ever-extending structure and malleable tendencies give endless possibilities, which is useful only if there are laws, limits, processes, and constraints in place that help give some sort of context to the working space and that separate the mix of concepts into containers of encapsulated logical boundaries, which are much easier to comprehend for the programmer.

This brings up another good point: software development, in essence, varies in complexity only for us humans who read and work on it, not for the machines that actually execute and run it. The distinctions, encapsulations, clarities, notations, specifications, and depictions we establish in the domain's design and its corresponding implementation inside the code are made specifically for human consumption. Machines, on the other hand, would theoretically rather be fed a never-ending supply of 1s and 0s so they can do the low-level processing that they were created to do. They don't care about function names or class namespace structures, which exist for us developers to read and gain insight into when we are modifying the code at a later time.

It is good to keep this in mind when developing applications because we need to be kind to the next person who looks at the code. It can also serve as a great reminder for ourselves when we forget that we put that extra call to doSomethingOdd() until we see a verbose comment like this:

```
/** !!!!IMPORTANT!!!! DO NOT, NOT CALL THIS FUNCTION! ITS MANDATORY*/
$this->value = doSomethingOdd() . doSomethingOdd();
```

Believe it or not, this is a sample from a *real* project I've worked on! It makes absolutely no sense and adds a lot of confusion for the next person who has to read it.

The names of variables, classes, and objects can give the developer an idea of what is happening in the code, which, depending on the complexity, can be written on every line to describe what each does. They are more or less explanatory comments that help describe the process's details in plain English. While comments can be immensely helpful, the over-usage of comments can litter the code, decreasing both readability and development speed. But comments are by no means useless. Like it or not, even the smallest application is always at risk of increasing in complexity as new features are created and new concerns added. In the end, its important to find a good balance of comments and source code which they describe.

What Not to Do

The worst thing you can ever do when building an application is to mismanage complexity—in either direction (either overestimating or underestimating). Attempts at avoiding complexity as it is materializing inside a project turns out to be just as bad as over-engineering software to handle *anticipated* complexity. With the latter, what tends to happen is that you waste precious development time creating something that may or may not be an actual concern in the future when you could have spent that time on *real* application requirements. Add to this the fact that the assumptions and preconditions made when first modeling a "might be" system have most likely changed as refinements and updates are made to the underlying business rules (domain model). It's only after just thrown away a bunch of time building code that the system cannot use that you realize you may have to rewrite that part of the system entirely because the solution you've built no longer satisfies the new problem scope.

Avoiding complexity is a phenomenon that can present itself during development and, oftentimes, without the developer realizing it, at least not at first. Initially, the developer starts out with good intentions, adhering to best practices and good architectural structures, but tends to falter somewhat and go against these best practices (in some cases by introducing an anti-pattern). But if the solution actually *works*, it gets shipped. This isn't a concern if the team regularly participates in code reviews and is constantly making an effort to refine and improve the core business model, because they eventually will refactor this code and implement a better, more knowledgeable solution than the first version that was just the first thing that worked.

However, when refactoring is not a standard practice when developing software, these issues will manifest themselves down the road as a big ball of mud that is heavily commented with stale, out-of-date comments that usually don't give the person reading them any better idea of what's really happening. In some extreme cases, the logic can reach a point where there is just too much complexity that has been shoved into monolithic structures housing many different concerns within the same file, class, or model. Adding complexity is no longer even possible without a large refactoring effort, usually spanning the course of several weeks or months.

Essentially, there are two main reasons this horrible situation can become reality The first is when best practices are not followed. The second is when the solutions were constructed without ample domain knowledge and experience that would otherwise be necessary for modeling the business domain (and operations on those models) correctly.

If the people working on the software do not properly understand the business concepts behind it and fail to invest the effort it takes to form a conceptual basis for said concepts, they will desperately attempt *any* solution that may help accomplish what they need to do. When this happens, code gets randomly inserted here and there to test various things or dump out values of variables that only actually exist under certain conditions or under a specific state (due to the stateless nature of PHP and web development as well). Testing becomes so involved and cumbersome that the tests themselves are all but ignored entirely at some point, leaving a large gap in the test coverage of the system's codebase and slowly deteriorating the CI/CD pipeline and all the cool things that your DevOps engineer has spent weeks getting ready as completely useless.

If this happens, it *almost always points to a lack of clear boundaries, usually caused by violation of the separation of concerns* on a domain level or using incorrect components that were not properly defined in a ubiquitous language.

You know you're working on one of these hellish applications when the concept of "debugging the code" equates to relying on the old "dump and die" or `print_r($var);die;` command to poke at the code and attempt to figure out what is going on at this particular place in the code's execution because the environment is made in such a way that any error output is all but nonexistent, not to mention the lack of any means to properly debug code.

Dealing with Complexity

Domain architecting is all about tackling complexity as it arises and putting naive instances into place at first, with an attentive focus and aggressive refinement of those instances as additional insight is gained regarding the business domain. DDD has various techniques and steps to help us get started in building a solid foundation for our application.

The DDD Flow

The best way I've found to implement DDD in my day-to-day web development projects is by following this general process. Keep in mind that these steps are free from the technical aspects of DDD (we will go over those later).

1. **Deep dive into the domain you are working in.** Immerse
    yourself in it so that you become intimately familiar with the
    domain's problems, solutions, and architecture. If you work in the
    healthcare billing industry, for example, you probably have CPT
    codes memorized and can recite the MediCal patient eligibility
    address by heart. If you are in the financial industry, you probably
    know how loans are structured and how to distribute cost
    depreciation across the lifetime of an asset.

2. **Work with domain experts to create a ubiquitous language.**
    Since you are most likely *not* an expert when it comes to the
    domain that you are working in (especially if you are just starting
    out on your web development career), you will need to rely on the
    people who are experts to construct a general-purpose, company-
    wide set of terms and definitions along with accurate depictions
    and documentation regarding relations that may exist between
    them.

3. **From your derived learning and partial understanding of the
    system gained in steps 1 and 2, construct a rough design of the
    system as it is depicted by the business's solution space and
    as you understand it to initially be.** Even if the initial design
    has missing parts or doesn't clearly indicate the boundaries
    that separate its various pieces at first, get some sort of design
    conceptualized that is based on the core domain model and
    described in terms of the ubiquitous language.

4. **Refactor and refine the model's design frequently, and fail
    quickly.** Because we value agile development practices and are
    suckers for iterative development, we keep our model constantly
    up-to-date with our understanding of the business domain.
    The design of the domain model should always reflect the most
    currently gained and accepted knowledge of the domain itself.
    We do this by "failing quickly." If we fail as fast as we can when
    developing some system, we are forced to fix these failures equally
    as fast, each one enriching the domain model and refining its
    structure (even if as a way of how *not* to do something).

5. **Repeat step 4 each time new insight into the domain model is gained, and create a series of repeatable steps that can be used to continually deploy the domain changes to your production environment (CI/CD pipeline).** Having a good continuous deployment pipeline in place allows us to maintain a level of continuity between our conceptual understanding of the domain and the code that implements it.

What tends to happen, every once in a while, is that there will be a realization of an important overlooked step within the domain model itself (a process, a redefined mapping of an assumed property, or even a misidentification of an item in the ubiquitous language) that will be big enough to mandate a significant update or refactoring to accommodate. It will most likely come as a realization to something unrelated happening, like, for example, the effects of an event being fired off that have listeners scattered across multiple bounded contexts. The changes that scream out "refactor me" are the first ones to look at, because they often are masking a true deeper meaning and may not be represented in full light in the currently implemented domain.

Each refinement made to the domain is another small step toward creating a domain that represents the core values of the business and represents it, mirrors its composure and conceptualizes its very nature of existence. That implies that every update or change to the application is important because each one represents some gained insight or understanding in the business model.

Deep Dive into the Domain You Work In

You most likely know very little, if anything, about a given domain that you just got hired to be involved with. You most likely are familiar with software development (at least I hope so if you've actually gotten a development job) and are armed with various patterns, frameworks, tools, and idioms to help manage complexity as it creeps into the application scope. Still, there is a good chance that you know very little about the core business domain you are working in.

I encourage you to embrace your company's domain to the fullest extent. Your goal should be to eventually become a domain expert yourself and acquire an intimate knowledge of the business's domain model. Then you will be considered an asset to the company you are working for and be in a good position to craft a domain-driven design for that company.

If this isn't the case and you have no idea what you are doing, you are going to have a hard time implementing a domain-driven design for *any* project. After all, how can you possibly build the implementation details that only exist to facilitate the corresponding business objects that they represent when you have little to no understanding of the domain model itself? The answer to this is the same answer to the question in pretty much any domain imaginable: you are at the whim of your domain experts, as they are the key to gathering enough information about the domain and business to actually craft a domain model that represents it. Conversations with domain experts help for sure, but they, depending on the domain's complexity, can easily overwhelm to a new developer, and it may take time for them to truly get a good grasp on the information.

Work with Domain Experts to Create a Ubiquitous Language

Domain experts eventually become a developer's best friend, for it is the domain experts that hold the source of truth regarding every aspect of the business, usually in their head. It is our job as developers to pull that information out of their minds and into the software so that knowledge can be shared with all other aspects of the application. There's a certain way to go about getting information from domain experts, which I have summarized in the following list:

- Try not to overwhelm them with complex technical details and developer-lingo. Instead, attempt to match up the terms and language used by the experts to describe the business, mimicking the contexts and components that they use to describe the business aspects of the system.

- Do well to ensure clarification about any concepts or elements of the business model that are unclear or hard to understand.

- Use the domain expert's own jargon as a basis for forming a ubiquitous language and make the resulting entry in the ubiquitous language exist in a narrow scope so that its definition cannot be mistaken for another term in the business dialect.

- Work to establish clear domain model terminology definitions and a company-wide accepted set of agreed upon specifics that belong to the definition that make it unique.

Construct a Rough, Naive Design of the Domain

Once you get some kind of feel for the high-level aspects of the domain, use that to create a bare-bones, skeletal sketch of the domain model. This will initially be a naive attempt at describing how the business operates on a technical level, but don't be too concerned about how minimal it turns out to be for early versions. Keep in mind that a domain-driven design is one that is never actually "finished." Once we have everything we need in place for a DDD, we then employ techniques related to continuous integration/continuous deployment (CI/CD) to ensure that our domain model is continuously being refined, updated, and made better as new insight gained by the team is portrayed within the application itself (via its implementation in code).

Note   Initially, your domain model could be constructed of various documents, drawings, and notes written on paper. It can be composed of really anything that you need in order to successfully describe the business domain in terms of the model that is being built to satisfy it.

Refactor Frequently (Fail Often)

The great Thomas Edison had this to say after finally succeeding after some 10,000 or so attempts at creating a working light bulb:

"I have not failed. I've just found 10,000 ways that won't work. Many of life's failures are people who did not realize how close they were to success when they gave up."

—Thomas Edison

In the process of success, failure is an inevitability. What is important is that you *learn* from these failures and use that knowledge to help find a working solution. The concept of "failing fast," then, aims not at succeeding, but at failing. In failing over and over, you get a pretty good idea about how *not* to do something, which would take you one step closer to success because, if anything, it is an example of how not to do it. It would stand to reason, then, that failing faster will bring you to realize the solution that actually works sooner.

This is an important concept in agile development because the core of being agile means to give and receive feedback constantly. The flow of information and knowledge should flow freely in all directions, from the developers to the domain experts to the top-level executives. Failing fast gives you the ability to gain insight, even if it's in the form of what *doesn't* work quickly, so that knowledge can be encapsulated within the domain model and all who use it. Tools of the trade that help in these areas are SaaS such as Atlassian's Asana coupled with Jira for task management and Confluence for building custom documentation and how-to libraries. Other good products are Invision for design, GitHub and Bitbucket for repository management, MySQL Workbench or Sequal Pro for database navigation/design, and Slack for team communication and collaboration.

Technical Aspects

Up to now, I have been focusing our discussions on the strategic portions of DDD. The "technical aspect" of a software system can be thought of as the *how* and is basically a set of structures for you to use as tools (templates) for realizing your domain model in code form. The tools include various concepts that we will go over and that are all based on solid best practices.

In this book, I will give you the tools that will be useful in keeping your code aligned to the business needs and requirements so that the software will be a spitting image of the business itself. I will show you how to rely on your ubiquitous language to build out the components that will drive your application and your software development in a domain-driven way. You will learn to stay focused on the various aspects of the business itself and use that knowledge to build the skeleton of your initial domain model. Then you'll use the technical designs and practices offered by DDD to actually express these domain concepts in code, as well as define any operations on them, services that use them, or database schemas that they represent.

Frameworks give you controllers, routes, responses, and all kinds of other things that are meant to be used as tools to facilitate the interactions and usage of the objects in your application. These tools usually employ some form of object design pattern. These are patterns that exist at an object/class level, and they are generic. In domain-driven design, there are many components that are modeled using one or more of these design patterns. For example, DDD presents the following architectural components to aid in the interactions and usage of objects in your domain layer:

- Entities

- Factories

- Repositories

- Value objects

- Aggregates

- Domain events

- Domain services

- Modules

These are all important concepts and are aimed at facilitating the domain model, separating the different concerns of the system, and establishing some standards in the way objects in the system exist and interact, by using best practices. They are generic enough so as not to hold the actual domain or context in which you are working in as any sort of particular type or fashion. They are meant to be domain-agnostic solutions to common business problems that arise in a typical web development or software application project.

In regard to what they mean to us in terms of domain-driven Laravel, they are basically key to the idea and implementation of DDL and, as such, are given ample room for discussion (each taking up an entire chapter to introduce and discuss the finer details). We will work through these and create reasonable implementations of them inside Laravel, using the customized framework we are going to create in the next chapter.

For now, I'll give you a little context for what I've discussed thus far using the following project.

Example Project 3-1: Warehouse Management

This sample project will introduce a fictional warehouse management application that we are in charge of developing from the ground up. This example will serve as a sort of guide to help capture the intent of the software, gain knowledge of the background information needed to solve software problems, and form a ubiquitous language, which we will then transform into a rough architecture to make it work in the real world. We will mostly be focused on the information gathering and high-level shape of the system we are designing. We won't actually be writing code for use with the Laravel framework until later in the book. I do use PHP code in the example to demonstrate various concepts, but these ideas are more generic in nature. No previous experience with Laravel is needed at this point (but never hurts!).

During the knowledge gathering phase, we want to focus on the model in a nontrivial, nontechnical sort of way. By initially modeling the project in plain English and with flowcharts/diagrams, we rid ourselves of the overhead of designing all the classes, interfaces, and object graphs that the system needs to run, by delaying them. This allows us to model the domain in terms that everyone can understand (not just developers). We then will create a sort of catalog for all these common business terms; this is what is referred to as a *ubiquitous language.*

This catalog of business terms and concepts is important to get correct because it is the literal foundation that we will use to model all relevant aspects of the system and, as such, will be utilized by all members of the organization to relay business ideas and describe internal operations. This language is at the heart of the domain.

Note   Understand that the items in this glossary can only be defined perfectly by having countless discussions, debates, research, and planning sessions with domain experts and other members of the organization. One approach I've seen in the real world is to have one person from each department in the same room with the domain experts and developers. Magical things can happen. For this example, I have omitted that aspect.

Requirements Overview

We are going to build a sort of warehouse management system. Let's imagine we have a customer who wants to automate their day-to-day processes to be more efficient, ship more products, and make more money. They already have in place an analog, archaic system using a combination of printed paper and manual processes. Even though the orders and shipping are managed by an e-commerce platform, the system lacks any sort of tracking capabilities or inventory management and therefore is done by hand. The so-called reporting features of the app consist of a multicolored Excel spreadsheet that has a variety of formulas and summations that can also be calculated only once the proper entries are made to the subsequent cells involved in a formula's calculation. What's more, their recent expansion into a larger warehouse has created a new challenge when the workers fulfill the incoming orders. The (now much larger) warehouse lacks a proper product location management solution, and therefore the fulfillment process has slowed down drastically, taking between 10 and 45 minutes to complete just a single large order.

Basically, it's our job to create a new system that will be an all-encompassing solution for the standard concerns a typical warehouse would have, while addressing the issue of proper product location management by devising a new location scheme that will make it much easier for the workers to locate the products and fulfill the orders. We will discuss things like the following:

- Order management

  - Inventory updates/audits

  - Order tracking lifecycle/workflow

- Inventory management

  - Item tracking

    - Location in warehouse

    - Quantities

    - *Reserved*: Amount of a product that's already spoken for

    - *Available*: Amount of a product that is in stock and ready to be sold

    - *Expecting*: Amount of a product that is on order (backordered)

  - Item lifecycle process/workflow

- Fulfillment

  - Pick and pack

  - Shipping system

  - Order fulfillment process/workflow

These are the central concepts we will focus on in this example.

Order Management

A warehouse makes its money by receiving and shipping orders to its customers. The amount of time taken to successfully process and ship an order has a significant impact on the bottom line, so the warehouse needs the order workflow to be exact, repeatable, and fast so it can hit the revenue goals.

Currently, the warehouse has an e-commerce platform that accepts orders and payments, so we don't have to be concerned with the placement of orders and billing—which leaves us to focus on managing and tracking the order's fulfillment and its lifecycle, from tracking the inventory adjustments that must be made when we process an order to picking and packing the line items on that order and shipping them to the customer. This process is the *order workflow*.

There exists a need to track state within the context of the order workflow. Orders are entities that go through different stages throughout their lifecycle. Figure 3-3 shows a basic flow of the lifecycle that an order goes through (based on our initial assumptions with how the process of ordering something would normally flow).

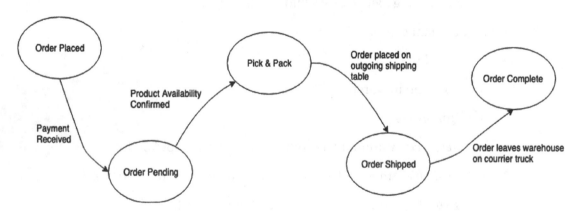

Figure 3-3. *Order workflow/lifecycle*

Basically, we have a fairly simple order flow. You can just as easily call it an *order lifecycle* (with the events modeled as the lines in the diagram) or *order process* because it doesn't really matter all that much. What does matter is that you stay consistent with that name throughout the documentation and ubiquitous language (UL). There must be consistency of the terminology spoken by the domain experts in common business-related lingo and the software model in terms of the agreed-upon concepts in the UL.

What that usually equates to is taking a consensus on which terms to use to refer to which business objects and coming together on an agreed-upon verbiage and definition that is spoken and used throughout the entire organization. We cannot have duplicate definitions inside our UL, mainly because it adds unneeded copies of the definition, which is just one additional thing in the system that could possibly be mistaken, misrepresented, or misconstrued. It is simpler and better to clearly define a term's definition that will not be shared in the same form within another term's definition.

Note   What we eventually will create in software should be an almost mirror image of all those real-life, standard objects and processes living inside the business domain. Sometimes modeling a domain reveals errors in logic or processes that need to be resolved so that the same errors do not show up in the code.

Getting back to Figure 3-3, an order gets placed on the online e-commerce system, and the warehouse receives the order and immediately marks it as being in the Order Pending stage once payment for the order is confirmed using automated banking and payment gateway plugins. At this stage, the order is not considered to be eligible for completion (pending the remaining steps after Pick & Pack). The way they become eligible for the Pick & Pack step is after the warehouse workers verify that the products on the order are physically available in stock and the quantities for each item can be accounted for.

Once that happens, the order moves to the Pick & Pack stage, where it is now on the "pick list" and queued up for physically locating the item in the warehouse (aka *picking*) and placing it in a box for transportation to the customer (*packing*). After this happens, there may be some additional verification steps to ensure that the correct items are in the box and they are in the proper quantities such as a manual secondary check performed directly before taping up the box that goes out to the customer. Other than that, the package is ready to be shipped and is carried off by a daily pickup provided by a courier (UPS, FedEx, whatever). At this point, the order finally moves into the Order Completed stage. This would seem like a pretty easy and semicomplete model (at least for the purposes of this example).

> **Note**   The scope of the project thus far is deliberately made to be bite-sized so
> I can demonstrate how to go about modeling a domain in software (or at least
> where to start) while not using precious page space describing every intricate
> aspect of the warehouse management system.

Inventory Management

Now that we have our basic outline of the order workflow sketched out, we can start diving into a little more detail in the system. In the real world, features and requirements may present themselves at any time and can be completely unpredictable in size, scope, or importance. For our purposes, we are going to have to build into the system more complexity, which will be in the form of additional components that facilitate and manage the warehouse inventory (because that's what warehouses *do*), of course.

This would mean that we have to account for all items inside the warehouse so that we can manage the physical quantities properly and get answers to questions that help make decisions that the business relies on in order to be successful. A perfect example of that in the context of inventory management is knowing when to order additional stock, because (obviously) if we don't have any inventory, we can't fulfill orders. The team responsible for purchasing truckloads of stock in a typical warehouse use the data provided by this inventory management *context* as a means of determining what needs to be on a vendor order for the stock we are out of, and how many of them should be ordered. (This could be ascertained by looking at the *backordered* quantity listing that has been made available via the inventory management component in conjunction with the sales report covering the last 30 days, which gives an indication to the product's recent demand.)

In fact, our e-commerce team most likely relies on some sort or reporting or notification regarding the quantity of products the warehouse has in stock at any given time so that they can properly list products on the website and mark the ones for which there is no inventory as "Sold Out" (although this would be a great place for some automation). This is a slight detail that, on a real project, would require additional clarification because we have the same data driving multiple needs that can, at any given time, be out of sync with the source of truth, which in this case is the actual number of physical products in the warehouse. We will overlook this detail for now and revisit this later.

Just like the order management component described earlier has a workflow (or state machine), the inventory component will also have one, only applied to the context of an item or product. It's important to notice here that there has to be some collaboration between the inventory management components.

Knowledge gathering is one of the most important things to do when modeling software. It is what eventually shapes the internal structure of the objects (in regard to their namespacing), and it is the first step in creating a usable UL. We are going to cheat a little for this example and pretend we've already discussed enough with domain experts to build a rough UL.

Fulfillment

So, we have covered the order management aspect of the system, which is going to deal with the order's lifecycle and track it from receiving the order to shipping it out. We also have the inventory management aspect of the system, which keeps a record and count for all products inside the warehouse, along with their location (which is an important detail).

Fulfillment will be "absorbed" into the order workflow, which will basically contain all the items originally listed as "fulfillment." The fulfillment process is just an active order going through its workflow. These are the steps of this workflow:

1. Locate each product on the order form.

2. Grab or pick the item in the specified quantity (the item's quantity affected would be listed under "Quantity Expected").

3. Place said items in a packing box, seal the package, and send it out via courier.

So far, this seems fairly straightforward. One thing you probably haven't considered is the involvement of the first step. In real life, I've seen in many warehouses a proper "map" or location reference for the products on the shelves. Oftentimes, this knowledge is contained inside a domain expert's head, making teaching new hires extremely difficult due to a lack of proper documentation. There is a pain point here.

For our example, let's say that this pain point existed and that the warehouse workers were taking far too long to find the products so they could ship the order. The root cause of this is a lack of a proper coding system or product map that would aid the workers in quickly finding and selecting the item from the shelf. So, we need to be able to adequately track an item's location in the warehouse.

Where to Start

This may seem like a lot to deal with all at once, but in the real world, requirements like this are usually much more involved and detailed, and in the case of creating a new system from scratch, they seem to all come at you at once. Sometimes it can be overwhelming, and we often are all too eager to transfer this knowledge from our brains into the physical world. In this case, it may be tempting to start the system's architectural solution with each of the listed concerns in the requirements as a single group (Figure 3-4).

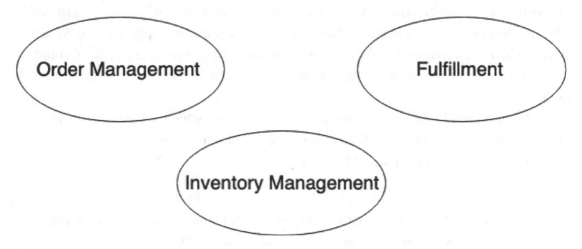

Figure 3-4. *Possible architectural groupings*

But think about this: we have separated out fulfillment from the order management concerns of the system, which are indeed separate requirements, but they should be part of the same context. In this case, what we are trying to do is track the order's lifecycle from the time it enters the warehouse to when it leaves (i.e., gets shipped). There are multiple stages to the lifecycle, and the entire lifecycle (workflow) can be thought of technically as an order's fulfillment.

One way to get a better understanding of the mountain of requirements and domain knowledge and start separating out what actually needs to be done is to find where the problem space and solution space are.

Problem Space

The problem space can be thought of as all the things the company wants to solve. It holds the requirements and is broken down into domains and subdomains. In our case, the problem space contains the three main ingredients to our warehouse management software: order management, inventory management, and fulfillment. Basically, the diagram in Figure 3-5 would serve well as a representation of the problem space, or the main objectives/acceptance criteria required for the project to be considered complete, if only it had the two similar requirements in a single subdomain. We will start referring to those three items in the problem space as the model's subdomains from this point forward. Once we have made this adjustment, we come to understand there are, in fact, two subdomains that can be derived from the list of requirements.

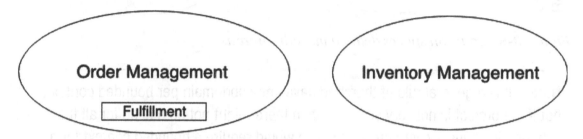

Figure 3-5. *Problem spaces*

Solution Space

The solution space is, if you haven't guessed, the resulting effort of solving the problems grouped into the subdomains we listed earlier. To know where to start with modeling your solution to the requirements of the project, you can model one solution group (also called a *bounded context*) per subdomain. In our case, we come to conclude that two bounded contexts exist for this project, one for each subdomain (Figure 3-6).

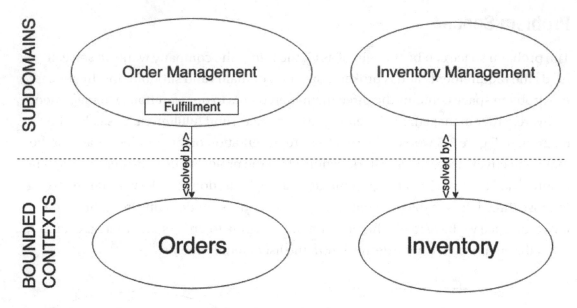

Figure 3-6. *Solution spaces defined via subdomains*

Note   It is a general rule of thumb to have one subdomain per bounded context, but if the project is not very complex, then there might not be a need for all the subdomains (where every problem space would require a bounded context for a solution).

In splitting up the project in this manner, we can get a clear picture of *which* work needs to be done (although there is not any such indication of the priority of any particular subdomain). We can also get a basic concept of the structure of the domain model we are going to need to create to adequately solve the problems in a logical and domain-driven way. That means shooting for reusability and creating a rich, robust domain model through refinement and refactoring, ultimately establishing a solid representation of the domain, modeled as software components.

Create a Ubiquitous Language

Now that we've defined the problems that our project needs solutions to and which solutions are needed to solve these problems, we can start creating a ubiquitous language for the software, derived from domain knowledge.

Please note (as I have mentioned) that a true UL only comes about after countless discussions with domain experts and by refactoring the definitions of business terms as additional insight is realized or made in the domain.

Right off the bat there are two important terms we need to define.

- *Order*: An incoming form containing a list of products and their corresponding quantities that have been requested by a customer

- *Inventory*: A log of all every product's *location* in the warehouse and *quantity* available to sell

After adding these, we see a few additional terms that we should add as well.

- *Product*: A single item for sale in the warehouse; contains such data as the item's price, name, and short description

- *Order Line*: A single line belonging to an order that is comprised of a single product and the quantity of that product

---

Note   Remember, these are not our domain objects and most definitely not the classes we will use in our code, although some of them very well might be, such as an `Order` and `Product`.

The UL is arguably the most important thing to get right in the design of the software. It is the foundation of the entire platform we are building and will be known throughout the company in terms of how the definitions relate to the business. We need to keep our model up-to-date at all times, even if it means removing or changing the terms in the UL to reflect better the business concepts that they were derived from.

The way to achieve this is to constantly refactor the UL and the domain model as a whole to best represent the business objects and processes that are involved in the business's operations. Even in each sprint and each pull request, we constantly refactor the application to be better. We want this for our UL also, which is why I'll be making corrections and modifications to it as we go.

Defining What to Build

So, we have a rough UL in place that seems to reflect the overall verbiage used to describe both the problem space and the solution. They are expressed clearly in the UL (which could be a document, spreadsheet, plain-text file, or paper) and are defined in terms that domain experts and developers have come to agree on. That's all gravy!

The next step is to get a feel for the operations that occur (and need to occur) to complete the required features of the application. We can take the requirements given at the start of this example and use them to describe what we want the application to do, in terms of how it should do them. This is best done by forming complete sentences in plain English, using the terms in the ubiquitous language to describe each requirement. We form the sentences from the vantage point of the user to capture their needs (these are called *user stories*).

- As an operations associate, I want to be able to quickly navigate to the product's location in the warehouse and be able to identify it on the shelf quickly so I can get the order ready for shipping.

- As a stocker, I want to be able to locate an item in the warehouse and adjust its inventory in a nonintrusive manner so that I may keep every growing warehouse stocked.

- As a sales representative, I want to be able to quickly identify a product and its inventory levels to coordinate orders with customers.

- As an operations manager, I need to track product quantities in real time, by how many we currently have, how many is on order from a vendor, and how many are in the order process so I can solve business questions.

Glancing over these user stories, we can get a pretty good idea of the features that we are going to have to create and can start putting together some actual architecture following some tried and true patterns used also in domain-driven design.

Figure 3-7 shows where they would fit on our earlier map of bounded contexts.

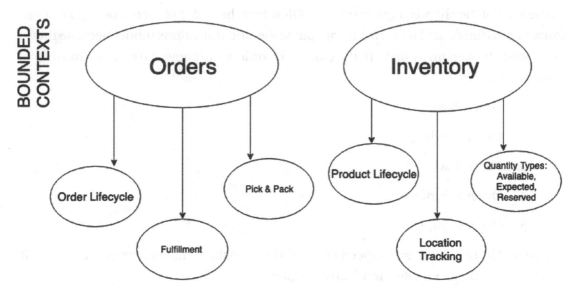

Figure 3-7. *Mappings from user stories to bounded contexts*

Workflows/Lifecycles

It appears we have two lifecycle workflows we need to define: one for the Orders context and the other for the Inventory context. What we need is a way to track an order's status through these transitions in such a way that creates a "flow" between statuses (stages). What we will make is known in computer science as a *workflow net*, which is a derivative of a *petri net*.

A workflow is composed of *states* as well as events that act on one state to get to the next (i.e., transitions). The transitions are important to us because they contain the specifications as to which transition(s) are valid for the particular state that the underlying entity exists in. It defines how the states and transitions interact and is what we will be using to control our work order workflow.

Order Workflow

At the start of the chapter, I gave you a workflow that the `Order` objects would go through from start to finish, and it fits nicely into our states and transitions model because they are already broken up as such. In the case of the orders workflow, we can assume the following states:

1. Order Placed

2. Order Pending

3. Pick & Pack

4. Order Shipped

5. Order Complete

For each state, we need to specify the event or transition that can be performed on it to advance to the next state. Here's an example:

- Going from stage 1 to stage 2 requires a *payment.*

- Going from stage 2 to stage 3 means that the product has been *confirmed* to be in stock.

- Getting from stage 3 to stage 4 requires the order to be pulled from the shelf and packed into a box that the customer would receive.

- Going from stage 4 to stage 5 would indicate that the order has been successfully sent out to the customer on a courier truck.

We will use this basic format to create the product's lifecycle also.

Product Workflow

The lifecycle of a product, in simple terms, starts with a product being received at the receiving dock, where it gets logged in to the system as received, and the proper entry to the quantities for that product will be updated (but only if that product is already in the system). If it is, we can assume there is already a quantity associated with it. Let's assume that the counts of these quantities are correct (i.e., the number of expected counts are accurate), which means we would subtract the quantity received from the Quantity Expected count in the system's books and then add that same number to the Quantity Available count for that product.

If the product is new to the system, we must create a new record for that product in the system and then add the received quantity to the Quantity Available count for that product. We can see right off the bat that creating a new product in the system is not as straightforward as receiving a quantity against a pre-existing one. We will most likely need to set up a system where the receiver could enter in the specifications for the new product and it can be added to the inventory log for future tracking. For now, we are going to overlook this complexity and just assume that there is an existing record for each product that is coming into the warehouse.

After this, the product is put on a cart, which the stockers then use to place the products in their respective location in the warehouse. It will wait there on a shelf, with an "available" like status, until an order is received that has a line in it for that product. At this point, the quantity is adjusted after the operations associate picks it from the shelf, and it marks the product's final state as "Product Sold." Figure 3-8 provides a map of the product workflow.

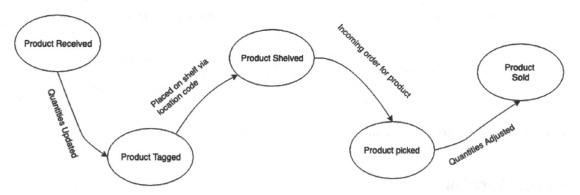

Figure 3-8. *Product workflow/lifecycle*

Note   This would be a good spot to stop and add the two new concepts of Product Workflow and the Order Workflow that we've established in the last few pages, along with a brief and accurate definition for both, to the ubiquitous language.

Fulfillment

This was listed on the software requirements; we decided earlier that "Fulfillment" was just an order going through its typical workflow. We captured the concern of fulfillment inside the Order-bounded context, so we can eliminate this from the UL and from the system the idea of fulfillment and instead just use "order workflow" to mean the same thing. Fewer objects in the system equals less stuff to keep track of for us humans when we are debugging it later.

The same is true for the Pick & Pack stage, which belongs inside the Order context and even exists inside the order workflow itself. So, we can just lump the act of picking and packing in the domain workflow, but the data surrounding the pick and pack phase is worth exploring. Figure 3-9 shows a diagram of our context and the features they support.

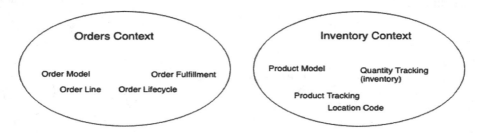

Figure 3-9. *Bounded contexts*

Product Location

As stated earlier in the example, one of the pain points that warehouse workers were having was that they were taking too long to physically locate the item on one of the thousands of shelves in the warehouse. As a small exercise, we will provide a reasonable solution that will help map out *where exactly* any given product is located so that it can be picked and packed. This is an example of providing a solution to a problem without using code. Remember, code as a last resort.

To add some context to the example, let's pretend this warehouse carries and ships shoes. The warehouse is 10,000 square feet, with about 8,000 dedicated to product storage. We need a way to identify a single shoe inside the warehouse's location quickly. This means we need some type of coding scheme that is attached to each product that specifies its location in the warehouse.

Note   I use the terms *shoe* and *shoes* interchangeably in this writing to mean a pair of shoes (we obviously have no use for a single, stand-alone shoe...except to maybe throw it at a politician or something).

To start out, let's think about the problem deeper. The shoes all need to be located in a reasonable amount of time, so we are obviously going to have to organize the shoes to *decompose* this organizational problem. Basically, we need to break this big problem of warehouse and order processing into smaller, more manageable units of work. One way to do that is by looking at ways the concepts in the domain model naturally separate. The first thing that comes to my mind is gender. The gender of the shoe is the most obvious way to split up the stock. It seems to be an easy and straightforward separation, that is, until we find out that certain shoe brands only deal with women's shoes, some strictly men's shoes, and some have both.

Note   For the time being, we are going to not consider the shoe's model, which would normally have to be accounted for in a real-world project like this. We are simply delaying it for now.

We could still make the gender separation work, which would give us something like Figure 3-10.

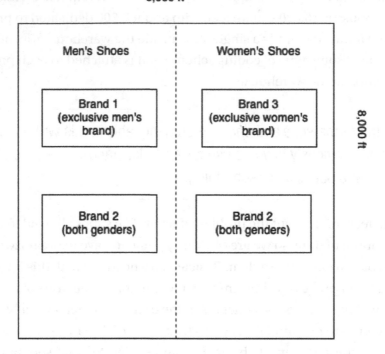

Figure 3-10. *Separating the warehouse by gender and brand*

The only caveat is that there will be a duplication of locations in which a single brand can be, which may or may not be a problem for the business, depending completely on its particular needs. Whatever the case, we would rely on conversation with a domain expert to see if this warehouse scheme is feasible for the company's day-to-day operations.

The domain expert tells you that the layout we've depicted will work because the gender is something that is attached to any shoe, so we could use it to divide the warehouse according to shoe gender. The brands duplicated wouldn't be too much of a concern, as long as there is an adequate system to track and label a shoe's location in the warehouse, which would depend on brand and gender.

Identity

So, what we need to come up with is an easy-to-read schematic of the warehouse that separates each shoe so that no two have the same identifier. We can assume that there needs to be an *identity* associated with each shoe in the form of an internal key that can be used throughout the rest of the system as a means of identification. Let's give the shoes an *internally generated identity*.

After thinking about this generated identity, you have a stock of brilliance. *What we need here is a barcode system!* That would allow us a means of tracking every shoe by giving that shoe an assigned identity in the form of a barcode. To ensure uniqueness, we decide to use a UUID scheme that can be translated into a barcode easily using a third-party package (to see the options available, do a Google search for *Laravel barcode generator*).

So, the barcoding system is the way to go. There is a problem, however. The UUID scheme is not at all human readable as its standard format is 32 hexadecimal characters in base-16 (here's an example: 123e4567-e89b-12d3-a456-426655440000). That doesn't exactly *roll* off the tongue. It would also cause an issue if (for whatever reason) we needed to find the location of a given shoe *without a barcode scanner.* Normally, we would invent some sort of internal mapping of UUIDs to locations on the shelf, which could only be deduced by scanning the barcode and retrieving the product's location from an internal database. In short, it would make the location of a shoe coupled directly to a barcode scanner. This may be a good solution for some, but for this example, we can do better.

What we want to create is a standard way of identifying a shoe in the warehouse that is both barcode scannable and human readable. We scrap the UUID implementation and instead decide to create one of our own. This scheme must have the gender, brand, and sizing information to make it obvious what shoe it is. Then we can tie this code to the warehouse shelves, with each shelf representing a particular group of shoes.

We quickly put together a rough draft of the coding system.

```
(gender: m/f) - (brand: first 4 letters) - (size: 2 digit integer)
```

This would seem to cover almost all the requirements. It has the three data points built into it and is easy to read and understand by a person without a barcode scanner. The only problem is that the same brand of shoe in the same gender and size would have the exact same ID number. This is no good because we want to uniquely identify each shoe.

Taking that into consideration, we make an amendment to the code scheme.

```
(m/f) - (brand: 1st 4) - (size: 2 digits) - (Unix timestamp)
```

I think we may have a solution that works. By adding the Unix timestamp onto the end of the ID number, we have maintained a unique way to distinguish one shoe from all the others in the large warehouse in addition to preserving human readability.

Figure 3-11 shows a broken-down identification number for a single pair of shoes. (I realize that last sentence would make absolutely no sense in pretty much *any* other context, but it works here.)

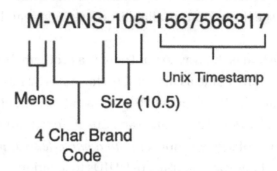

Figure 3-11. *Breakdown of a unique identifier for every shoe*

The Unix timestamp is what guarantees our unique identification number required for each pair of shoes, at least *virtually*, because there can be two new products that are the same that get added to the system the very same second, resulting in the same unique identifier. However, the chance that this will occur in real life is small enough to take on the risk. It most likely will never happen.

Now that we have a standard identity for each pair of shoes entering the system (i.e., receiving), we need to transfer this string into a barcode for easy scanning and retrieval.

Generating the Barcode

Because a barcode is going to be used simply to tell the difference between each product, all the work is basically already done because we've created the coding scheme for the shoes that identifies them uniquely. Now all that is required to start putting this plan into action is generating the barcode from that identity information. One way to do this is using a QR code (or "quick response" code).

QR codes are universal, are well supported, and can hold any arbitrary data that we want, including the identifying string on a pair of shoes! We won't go too much into the implementation details at this point, but if you're curious, you can always do a Google search for *Laravel QR Barcode Generator* to find a supporting library that will handle the conversions from identity to a barcode image automatically. This is what would be ultimately required for a system like this to work in production, mostly because a barcode would need to be printed out at the time of identification and physically placed on the shoebox, with all the data points included in the identification number. Figure 3-12 shows the resulting QR code from translating the identifier M-VANS-105-156756631.

Figure 3-12. *The barcode image produced from the string M-VANS-105-1567566317*

This is an extremely handy solution that can basically be applied to anything that needs to be tracked or accounted for. The best part is that you can encode any data into this barcode! Whatever you use to generate the image can be decrypted after you scan it with a barcoding app. (You can use your phone for development purposes, but in a real-world scenario, you will probably want to invest in some professional 3D barcode scanners for performance and ergonomic reasons.) In our case, we can use the identity coding scheme we created earlier to generate a valid, human-decipherable, unique string that can be converted and reversed by a scanner.

Bridging the Disconnect

We have the following so far:

- A unique identifier for each shoe

- A well-formatted string representing the identifier that is human-decipherable and containing a variety of information within it (gender, size, and brand).

- An innovative and well-thought-out means of reading the barcodes

What have we been overlooking the whole time? Implementation details!

It has not been clear up to this point how the barcoding system is going to work in practice. Specifically, we have an ongoing disconnect between the software that actually runs the system's backend and the business rules for which they are built on. We need to elaborate on the details of the shelving organization and how we can use the barcoding system to manage those details.

Shelving System

The shelving scheme we decide on will need to support human-readability, just like our product identifier. To make the system work autonomously, we need a way to relate a given shelf with a section of the products in the warehouse. The sectioning in our case is already done, via gender and brand. We just need our warehouse to physically reflect this qualifier.

Let's divide the warehouse with a theoretical number of shoe companies in respect to their locations on the shelf (Figure 3-13).

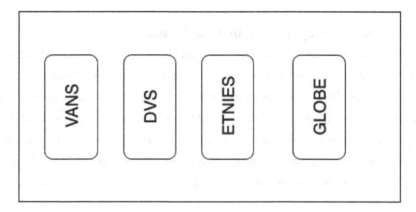

Figure 3-13. *Rough draft of warehouse structure*

This could work, but one may argue that you don't know how *much* of any particular brand is going to take more space (if any). That would be a legit concern if the company were new, but really, how are you going to know how much of any particular brand is going to be inside the warehouse at any given time, and at what interval should you space the brands apart from each other?

Given our ongoing lesson of "code as a last resort," I would argue that this problem can be easily solved by looking at the sales reports from the last year and estimating the inventory at roughly the same levels.

The rough draft in Figure 3-13 depicts the warehouse shelving split by brands (in reality there would be more than four, but work with me), and the space is spread out equally for all brands. This could work for a solution, but what about gender? We have gender inside the barcode stamp, so we can use it as a means of separating the physical stock. See Figure 3-14.

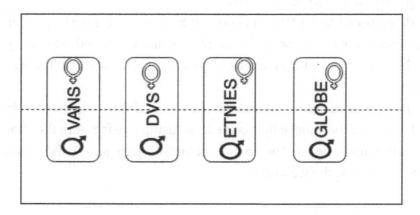

Figure 3-14. *Brands split by gender*

As you can see in Figure 3-14, the brands themselves are split up between men's shoes and women's shoes. This gives us all the possible combinations of products (assuming there are only four brands).

A Real-World Scenario

You are a warehouse stocker, and a shipment of shoes arrives for receiving. The receiver handles his part of logging the items and their counts into the system, which means there is already a barcode on each box for you to scan. However, your company's web developers were pretty smart, and they included the English version of the barcode right above the image. The shoes belong to the following category:

W-GLB-65-1567566899

You tell yourself, "No problem, I've got this," and read the translated version of the code to yourself: "Women's Globe, Size 6.5." You go to the designated shelf holding all the Globe brand shoes, go to the women's half of the Globes, and do what with it?

Oh no! We've left out a critical detail in the design of the system. We didn't explore the shelf problem deep enough. We stopped at a more coarse-grained solution that left a hole in the implementation. It's not a huge deal, though, because all it takes is to add another data point to the system that will serve as the additional divide for organizing our shoes.

What could we use to separate the shoes on the shelf that each shoe has and that varies enough between individual shoes so as to act as a good separating mechanism? If you haven't guessed it, it's simple: the size!

Brilliant deduction, Watson! We can chop up each shelving area by gender, with the individual shelves made up of a single brand of shoe and separated into various "size holes" (to be blunt about what they are; I was going for the most direct thing I could think to call it).

Figure 3-15 is just a sample solution to the problem of shoe organization in finer-detail, with the sizes of the shoe acting as the final distinctive factor in the shoe's attributes such that it can be used as a means of further segregation of the massive volume of shoes entering the warehouse.

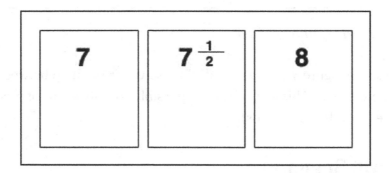

Figure 3-15. *Individual shelf organization via shoe size*

This diagram is the layout of the shoe sizes *for a single row* on a shelf. The spacing between the sizes would come into question right away, and that is a detail to consult with a domain expert on.

As programmers, we can and do make some assumptions about the work we are doing. This is perfectly fine for development. If a situation arises that must be accounted for by the software but cannot be defined in a precise manner or is otherwise unknown at the time, make an educated guess and fill in the missing gap with this guestimate until you have the chance to go back through and determine the proper result, which usually comes about through further conversation with domain experts or could require a much larger level of investment to determine.

Let me rephrase what I said earlier: it is perfectly fine to make assumptions as a placeholder for values/processes that are not yet known, assuming the group/person creating it has regular code reviews and tech debt elimination sessions, as well as allocating enough time for refactoring. These should happen on a regular basis, religiously.

After speaking with a domain expert about how much space each size should be on a per-brand basis, you have come to the understanding that they should be split up into groups of shoe sizes, as shown in Figure 3-16.

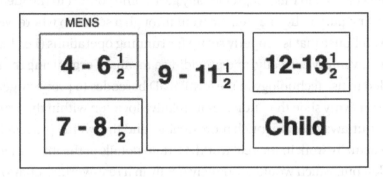

Figure 3-16. *Shoe size distribution per rack of shelves belonging to one brand*

This size distribution indicates that the majority of the sizes for men will be in the 9 to 11.5 range. There is also a place for child sizes (in this case, a boy). In this case, we made an assumption as to what the organizational factors should be, and we were correct in our design; however, we did not know how to model the shelving system in a manner that would be best for the business, so we established a reasonable estimate of what it may look like, and then we modified it again once we had the time to discuss the matter with the domain experts, who let us know that the sizes should be segregated based on the popularity of the sizes, which we were able to correctly portray in Figure 3-16.

Conclusion

This chapter took up quite a few pages mainly due to our example scenario (which we solved completely, by the way). In programming, we are often faced with choices pertaining to quality of code, time estimates, and cost of development. Leaning toward one quarter of the triangle can cause a downplay of another. Quality, cost, and time are always going to be surrounding issues that you will get better at estimating over time.

In addition, we went over some possible fires that could arise out of not maintaining your codebase properly and not frequently taking part in code reviews. Not refactoring regularly falls into this same category. The DDD model works well only if a correct development cycle is in play, and the component design is iterative, composed of small wins and "low-hanging fruit." Splitting the larger issue into smaller, bite-sized pieces makes developing a solution for it much easier and manageable. Trying to lump together different components can lead to disaster, and the principle of the separation of concerns should always be attempted, if it makes sense to the *contextual contours* of the system's overall strategy.

The example I created in this chapter ideally gave some context to the ideas I've expressed in the first part of the chapter. We went through a scenario where we had to design a shoe warehouse that is properly set up for running operations (i.e., facilitating orders), tracking inventory correctly, and providing a means of organizing the shelve racks. We decided to use technology in the form of 3D barcodes to properly generate an encrypted code on every shoe that indicates its relative location within the warehouse. We've made the put-away feature much more doable, and the overall process has been tightened up to actually work in the real world. Certain details of the implementation we've designed were left out, which would absolutely not fly in a real-world scenario. Ensure you are going the right direction with frequent conversations and confirmations by the domain experts. They are your source of truth in most domain-related matters. Documentation could also be written in tune with the domain experts' thoughts on a given concept or process. We can use logic to make an educated guess for development, but always make sure to revisit the design regularly and establish proper constraints on the values and variables you are working with (or details you've chosen to ignore at the time).

As a side note, this example was derived from a company I really worked for as a PHP developer. I left out some minor details to focus more on the concepts I've been discussing thus far in the book.

Note   I did leave one detail out, the "pick and pack" issue where workers were having to spend too much time actually searching on the shelf for a given shoe, in a certain size and brand. I will leave this for you to think about and come up with possible solutions for. What you should be thinking about is how to express the shoe's location on an even *finer* level of detail than the shelving system we devised earlier.

Now that we have a design for our system in place, we will continue with the technical concerns later...but, first, an introduction to Laravel.

CHAPTER 4

Introduction to Laravel

In this chapter, you will learn the ins and outs of various Laravel facilities that, when used in combination with best practices, can have remarkable results in a relatively small amount of time. It is important that you set up your environment correctly, and there are many tutorials online (or visit Laravel.com and read the installation documentation, which is great). We will go over how to install Laravel on your local environment (using Composer with the Laravel installer script).

Note If you read the install documentation and decide to go with the `homestead` virtual host option, then you don't need the installation process that I've outlined in this chapter, so feel free to skip to the next section.

After we get ourselves set up properly for Laravel development, we will go through another example scenario that you may encounter at some point. We will build a simple form that accepts and validates a file of a specific type and hits various endpoints defined as routes that will forward the request to the controller, which will then handle generating a filename and storing it in the filesystem.

We will go over Laravel basics such as the following:

- Routing configuration
- Controllers
- Artisan command-line utility for generating scaffold code
- Request and request validation

J. Griffin, *Domain-Driven Laravel*, https://doi.org/10.1007/978-1-4842-6023-4_4

- Front-end and blade templating

  - Setting up Ajax requests and response (The example I give is a bit archaic in terms of the front-end aspects, but I'm not focusing on the front end much in this book. For more on the latest and greatest front-end technologies, I recommend you check out *React*.)

- Laravel's request/response cycle

- A basic "flow" that you can repeat to start your own projects

We will be modifying the scaffolding that the Artisan tools provide to tweak things such as routes, requests, controllers, and other prebuilt templates. We will allow outside access *into* the application by means of URI-based routes. We will learn about requests in Laravel, including the request/response lifecycle and validation of incoming request data. I will show you how to seamlessly validate your requests by simply type-hinting them inside your controller methods, as well as how to go about setting up the proper validation constraints in the request's `rules()` method to automatically validate entire request objects. We want our API and our application to be as secure as possible, and Laravel has many great features to easily implement best-known security practices with (usually) just a few lines of code. I will dive into these a little and discuss some considerations and background knowledge that will help you start making sense of things.

You will learn about the *way* Laravel operates as well. If we are to create an application that has a model-driven design that is implemented using the Laravel framework and best practices, we need to gain a well-rounded understanding of both Laravel *and* those practices. Laravel will be the subject matter of this chapter, but we will follow the best practices that Laravel itself is established on.

I've included several sections that go off on a few select tangents but are nonetheless important concepts that you shouldn't skip over. These sidebars are meant to make you think more deeply about a specific concept, including the pros and cons of the decisions we make regarding the implementation of software, and to give you a few ideas for finding alternative means of accomplishing the same task in different ways. In Laravel, you are granted many freedoms to customize the way your application behaves, what it does, and how it does it. Of course, there is a standard "flow" to a Laravel application that is built into the framework itself (otherwise it wouldn't really be a framework), but it provides enough extension points and means of diverging execution of a program that allow us to accomplish virtually anything we could in standard PHP, only through a clearly defined API built on top of solid components.

I have left out the Eloquent ORM concepts for this chapter; however, we will discuss Eloquent in depth later because it is a key player in DDL.

Note   It is assumed that you already have a copy of PHP installed on your local system. If not, you can read how to install it here: `http://php.net/manual/en/install.php`.

Now then, let's get on with the Laravel setup and start learning some cool stuff.

Why Laravel?

In two decades, we've seen some quite extreme changes to the playing field that is web development—on an epic scale. These came in the form of front-cnd and backend advancements, systems design patterns, and new dialects and libraries. In 2000, Cake PHP introduced the first PHP web framework and enjoyed a worldwide reaction to what was an entirely *new* way of reasoning about and designing web applications. Included in the core of the system were implementations of a wide variety of tried and tested design patterns, and it was itself modeled as an MVC framework. The most important thing, in my opinion, was that it was a clear way to separate architectural concerns, allowing developers to start veering away from creating tangled spaghetti jungles of mixed layers (UI+data+infrastructure) jammed into a single file.

Before MVC, most PHP code was procedural in nature. Even complex web applications had little to no partition of layers. The real world required something better. The decision to implement the MVC pattern was one that had a viral response in the form of new (competing) PHP MVC frameworks. This is most likely what inspired Fabien Potencier to start the Symfony framework project and also is what fueled the Zend company to build out the Zend Framework. With the release of PHP v5.3 came an assortment of more evolved PHP frameworks. Symfony 2 and ZF 2 were complete rewrites of their former selves and embraced the new namespacing features available in PHP 5.3. Hidden away in the midst of this stuff going on was mastermind Taylor Otwell, who concocted the famous Laravel framework.

I'm a firm believer in the idea that practice makes better. That being said, the best way for you to gain anything from this chapter is to follow along and practice coding the examples. It is much easier to copy and paste the code (if you're reading a printed version of this book, even better), because you will learn faster and better by actually trying it on a computer and attempting to get the expected results, which I have provided as well. Reading code is good, but writing code is better. I've kept the content in this chapter very hands-on to better give you an idea of how things may go in the real world.

Installation Using Composer

Composer is both a package and dependency manager. To install it, open a terminal and cd into a new directory. Run this command:

```
curl -Ss getcomposer.org/installer | php
```

You should see something like the following:

```
All settings correct for using Composer
Downloading...
Composer (version 1.9.0) successfully installed to: /home/vagrant/Projects/
laravel/composer.phar
Use it: php composer.phar
```

Although there are numerous ways to set up a new Laravel application, we will do it via the Laravel Composer script. To install this script, run the following:

```
php composer.phar global require laravel/installer
```

This will not only download the packages you specify in the composer.json file but will also generate a nice little autoloader that you can "plug and play" in one line of code.

```
require_once('vendor/autoload.php');
```

In the Laravel stub project we are about to set up, this file is already included in the system inside the public index.php file, so we don't have to worry about it; just know it exists. Type the following command to initiate the Laravel installer, which should result in the latest framework version being installed (at the time of this writing, it's 6.0):

```
laravel new ddl
```

This command will generate a wealth of screen output similar to the following:

```
Crafting application...
Loading composer repositories with package information
Installing dependencies (including require-dev) from lock file
    1/3: https://codeload.github.com/laravel/framework/legacy.zip/
    f38711564c642ee88a58bf180010a0c7a7ab062e
    2/3: https://codeload.github.com/facade/flare-client-php/legacy.zip/
    a276603dbb7b9b35636d573d5709df5816dd4d2b
    3/3: https://codeload.github.com/facade/ignition/legacy.zip/1f92a209c1a
    5a60f43c5bbff196177810e817095
    Finished: success: 3, skipped: 0, failure: 0, total: 3
Package operations: 84 installs, 0 updates, 0 removals
  - Installing doctrine/inflector (v1.3.0): Loading from cache
{LONG LIST OF OTHER DEPENDENCIES INSTALLED FROM CACHE OR DOWNLOADED}
facade/ignition RUNS)
Discovered Package: suggests installing laravel/telescope (^2.0)
(LONG LIST OF OTHER SUGGESTED INSTALLS - IGNORE THESE)
Generating optimized autoload files
(A FEW COMMANDS THAT COMPOSER nunomaduro/collision
(A FEW OTHER DISCOVERED PACKAGES)
Package manifest generated successfully.
Application ready! Build something amazing.
```

If this is your first time installing the application's dependencies, you may see a bunch of Downloading... lines instead of Loading from cache.... If this is the case, just be patient; there are quite a few packages it needs to make Laravel run and could take several minutes.

You can investigate *what* actually went down in the filesystem by issuing an ls command.

We've already taken a pretty good look at the Laravel directory structure in Chapter 1, but here is a little more detail on the matter:

- app/: This is the source folder where our application code and domain model live. It is the location of the majority of the custom code found inside a typical Laravel app.

- `bootstrap/`: This holds the application's startup script and a few class map files.

- `config/`: This holds the app's default configuration and is overwritten by the parameters defined in the `.env` file.

- `database/`: This houses the database files including migrations, seeds, and test factories.

- `public/`: This is a publicly accessible folder holding compiled assets and of course the front door to Laravel, the `index.php` file.

- `resources/`: This holds front-end assets such as JavaScript files, language files, CSS/SASS files, and blade templates.

- `routes/`: All routes in the application are inside here; they are API or browser specific.

- `storage/`: This holds all the temp files in the system including cache data and sessions generated by the application, along with compiled view files and log files.

- `tests/`: This holds unit and functional tests.

- `vendor/`: This holds Composer-installed dependencies.

Now then, let's set up the rest of the app with an Artisan command. Artisan is the command-line utility that comes with Laravel and is extremely handy when developing Laravel apps. The `.env` file contains all the values required by the app and external packages and is used as a means of overwriting the default configuration found inside the `/config` folder.

Something important to note is the structure of the `Http` components inside Laravel. The concepts of a controller, route, and middleware have been grouped into a single parent namespace known as the application's `Http` namespace. It is located at `/dll/app/ Http` and is broken down like so:

- `App\Http\Controllers`

- `App\Http\Middleware`

- `App\Http\Requests`

Besides the domain model itself, we will be interacting with items inside the App\Http namespace a lot, so it's best to get good and familiar with this structure and the items found within it. I recommend going through all the files in the namespace first, just so you can get an idea of how Laravel is structured and how it handles HTTP requests.

Project 4-1: Laravel File Upload

Note   While working through the example projects (and indeed all projects in this text), I recommend actually taking the time to type the source code into the local environment we set up earlier in the chapter. I do not recommend you type the PHP doc blocks that annotate each class and method, as these were generated by an IDE (specifically, JetBrains PHPStorm, which I highly recommend you try). VSCode is an alternative IDE that is made by Microsoft. It's not worth it to type in all the comments either, unless you feel the need to do so. Note also that there are *no* annotations used in any example in this text; there is a reason for this that I will explain later.

In this tutorial, we will be building a simple application that will do the following things:

1. Display a web form via an HTTP route.

2. Provide a means of submitting the form via Ajax on the client side and return a valid response to the user indicating success or failure along with the name of the saved file.

3. Create a form request object that handles validation of the incoming data (including the validation of any attached files), which then gets injected into the controller.

4. Extract the file from the request, generate a filename, and store it in the filesystem under a new name.

5. On the client side, the response to the form submission request will be sent and received via Ajax, of which the response will be parsed and the user properly notified in either event: success or failure.

Note   For this example, I haven't included database-level or user-level security concerns. In a real-world application, these types of things should be put as a top priority *at all times*.

Table 4-1 describes the various components that we will need to tackle this beast.

Table 4-1. *Components Needed for the File Upload Demo Application*

Component Type	Component Name	Description
Route	/upload /process /list	Defines endpoints that are utilized by clients that point to some method located on the specified controller (in this case, the UploadController)
Template	upload.blade.php	Holds the web form and the Ajax calls used to submit the form and retrieve a response
Form Request	UploadFileRequest	Used to describe what is expected from the form and also validates the data and provides a mechanism for adding custom authentication logic
Controller	UploadController	Handles the request/response cycle

Configuring a Route

A route in Laravel is basically a URI or endpoint that allows communication from the outside world via a known URL address to a particular controller method and may contain URI parameters (query string). It is basically a client issuing a request to a defined route, which validates the form data based on a set of requirements and forwards the request to the proper location on the controller, which then delegates the logic used to store the uploaded file and return some type of response indicative of the success of the request (success or failure).

Either a route can be self-contained, with the logic needed to fulfill the request within a passed-in closure function that gets run and returned to the client, or a route can simply forward to a particular method on a controller, which accepts a request and returns a response. It's the same when using closure-defined routes, but the big difference is that you cannot use Laravel's caching facilities to cache closure-based routes. You can also declare the specific HTTP methods that are able to be hit with the namespace defined in the route group. See the section on routes in the Laravel documentation at `https://laravel.com/docs/6.0/routing#basic-routing`.

Laravel provides a means to restrict the given route to be available only via a specific HTTP verb, attach runtime logic to groups of routes via middleware, and tag any route with an easy-to-remember (and type) name so you don't have to remember long strings of URLs when referring to different endpoints within the code. It also gives us many additional options regarding how to structure the route and define the route-level parameters—there is a lot of flexibility in this component. I recommend checking out the documentation to get an idea of the raw power that the Routing component offers right out of the box. Routing configuration for the entire application is located in two central files (but can be customized to be structured in any way you'd like): `routes/web.php` and `routes/api.php`.

Later in the book, we will be restructuring the entire Laravel framework's directory and namespace map to be more domain-driven by separating out each defined set of routes into corresponding modules inside our domain model. We will use the modules defined within our domain model as direct "groups" of routes. This task is made easily in Laravel thanks to the robustness and flexibility that its Routing component offers.

Note   If you read the install documentation and decided to go with the `homestead` virtual host option, then you don't need the installation process that I've outlined in this chapter, so feel free to skip to the next section.

As I mentioned earlier, not only can a route be forwarded to a controller method, it can also be self-defined with a *callback function*. The idea is the same: run the logic within the callback function and return some type of response. Here is an example of a simple route defined as a closure function:

```
Route::get('/uri/something', function() {
    return 'You are at the path : /uri/something';
});
```

This is the simplest route there is. It matches up the URL string /uri/something and returns a simple "You are at the path : /uri/something." The way you can think of it is that there is some URI that, upon invocation, will return whatever the resulting calculation is from the callback function. It offers the same kind of request handling as using a controller, and it's just as convenient as using a controller to define the logic of that particular route, so it's really up to you and your team to use. However, I suggest using controllers to define the logic that your route runs so that it is separate from the route definition itself.

If you are like me and don't like mixing route configuration and controlling logic in one (or many) route file(s), you can elect to have the route dispatch the request to a controller, where you can add any other validation (which we will see in a bit) or custom logic that you need to generate a proper response to the request.

```
Route::get('/uri/something', 'SomethingController@something');
```

I personally think that this is a better approach because it does *not* bloat the route files with business logic and instead uses the controller and route-file approach, like so:

```
/**
 * Something Controller - something()
 */
Public function something()
{
    return 'You are at the path : /uri/something';
}
```

This achieves the same effect as the closure-defined route.

Note   There are other approaches and theories regarding the way routes should be specified when routing requests to controllers. For example, Symfony's take on it is to have your "controlling logic" and your route definitions together, but existing within the controllers as annotations, which are comments with code that get parsed and used. In this regard, it would make sense to have them together because they are in different context than being inside a routes file. My perspective on it is it's simply too verbose in the way it uses annotations for validating parameters and passed-in data. Laravel offers a much better and cleaner solution than this, which I will demonstrate later in the chapter. To that point, annotations are extremely ugly and make the code literally look like a tangled mess of crap that appears to be commented out at first, so it's not always obvious they are actually doing anything at first glance.

We have multiple routes to define that do different things. Keeping them grouped in a controller keeps a clean separation of concerns, although it is discouraged to use controllers to house core domain logic. Remember, the proper place for business logic is in the domain model; controllers live outside the domain model and are responsible for "shaking hands" with clients via a request, dispatching whatever work needs to be done to other components, and returning a response indicative of the success or failure of the request. Also, it is better to use controllers to define your route's behavior rather than inline closure functions because routes in Laravel can be cached only if there are no inline callbacks in your route definitions.

Route Files

Routes are stored inside files under the `/routes` folder inside the project's root directory. By default, there are a few different files corresponding to the different "sides" of the application (the term *sides* comes from the hexagonal architecture). Together, these sides form a boundary that encapsulates the application's business logic inside an imaginary shape (perhaps in the shape of a hexagon), with the domain model in the very center of that shape, and all requests into it must use some type of adapter that will allow them to cross the boundary into the application.

In Laravel, there are a few different route files that come out of the box.

- `web.php`: This has the public-facing browser-based routes. These are the most common and is what gets hit by the web browser. They are run through the web middleware group and also contain facilities for CSRF protection (which helps defend against form-based malicious attacks and hacks) and generally contain a thread of "state" (by this I mean they utilize sessions) in order to persist data between requests.

- `api.php`: This has routes that correspond to an API group and thus have the API middleware enabled by default. These routes are stateless and have no sessions or cross-request memory (one request does not share data or memory with any other request; each one is self-encapsulated). API routes commonly sit behind an authorization mechanism (such as a bearer token) that must be included in every request header.

- `console.php`: These routes correspond to custom Artisan commands that we have ran to generate the scaffolding of our Laravel components. Later, we will create our own Artisan commands that can be ran via the command line to build numerous quick and dirty procedures that can be scheduled or sent to a message queue.

- `channels.php`: This registers routes for event broadcasting. We won't go too far into event broadcasting in this book, but Laravel does provide built-in support for it. To learn more about event broadcasting in Laravel, check out the documentation.

The main file to be concerned with at this time is the browser-specific one, `web.php`. There is already one route defined by default, which is the one that gets hit right when a user navigates to the web root of your application (the web root is in the public directory) or the home page. It is worth mentioning that an API-specific route would not be appropriate to return a full-fledged HTML page meant to be rendered in a browser window. APIs have generally simpler responses, often consisting of a JSON-encoded string with metadata such as status code, human-readable message, or error notifications. That's why there are two separate route files. When you hit a web page, that route came from the `web.php` route file. However, if you were to submit a form on that page, you might actually hit an API route (in `api.php`) that actually carries out the processing of the form. We are going to need three different routes for our example upload application to function (see Figure 4-2).

Table 4-2. *Route Configuration for Our File Upload Example Application*

Route Name	Route URI	Purpose
upload	/upload	This will be the main page displaying our web form for uploading files.
process	/process	This is where the form (located at /upload) initiates a post to submitted data to the path inside the form's `action` value.
list	/list	This lists all uploaded files in the system.

Note   The /list endpoint may not be needed if we wanted to put all the logic for displaying the upload form *and* the list of files on a single page; however, I kept them separate for now to add some additional context and scope to our demo. We will revisit this later.

Let's create our basic HTML upload form, starting with the route definitions. Open your routes/web.php file and enter the code from Listing 4-1 into it.

Listing 4-1. The Routes We Use in the Example file-uploader Application

```
// routes/web.php
Route::get('/upload', 'UploadController@upload')->name('upload');
Route::post('/process', 'UploadController@process')->name('process');
Route::get('/list', 'UploadController@list')->name('list');
```

For each desired route, we make a separate entry for it explicitly in the corresponding routes file (in this case, web.php) using one of the available HTTP-specific request methods (get(), post(), put(), patch(), delete(), and options()). For a breakdown of each of these, check the Web. What these methods do is specify which HTTP verbs are allowed to access that given route via the defined URI (or endpoint). If you need a route to be able to accept more than one HTTP verb (which could be the case if you are using a single page to both display the initial data and post submitted form data), you could use the Route::any() method. Generally, GET routes are used to ask a question or retrieve/read some data from the application, whereas POST routes are used to submit forms updates of some model or data structure inside the application. PUT is used to create a new instance of that model or database entity.

The first argument to these route definitions is the URI or endpoint at which you want the route to be accessed at (the physical location on the web server). The second argument to both the Route::get() and Route::post() methods (and any of the other HTTP-verb-related methods that the Route facade supports) is the location of the code that gets executed upon hitting the route's endpoint with the allowed HTTP verb (GET, POST, PATCH, etc.). Laravel provides an easy means of specifying the controller/controller method combination that the router will forward the request. We are using the `UploadController` for all three routes and have specified them in the following fashion:

```
Route::get('/upload', '{CONTROLLER_NAME}@{CONTROLLER_METHOD}`)
```

The last method we call on each route is its `name()` function, which accepts a single string as an argument and is used to more or less "tag" a particular route with an easy-to-remember name (in our cases, upload, process, and list). I realize it doesn't seem so great of a feature to give each route its own name when the URL is named the same, but it really comes in handy when you have a specific route like `/users/profile/dashboard/config`, which would be easier to remember as `profile-admin` or `user-config`.

Note   The type of method chaining available on many of Laravel's components that allow you to call additional methods on the returned object in an easy-to-use way that pretty much mimics the English language. This is known as a *fluent interface*. Here is an example of one, taken from a Laravel migration, which is used to define and track changes to a database schema (in the following case, we are defining a foreign key constraint):

```
$table->foreign('user_id')
->references('id')->on('users')
->onDelete('cascade');
```

As you can see, the "language" of the method chaining makes a complete English sentence, which is usually a lot easier to remember than arbitrary method names.

A Note on Facades

"Facades provide a 'static' interface to classes that are available in the application's service container.

"They provide a terse, memorable syntax that allows you to use Laravel's features without remembering long class names that must be injected or configured manually."

—Laravel docs

In the previous route definitions, we use the Route facade instead of manually instantiating a new `Illuminate/Routing/Router` object and calling the corresponding methods on that object. It's just a shortcut that saves typing. Facades are used heavily throughout the Laravel framework; you can and should get more familiar with them. The docs for Facades can be found at `https://laravel.com/docs/6.x/facades`. If you don't like facades, you can just as easily use static method calls instead.

Generating the Controller

Enough small talk (although this book is primarily in PHP, not Smalltalk), let's continue and generate the controller that will be part of the application layer that will act as a mechanism for handling the request, that is, accepting a request and returning a response. This is all any controller should ever do!

It bears repeating: the following are the *only* things that a controller should do:

- *Accept a request*: The route wires up a URI to a general-purpose or specific `Request` object, whose data is validated *before* it is auto-injected into the controller method defined in the route (accomplished by simply type-hinting the request object in the controller method). This part of the request/response lifecycle can also be thought of as a handshake-type mechanism between the client and the application.

- *Return a response*: After dispatching work (most likely in the form of jobs, commands, or some other actionable domain object or facade), a response is needed to give the requesting user in accordance with the particular method they used to access the system. For example, calls made to an API that is offered by a web application typically require some sort of JSON-encoded response with a human-readable success message, HTTP status code, and maybe some additional data about the status of the request. On the other hand, a response to a browser request could be a slew of different HTML, CSS, and JavaScript code that gets parsed by the browser and displayed within a window.

The good news is that Laravel provides easy-to-use facilities to do all this and more! To get the basic structure of a controller, we can use for the purposes of this example, run the following command from within the project's root directory:

```
// inside the directory "ddl/"
php artisan make:controller UploadController
```

Essentially, what this command does is generates a *stub* for a controller named UploadController inside of the main controller directory at /app/Http/Controllers/UploadController.php. Open it up and take a gander. It's simple because it is only a stubbed-out version of the controller, with the correct namespace path and the required classes that it extends from (see Listing 4-2).

Listing 4-2. Generated Controller Stub From

```
// ddl/app/Http/Controllers/UploadController.php

<?php
namespace App\Http\Controllers;
use Illuminate\Http\Request;
class UploadController extends Controller
{
    //
}
```

Generating the Request

Before we continue making a few changes to the UploadController's generated stub, let's get all the scaffolding code generated at once. That way, we can get a clear, high-level picture of the overall process without getting lost in the finer-grained details that make it work internally.

Note   It's important to understand the difference between a form request and a request object. A *form request* is a type of request that's specific to a standard HTML web form and contains the submitted data and any attached files, along with the validation requirements specified inside the request's `rules()` method. On the other hand, a request object is Laravel's extension of the Symfony request object, which encapsulates a real HTTP request (via, for example, a `curl` command) and packages it with easy-to-use accessors and manipulators (more on these later), as well as contains such data as header information, query parameters, request body parameters, cookies, session values, and the HTTP verb, the URL, and the referring URL.

The controller method that handles the request must type hint the specific request class in its signature. There are a few shortcuts available in Laravel that give you access to awesome validation features, targeting such concerns as request validation, database validation, and parameter validation, and they give us opportunities to create additional complex domain-level validation using implementations of the `Illuminate\Contracts\Validation` contracts. (You'll learn more about this later in the chapter.) For now, let's use the Artisan command again to generate our request stub.

```
php artisan make:request UploadFileRequest
```

This command will generate a file called `UploadFileRequest` inside app/Http/Requests/UploadFileRequest. Open up the stub and take a peek. You will find it simple, containing only two methods, `authorize()` and `rules()`.

What we have just generated is known as a *form request*. It is meant to capture any passed-in data from an HTML form, validate the incoming data based on our specified validation checks, and be injected into a controller method where it can be used or modified (although the latter isn't recommended due to the request being immutable).

Listing 4-3 shows what the generated request will look like out of the box.

Listing 4-3. A Generated Form Request Stub

```
// ddl/app/Http/Requests/UploadFileReq    uest.php
<?php
namespace App\Http\Requests;
use Illuminate\Foundation\Http\FormRequest;
```

```php
class UploadFileRequest extends FormRequest
{
    /**
     * Determine if the user is authorized to make this request.
     *
     * @return bool
     */
    public function authorize()
    {
        return false;
    }
    /**
     * Get the validation rules that apply to the request.
     *
     * @return array
     */
    public function rules()
    {
        return [
            //
        ];
    }
}
```

Customizing the Generated Request

Let's modify the previous request stub to meet the needs of our application. The scaffolding code is nice to have because it allows you to basically prototype the various components you will need to make your application do what you need it to do.

Creating the Validation Logic

Open the UploadFileRequest file and change it to look like Listing 4-4.

Listing 4-4. Modified Request Stub for Our Upload Application

```php
// ddl/app/Http/Requests/UploadFileRequest.php

<?php

namespace App\Http\Requests;
use Illuminate\Foundation\Http\FormRequest;
class UploadFileRequest extends FormRequest
{
    /**
     * Determine if the user is authorized to make this request.
     *
     * @return bool
     */
    public function authorize()
    {
        // NOTE: This is a convenient location to include any auth
        // checks or other authentication logic specific to this
        // specific form request.

        return true;
    }

    /**
     * Get the validation rules that apply to the request. It is here
     * that we specify how we want the data to be structured and what
     * it should look like.
     *
     * @return array
     */
    public function rules()
    {
      return [
            'fileName' => 'required|string',
            'userFile' => 'required|file'
      ];
    }
}
```

There are not a whole lot of changes in Listing 4-4. First, the `authorize()` method now returns true instead of false. This method is responsible for allowing the request to pass into the application. If it evaluates to false, it stops the request from entering the system (i.e., does not pass the request to the corresponding controller method defined in the route) and instead returns some sort of error response. This response will be specific, again, to the type of request made: web, API, or . This would be a handy place to put any authorization checks on the user or any other logic that may need to occur to decide whether the request can move forward to the controller method, where it is processed and a response returned—or, the logic may determine that the request isn't valid and instead issue an error response with some 4xx or 5xx status code (indicating a "not found" error or a server issue), which may be described using a specific `Exception` class to log the error on the backend, but may appear as a generic error page on the browser.

For now, we just return true here to allow anything and everything to use the request, but it's also a great place to add authentication logic and other validation checks relating to authentication or authorization. See a more in-depth example in the following section.

The other method, `rules()`, is where all the magic comes into play with regard to validation. The idea is simple: return an array containing a set of rules in the following form:

```
'formFieldName' => 'pipe-delimited validators'
```

There are a variety of constraints that are supported by Laravel right out of the box. For a full list of them, check out the online documentation at `https://laravel.com/docs/6.x/validation#available-validation-rules`. For our upload application, there are going to be two fields that are passed in via a POST request from a form on the front end. The `fileName` parameter must be included inside the form body (i.e., required) and is used as the filename we will store the file under in the storage (this is done in the controller—we will get to it a little later). We also specify that the filename must be a string by adding a pipe character (|) and the word `string`. Constraints are always delimited by pipes, allowing you to specify many additional criteria for the given field in a single line. That is some powerful stuff!

The second parameter, `userFile`, is the actual *file* that the user uploads from a form on a web page. `UserFile` is also required and must be a file.

Note   If we were expecting the uploaded file to be an image, then we would use the image constraint instead, which would limit the file types accepted to be one of the most popular image types (JPEG, PNG, BMP, GIF, or SVG). Since we want to allow the user to upload *any* type of file, we will just stick with the file validation constraint without checking the extension. Is this a valid security measure or a potential security flaw that we introduced by now specifying the type of allowable file extensions we accept into our application? I discuss this later in the chapter in the section titled "The Bigger Picture," but, more specifically, I include the section "Using MIME Types to Verify Uploaded Files" next that will demonstrate how to use MIME types to validate the files are what they claim to be.

Something else to note about the request object's `rules()` method is that if for some reason we omitted a parameter that we *did* want to validate inside the request, it obviously would not have any requirements and would be passed along to the controller with the rest of the other parameters the user submitted using the form. The automatic validation will work correctly only if you specify all fields in the form, along with their constraints, inside the `rules()` method of the request. Also, when you do include a parameter in the `rules()` method that's not present in the form's incoming values, Laravel will stop the request short of hitting the controller method defined in the corresponding route definition.

That is about all there is to the request object. Its main job is to simply hold the acceptable set of criteria (constraints) that the form's body parameters must satisfy in order to proceed deeper into the application. Another thing to note is that these two fields (`userFile` and `filename`) must also be specified inside the HTML code in the form of input fields (with the field name corresponding to the name inside the request object).

You might be asking: sure, this defines the characteristics of what a form request should contain, but where is the actual check of these constraints performed? We will discover the best way to perform these checks in an automated fashion by using the validations configured in our request; however, the manual way to perform an auth check looks something like the following:

```
$validatedData = $request->validate([
    'fileName' => 'required|string,
    'userFile' => 'required|file',
]);
```

Customizing the Generated Controller

We are ready to customize the controller logic. Open app/Http/Controllers/
UploadController.php and modify it so it looks like the one listed in Listing 4-5.
Remember, if you are following along in the example and manually typing the application,
you do not have to worry about transcribing the comments because I do not use
annotations in this book for any kind of special functionality. Avoid the extra keystrokes for
something more useful. In a production environment or part of a published language or
API documentation, however, the docblocks should be included on every class, method,
and package.

Listing 4-5. The Modified UploadController That Handles the Persistence of the
Uploaded File

```php
<?php
namespace App\Http\Controllers;

use Illuminate\Contracts\Container\BindingResolutionException;
use Illuminate\Http\Request;
use App\Http\Requests\UploadFileRequest;
use Illuminate\Support\Facades\Storage;
class UploadController extends Controller
{
    /**
     * This is the method that will simply list all the files uploaded
     * by name and provide a link to each one so they may be
     * downloaded
     * @param $request : A standard form request object
     * @return \Illuminate\Contracts\View\Factory|\Illuminate\View\View
     * @throws BindingResolutionException
     */
    public function list(Request $request)
    {
        $uploads = Storage::allFiles('uploads');
        return view('list', ['files' => $uploads]);
    }
    /**
```

```
 * @param $file
 * @return \Symfony\Component\HttpFoundation\BinaryFileResponse
 * @throws BindingResolutionException
 */
public function download($file)
{
    return response()->download(storage_path('app/'.$file));
}
/**
 * @return \Illuminate\Contracts\View\Factory|\Illuminate\View\View
 * @throws BindingResolutionException
 */
public function upload()
{
    return view('upload');
}
/**
 * This method will handle the file uploads. Notice that the
 * parameter's type-hint is the exact request class we generated
 * in the last step. There is a reason for this!
 *
 * @param $request : The form request for uploading a file
 * @return array | \Illuminate\Http\UploadedFile |
 * \Illuminate\Http\UploadedFile[] | null
 * @throws BindingResolutionException
 */
public function store(UploadFileRequest $request)
{
    $filename = $request->fileName;
    //the request is valid at this point because of the defined
    //parameters we specified in the form request
     $file = $request->file('userFile'); //no isset() req'd

    //retrieve the original extension of uploaded file
     $extension = $file->getClientOriginalExtension();
    //create a new file name
```

```
        $saveAs = $filename . "." . $extension;
        //save the file to the local filesystem, inside uploads/
        $file->storeAs('uploads', $saveAs, 'local');
        //return a success message
        return response()->json(['success' => true]);
    }
}
```

So, it's a fairly straightforward approach to saving the uploaded files to disk. Here is a breakdown of the upload() method:

1. Type hint the request class in the controller method that is doing the heavy lifting functionality so we can auto-validate the incoming data.

2. Grab the file out of the (now validated) request object inside the controller method.

3. Grab the filename out of the request.

4. Generate the final filename that will be used to save the file under. The getClientOriginalExtension() method retrieves the original uploaded extension of the uploaded file (if you can't guess at the obvious functionality implied by the name, of course).

5. Store the file to the local filesystem using its storeAs() method, passing in the named path inside the /storage directory as the first argument and the filename to save it under as the second.

6. Return a JSON response indicating the request was successful.

Also included in the controller are a few methods to facilitate the user interaction between the browser and the application, like for downloading a given file, viewing a list of past uploaded files, or displaying the form on a page that the user can access.

Figure 4-1 shows what's going on.

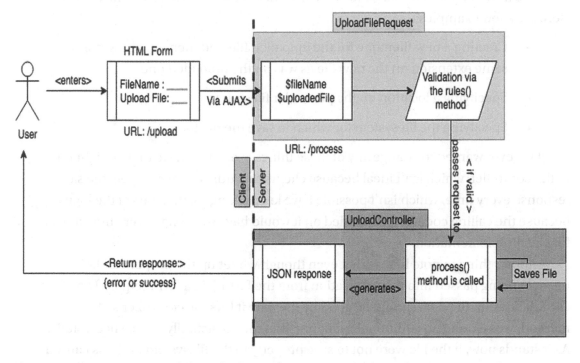

Figure 4-1. *Overview of the whole application including the request and response*

This design will work, but it's not perfect. There is still room for improvement. Can you identify where? If you can't, I'll give you a few hints (so that you can better handle these types of things as they occur in real-life situations). One of the most important pieces of advice I can give you is this: make it a habit to fall back on best practices and become familiar with design patterns, architectural patterns, and core software design principles so that you have a place to go when you are stuck or confused about how to go about structuring your application (the correct answer to that is inline with the domain model).

If you remember from earlier in the chapter, I made it a point to inculcate that controllers should be limited to doing one of two possible things: accepting a request or returning a response. The controller I have created earlier does work and all, but the issue lies in a violation of a core software design principle: separation of concerns. The controller's `store()` method contains the actual business logic involved in saving the uploaded file (in its entirety!) when it should actually be separate from the controller, as part of the domain model. The fact that there are multiple concerns within the central topic is a hint that they should be located elsewhere besides inline with the controller. Here are a few examples:

- Creating a new filename for the uploaded file and then attaching the same extension on the new file as was on the uploaded one

- Specifying a location on the particular filesystem

- Specifying the filesystem for which to save the file to

If we ever wanted to change any of these things, we would have to do it right there in the controller, which isn't ideal because clients that utilize it may expect the same response every time, which isn't possible if we keep changing that part of the logic, because the calling code that depended on it would have to change every time as well, for each implementation.

Another thing to note here is that even though we set up the proper validation for the data being passed into the application from the form (via a form request) and have confidence that the data should be good by the time it hits the controller's store() method, we've done no additional validation that the file actually saved successfully. As it stands now, if the file were not to save properly to the filesystem and this caused a silent error that went to a log rather than display on-screen as well, you would have no indication that saving the upload file had actually not occurred and would go on with the assumption that everything is just dandy because the only response being returned from that method is a basic JSON-type API response, only viewable by opening up the developer tools add-on of your favorite web browser and searching through a heap of network calls, which is utterly inefficient for a practical implementation in the real world. We are literally lacking any validation of the file being saved to the specified filesystem. Because we are professional, highly skilled (and damned handsome) developers who appreciate the quality of their work, we will go through this shortcoming and fix it up.

If something else has been bugging you this entire time, it probably is the fact that we've used our controller's method body to house our main concern of the application: the process of accepting, verifying, and storing an uploaded file. These are *domain concerns* that should be handled in the *domain model*. There are many different ways to handle this scenario.

Let's start with the misplacement of the logic within the body of the upload() method within the UploadController. We know that there is too much going on in this controller, so we decide to split apart the domain *logic* involved in saving an uploaded file to storage, which we will delegate a call from inside our controller. There are a number of other ways we could approach this problem that would force us to push the file processing and storage logic down to the domain layer. I will highlight several ways to do this (and there are many, many other approaches that could work just as well).

We can choose to implement some sort of command bus. Essentially, a command bus is a design pattern that has two components that are used to facilitate operations involving the service layer of the application as well as facilitate responses going out of the app: the `Command` object and the `Handler` object. The `Command` object simply holds a user request (or client request), and all parameters and passed-in user data gets encapsulated into this `Command` object—it's the what. The `Handler` component is the doer (or the how) and encapsulates any logic that is to be run that directly corresponds to a `Command` object's request. Each `Command` has, in theory, one handler object that is specific to that `Command` object. Think of a handler as a means of carrying out a request encapsulated inside a `Command` object.

Because of the popularity of the command bus architecture, several PHP-specific libraries have emerged that handle the various topics and ins and outs of a working command bus. They are Broadway (`https://github.com/broadway/broadway`) and Tactician (`https://tactician.thephpleague.com/`). Both packages are well written with quality code and the tests to back them both, and if you are going to build out a full command bus pipeline with event sourcing, CQRS support, event replays, and projections, you may want to consider giving Broadway a look because it supports all that and much more.

If, on the other hand, you are looking to implement a smaller, microservice-based architecture that would have the basic command and handler setup for a relatively low number of recent possible requests and responses, then Tactician may be a better choice. Tactician has a small size on disk and is super-fast, effective, and easy to learn. It supports a variety of different middleware (or you can roll out your own) and supports custom extension points for such concerns as logging, caching, and support for firing and tracking events.

The League of Extraordinary Packages is the group that created and maintains Tactician and other high-quality stand-alones for the PHP community. You can find all of them here, along with very high-quality documentation: `https://thephpleague.com`.

Another possible way to handle this scenario is by placing the code relating to the processing and storing of files uploaded via the form in a *domain service*. Whenever we are modeling out systems and the interactions the system has with our domain objects, there isn't always a clean-cut, surefire answer to the basic question we ask of all our application components: what is it, and where does it belong? If it isn't a thing and instead falls under the category of a business process, make a service to encapsulate the business logic and call it from the controller, passing along any required variables or data that is needed to fulfill the request. The service then does its thing and either returns a result to the controller, which then gets returned to the client, or writes the result to a separate log or even logs an event to a task or message queue.

One other possible solution would be to create a *job.* Jobs exist within the domain model and are run as independent units of work, callable from anywhere in the codebase. Laravel has full support for creating and managing jobs and even has a separate prebuilt application that offers a powerful UI that allows administrators a visual way to view and manage different jobs running in the system. We will dive into jobs in later chapters, but one thing to note is (like most other things in Laravel) there is a mechanism for generating jobs that will generate a scaffolding of a generic Job class via an Artisan command. We will go over a possible implementation of one such job later in the chapter, in the section "Using Laravel Jobs to Encapsulate Business Logic."

USING MIME TYPES TO VERIFY UPLOADED FILES

I want to step back for a moment and revisit the issue of accepting nonvalidated file types into the system. We basically have no other validation in our system at this point other than the answer to the simplest possible question: "Is it a file?" This should have been a very loud indicator that additional security is going to be needed so that we don't create a huge security vulnerability in our system by being too liberal on the types of files we want to allow users to upload.

Given the fact that validating a file extension provides some level of security against malicious files entering the system, it can and should be verified so as to "weed out" any file types other than ones having a specific extension appended. However, aside from preventing legitimate users from selecting the wrong file, it doesn't do us a whole lot of good against, say, a user actually attempting to upload a malicious file. One could just as easily change the extension of a known malicious file before they uploaded it via a web form. Without any proper validation, a user could, in theory, be able to upload a file containing a worm algorithm to our system because we decided not to implement a more advanced method of verifying the file's true type.

Laravel does provide us with a few tools we can leverage to beef up the security of the application. We need to validate the incoming file by using its declared MIME type to ascertain the true file extension (as opposed to the extension provided in the name of the file corresponding to everything after the last period, which is as easy for a user to change as it is to rename a file before uploading it). The extension type that is pulled off the file is then compared to the file's extension as specified by the suffix of the filename.

This is done automatically when using a method on the `File` facade named `putFileAs()` or by calling the `store()` method on the file located directly inside the request.

```
//calling the store() method in a chain-like manner from the request
$path = $request->file('customers')->store('customers.csv');
```

```
//explicitly using putFileAs() on the Storage facade
Storage::putFileAs('customers', new File('/path/to/customers'), 'customers.csv');
```

The only problem with this is that the MIME type that gets validated is actually obtained from the MIME type that the file in question indicates, which can be easily modified to appear to be something else. Laravel provides a MIME-type validation that we can use that will actually attempt to guess the MIME type of any given file from that file's contents rather than rely on its metadata. All we have to do to tap into this validation is simply by adding the following to our form request object, inside the `rules()` method:

```
//in ddl/app/Http/Requests/UploadFileRequest.php
```

```
//replace the rule for userFile to look like the following in the
public function rules() {
//...
'userFile' => 'mimetypes:video/avi,video/mpeg,video/quicktime,image/
bmp,image/jpeg,image/gif'
//...
```

IMPORTANT: Although this provides additional security for our application, we do lose a bit of flexibility as a trade-off because the changes made restrict the file's MIME type to be one of the supported video or image formats listed in the `rules()` method at the key `userFile`. This is a never-ending struggle that you will face in the real world constantly: *security versus convenience*. We will discuss this more in depth in later chapters.

The Blade Template

The last part of the application that we need is the part that actually displays the form inside a browser and handles all the Ajax calls that actually perform the logic needed to submit the form and upload the file to the server. Create a new file located at ddl/ resources/views/upload.blade.php (Listing 4-6).

Listing 4-6. The Blade Template

```
<!-- ddl/resources/views/upload.blade.php -->
<body>
    <h1>Upload a file</h1>
    <form id="uploadForm" name="uploadForm"
action="{{route('upload')}}" enctype="multipart/form-data">
        @csrf
        <label for="fileName">File Name:</label>
        <input type="text" name="fileName" id="fileName" required />
          <br />
          <label for="userFile">Select a File</label>
        <input type="file" name="userFile" id="userFile" required />
        <button type="submit" name="submit">Submit</button>
    </form>
    <h2 id="success" style="color:green;display:none">Successfully uploaded
    file</h2>
    <h2 id="error" style="color:red;display:none">Error Submitting File</h2>
    <script src="//ajax.googleapis.com/ajax/libs/jquery/1.9.1/jquery.min.js">
    </script>
    <script>
        $('#uploadForm').on('submit', function(e) {
            e.preventDefault();
            var form = $(this);
            var url = form.attr('action');
            $.ajax({
                url: url,
                type: "POST",
                data: new FormData(this),
```

```
                 processData: false,
                 contentType: false,
                 dataType: "JSON",
                 success: function(data) {
                     $("#fileName").val("");
                     $("#userFile").val("");
                 }
          }).done(function() {
              $('#success').css('display', 'block');
              window.setTimeout(()=>($("#success").css('display',
              'none')), 5000);
          }).fail(function() {
              $('#error').css('display', 'block');
              window.setTimeout(()=>($("#error").css('display',
              'none')), 5000);
          });
      });
  </script>
</body>
</html>
```

This is a typical example of a blade file containing an HTML form and JavaScript/jQuery for adding asynchronous functionality (so we can make calls to the server endpoints and receive data from those calls without ever refreshing the current page). There is a basic `<form>` tag with no method attribute (which I'll explain in just a second) and with a curious `action` attribute with the value `{{route('file.upload')}}`. In a blade, this is what is known as a *directive*. A directive is just a fancy name for function; there are functions specific to blade templates that perform different operations that are common to constructing web pages and web applications. For a better understanding of all the cool stuff that blade can do, check out `https://laravel.com/docs/6.x/blade`. In the previous case, we are using the route directive to generate a URL for our form submission.

Remember that we defined our routes earlier in the application inside the `web.php` file, specifying an easy-to-remember name for each of them. The `{{route()}}` directive accepts a name of a route, looks it up inside the internally cached routes list, and generates a full URL based on the definition of that route in the `web.php` file. For this first case, we are specifying that we want the form to send its submitted data to the /process endpoint, which is defined as a POST route.

The next weird thing you may have noticed is the @csrf tag right below the opening form tag. In blade, this tag generates a _token parameter on the form, which gets checked inside the application before the form data is allowed to be processed. This ensures that the data inside the form is of a valid origin and prevents cross-site request forgery attacks. For more information on this, see https://laravel.com/docs/6.x/csrf.

Note   If we omit the @csrf tag in the previous template, Laravel will not accept the form and instead will return a "419: Page Expired" error *unless* you add the specific page that the form lives on to the $except property of the VerifyCsrfToken middleware, located at app/Http/Middleware/ VerifyCsrfToken, like so (do not actually do this in the example project we are building; this is for demonstration purposes only):

```
//inside VerifyCsrfToken.php
/**
 * The URIs that should be excluded from CSRF verification.
 *
 * @var array
 */
protected $except = [
    '/payment-gateay-url'
];
```

Now you should be able to start your local development server with the following command:

```
php artisan serve
```

This should give you a message similar to this one:

```
Laravel development server started: <http://127.0.0.1:8000>
```

When you navigate to this page in the browser, you will see the Laravel default splash page displayed on the screen. Go ahead and navigate to http://127.0.0.1:8000/ upload to see a basic form on the screen. Fill in some type of filename, select any type of file from your computer for the upload input, and click Submit. Once you do this, you should see the success message we defined earlier on the screen, or you may get the error message if something didn't go right (for whatever reason).

Something to be aware of is that if after submitting the form you receive a "403 : Unauthorized" error, it's most likely because you forgot to change the form request's `authorize()` method to return true instead of false.

If for some reason you do not see what you were expecting to see or if the form process fails for some reason, be sure to verify that all code you've transcribed into your own editor is correct. There may be a few other potential points of failure that we did not think of initial or anticipate when writing this piece of functionality. This is an accurate depiction of web development in the real world. We are given a list of requirements, have conversations and meetings to nail down the *exact* requirements, design the means of *meeting* those requirements, and build an implementation of a solution that resolves the requirements. There is *no way* we can think of everything that could possibly happen to a request when we are writing the specifications for it in our software. It's simply impossible.

Instead, what we are left with is to fall back on good programming standards and best practices. In this case, the concept we need to remember to apply is *iterative development*, or small, incremental changes, to the application to flesh out all the requirements in code.

The Bigger Picture

Let's look at what we've done.

You should recall that the request object we constructed at the beginning of this tutorial should have the same parameters defined in its rules method as on the form in the blade template (if not, reread the section "Creating the Validation Logic"). The user fills the form on the web page located at /upload that is rendered via a blade template engine and submits the form. The template's jQuery code at the bottom stops the default submission (which would automatically redirect to the page specified in the form's `action` parameter), creates an Ajax POST request, loads the request with the form data and uploaded file, and sends the whole thing into our application, which creates the internally used request object that gets fed into the route or controller method containing logic for this endpoint.

The request object gets populated by associating the parameters inside the `rules()` method with the submitted form parameters and then validates the data according to each specified rule. If all the rules are satisfied, the request gets passed along to whatever controller method corresponds to the values defined in the route file `web.php`. In this case, it is the `process()` method of the `UploadController` that does the work. Once we hit the controller, we already know that the request passed validation, so we don't have to retest if the filename given is in fact a `string` or the `userFile` parameter actually holds some type of file. We can continue as normal.

The controller method then grabs the validated parameters out of the request object, generates a filename by concatenating the passed-in `fileName` parameter with the `userFile`'s original extension, stores the file inside a directory in our application, and then returns a simple JSON-encoded response verifying that the request was successful.

A NOTE ON SECURITY CONCERNS

Question: Is there any part of the system we have implemented (thus far) that jumps out at you as being a potential source of error or confusion?

Answer: Along with additional concerns that could very well be valid but are not listed here are the following scenarios that we have *not* yet accounted for or protected against in our application:

- Security concerns

    - There is no user-level authorization that takes place in the application, although a possible solution for this could be to implement a policy, which I discuss briefly in the example found in the "Authenticating Form Requests and Using Policies" section later in the chapter.

    - There is a lack of constraints specified in the form request, particularly surrounding the file that is uploaded to the server. If left as is, there would be no checks to guarantee that the file didn't contain malware or some type of botnet replication software. Checking the extension only gets you partway there. The solution to this can be found in the section "Using MIME types to Verify Uploaded Files" included earlier in the chapter.

- Persistence concerns

  - A less obvious concern would be the other user-input parameter in our form. fileName, a required string, is the corresponding name given to the saved file once it enters the system. As it stands, the user can submit *any* valid string, as long as it's neither blank nor omitted, and our application will gladly accept it, validate the string, and attempt to use it to save the file inside a given filesystem. This filesystem could be a Dropbox account or perhaps a local place on the hard drive—we don't know. As such, these platforms all have certain restrictions on how a file can be named, how long the name is allowed to be, and the character set that is allowed to make up the name. One solution to this issue is to utilize Laravel's nifty League\Flysystem\Util::normalizePath() method simply by adding the following code to the UploadController's store() method, right after the $filename variable is defined.

- Architectural Concerns

  - The location of the business logic (which lives within the controller itself) throws a red flag that screams "refactor me" because of the obvious neglect of the separation of concerns. The most important logic related to the business or underlying domain should be moved elsewhere, within the domain layer. The controller lives in the Application layer while the domain logic should be segregated into...well, a domain layer.

Note   I encourage you to check out the other cool ninja-like tools available in the Flysystem library from The League of Extraordinary Packages, which I already introduced to you earlier. Just in case you forgot, here's their website again, specifically for their Flysystem library, which helps manage and carry out modifications and additions to some type of supported filesystem: https://flysystem.thephpleague.com/docs/.

```
$filename = League\Flysystem\Util::normalizePath($filename);
```

This simple line of code accepts a given string and modifies it based on an internal process that strips away any illegal characters and limits the string to a particular length so that it may be used as a valid name for the file being uploaded. The only downside of this is that because the user specified the file's name inside the form, they would be expecting the file to be named exactly as they entered it unless they were notified otherwise after submitting it. We can solve this issue a number of ways, including simply notifying the user that the file was stored under a different name because the one they provided was invalid, and included in the response would be the name which their file was actually stored under. Another solution would be to not even allow a user to name the file, but have the filename generated and then store the generated filename in a relational database along with the owning user's ID and the file's location on the filesystem. Listing 4-7 shows a possible solution for implementing an autogenerated ID number for the given upload instead of allowing the user to specify the name parameter.

Listing 4-7. Possible Solution

```php
//in ddl/app/Http/Controllers/UploadController.php

use App\UserUpload;
use Illuminate\Support\Facades\Auth;
//..
class UploadController extends Controller
{
    public function store(UploadFileRequest $request)
    {
        $file = $request->file('userFile')
        //save the file to the local filesystem, inside /uploads
        //*NOTE*: this also runs the MIME type check automatically:
        $path = $file->store('uploads');

        // $path will be a string returned from the store() method
        // corresponding to the saved path of the uploaded file
        $upload = UserUpload::create([
            'user_id' => Auth::user()->id,
            'filename' => $path,
            //a way to track the source of the uploaded file
            'form_id' => $request->form_id //this is arbitrary
        ]);
        //return a success message
        return response()->json(['success' => true, 'upload' =>
            json_encode($upload)]);
    }
}
```

The response is received by the jQuery logic (which resides in the blade template, shown later in the example), which does a few more UI-related tasks such as displaying the success (or error) message for five seconds and then hiding it as well as clearing out the previous form entries. This is so the user knows for sure that the request was successful and can upload another file, if they want.

Also, take note in Figure 4-1 just where the line is drawn between the client and the server. This concept is absolutely critical for you to understand and will help you solve problems and issues you may have in the future when juggling, for example, multiple asynchronous requests that can occur at any given time.

The separation of the client concerns from those on the server side exists right at the boundary of our application, via a request object. The request object itself can be thought of as the client's actions they want to take against (or on) our application that the route somehow uses in order to generate and return a response to the client (user), thus completing the request/response lifecycle. It does the initial validation and registration of form values passed in from the web browser automatically by running them through the validations we specified in the `FormRequest`'s `rules()` method.

If they are deemed valid, then they get passed along to the controller (or the body of the route definition if it's configured with a closure function). Everything before that is on the front end (the "client" literally means "on the user's computer"). The response is returned from the app back on to the client side, where our jQuery code patiently listens for its arrival and does a few simple UI tasks once it receives it in order to properly notify the user that the request was a success or that an error occurred.

Additional Considerations

In the first part of this chapter, I wanted to focus on the core functionality of this sample project to give you a clear picture of how the process works on a high level, in its entirety, without getting too heavily involved on the details and considerations that the project would have if it were developed in the real world. In doing so, however, I've left out a few important pieces that are, in a real-world implementation, important things to get correct. For example, in the `list()` method we are just grabbing all files in a specific directory and displaying all of them to the end user. In real life, we obviously wouldn't want to display other users' files publicly. In that situation, we might have chosen to save the file in a particular format so as to easily determine which user the file belongs to. Here is a filename format that would allow us to determine which files belonged to which user:

```
{user-specified-file-name}.{userId}.{extension}
```

By hard-coding the user's ID into the filename, we can determine the owner of each file. This approach will have some other issues, however. If we consider the fact that the application might house many users and hundreds of files, we would have to loop through each of them inside a given directory to separate the files by owner. A better approach might be to allow each user to have their own private directory that is named with a standard format, perhaps including their user_id or username to identify each one. That way, we could just look up the directory by name and return a collection of all files that exist in that directory.

A more sophisticated approach would be to store a record inside a relational database table that basically links each file to its corresponding owner (most likely through a foreign key on the user_id field). This would be the best way we could solve this issue because instead of doing a glob on a directory and looping through each of the files and then checking which filenames match up to which user_id, we could simply issue a query to grab all filenames that belong to a given user and use the file's path to display a link for each one that the user could then click and download or receive metadata about.

This is something that can come up in a real-life application at some point (that is, saving a file on disk or even in off-site storage and managing the files via some type of interfaces). The documentation at https://laravel.com/docs/6.x/ filesystem#storing-files has all the specifics for how to store and retrieve data to different types of filesystems (local and remote), how to handle and change the file's metadata, how to upload and download files, and how to manage access to the files through file permissions.

There is still the problem of the mix of concerns inside the controller. The logic used to store the uploaded file is inline with the controller method. This is an issue because we have come to an understanding that the controller is simply a place to receive a request and return a response; in our example, however, this is clearly not the case. The controller is handling all the logic involved in the processing and storage of the uploaded file, which, in our case, is the core domain logic. We discuss different solutions to this dilemma in this chapter and future ones.

Introduction to Policies

The following section depicts a common problem found in enterprise web applications related to security constraints for which the only clear solution is to implement some sort of have robust user management and authorization system to deal with the management of the users as well as managing the permissions of each user through a Role entity. Oftentimes, you will need to know who the user is and what the user can do before executing the required logic to complete the request. We could use that nifty little spot in the request object (within the authorize() method) as a means of properly checking the user type before allowing the user to access and submit a particular form, but what if we wanted to implement such business policies as authorization on a per-domain-model basis so that any given instance of a domain class will have the same set of security settings as any other instance of the same type? We can use Laravel's policies to do just that, which we will discuss next.

AUTHENTICATING FORM REQUESTS AND USING POLICIES

For example, let's say that your application supports an enterprise, corporation, or some other mid- to large-sized company. In this enterprise, there is a custom authentication layer that is built into the very core of the application that has a defined set of user types and a corresponding table of permissions, roles, and/or groups that together define all the actions that each individual user is allowed to access, see, and do inside the application.

Let's say that this application manages a claim submission process used by different doctors that allows them to bill the federal Medi-Cal program for medical services and treatments given to people meeting certain income and poverty levels. The way it works is that patients schedule an appointment with a contracted provider in the system, and they show up and receive care at the doctor's office for some medical need. After the care is given, the way the doctor gets paid for his services is by submitting a medical claim to the Fully Qualified Healthcare Centers (FQHCs), which is in charge of reimbursement payouts to the providers that operate under the Medi-Cal service umbrella.

The federal government has no leniency for inaccurate claim submissions and accept them and pay them out only if they are 100 percent accurate. The required data, documents, and procedures done for the patient (modeled in a complex system known as the CPT coding system), patient information, provider information, and a slew of other checks and balances ensure that a patient is eligible to receive care *before* the FQHC will cut a check to the provider.

To help with this process, an application was created that allows different user types to log into separate parts of the application so they can do their work without disrupting other users of the system. A set of available permissions determines what each user has access to do or see. These user types include the doctor giving care, billers from the FQHC that manage payments, reviewers that have access to every claim so they may "clean" it and verify all the data is 100 percent accurate, and administrators of the system whom can access everything.

Let's pretend we are in charge of properly constructing a form that accepts a set of (fake) data normally found on one of these medical claims. We know we only want to allow doctors and administrators to have the ability to actually submit a medical claim form into the system. Doctors obviously need to submit claims to get their money, and admins obviously need to be able to send fake claims into the system for testing purposes. How would we go about doing such a thing?

Utilizing the Form Request's authorize() Method

As explained previously, the form request that is responsible for representing (and validating) a claim form could be restricted based on the user type, which can occur inside the form request class itself. We will also use the Auth facade to help us accomplish this task, because it is a straightforward way to access pretty much any information about the currently logged in user that we would ever need.

```
public function authorize()
{
    $user = Auth::user();
    switch ($user->role) {
    case 'Administrator':
    case 'Provider':
        return true;
        break;
    default:
        return false;
        break;
    }
    return false;
}
```

This `authorize()` method found inside a typical form request class first grabs the logged-in user who is attempting submission of the form and then checks that user's role attribute (which in this case evaluates to a simple string depicting an English word describing the type of user) to see if that user is either an administrator or a medical provider.

Note   The user's role in our Laravel application is most likely to be some set of records stored inside the database. For example, let's assume there is a `user_roles` table in a MySQL database that contains two foreign keys: a `user_id` field to represent the user and a `role_id` field to represent the specific role that the user belongs to. There could be many roles assigned to a user or just one, depending on the needs of the application.

If the user is either one of the accepted user types, then the method returns true, and the request is authorized, forwarding the request itself to the controller method defined in the route. If any other condition is true besides the user having one of these two possible roles, the method returns false, and execution of the form is halted with a pretty exception describing that the form request was not authorized (or, if in a production environment, the exception information and stack trace are instead written to a log file).

Let's add some complexity to the mix and say that there is an additional user type in the system corresponding to an office assistant inside the doctor's office who enters updated information to an already submitted claim—say, for a correction—into the form for the claim instead of the doctor (which is common practice because a doctor's time is obviously more valuable doing doctor-related things versus entering data into the system via a computer). These office assistants are allowed to submit claim forms into the system and update pre-existing claims only if they are registered as being part of that particular office (i.e., on the doctor's payroll). This is to prevent any possible means of allowing assistants from different offices to update claims on behalf of a doctor whom they do not directly work for. Privacy is a huge thing in the medical industry, and certain measures need to be met to protect patient privacy and establish protected health information (PHI) guidelines.

We need our application to be able to handle this constriction and only allow users of type `OFFICE_ASSISTANT` to submit forms for an office only if they are a registered user working for that office. We may be tempted to jump back into that form request class and update the `authenticate()` method to include an additional check for this requirement. The problem with this is that we don't actually have access to the imaginary `Claim` object that the system creates *with* the submitted form data, nor do we have the actual data being passed into the request at the time that the `authenticate()` method is called, so we have no way to validate that the data is coming from a corresponding office assistant who is employed by the provider on that same account. To properly construct this authentication feature requirement, we would at some point need both the logged-in user object as well as the object that we are validating against *in the same context* so as to properly check them and resolve if that user is allowed to submit the claim.

Laravel Policies to Protect Resources

Luckily for us, Laravel ships with a component called a *policy*. A policy is a class that is responsible for the validation of a single specific type of domain object. It is basically a means of organizing any given authentication or permissions checks relating to a particular resource or entity. For example, to create a protective wrapper around a core business object (like the `Claim` model), we would use an Artisan command (like we usually do when creating new Laravel files) to create the scaffolding of what will be `ClaimPolicy`.

Note   Don't worry about running any of these commands or typing any code inside this section. It is for reference only and is used here to give you more context for the topic of model-level security and policies.

```
php artisan make:policy --model=App\Claim ClaimPolicy
```

This command creates for us an `UploadPolicy.php` file inside the directory `ddl/app/Policies/UploadPolicy.php`, which will look like Listing 4-8.

Listing 4-8. A Generated Policy Class That Provides Authentication for Claim Objects

```
// ddl/app/Policies/ClaimPolicy.php

<?php
namespace App\Policies;
use App\User;
use App\Claim;
use Illuminate\Auth\Access\HandlesAuthorization;
class ClaimPolicy
```

```
{
    use HandlesAuthorization;
    /**
    * Determine whether the user can view any Claim.
    *
    * @param  \App\User  $user
    * @return mixed
    */
    public function viewAny(User $user)
    {
        //
    }
    /**
    * Determine whether the user can view the Claim.
    *
    * @param  \App\User  $user
    * @param  \App\Claim  $claim
    * @return mixed
    */
    public function view(User $user, Claim $claim)
    {
        //
    }
    /**
    * Determine whether the user can create claims.
    *
    * @param  \App\User  $user
    * @return mixed
    */
    public function create(User $user)
    {
        //
    }
    /**
    * Determine whether the user can update the Claim
    *
```

```php
 * @param  \App\User   $user
 * @param  \App\Claim  $claim
 * @return mixed
 */
public function update(User $user, Claim $claim)
 {
    //
 }
/**
 * Determine whether the user can delete the Claim.
 *
 * @param  \App\User   $user
 * @param  \App\Claim  $claim
 * @return mixed
 */
public function delete(User $user, Claim $claim)
{
    //
}
/**
 * Determine whether the user can restore the Claim.
 *
 * @param  \App\User   $user
 * @param  \App\Claim  $claim
 * @return mixed
 */
public function restore(User $user, Claim $claim)
{
    //
}
/**
 * Determine whether the user can permanently delete the Claim.
 *
 * @param  \App\User   $user
 * @param  \App\Claim  $claim
 * @return mixed
 */
```

```
public function forceDelete(User $user, Claim $claim)
{
    //
}
}
```

The general concept is composed of two standard objects in an application: a user object (representing the user attempting to access our resource) and a Claim object (the resource we are protecting). The scaffolding code has all the type hints pre-created for us because we specified the resource when we generated this class, via the passed-in parameter --model= from the initial command. All the methods within the policy correspond to the various "actions" that can be taken on any given Claim model (business object). We have methods for viewing, updating, storing, and deleting our Claim resource. All that is left to do is specify how you want each actionable scenario to behave in terms of the required logic that runs in order to determine whether a user is allowed to do something.

In this case, we want to only allow the storage of a given claim model if the user's role is either an administrator or a provider, or if the role is Office_Assistant when and only when that assistant is considered to be a registered employee of the same provider's office. Initially we stuck the logic inside the request object's authenticate() method, but policies offer a more robust, customizable approach to validation that is better to use for a higher degree of control when dealing with *resources* (business objects).

To make the most out of this discussion, we are going to focus on the updating portion of the requirement. An office assistant may update an already submitted claim if they are a registered user of that office. Listing 4-9 shows how the create() method could look like for this requirement.

Listing 4-9. Possible Implementation of a Policy's update() Action on a Given Claim Object

```
/**
 * Determine whether the user can update the Claim
 *
 * @param  \App\User  $user
 * @param  \App\Claim  $claim
 * @return mixed
 */
```

```php
public function update(User $user, Claim $claim)
{
    switch ($user->role) {
        case 'Administrator':
        case 'Provider':
            return true;
            break;
        case 'Office_Assistant':
            $employeeManager = (new EmployeeManager());
            $providerOffice = $employeeManager->
                findRegistrationFor($user);
            if ($claim->provider === $providerOffice->provider) {
                return true;
            }
            Return false;
            break;
        default:
            return false;
    }
}
```

This example defines an update() method that takes a User object and a Claim object to
determine whether the request should be allowed to proceed. If the user has a role of either
administrator or provider, then they are allowed to update a particular Claim. If the user is
of type Office Assistant, there is additional logic inline within the switch statement
that creates a new instance of a domain service, EmployeeManager, which in turn finds
the provider's office that the assistant is registered to and compares that against the provider
attached to the claim. Only if these values are the same does the application allow passage of
the request into the insides of the system. I will show you how to employ your own policies later.

Also, I've left out all code related to actually implementing this policy, but for now just know
that they can be implemented in a few different ways, depending on the context of what you
are trying to accomplish.

- Via the User model using the methods can() and cant(), which accept the
  model to check against and the action within that model corresponding to the
  policy method that will be used for the auth check

```
if ($user->can('update', $claim) {
    // perform update logic after the "update" method has
    // been called on the ClaimPolicy
}
```

- On a given route, via middleware

```
Route::post('/claim/{claim}', function (Claim $claim) {
    // perform update logic
})->middleware('can:update,claim');
```

- Inside a controller via a helper method

```
/**
 * Update the given claim
 *
 * @param Request $request
 * @param Claim $claim
 * @return Response
 * @throws \Illuminate\Auth\Access\AuthorizeException;
 /*
public function update(Request $request, Claim $claim)
{
    $this->authorize('update', $claim);
    //the current user can update the claim
}
```

Table 4-3 shows the mapping of the controller method to its corresponding method used to authenticate.

143

Table 4-3. *Mapping of Controller Methods to Their Corresponding Methods on the Policy*

Controller Method	Route-Defined HTTP Verb	Policy Method
index()	GET	viewAny()
show()	GET	view()
create()	GET	create()
store()	POST	create()
edit()	GET	update()
update()	PUT/PATCH	update()
destroy()	DELETE	delete()

Note that with any of these options, Laravel will automatically check to see whether there is a policy for the given model that is being requested access to; however, if there is not, it will fall back to any defined gate authentication closure defined in the `AuthServiceProvider`.

One other thing to note about the policies is the type of domain object that gets passed into the policy's methods that allow for modification or deletion of that object type. The type of object that gets passed into the policy methods is the model (or resource) for which that policy is protecting. This is not to be confused with a resource model, which is defined using a resource controller that is specific to actions on a particular model.

Another really great thing about them is that they support Eloquent relationships, making it easy to transform objects that correspond to relations of other objects in a straightforward and nonintrusive manner. We will touch on all of this later in the book.

Designing an API-First Application

At this point, we know most of our request details (like what they are and how to validate them), so we can now start to see a mental picture of the overall structure of the application at this point. We have included proper definitions of what we are expecting from the form as it comes into our application, which serves as a good high-level overview of the data types you will be interacting with. This is the way to go about building out your application, so if you are ever confused about exactly where to start on a project, a good candidate would be the API.

We will go over how to build and implement an actual API using the provided facilities and plumbing setup in Laravel later in the book, but to whet your appetite, I've included a sidebar on something called *API-first design*.

API-FIRST DESIGN AND THE OPEN API SPECIFICATION

In professional web development, API-first design is quite a bit different than the process I have depicted in this chapter. The reason for this is because I wanted to get you acquainted with the way Laravel flows; the best way to do that is by allowing you to concentrate on that specific conceptual group of elements, without being distracted with more architectural practices and patterns. We will learn these in due time as the book proceeds.

The main difference is that in an API-first design, it is common to start by creating the schema that the API will follow in order to complete the various application tasks required by the model. This is typically done in a language-agnostic and database-agnostic way so that what you end up with are strict guidelines of what the API layer is, down to the nitty-gritty details like the types of parameters requested and indeed the entire defining structure of both the requests and responses that enter and leave the application, grouped into similar focuses of functionality via endpoints. You define all the endpoints in the API first, before a single line of actual code is written to consume it.

The Open API Specification and Swagger

There are a variety of ways to do this in the real world. One solution I propose to you is utilizing what is known as the Open API Specification, as used by API design tooling applications like SwaggerHub (`https://swagger.io/tools/swaggerhub/`). There is somewhat of a learning curve to start using Swagger inside your own applications, but it is well worth the time it takes to learn. The neat thing about SwaggerHUB is that it offers you a unique way of viewing the data structures you define inside the API (using the Open API specification as a means to do so). It also offers a wide array of cool features such as snapshot creation, version tracking, forking/merging, and publishing features. The version tracking is particularly useful in a team environment because it makes it easier for all members of the team to use the newest version of the API standards as it gets built.

here's something I find incredibly cool: the visualizations SwaggerHub provides are useful when looking at the API from different perspectives and navigating to specific definitions, and they are all generated using the Open API markup language. It takes a little time to learn how to define the various structures, requests, and responses you will need in your own application, but it is well worth the effort. Once you get the hang of it, you can pretty much fly through defining the API design details that are centric to your application's success. Using tools like SwaggerHub and the Open API specification, you can guarantee that the definition makes sense (because it is parsed and validated every five or so seconds, regenerating the visual tools corresponding to the route definitions) and that you are not repeating definitions of the entities that are involved in each particular request and response.

You define such structures once (from within the *components/schema* node) and can then reference them in any endpoint, request, or response definition in the API. If you reference a particular structure that is *not* defined, you will get a friendly error markup with an explanation as to why the issue exists. Validation is helpful because the API definitions that you specify for your application are followed *exactly* by client-side implementations, meaning that the definitions, types, and data structures you lay out for your own API must be accurate.

Once you are satisfied with the definitions of all the structures that comprise your API, you can then "publish" the changes to a specific released version, preventing further modification of that version unless a new version of it is created (using incremental versioning in the form *version.major.minor*, for example, 1.0.3). You can specify which version to use as the default as well, enabling you to have as many "in-progress" versions as you want, while forcing a specific version to be shown to and used by the team to develop other areas of the application that consume the API.

Middleware

Middleware is a concept that has gained widespread support in the PHP world, specifically within MVC frameworks such as Laravel and other server-side frameworks like Node's Express. Middleware is used as a mechanism to filter incoming HTTP requests entering your application, and they can be used for pretty much anything and everything you could possibly want to do, whether before, after, or in between.

They are commonly used for a variety of valid and legitimate purposes in web applications, including the following:

- Authentication and authorization checks

- Session validation and modification of session variables

- Reading, setting, or modifying request and response headers (corresponding to before- and after-middleware)

- Logging transactions and API calls

- Redirections and inner-site "flow" customization and interrupting the standard request/response lifecycle to completely replace either one

- Emitting or reacting to specific domain events

- Modifying the request or response for every call to the application or only on specific endpoints, from specific IP addresses that also limit requests so they must include a valid request header with a proper value, and pretty much any other security concern you could ever need

- Much more

As another example, in Laravel, the checks and balances (so to speak) that operate from within the application ensuring the request's validity and authenticity do so through a required authentication session (using a Cookie header), normally implemented as some type of token authentication to restrict parts of the application that shouldn't be available to nonusers of the system. Laravel uses middleware to establish virtually *all* authentication operations throughout the system.

To get a high-level overview of the middleware that is configured in a Laravel application by default, you can check out the `Kernel` class of the Laravel application, which is located at `/ddl/app/Http/Kernel.php` and is an extension of Symfony's famous `HttpKernel` implementation that is pretty much the de facto standard `Kernel` in virtually all modern-day web application frameworks.

```
// ddl/app/Http/Kernel.php

<?php
namespace App\Http;
use Illuminate\Foundation\Http\Kernel as HttpKernel;
class Kernel extends HttpKernel
```

```
{
    /**
     * The application's global HTTP middleware stack.
     *
     * These middleware are run during every request to your application.
     *
     * @var array
     */
    protected $middleware = [
        \App\Http\Middleware\TrustProxies::class,
        \App\Http\Middleware\CheckForMaintenanceMode::class,
        \Illuminate\Foundation\Http\Middleware\ValidatePostSize::class,
        \App\Http\Middleware\TrimStrings::class,
        \Illuminate\Foundation\Http\Middleware\ /
        ConvertEmptyStringsToNull::class,
    ];
    /**
     * The application's route middleware groups.
     *
     * @var array
     */
    protected $middlewareGroups = [
        'web' =>
      \App\Http\Middleware\EncryptCookies::class,
        \Illuminate\Cookie\Middleware\AddQueuedCookiesToResponse::class,
        \Illuminate\Session\Middleware\StartSession::class,
    // \Illuminate\Session\Middleware\AuthenticateSession::class,
        \Illuminate\View\Middleware\ShareErrorsFromSession::class,
        \App\Http\Middleware\VerifyCsrfToken::class,
        \Illuminate\Routing\Middleware\SubstituteBindings::class,
    ],

        'api' => [
            'Throttle:60,1',
            'Bindings',
        ],
```

```php
    ];
    /**
     * The application's route middleware.
     *
     * These middleware may be assigned to groups or used individually.
     *
     * @var array
     */
    protected $routeMiddleware = [
        'auth' => \App\Http\Middleware\Authenticate::class,
        'auth.basic' => \Illuminate\Auth\Middleware\AuthenticateWithBasicAu
        th::class,
        'bindings' => \Illuminate\Routing\Middleware\SubstituteBindings::class,
        'cache.headers' => \Illuminate\Http\Middleware\SetCacheHeaders::class,
        'can' => \Illuminate\Auth\Middleware\Authorize::class,
        'guest' =>
\App\Http\Middleware\RedirectIfAuthenticated::class,
        'signed' => \Illuminate\Routing\Middleware\ValidateSignature::class,
        'throttle' =>
\Illuminate\Routing\Middleware\ThrottleRequests::class,
        'verified' =>
\Illuminate\Auth\Middleware\EnsureEmailIsVerified::class,
    ];

    /**
     * The priority-sorted list of middleware.
     *
     * This forces non-global middleware to always be in the given order.
     *
     * @var array
     */
    protected $middlewarePriority = [
        \Illuminate\Session\Middleware\StartSession::class,
        \Illuminate\View\Middleware\ShareErrorsFromSession::class,
        \App\Http\Middleware\Authenticate::class,
        \Illuminate\Routing\Middleware\ThrottleRequests::class,
```

```
        \Illuminate\Session\Middleware\AuthenticateSession::class,
        \Illuminate\Routing\Middleware\SubstituteBindings::class,
        \Illuminate\Auth\Middleware\Authorize::class,
    ];
}
```

The Kernel class provides the assignment of a particular middleware to a given route type. I use *route type* here to mean web routes versus API routes. In contrast, I use *route group* to refer to individual route groups that are defined in one of the central route files. Each middleware is given a shortcut syntax that you can see in the previous code that corresponds to the array keys for which each route type is defined. We will discuss the difference between the two route types at the end of the chapter.

Listing 4-10 shows an example of middleware. Take a look at the file dll/app/Http/Middleware/RedirectIfAuthenticated.php. This middleware corresponds to the guest key within the web route configuration group (Listing 4-10).

Listing 4-10. An Included Middleware in Laravel That Redirects Users Already Authenticated to the /home Route

```php
// dll/app/Http/Middleware/RedirectIfAuthenticated.php

<?php
namespace App\Http\Middleware;
use Closure;
use Illuminate\Support\Facades\Auth;

class RedirectIfAuthenticated
{
    /**
     * Handle an incoming request.
     *
     * @param  \Illuminate\Http\Request  $request
     * @param  \Closure  $next
     * @param  string|null  $guard
     * @return mixed
     */
```

```
public function handle($request, Closure $next, $guard = null)
{
    if (Auth::guard($guard)->check()) {
        return redirect('/home');
    }
    return $next($request);
}
}
```

Middleware is convenient in that it sits between a request entering the application and the domain model (or the application's core), and it can act as a mechanism for any type of authentication/authorization checks, caching mechanisms, application logging, session/cookie parameters, or ensuring a form's validity to prevent XSS attacks via CSRF protection checks. These are all examples of how these things get called and established within a Laravel app. However, the actual definitions, collaborations of, and dependencies of a specific implementation of a given feature more often than not will be located in some other class or component. Middleware is only a mechanism for implementing those listed concerns but should not directly implement their corresponding logic inline. Instead, design the architecture to house such concerns within the domain layer, which you can then call from a particular middleware or controller method, but only if it makes sense to do so in the context of the problems you are working on.

Keeping this separation of concerns allows us to better organize the core logic of the application and gives us a clear boundary of which logic needs to be in which layer and even allows finer-grained control when the domain model is implemented as a series of independent and specialized modules that span multiple bounded contexts, and each of those bounded contexts can be considered part of their enclosing module. This helps to organize code on a domain level, which is exactly what we want.

Another important thing to note is that this mechanism gets fired (called) on every single request going into the application, as well as every response going out of the application. There are, of course, ways to configure middleware so that they only "activate" for portions of the applications instead of each and every request/response, but really the way to handle additional filtering of the request is to add the logic that determines whether the middleware should be run or skipped—that logic should be placed within the body of the middleware definition and should either return the next callable middleware right away (before-middleware) or at the end of the middleware's body (after-middleware) that is on the stack either before or after the check is performed.

I will show you how to configure both before-middleware and after-middleware a little later in the book.

You can also specify a route or groups of routes to force the usage of a particular middleware if you don't want that middleware to fire on every single request, like the one in Listing 4-10 does. What better way of assigning specific middleware to its relative portion of the application than using a route configuration? Since we group all of our different sections (components) together using route-specific URIs anyway, Laravel provides an intuitive and straightforward means of enabling specific middleware to run only when a specific route gets hit by the client.

Although we won't be diving into the details of implementing a middleware in your own application just yet, it is important that you have a basic understanding of what they are so you can follow the discussion on route files in the next section of this chapter. There are two main groups of middleware in Laravel corresponding to the scope of what the middleware actually touches, defined by default: the API middleware group and the web middleware group. These groups can be configured (and changed) from within the service provider located here: `app/Providers/RouteServiceProvider`. If you open up this file and take a peek, you will notice a basic `map()` method that calls two default methods within the same class: `mapWebRoutes()` and `mapApiRoutes()`. These two middleware groups are determined by two URIs, which is what is used internally as the mechanism for mapping a given middleware to its corresponding group of routes for which it is activated (Table 4-4).

Table 4-4. Laravel's Default Middleware Configuration

Middleware Group Name	Route Prefix	Example Valid Route	Route File
Api	/api/	/api/users/create	routes/api.php
Web	/	/about	routes/web.php

In a typical real-world scenario, an application would most likely contain separate versions of its API, which could be signified by adding a route prefix to a select group of routes that indicated which version of the API a given client was using. The following are typical examples of API route endpoints:

- `http://mysite.com/api/v1/`

- `http://mysiteapi.io/api/json/v1`

- `http://api.yoursite.com/v1/`

- `http://yoursite.com/api/v2/files`

Web Middleware ➤ For Web-Based Routes

The web middleware group is configured in the `routes/web.php` file and is considered to be the "public" scope of an application that users interact with through a browser. By default, it corresponds to all URIs that do not start with `/api`, which usually ends up being the majority of URIs found in a web application. Anything starting with a `/` (except `/api`) is considered to be a member of the Web route group and thus has more of a public setting, which, in this case, allows a non-logged-in user to view standard web routes. The most basic example of this is an application's home page or its about page.

API Middleware ➤ For API-Based Routes

No matter what, we are not going to ever want all of the application's URIs (routes) to be available to nonauthenticated users (*guests*). This is true also of an application's API, which generally contains defined REST interfaces that allow a client to access and modify the core parts of a system or domain. For example, if we were to build out an implementation for setting up a new user account in our application, we would want to put the URIs (routes) *behind* some sort of protective barrier so as to provide means of security when unauthenticated users attempt some malicious acts (and you always have to assume they will attempt such things). In this case, we would perhaps specify a `/api/users` route that would correspond to a REST-ful implementation of an API, allowing the route to carry out the required functionality, based on the HTTP verb, by means of either a route-based closure or a reference to a controller method defined in Laravel's shortcut syntax for referring to a single method on a particular controller.

This is easy to configure in Laravel, and I will show you specifics later. For now, just make sure you understand what middleware is and acknowledge the types of things that can be (and are) configured through each middleware group within a Laravel application. We will return to the middleware concept later.

Intro to Laravel Jobs

This section introduces the concept of a *job*, which is basically a set of transactions or operations that are encapsulated into a single object and whose inner processes are created to solve business problems at the domain level. Jobs can be used similar to commands, can be easily called inside a controller, can be placed on a queue, and can monitored with supervisorD in order to process them concurrently (i.e., *asynchronously*). You could set up one of the popular choices for modern-day task and message queues sch as RabbitMQ, Kafka, or ActiveMQ, to handle the communication, management, and reporting of the individual tasks in an asynchronous way so that operations appear to be more fluid and the wait time is less than with synchronous processing. However, for this example, we will just create a synchronous implementation and return the result of the job back to the calling code (within the controller) immediately, rather than the "set it and forget it" technique that makes asynchronous processing so popular. We will dive into working with message queues.

USING LARAVEL JOBS TO ENCAPSULATE BUSINESS LOGIC

As we now know, a controller's purpose in an MVC architecture should be *only* to shake hands with the client, delegate any domain work to the domain layer (that in turn handles them one at a time or uses an application service that consumes the domain layer directly), and return a response that indicates the success or failure of a given request. That being said, our initial design of the UploadController's store() method contained all the logic needed to process, name, and store the uploaded file. This domain logic should be encapsulated somewhere besides the controller method body, and one possible way to do that is to create a job.

To generate a new job scaffold, use this:

```php
php artisan make:job SaveUploadedFile
```

This command will produce the code inside a file at app/Jobs/SaveUploadedFile.php (Listing 4-11).

Listing 4-11. Scaffold Code Generated from make:job Command

```php
// ddl/app/Jobs/SaveUploadedFile.php
<?php
namespace App\Jobs;
use Illuminate\Bus\Queueable;
use Illuminate\Queue\SerializesModels;
use Illuminate\Queue\InteractsWithQueue;
use Illuminate\Contracts\Queue\ShouldQueue;
use Illuminate\Foundation\Bus\Dispatchable;
class SaveUploadedFile implements ShouldQueue
{
    use Dispatchable, InteractsWithQueue, Queueable, SerializesModels;

    /**
     * Create a new job instance.
     *
     * @return void
     */
    public function __construct()
    {
        //
    }
    /**
     * Execute the job.
     *
     * @return void
     */
    public function handle()
    {
        //
    }
}
```

The class is simple enough and contains just two methods: the constructor and the `handle()` method. The constructor is used as a means of dependency injection. Any additional objects you may need to fulfill the job are type-hinted in the constructor's signature and resolved automatically by Laravel's dependency injection component. In fact, if you need even more customization with regard to the objects fulfilling a particular task, you can specify *how* you want the objects built that are injected into a service or job using Laravel's service container (read about it at `https://laravel.com/docs/master/container`). We will go over more advanced usage of the service container later in the book.

The constructor is also the place where you pass in any data from the request that is needed to fulfill the task encapsulated within this job. Because we are concerned with storing user-submitted files, we need to include any parameters that used to be inline in the controller's `store()` method and put them as separate items inside the constructor of the `Job` class. We do not pass the entire request object into the constructor; it's bad practice.

The second method in Listing 4-11 is the `handle()` method, which is the meat and potatoes of the job definition. This is where the main logic runs when the job is called. It basically utilizes any objects you've specified in the constructor (which should also be included as class member params in the job definition). When the job gets dispatched (usually from a controller), it injects whatever is needed in the constructor and calls the `handle()` method. Let's see what the job looks like for saving a user's uploaded file and storing the generated file ID in the database to track which user owns which files.

```php
<?php
namespace App\Jobs;
use Illuminate\Bus\Queueable;
use Illuminate\Queue\SerializesModels;
use Illuminate\Queue\InteractsWithQueue;
use Illuminate\Contracts\Queue\ShouldQueue;
use Illuminate\Foundation\Bus\Dispatchable;
use Symfony\Component\HttpFoundation\File\File;
use App\UserUpload;
class SaveUploadedFile implements ShouldQueue
{
    use Dispatchable, InteractsWithQueue, Queueable, SerializesModels;

    protected $fileName;

    protected $upload;

    /**
     * Create a new job instance.
     *
     * @return void
     */
```

```php
    public function __construct(File $upload)
    {
        $this->upload = $upload;

    }
    /**
     * Execute the job.
     *
     * @return void
     */
    public function handle()
    {
            //save the user's file and grab its path on the filesystem
            $path = $this->upload->store('uploads');
            //create a record to track user's uploaded files
            $upload = UserUpload::create([
                    'user_id' => Auth::user()->id,
                    'filename' => $path,
            ]);

            //do a final verification check that the saved file exists
            if (!is_file($path)) {
                    throw new Exception("Problem with saving the file");
      `}

            return $path;
    }
}
```

With this new job in place, we can modify our controller and remove any concerns relating to file storage and instead simply delegate that task to the new SaveUploadedFile job. Here is what that might look like (we've actually used the built-in method that comes included with all job classes in Laravel), via a static method:

```php
public function store(UploadFileRequest $request)
{
    $file = $request->file('userFile');
    $filePath = SaveUploadedFile::dispatchNow($file);

    return response()->json(['success' => true]);
}
```

As you can see, our controller method has been reduced in size and complexity because we've now delegated the task of storing the uploaded file within a job class rather than inline with the controller method handling the request. Now we have a clear separation of concerns, plus we are practicing something called *intention revealing interfaces*, where we name classes, objects, and parameters in a way that clearly indicates their purpose while also making the actions taken on those parameters as clearly defined and revealing as possible.

Maintaining Quality in the Real World

The best way to manage this iterative development process and help keep you focused on solving the domain concerns of the system is to employ concepts found in an application of continuous integration techniques such that you are constantly evolving the software with quality code that includes unit tests as well as an automated testing mechanism that you set up to run on every commit to the codebase or every merge from a pull request. This helps to ensure the new code you write doesn't break any old features and gives you a clear road toward upgrades and maintenance of the application after it is being used in production. Not breaking old code is crucial to maintaining quality web software, and a solid CI/CD pipeline can definitely help with that.

Overall, the process that I've outlined in this chapter goes like this:

Design domain and architecture ➤ generate generic code ➤ customize generic code ➤ reiterate system design ➤ refactor toward new insight.

From a higher level, it would look more like this:

Design ➤ prototype ➤ implement ➤ refactor.

The concept of incremental changes are core foundational points of several popular programming paradigms. Extreme programming (XP) and agile development are both dependent on the value that iterative cycles of development bring to a web application development effort. There is even a blog on the subject by yours truly, which you can find at `http://continuousiteration.com` (← not "continuous integration" but "continuous iteration"). All the good domains were taken, so I tried to come up with something that meant the same thing and sounded close to the same thing, and that's what I came up. Don't hate.

Conclusion

In the chapter, I went over the installation of Laravel onto your local system using the Composer package manager to resolve dependencies. After that, we took a look at an example application built using Laravel, attaining a good idea of the main components involved in a Laravel application. I showed you how to use the Artisan command-line tool that comes with Laravel to generate scaffolding code for these components, and then we used them to implement the functionality we required. We went through the example in more or less the same manner as we would in a real-world scenario: we created a naive implementation to meet the requirements of the system, and then we went back and put some additional thought into the design and realized it was lacking a few important things and breaking some important rules.

We make the prototype of the model in code, knowing full well that it is not perfect. We slowly start chipping away at the weak points or inaccurate expressions of the business model over and over, until we end up patching all the holes. In the end, this leaves us with a working piece of software that is aligned to the business model it was built from.

After we built the rough draft of the implementation for our upload application, we went over some additional considerations for the application's structure and components and also discussed some shortcomings of the initial version. You learned how to possibly mitigate some of these shortcomings and make adjustments to both the structure and logic of the code, giving you (I hope) a solid grasp about how to do basic requests, validate incoming request parameters, use jobs to encapsulate business logic, use controllers as a means of completing the request/response lifecycle, and use a few other tools of the trade that Laravel provides.

Now that you have this understanding, we can get into the meat and potatoes of this book and discuss what it is we are actually trying to do in regard to domain-driven Laravel; then we'll tackle what it's going to take to implement it, of course, in the real world.

CHAPTER 5

Advanced Laravel

In this chapter, we will explore some of the more advanced topics of Laravel. We will be focusing on the Laravel features, tools, and shortcuts that are directly relevant to the examples and supporting code used throughout this book. This is not meant to be an in-depth, all-encompassing explanation of every feature Laravel has, and you should reference the Laravel documentation directly when you need clarification on anything Laravel.

For our purposes, we will focus on these topics:

- The cycle (flow) of a Laravel application

- Service providers

- The service container and the $app variable

- Queues and Laravel jobs

- Contracts

- Events

After you get a better understanding of some of the more advanced features available in Laravel, we will tie all the topics together by the end of the chapter and discuss some high-level approaches to building the different parts to meet our application's requirements. The tools within Laravel are available for you to use as you want. What we want to eventually accomplish is not just having a group of tools at our disposal, but to position those tools in a manner that would allow us to form a solid development pipeline for the various commands and services that need to be run to fulfill requests from the client. We just need to use them in accordance with domain-driven approaches to forge a solid, reusable foundation that we can push additional requirements through again later. Think of this pipeline as a sort of repeatable set of steps that achieves some domain-related task or process that can be repeated an infinite number of times to achieve a similar structure but supporting a completely different directive. They are not

© Jesse Griffin 2021
J. Griffin, *Domain-Driven Laravel*, https://doi.org/10.1007/978-1-4842-6023-4_5

set in stone, but they should provide ample guidance for you when you are working on real-world projects that are written using Laravel.

The Cycle of a Laravel Application

Laravel operates in a predictable manner via a series of operations that occur during the bootstrap of the framework. All incoming requests first hit the /public/index.php file (sometimes referred to as a *front controller*), which loads the Composer autoloader (/vendor/autoload.php) and then loads the application from the bootstrap/app.php file. The first action taken by this file is creating an Application instance (an instance of the service container). Here is what that looks like:

```
// ddl/app/bootstrap.php
$app = new Illuminate\Foundation\Application(
    $_ENV['APP_BASE_PATH'] ?? dirname(__DIR__)
);
```

This code creates a new instance of the main Application class, which accepts as a parameter the location of the Laravel application. This can be configured inside the .env file, which holds the main configuration values used throughout the entire application. These values will get picked up by Laravel and injected into the various parts of the application. In the previous instance, it will default to the current directory if $_ENV['APP_BASE_PATH'] hasn't been defined (i.e., is not in the .env file).

Depending on the type of request (be it from a normal browser or via a console command), Laravel will utilize either the app\Http\Kernel class or the Console/Kernel class, respectively. Whichever Kernel class is used, Laravel passes the incoming request to the kernel, which then loads the appropriate configuration and settings for the specific environment. The kernel defines all the middleware used in the application and registers them in a sort of stack-like structure within the framework's Application object. The middleware layer in Laravel is important because it provides the application with the specific environment being requested based on the type of Kernel class used in the process and the type of request coming into the application. There are two main types of requests: web requests (browser based) and API requests (based on HTTP verbs).

Middleware in Laravel is responsible for handling a variety of tasks and setting up some of the fundamental features of Laravel. These include but are not limited to the following:

Web request middleware

- Session setup

- Cookie encryption

- CSRF protection

- Authentication

API request middleware

- Throttle requests

Route middleware

- Cache headers

- URL signature validation

- Authorization

Route middleware can be attached to individual routes or groups of routes defined within the route files (the main ones being `/routes/app.php` and `/routes/web.php`). Middleware is also responsible for determining whether the application is in maintenance mode and, if so, redirecting users to a temporary maintenance page.

The key player in all of this is the `Application` kernel. At a high level, the kernel's `handle()` is responsible for two things:

- Receiving a request

- Returning a response

The kernel is the foundation for almost every major PHP web application framework in existence and actually was originally developed by and for the Symfony framework. After deciding which kernel to use, several additional bootstrapping tasks are carried out, including reading environment variables, loading configuration defined in the `/config` folder, registering application facades, and bootstrapping service providers.

Service providers are specified in the `config/app.php` file and are loaded by the application by running each provider's `register()` method and then each provider's `boot()` method, respectively. We will go into more depth on service providers in just a little bit. After the service providers have all been loaded, the request is sent to the router to be dispatched according to whatever is configured in the respective routes file. The router accepts the request and forwards it to the specified controller for processing or may even handle the meat of the request inline inside the route definition. We covered some routing principles in the previous chapter, but just to recap, the route forwards the request to the specified controller to be processed and acted upon and to then return some kind of response (be it a JSON object responding to an API call or a complete web page displayed on the browser).

Service Providers

Service providers hold all the major features of the framework and are arguably the most important aspect of the framework. The default providers are located inside the `app/Providers` directory. Here is what the Laravel documentation says in regard to service providers:

> *"Service providers are responsible for bootstrapping all of the framework's various components, such as the database, queue, validation, and routing components. Since they bootstrap and configure every feature offered by the framework, service providers are the most important aspect of the entire Laravel bootstrap process."*

—Laravel documentation

From that statement, we can conclude that service providers are the means for which to define a specific portion of functionality's configuration details so that it can be picked up and recognized by the framework and then made available to the rest of the application by means of autoloading or service container bindings. You can think of service providers as the glue that holds together the application and allows for the extensions and additions to the framework and the application. They are also utilized by the framework itself to register the lower-level components that make up the feature set offered by Laravel. Some service providers are set up in such a way that cause them to be loaded only when needed (called *deferred loading* or *lazy loading*).

Each service provider contains two main methods on them: `register()` and `boot()`.

register()

The register() method is the first thing that is called in any service provider on bootstrap of the framework. This is where you would include any logic for a service provider that can be done *without* the use of any other service provider. The register method gets run before the service container is fully instantiated and is meant to do any prerequisite logic for whatever portion of the application the service provider provides service.

You should bind things only into the service container, such as classes or services, and should not pull things out of the service container (because it hasn't been fully built or instantiated at the time that the register() method is called on each provider. If you need to use other services or need to use something that is already bound to the container or register any routes, listeners, or anything of the sort, use the boot() method.

Listing 5-1 provides an example ServiceProvider for some application that instantiates a class used to interface with some Redis database.

Listing 5-1. Service Provider's register() Method

```
// An example service provider

<?php
namespace App\Providers;
use Illuminate\Support\ServiceProvider;
use Predis\Client;

class RedisServiceProvider extends ServiceProvider
{
    /**
     * Register any application services.
     *
     * @return void
     */
    public function register()
    {
        $this->app->singleton(Redis::class, function ($app) {
```

```
        return new Client(
            config('database.redis.options.default'));
    });
  }
}
```

In Listing 5-1, we have a standard service provider that is defining a service that is a singleton (a singleton is a specific class where only one can exist at any given time). This service makes use of the `Predis\Client` class by creating an instance of it with the configuration defined in `/config/database.php` under the `redis` key, which looks like Listing 5-2.

Listing 5-2. The Default Configuration for a Redis Connection, Located in app/config/database.php

```
// /ddl/config/redis.php
return [
    // ...
     "redis" => [
    "client" => "phpredis",
    "options" => [
        "cluster" => "redis",
        "prefix" => "laravel_database_",],
        "default" => [
        "url" => null,
        "host" => "127.0.0.1",
        "password" => null,
        "port" => "6379",
        "database" => 0,
        ],
      "cache" => [
        "url" => null,
        "host" => "127.0.0.1",
        "password" => null,
```

```
        "port" => "6379",
        "database" => 1,
      ],
    ]
  ]
];
```

If you haven't already guessed, the argument to the config() method corresponds to the location of the particular setting within a specified configuration file (.php), located within the app/config directory, which returns a single, multidimensional array with keys corresponding to the config "node" that the configuration values correspond to. The first part of database.redis, which is everything to the left of the period (i.e., database), corresponds to the filename. The second part, which is everything to the left of the period, corresponds to the key of the array returned from that file. In the previous case, it is referring to the redis['options']['default'] key within the config/database.php file.

boot()

The boot() method is where you can include any logic that is dependent on other configuration, services, or other aspects of the system. It is run *after* the service container has been instantiated by Laravel and, because of that, is allowed to utilize any other functionality provided by other service providers or things existing within the service container.

When you have dependencies that you need for the service provider to configure that part of your application, you may inject them into the boot() method, and they will be automatically passed in as arguments for you to use, like in Listing 5-3.

Listing 5-3. Example boot() Method in a Service Provider

```php
<?php

class ClaimServiceProvider {
    // properties and register() method

    public function boot(ClaimRepository $claimRepository,
    CptCodeRepository $cptCodeRepository)
    {
```

```
$claim = $claimRepository->findBy('patient_id', 3345);
$cptCode = $cptCodeRepository->whereIn('cpt_code',
$claim->cpt_codes);
//... additional logic
}

}
```

This is made possible thanks to Laravel's service container, which we will get into next. We will start discussing the many different aspects of Laravel's service container that make it unlike any other you've probably used in the past (it puts most of them to shame). A ServiceProvider's boot() method can be used to configure virtually any aspect of the system, and because the service container is fully loaded and ready at the time this method is called, you are able to inject any dependencies or utilize any other services in the system as you want. You will likely find working with the service container somewhat difficult at first, so don't worry if you don't get how everything kind of plugs into everything else. Focus on the high-level topics we discuss in the chapter before attempting to write your own service provider or attempting to set up an injection strategy for a service's dependencies.

Service Container

Laravel's service container is truly remarkable, and the benefits of using it are partly what makes Laravel such an awesome framework. Dependency injection throughout the entire application is handled by the service container, as is the management and definition of "services" (for lack of a better word), by means of instantiating objects or resolving dependencies in a specific manner.

It's important to note that simple dependencies, such as those not requiring any additional configuration or parameters to be instantiated, are handled automatically by the service container and are injected without any additional logic in the code. Listing 5-4 shows an example for service containers from the documentation.

Listing 5-4. Controller with Dependencies Injected That the Service Container
Can Resolve by Itself

```php
<?php
namespace Claim\Submission\Application\Controllers;

use App\Http\Controllers\Controller;
use App\Repositories\UserRepository;
use App\User;
class UserController extends Controller
{
    /**
     * The user repository implementation.
     *
     * @var UserRepository
     */
    protected $users;
    /**
     * Create a new controller instance.
     *
     * @param  UserRepository  $users
     * @return void
     */
    public function __construct(UserRepository $users)
    {
        $this->users = $users;
    }

    /**
     * Show the profile for the given user.
     *
     * @param  int  $id
     * @return Response
     */
```

```
    public function show($id)
    {
        $user = $this->users->find($id);
        return view('user.profile', ['user' => $user]);
    }
}
```

The $app Variable

In Laravel, the $app variable isn't just some run-of-the mill configuration object or data container but rather a global state of the application at any given time. If you have access to the $app variable, you have access to literally every single component, configuration setting, framework-specific functions, and any object or service registered with the service container, because it is, in fact, the service container. All service providers come with an $app property that gets set in their parent class.

Tip   Be sure to check out the class Illuminate\Support\ServiceProvider; its source code is located at /vendor/laravel/framework/src/ Illuminate/Support/ServiceProvider.php. There are many interesting things in this abstract parent class, including how it loads views, routes, language settings, configurations, commands, and other aspects of the system's vital functionality and settings. These are the default parameters and behaviors that each service provider in the system inherits, so it's well worth the extra effort to read and understand the source code.

The $app variable is also used to "bind" classes and objects to the service container in such a way as to abstract the setup, bootstrapping, or pre-invariant checks of those classes and services so as to provide means for their instantiation. The way you bind things into the service container is by writing a ServiceProvider that will handle all aspects involved in both setting up/configuring your service and providing a way to acquire specific instances of the objects included within the context of your service. Ideally, but not always, these class groupings and implementations would have been created in alignment with the domain. That is, we want to use the ideas, concepts, business rules, and invariants that are all involved in the core domain as a guide to distinguish between our classes, modules, and any other concepts.

> **Note**   I use the term *service* to refer to a specific context or group of classes that make up a specific feature or accomplish a specific goal. It is more granular than a module and less granular than a single object or class.

Simple objects that do not inherit an interface or that do not need any configuration or additional parameters to be instantiated can be built by the service container using reflection (Listing 5-5). Something as simple as this does not need a service definition.

Listing 5-5. Service Requiring a Dependency on a ClaimRepository Class That Can Automatically Be Resolved Using Reflection

```php
<?php
namespace Claim\Submission\Application\Services;
class ClaimNotificationService
{
    protected $claimRepository;

    public function __construct(ClaimRepository $claimRepository)
    {
        $this->claimRepository = $claimRepository;
    }
    public function doStuff()
    {
        // do something with $this->claimRepository...
    }
}

class ClaimRepository extends Repository
{
    public function findBy($field, $value)
    {
        return Claim::where($field, $value)->get();
    }
}
```

In Listing 5-5, all that would need to happen to get an instance of `ClaimNotificationService` (without manually providing its dependency inline with wherever you actually use) is the following:

```
use Claim\Submission\Application\Services\ClaimNotificationService;
// anywhere in the code where you would have access to $app – like a
// service provider, or anywhere the helper method app() is available
$claimNoticationService = $this->app->make(
    ClaimNotificationService::class);
```

As you can see, we can simply pass the class name to the `$app`'s `make()` method to resolve the particular class instance that we need, without specifying the dependencies manually. Behind the scenes, this is made possible through reflection, which we won't be covering in this book. For now, just know that some magic happens in the backend that allows the service container to resolve simple dependencies, like the previous one.

Binding to the Service Container

According to the official documentation, the majority of all bindings in the system will be done inside service providers. There are different ways to bind something to the container so you can use it at a later time (with little up-front work), but the whole idea is to basically set up how a service or class is instantiated; then, instead of manually doing all that work again in multiple client contexts, you would simply refer to the service container's particular binding name, which would compose your service or class exactly as you defined it to be built from within a service provider. It's basically a registry of defined instances of any class or object that you would need along with instructions on how to properly configure those classes.

If a service provider implements the interface `\Illuminate\Contracts\Support\DeferrableProvider`, the instructions on how to build a particular object would only be run and acquired on demand (that is, lazy loaded). If the service provider does not implement this interface, then the object in question would be built and stored in memory on every run of the service container.

Let's say that we had a class named `CoolService` with a method `doCoolThing()` that we wanted to bind to the container for easy access. To bind a single class or object into the service container, we would use this:

```
$this->app->bind('CoolService', \App\Services\CoolService::class);
```

Later when we want to use this cool service, we must extract it from the service container like so:

```
$coolService = app()->make('CoolService');
$result = $coolService->doCoolThing();
```

If for some reason there was additional setup or configuration that the CoolService class needs in order to be instantiated, simply provide a closure encapsulating the code needed to set it up (this is shown in detail in the next section).

Using the Service Container

As an example, let's say we want to have our notification service in Listing 5-5 to be able to support SMS notifications, email notifications, and Slack notifications. We don't want to duplicate the code between each class that should be the same. One way to ensure this is by abstracting away the delivery mechanism of the notification (which in this example I call *handlers*).

One way to handle this is to add a method inside the notifier service that would accept the particular type of notification to be sent. Then, we could encapsulate the entire "how" part of the notification service into a set of three behaviors, one for each type, which would get loaded based on the type parameter passed into this new method. The UML for this theoretical class map would look something like Figure 5-1.

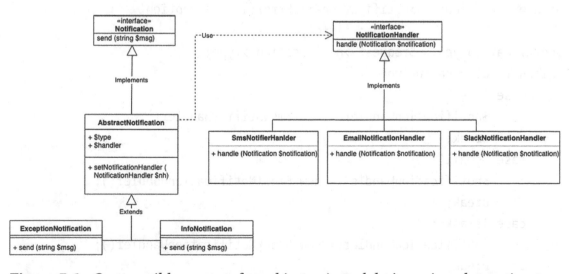

Figure 5-1. *One possible means of an object-oriented design using abstraction to solve the requirement of having multiple notification types*

Basically, we have two defined interfaces, `Notification` and `NotificationHandler`. `AbstractNotification` implements `Notification` and adds in the notion of a notification "type" and "handler" that are extended by the `ExceptionNotification` and the `InfoNotification` classes. These classes represent the means to send a message via the `send()` method but relies on the other set of classes on the left side of the diagram to actual do the sending part. The `Notification` handler interface in Figure 5-1 has three child classes, one for each message type. Each class has a `handle()` method responsible for transmitting the message to the desired medium (either a Slack notification, an email, or a text message). The abstract class uses the interface so that the implementation can be swapped out easily to replace the delivery mechanism without the rest of the application falling apart or breaking. We've encapsulated what can change about the notification system fairly well with this design.

Now that we have our overall architecture of the notification system, the code to actually instantiate such a system for the purposes of sending a single message seems a little extensive. For example, as it stands now, you would have to run something like the code in Listing 5-6, for every notification message you wanted to send via the application.

Listing 5-6. A Possible Usage of the Design in Figure 5-1 as Done by Hand, Not Using the Service Container or Dependency Injection

```
// example of using the above design
$context = $request->notification->isError() ? 'exception'
                             : 'info';
$notificationType = $request->notification->type;
switch ($notificationType) {
    case 'sms':
        $notificationHandler = new SmsNotifierHandler();
        break;
    case 'email':
        $notificationHandler = new EmailNotificationHandler();
        break;
    case 'slack':
        $notificationHandler = new SlackNotificationHandler();
        break;
```

```
        default:
            throw new InvalidNotificationTypeException();
}
if ($context == 'exception') {
    $notificationContext = new ExceptionNotification();
} else if ($context == 'info') {
    $notificationContext = new InfoNotification();
}
//finally, send our message
$notificationContext->setNotificationHandler($notificationHandler)->
    send($request->notification->message);
```

This is simply an impractical solution. How could we use Laravel's service container to help us?

We can create an alias of an FQCN (using any namespace we want, even if it's completely imaginary) that will point to either the InfoNotification or the ExceptionNotification and then call its corresponding setNotificationHandler() method automatically to set the proper type. Listing 5-7 shows an example of how that may look using a closure as the means of defining the logic that will be executed to build the desired object/service. (Most likely this would be done inside AppServiceProvider, which is the provider that is used by the entire system for application concerns and configuration.)

Listing 5-7. Example Service Container Binding for the Aforementioned Notification System

```
$this->app->bind('SlackExceptionNotifier', function($app) {
    $notificationContext = new ExceptionNotification();
    $notificationContext->setNotificationHandler (new
        SlackNotificationHandler());
    return $notificationContext;
});
```

175

Basically all we've done here is created an entry in the service container under the identifier SlackExceptionNotifier, which, when run, will perform the logic enclosed inside the anonymous function and return the result, in this case a fully instantiated, licensed, and certified notification object for you to use to send Slack notifications. Here is an example of its use:

```
$slackExceptionService = app()->make('SlackExceptionNotifier');
$slackExceptionService->send("Some slack message");
```

Note that this isn't the best way to handle the use case mentioned for this example, mostly because you would have to write a total of six services (three notification types * two notification contexts) to handle every possible combination. In the real world, this would be overkill; however, it serves the purpose for what we needed it for: to demonstrate binding and retrieving objects/services in and out of the service container. Don't look into it too much past that, because you will probably find flaws even in the initial system design.

Objects and services are not the only things you can bind to the container. You also have the option of binding a singleton class, which implies that there is only one single copy of an object of that class at any given time in the application.

```
$this->app->singleton('ClaimsApi', function ($app) {
    return new Claim\Application\Api($app->make('ClaimHttpClient'));
});
```

You can also bind specific instances to the container and expect to get that same instance handed back to you after retrieving it from the container.

```
$notifier = new ExceptionNotification();
$notifier->setNotificationHandler(
    new SlackNotificationHandler()
);
$this->app->instance('SlackExceptionNotifier', $notifier);
```

As you can see, we have simply instantiated an instance of ExceptionNotification and have stored this instance using the container's instance() method under the identifier SlackExceptionNotifier, which is what you pass as an argument to $app's make() method when retrieving an instance of 'SlackExceptionNotifier':

```
app()->make('SlackExceptionNotifier')->send('some slack message');.
```

Binding Interfaces to Implementations

This is arguably the coolest thing about Laravel's service container and is what makes the framework so powerful and flexible. So, we now know how to bind things to the service container such as classes, instances, and objects that need additional logic to be created and used virtually anywhere in the system.

There is another feature of the service container that allows you to bind interfaces to implementations. The reason this is powerful is because it allows you to dynamically pass in a concrete class that acts as an implementation to a given interface. Once you have it set up, Laravel will provide the application with that implementation wherever the interface that it is implementing is referenced within the application. This allows you to have different implementations of a single interface and gives you the power to swap out implementations by simply modifying just one line of code inside a service provider.

To bind implementations to interfaces, you would use this syntax:

```
$this->app->bind('Claim\Submission\Domain\ClaimRepositoryInterface',
    'Claim\Submission\Infrastructure\Repositories\ClaimRepository');
```

Laravel will see this code and automatically inject the implementation (`Claim\Submission\Infrastructure\Repositories\ClaimRepository`) anywhere and everywhere it finds a reference to `Claim\Submission\Domain\ClaimRepositoryInterface`. This is a powerful feature and is partly what makes Laravel so powerful.

Let's go through an example. Let's say you had an open source codebase that included a model for books that needed to be persisted to track the information about the book such as author, ISBN, and other defining characteristics normal books would have. You also have consumers of the model that use the book information for research and tracking purposes. The problem is that because the code is meant to be shared, you don't know the exact way that the book information is going to be persisted. Most of the time, the user is predicted to utilize MySQL for its storage and persistence needs, yet there are users who'd rather be able to store the books in Redis and even other nonrelational persistence mechanisms like MongoDB and Elasticsearch. You don't know which one the user will end up utilizing for its own implementation, so you need to account for all three variations to make your code super useful to others.

What we could do is create an interface to handle the persistence of the books and then implement that interface for each client's specific persistence mechanism. In doing this, we can provide each client with the specific entry points they need to interface with our book model. Once we have our implementations defined, we simply need to bind the interface with the implementation for the selected mechanism in the service container, and Laravel will take care of the rest for us!

Figure 5-2 provides a diagram of the system for clarification.

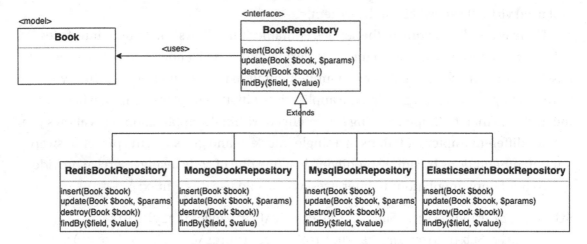

Figure 5-2. *An interface BookRepository with its possible implementations, each one specific to a given persistence layer*

That looks pretty good: we have an implementation of the BookRepository for every persistence mechanism we can think of (obviously there's more, but this will work for the demonstration). The only piece that would be missing is the setting that told the application which repository implementation to use. That could be solved in a number of ways (this list is noninclusive).

- Providing a BOOK_REPO_TYPE parameter in the .env file, which would be picked up via a config file and loaded into the application's memory

- Have the user hard-code their specific repository directly in the service container via the AppServiceProvider

- Have the user specify the repository in a separate service provider

Whichever way you decide to integrate a specific repository version, you would then configure the type of repository by defining this in a service provider so that it uses that repository anywhere it finds a BookRepository interface as a type hint (Listing 5-8).

Listing 5-8. The Service Container Configuration Needed to Support All Possible Repositories in the Application

```
$bookRepoType = "RedisBookRepository"; // this is derived from one of
                                       // the methods listed above
$this->app->bind('Domain\Books\BookRepository',
    'Interface\Repository\RedisBookRepository');
```

Once we have that in place, the only thing left to do would be to simply ensure that we are not depending on any of the children repository classes directly (Listing 5-9).

Listing 5-9. An Example of What Not to Do…Rely on a Concrete Method

```
// ..some controller
// EXAMPLE OF WHAT NOT TO DO
public function generateBookList(
    RedisBookRepository, outputFormat='csv') {
        // do stuff
}
```

Besides the obvious issue of the system not working, this code is breaking an important principle in programming. Don't rely on concretions, rely on abstractions. To put this principle in practice for the previous piece of code, we would simply swap out the RedisBookRepository with something more abstract so that we could utilize this generateBookList() method. The BookRepository class fits nicely here as it encompasses all implementations while leaving the actual details to the child classes. Instead of the code in Listing 5-9, using a coarser class definition as the argument would yield the code in Listing 5-10.

Listing 5-10. A Better Approach to Defining the Dependency of a Book Repository

```
public function generateBookList(
    BookRepository, outputFormat='csv') {
        // do stuff
}
```

179

Note   Can you identify the different principles that are in effect in Listing 5-9 and Listing 5-10? I'll give you a hint: there's more than one, and they fall within the SOLID principles.

What's important to remember is that definitions like these should be done only when necessary, because nine times out of ten, simply type-hinting the arguments with the proper dependency will suffice for what you are trying to do. This is known as *automatic injection*, and most of the time, you won't even need to tell Laravel how to build a particular object...it will determine this by itself via reflection.

Queues and Laravel Jobs

In Laravel, you have the option of incorporating some logic that needs to be run inside a Job class. You may want to run this job asynchronously or even defer the job to be run at a later time. A *queue* is usually some external queue system such as Amazon SQS, RabbitMQ, Redis, or MySQL. Laravel provides quick and easy methods for connecting such services to your application. The configuration for such services can be found in the `config/queue.php` file. Although we won't be going to deep into setting up a queue system until later in the book, we will be using jobs to encapsulate one-off tasks, and you could use a queue system to handle the processing of those jobs. For more information on configuring a driver for one of the supported queue systems, see the Laravel documentation at `https://laravel.com/docs/6.x/queues`.

A queue is simply a stack of jobs that are waiting to be dispatched and handled by some configured queue system, as described earlier. Queues are usually grouped in a manner easily recognizable as to what kind of jobs that particular queue handles, such as "default" or "primary." The ability to push jobs onto different queues segments the jobs in a way that's easier to manage and helps to identify where those jobs are needed. This is especially true for larger applications where you have multiple jobs firing off at different times and for different reasons. Sometimes the jobs you will need performed are resource intensive and could take a long time to run (at least from the perspective of the user). With PHP being an interpreted language, queues can be used to send out the job and immediately return a response to the user so they are not waiting there wondering why your application or page is "broken."

Response time and page load time are important to not only the user experience but also to the quality of your site as ranked by the Google search engine. Web pages with long response times are usually a source of errors in the application, and as a developer, many of the debugging items that I'm tasked with relate to parts of the codebase that take "forever" to load. When this happens, a queue system can be the answer to many issues stemming from something taking too long to load.

How Queues Work

In a nutshell, queues operate in respect to a selected *queue driver*. As described previously, Laravel has built-in support for a number of queue managers. You can think of a queue driver as one that handles the dispatching of your jobs and tracking them so they don't run more than once (also to keep a log of what's been dispatched). Other than that, the job itself can contain all the logic that you need to handle that specific task. If you need to dispatch an event so that an *x* number of listeners can hear it and act accordingly, you would do so within that handle() method. If you needed another job to be dispatched after the current one, simply put that logic in the handle() method of the job. You would include any dependencies you need as constructor arguments that you assign to properties of your Job class so that they are ready to roll when the code gets to handle().

When dispatching a job, if you don't specify a queue identifier (queue name), it will default to the "default" queue using whichever queue driver you have enabled in the configuration. All that driver really does is tell Laravel *where* to store the jobs that have been processed and the jobs that are currently on the stack. When using the "database" queue driver, the jobs will all be stored in a SQL table named jobs. Here is how you would configure that in your config/queue.php file:

```
'default' => env('QUEUE_DRIVER', 'database')
```

However, this table is not included by default, so you would need to run the command needed to create it, shown here:

```
php artisan queue:table
```

This will create a migration with the name _create_jobs_table.php, prefixed with the current timestamp. After this, you will need to run the migrate command to create the table in the database.

```
php artisan migrate
```

To create a job, you can issue the following Artisan command:

```
php artisan make:job JobClassName
```

This will yield a `JobClassName` class inside `App\Jobs` (keep in mind that this is the default directory and not necessarily the one we will use in this book). To create the meat and potatoes of what the job actually does, you simply inject any dependencies into its constructor and put the logic that you want executed within the `handle()` method. Laravel will auto-inject the dependencies directly into the job for you to use inside `handle()`.

As an example, Listing 5-11 shows a job that is used to update some patient's primary care physician.

Listing 5-11. An Example Laravel Job That Accepts $patient and $provider Objects, Then Modifies the Patient's Set Provider to Be the One Passed into the Handle Method

```
class ChangePatientPhysician implements ShouldQueue
{
    use Dispatchable, InteractsWithQueue, Queueable, SerializesModels;

    protected $patientProviderRepository;

    /**
     * Create a new job instance.
     *
     * @param  Patient $patient
     * @param  Provider $newProvider
     * @return void
     */
    public function __construct( PatientProviderRepository
        $patientProviderRepository)
    {
        $this->patientProviderRepository = $patientProviderRepository;
    }
    /**
     * Execute the job.
```

```
 *
 * @return void
 */
public function handle(Patient $patient, Provider $newProvider)
{
  //verify this patient is registered under this provider
  $isRegistered = $this->patientProviderRepository
                        ->patientRegisteredFor(
                  $patient, $provider);
  if ($isRegistered) {
      $patient->provider()->associate($provider);
      $patient->save();
  } else {
      throw new PatientNotRegisteredWithProviderException();
  }
  }
}
```

To dispatch the previous job, you would use the syntax in Listing 5-12.

Listing 5-12. Dispatching a Job from a Controller Method

```
// most likely in a controller somewhere
public function updatePatientsProvider($patient, $provider)
{
    //dispatch the job, passing in parameters that correspond to the
    //signature of the Job's  handle() method
    ChangePatientPhysician::dispatch();
    }
```

As you can see, creating and dispatching jobs is a cinch in Laravel using the underlying queue driver connection to facilitate the job through the work queue. If for some reason you didn't want to use a queue but wanted the job to be run right away, you could use the dispatchNow() method.

```
ChangePatientPhysician::dispatch();
```

We will be using jobs heavily later in the book when we are building our API for the Claims model.

Laravel Contracts

Laravel comes with a long list of standardized interfaces of some of the most common patterns, classes, and components used in any web application. The contracts all live in the `Illuminate\Contracts` namespace, and the features, tools, and support provided by the framework are specific implementations of a contract. You can also find them on GitHub at `https://github.com/illuminate/contracts`. You can find an implementation of every contract somewhere within the `Illuminate\` namespace. For example, Listing 5-13 shows a contract that describes a command bus, which is implemented by Laravel to dispatch jobs like the one discussed in the previous section.

Listing 5-13. Laravel's Contract for a Standard Command Bus

```php
// Illuminate\Contracts\Bus\Dispatcher
namespace Illuminate\Contracts\Bus;
interface Dispatcher
{
    /**
     * Dispatch a command to its appropriate handler.
     *
     * @param  mixed  $command
     * @return mixed
     */
    public function dispatch($command);
    /**
     * Dispatch a command to its appropriate handler in the current process.
     *
     * @param  mixed  $command
     * @param  mixed  $handler
     * @return mixed
     */
    public function dispatchNow($command, $handler = null);
    /**
     * Determine if the given command has a handler.
     *
     * @param  mixed  $command
```

```
 * @return bool\
 */

public function hasCommandHandler($command);
/**
 * Retrieve the handler for a command.
 *
 * @param  mixed  $command
 * @return bool|mixed
 */
public function getCommandHandler($command);
/**
 * Set the pipes commands should be piped through before dispatching.
 *
 * @param  array  $pipes
 * @return $this
 */
public function pipeThrough(array $pipes);
/**
 * Map a command to a handler.
 *
 * @param  array  $map
 * @return $this
 */
public function map(array $map);
}
```

Here we have a basic interface describing a command bus, including the methods required for implementing classes to define, along with details about what each should do in the commented-out docblocks. By glancing at this interface, we can deduce quickly that anything implementing it will have dispatch(), dispatchNow(), hasCommandHandler(), getCommandHandler(), pipeThrough(), and map() methods defined. The implementation that Laravel comes with to handle dispatching commands and jobs is too lengthy to put in this book; however, I urge to check it out at https://github.com/laravel/framework/blob/6.x/src/Illuminate/Bus/Dispatcher.php. Note that this class actually extends yet another interface with a single method dispatchToQueue(), which is required by the QueueingDispatcher interface.

Don't get confused with the nested interfaces. As of version 6, Laravel has revamped the way contracts are interfaces and implemented, but in the long run, they make more sense and have a logical structure. They have to, seeing as though they are all in use in some form or another to produce the features and functionality of the framework itself! Although we will not use contracts extensively in this book, it's an important fundamental to understand.

Events

Events in Laravel are a powerful tool to let other areas of your application know that something of interest has occurred. The other side of events are listeners, which follow the basic Observer pattern. Listeners (observers) are basically just simple classes that are set up to run after a specific event (observed) has occurred in the application. Notice I used the past tense when referring to the event, which is correct because, technically, all events have occurred in the *past.* That last sentence you read is, in fact, now in the past. As such, all events should have the past tense version of what it does. Here are some examples of common events:

- UserWasRegistered

- AccountWasDeactivated

- ChangedPatientsPrimaryPhysician

- ClaimWasSubmitted

- SomethingHasHappened

You get the point.

All event configuration is specified in the app/Providers/EventServiceProvider.php file. The class in that file has a protected property named $listen that is an array of arrays containing each event type and its subsequent listeners to that event. By default, that property has one element in it (Listing 5-14).

Listing 5-14. The Default Event Listeners That Come with Laravel

```
protected $listen = [
        Registered::class => [
            SendEmailVerificationNotification::class,
        ],
    ];
```

All this says is "Once the event defined by the Registered class occurs, fire off the listener contained in SendEmailVerificationNotification." You can manually add your events to this array as you are developing, along with their corresponding listeners. Another, much better option is to simply add the events (with fully qualified namespaces) and their corresponding listeners (observers), as shown in Listing 5-15. I created it simply for demonstration purposes, and I did so without having any of the classes I included within the $listen array.

Listing 5-15. Example $listen Array Inside the App\Providers\ EventServiceProvider Class

```
protected $listen = [
    //...
    ClaimWasSubmitted::class => [
        NotifyAccountManager::class,
        SendEmailSubmissionConfirmation::class,
        \Infrastructure\Services\UpdateElasticSearch::class,
    ];
    ];
```

After changing the EventServiceProvider to your liking, you can run the following Artisan command to generate all the classes included in the $listen array, in their respective default folders (App\Events and App\Listeners) or within the directory specified in the FQCN (assuming that directory has been properly configured with the autoloader in composer.json):

```
php artisan event:generate
```

Laravel's Stock Event and Listener

Another way to think of it is comparing it to the way newsletters work. A newsletter will have a list of subscribers (i.e., listeners) that receive it, so when the job gets distributed (i.e., dispatched), only the subscribers on the list will receive it, but to the rest of the world, it doesn't even exist. Listeners obviously would contain some logic to be performed once that event gets dispatched.

In Listing 5-16, for example, we can deduce that there is a `Registered` event that most likely gets dispatched once a new user registers with the system, and that event is listened to by a `Listener` named SendEmailVerificationNotification, which, in turn, most likely sends a confirmation email to that user (assuming that their email was a form on the registration page). By looking at the source code of the listener, we see that (of course), Laravel has already accounted for that (Listing 5-16).

Listing 5-16. Example $listen Array Inside the App\Providers\ EventServiceProvider Class

```php
<?php

namespace Illuminate\Auth\Listeners;

use Illuminate\Auth\Events\Registered;
use Illuminate\Contracts\Auth\MustVerifyEmail;

class SendEmailVerificationNotification
{
    /**
     * Handle the event.
     *
     * @param  \Illuminate\Auth\Events\Registered  $event
     * @return void
     */
    public function handle(Registered $event)
    {
        if ($event->user instanceof MustVerifyEmail && !
            $event->user->hasVerifiedEmail()) {
```

```
        $event->user->sendEmailVerificationNotification();
      }
   }
}
```

From this source code we can clearly see that it listens to the `Registered` event defined by the class `Illuminate\Auth\Events\Registered`. It also has the logic for sending the notification only if the user provides an email during registration. All logic that is needed to send the notification is contained within the listener's `handle()` method. It is self-encapsulating.

Instead of registering events manually in `EventServiceProvider`, as of Laravel 5.8.9, you have the ability to configure what's called *automatic event discovery*. When this is activated, Laravel will scan any listener directories you specify and auto-register any listeners to events. Whenever Laravel comes across a listener class with a defined `handle()` method, Laravel will register those methods as event listeners for whichever event is type-hinted in that method's signature (Listing 5-17).

Listing 5-17. Example Listener That Has the Corresponding Event Type-Hinted in the handle() Method

```php
<?php

use App\Events\PodcastProcessed;
class SendPodcastProcessedNotification
{
    /**
     * Handle the given event.
     *
     * @param  \App\Events\PodcastProcessed
     * @return void
     */
    public function handle(PodcastProcessed $event)
    {
        // do work here
    }
}
```

In the previous event, when Laravel hits this class and sees the handle() method, it will register the event (SendPodcastProcessedNotification) with the listener, PodcastProcessed. To configure this feature, you need to override the shouldDiscoverEvents method in EventServiceProvider (Listing 5-18).

Listing 5-18. Enabling Event Auto-registration in Laravel

```
public function shouldDiscoverEvents()
{
    return true;
}
```

To specify which directories you want Laravel to scan for auto-registering events (which only includes the App\Listeners directory by default), you override the discoverEventsWithin() method with the paths of the listeners you want Laravel to scan (Listing 5-19).

Listing 5-19. Specifying Locations Where Laravel Will Scan to Auto-register Events

```
public function discoverEventsWithin()
{
    return [
        'App\Listeners',
        'Domain\Listeners'
    ];
}
```

Events are generated with a trait that they use called SerializesModels. This trait makes it so the event can easily serialize any Eloquent models passed into it. If the event you are firing is one that should stop propagation of other events, simply return false from the handle() method.

If you are using a queue, you can get that functionality by adding a ShouldQueue trait to your listener class. For more information on customizing the specific queue, see https://laravel.com/docs/6.x/events#queued-event-listeners.

Dispatching Events

To dispatch events, use the event() helper, passing into it the name of the Event class.

```
$podcast = Podcast::find(345);
event(new SendPodcastProcessedNotification($podcast));
```

Events are often used to promote loose coupling within the application and helps keep things separated. For example, instead of sending an email confirmation directly from the register controller, thereby coupling the email logic and the registration logic, being able to dispatch an event from the controller that the SendEmailConfirmation listener will pick up on and act accordingly provides a completely decoupled solution that keeps your registration logic focused on registration. This is a common use case for events and listeners, and the functionality provided by Laravel to facilitate them is extremely useful.

Conclusion

This chapter covered some of the finer points of Laravel that we will be using throughout the rest of the book to realize a reasonable approach to a domain-driven design. By utilizing Laravel jobs, decoupled events, and listeners, along with Laravel's standard request/response flow and all the features of the framework, we can string them together to create a standardized "flow" of operations to encapsulate our business logic and allows us to create separated and loosely coupled components. We will discuss more in depth the overall flow of how we will create our business processes later in the book.

For now, think of how the different components available in Laravel suit the needs of a standard, modern web application quite well. Laravel itself is built on top of a dependency injection container, which can be configured on a per-service basis as needed by an application. We can also use the service container to bind specific instances of a specific type of object to any place in the code that references that object's interface. This gives us a flexible, clean, and concise way to manage dependencies and is partly what makes Laravel's service container so powerful. Laravel jobs are great for encapsulating well-defined, self-contained one-off tasks existing within the domain model in a way that can be easily integrated with a queue system to support asynchronous processing of jobs (which is also fairly easy to do in Laravel, as you will see in later chapters). When something interesting happens in the application (such as a job being dispatched to a queue and then actually run), we can use an Event to mark the occurrence of that job and then react to that event anywhere else in the application by writing an Event listener.

CHAPTER 6

Architecting a Claim Processing System

There are two central concepts in this book that are key to the successful design and implementation of a model-driven, well-architected web application using Laravel as the backbone framework. The structure of the book may seem a little weird at times, but I'm trying to balance all the prerequisite knowledge you need with the actual implementation you will be creating using that knowledge, all while juggling these two important topics. Frankly, there is a lot to learn, depending on the level of expertise you had when you started reading this book. I go into depth on the various concepts involved in DDD and the potential corresponding code relevant to Laravel in a manner that I think will be most beneficial to you when implementing these ideas and concepts in your real-life applications. I'll give you a solid understanding of these concepts by providing you with situations that they will make good use cases so that you can attempt an implementation yourself using the Laravel framework as a means of realizing a domain-driven design, whether it be in your own projects or your company's. The following are situations that make good use cases for selecting various patterns involved in DDD, so that we can fully explore the value they bring to our development efforts:

- Grasping each one's core use, as well as the pros and cons of employing each pattern (whether that pattern is from the technical, supple, or strategic pillar of DDD)

- Helping solve the types of issues that you may face (and I have faced) in the wild

- Giving you a clear mental picture of your application's inner workings and helping you define the high-level structure of your apps using DDD patterns to granulate the features across various domain layer components

© Jesse Griffin 2021
J. Griffin, *Domain-Driven Laravel*, https://doi.org/10.1007/978-1-4842-6023-4_6

- Considering architectural concerns when building out the core components using DDD's technical patterns as a means of their implementation while also keeping in mind that they are all simply possibilities and not concrete solutions

Also, remember that no idea should be dismissed without proper consideration of its potential impact on the rest of the system, based on core business rules described with terms found in the business's ubiquitous language. There is almost always more than one way to do something, and these potential solutions normally don't come about without hours of discussion, planning, prototyping, realizing that you messed something up along the way, and then correcting the mistake after you've gained additional insight into the more granular parts of the domain. This is no small feat and will (most of the time) require a whole lot of prerequisite learning, questioning, documenting, and refactoring to truly gain valuable insight into the domain model.

That being said, there can be (and most likely is) a better way of doing something than what I've outlined in the book, and I challenge you to be the one who comes up with it. I arm you with the information, best practices, and knowledge of the technical patterns found in DDD that you can use in your work projects or your own to create a well-constructed application with a rich model that fully captures the logic and rules that are expressed by the business to do what it does to make money. The best way I've found to do that is to give you good examples along with the thought process used to arrive at potential solutions—all clearly laid out so you can see the steps I took to reach the end goal. If you can understand the technical considerations (one pillar of the DDD structure) and use the model and architectural design techniques (another pillar of DDD) as a means of employing these technical patterns, then you can use these patterns as tools in your arsenal to build new requirements or features (the third pillar), which are the technical aspects and structures used to express a domain model in DDD.

That being said, this chapter acts as the glue that holds together the two central concepts I suggest using to build web application software (hint: they are in the title of this book). I will introduce to you some sample real-life problems that I myself have had the pleasure to work on. We will expand on the medical claim example I gave you in the previous chapter to discuss a variety of topics that we will design using DDD building blocks (i.e., those affiliated with the technical patterns of Domain-driven design), and we will implement the building block patterns using Laravel as a means to do so. We will do things in an API-first, test-driven way to fully establish the core business objects and processes that run on those objects, and we will be careful to follow the best practices and standards that we know any quality, maintainable code is written with.

We will be looking to use the teachings of DDD as a means of crafting quality into our software. Specifically, we will be focused on things such as the following:

- Developing a clean, language-agnostic API that will clearly describe the part of the system that we are building, giving the business a useful model of its domain

- Developing a refined and well-tuned definition of business terms, operations, and domain objects that are involved (ubiquitous language)

- Briefly defining the core concepts (tools) that are part of DDD

  - Repositories

  - Services

  - Domain events

  - Aggregates

- Describing what bounded contexts are and how to use them to section off domains and subdomains within our business logic and then utilizing these contexts to create a context map and, eventually, a set of models that will act as the backbone of our application's domain and namespace structure

- Remembering that we can use processes such as the agile methodology, iterative development, continuous modeling, and continuous integration to build high-quality, enterprise-grade web applications that are easily testable, cohesive, and loosely coupled and that fully represent the domain it was built from accurately and thoroughly

- Refactoring the code to be more on par with the business's domain model, which is important in creating maintainable software that can be expanded to solve problems imposed by new features requests in the future

Let's get started then!

Medi-Cal Claim Submission

We will expand our medical claim discussion from the previous chapter and go a little more in-depth with the required background information we will be using throughout the rest of the chapter.

How does our company make money? Normally, the claim submission process involved in the medical billing system tends to be difficult because it involves multiple steps and a precise system of checks and balances that must be adhered to for the government to cut a check to the provider for their services. Our company has created an application that helps alleviate the pain points in the manual process of submitting a claim. To do this, however, the application has to track and carry out various state management tasks required to verify the claim is 100 percent accurate and ready to be filed with the Federal Qualified Health Center (FQHC).

The way we will accomplish this is by establishing different statuses a claim can be in, which it also tracks for every claim going through our system. For example, there is a review process that must occur on a claim to ensure its accuracy so that it doesn't get rejected by the FQHC with a `CORRECTION_NEEDED` status, which delays the payment to the provider.

Basically, think of the service that our company provides as a clearinghouse for claims so they get accepted and the providers get paid the first time they are submitted to the FQHC. The reason this is important is because of the high level of returned claims (and delayed payments) that occur when providers submit the claim directly to the FQHC. There are simply too many errors that receptionists make when selecting the procedures that were done on each patient; this is known as a *pain point*.

Our company has found a niche in the market and has filled it with a spiffy new application that gives the provider's (doctor's) offices the ability to submit an entire claim using the tools and process that we've devised based on the federal claim review process. This process verifies all the required data is there and queues the claim for review. The review team handles verifying the claim as it goes through the review process, ensuring that all patient data, medical status, descriptions of received care, CPT codes representing the various procedures that were done on a patient, and a slew of other doctor/insurance provider information are all on hand and are all 100 percent correct before they mark the claim as "Reviewer Approved."

At this point, the claim is ready to be submitted to the FQHC for billing to verify the amount and then to process the payment and cut a check to the provider. We intercept the check, take our potion of the revenue, and then shoot the remainder of the money to the provider, after fees and expenses. For the federal entity to approve the payout reimbursement to the providers, however, the claim must be guaranteed to be correct. The claims are submitted and paid out in batches of anywhere between 100 and 1,000 separate claims.

It would take roughly five to ten times longer to submit the claims "the old-fashioned way," meaning via paper forms, a fax machine, and photocopied documents in comparison to our new claim submission system. The process used to be 100 percent hand, when there were no computerized checks to ensure that the data on the claim form was valid before actually submitting it to the federal government. There was nothing in place to ensure the procedure code combinations (aka CPT code combos) represented the actual payable work completed on a patient by a provider. There are numerous other (rather strict) requirements imposed by the official claim submission process that, if not met, would mandate a nonpayment return of the claim to the provider, requesting them to make the needed corrections before attempting to submit the claim again.

Medi-Cal Procedure Codes

Claims are paid out on a predetermined cost structure that is based on something called a *paycode sheet*. The way the FQHC determines how much to pay the providers depends on the type of cost structure the provider is registered under. The two structures are as follows:

- *Pay per visit*: This cost structure mandates that a predetermined, fixed amount is paid to the provider for their services for every visit they receive from a registered patient that has Medi-Cal benefits, no matter what routines, services, or procedures the patient received. They are paid the same fixed amount for each visit. The amount is agreed upon by the provider and the FQHC, but our company actually issues the checks to the providers. Usually, the pay-per visit amount ranges from $100 to $150. Note that although they do not determine the amount paid out to the provider, the pay per visit plan still requires that every procedure involved be tracked with a procedure code (aka CPT code).

- *Pay per procedure*: This is where it gets complicated. Doctors that are under the pay per procedure structure are paid based on the procedure they provided to the patient. The amounts are determined by analyzing a given set of individual procedures, which are known as CTP codes. Each CPT code represents one medical procedure completed on a patient (X-rays given, applied cast to mend broken arm, etc.). The way the amount is determined on a claim is by analyzing the groups of individual CPT codes listed and looking up that CPT code Combination in something called a paycode sheet.

CPT Code Groups

To make things even more complicated, the FQHC determines the payment based on groups of these CPT codes, known as *CPT code combos*. The big deal here is that these combinations are very specific, and most of them have requirements to be included on a claim. Some CPT combo groups may contain multiples of the same CPT code or may have a CPT code with a requirement that deems it valid only if another specific CPT code exists within the same group.

Other requirements exist as well. Each CPT code combo corresponds to one or more CPT codes, which in turn may have prerequisite requirements, may be contained only within another set of CPT codes, or may be used in a specific sequence of steps that each, in turn, have their own CPT-specific requirements. All available procedures that a doctor can possibly perform on a patient are modeled as a series of CPT code combos. This is how the FQHC determines the exact amount paid out for each of these procedures. All possible combinations, along with their predetermined cost amounts (paid to providers), are stored within a specific paycode sheet.

Paycode sheets track all these CPT combos that represent various procedures completed on each patient and that are modeled and expressed in a preset format that is not human-readable. This requires the providers' offices to look up each CPT code they wanted to use by hand and then ensure that the CPT combos they submitted with the claim correspond to valid entries within the specific paycode sheet.

For example, here is a list of (fake) CPT codes that correspond to a patient who was treated for breathing problems:

- Chest X-ray completed (code 3892)

- Blood work ordered (code 3332)

- Albuterol sulfate administered to patient via a nebulizer (code 4523)

These three codes are all found on a single claim, because they all occurred in the same visit. There is a strict policy by the FQHC that states that no patient can be seen more than once per day, so every procedure done for that patient on a given day must be included on the corresponding claim—hey will not accept more than one claim per patient per day.

These codes will be found inside a given paycode sheet with a specified amount the provider makes from treating the patient. Table 6-1 shows an example record in a paycode sheet that dictates the amount paid to claims having the previous three CPT codes together.

Table 6-1. *Record from a Paycode Sheet Corresponding to a Group of CPT Codes*

CPT Code IDs	CPT Codes	Amount
3; 38; 420;	3392, 3332, 4523	$150

As a feature for the providers of the system (which are the main users of the application and the central client that our sales team focuses on), the application should somehow house the paycode sheet data as well as the data submitted with a claim inside an internal relational database, parse out the code combinations on the submitted claim, look up this combination in the relevant paycode sheet, and attach to the claim's metadata the estimated amount that the claim is worth, in total.

Figure 6-1 breaks down the CPT coding system.

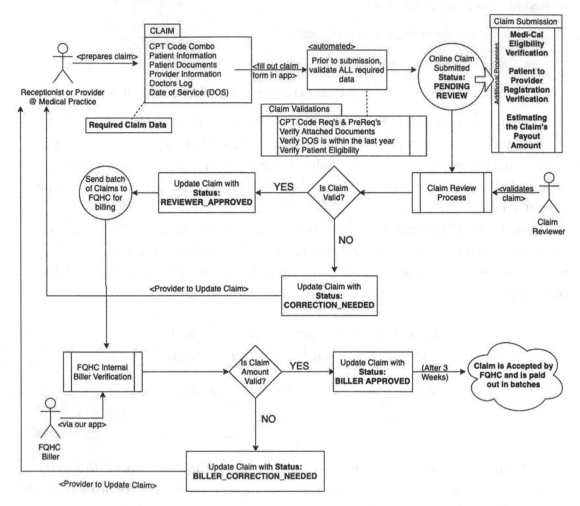

Figure 6-1. *Workflow involved in the Medi-Cal claim submission process*

In Figure 6-1, we start out at the top left, with the provider (or receptionist at the provider's office or practice) logs into our application and goes to the Create New Claim page. On this page are all kinds of form inputs for the various pieces of required information the claim needs to be processed successfully. The following pieces of data are needed to complete and submit the form:

- The patient's documents must be on file. This includes the following:

  a.   Photocopy of patient's ID or DL

  b.   Photocopy of patient's Medi-Cal benefits card

  c.   Copy of (or electronically stored) contract to receive care

- Basic patient information

  a.   First name, middle initial, last name

  b.   Date of birth, gender

  c.   Hair color, eye color, weight

  d.   Social Security number

  e.   Current street address

  f.   Emergency contacts

- Procedures completed on patient, tracked via CPT code combination that must be valid according to the amounts corresponding to the CPT code combo defined inside a given paycode sheet

- Provider information

  a.   NPI number (national provider identification number)

  b.   Provider's name, location, license/medical degree

  c.   Associated practice that the provider is practicing under

- The date of service (DOS), which is the date that the procedures were completed on a patient

- Associated doctor's log/history of treating the patient, known as *progress notes*

In addition, there are a number of automated validation tasks that occur when a user submits a claim, including checking the claim for all the previous requirements, verifying the DOS falls somewhere within the last year, and verifying patient eligibility via looking for an uploaded document provided by the provider's office.

After all data on the claim has been verified as best as the application can without human involvement, the claim is physically submitted to the system and gets saved with the status of PENDING_REVIEW. Once the claim is officially submitted, on the backend, we have a few additional processes that run on it before it gets to a reviewer. First, we want to automate the patient eligibility requirement so that the application actually goes to the Medi-Cal page online, submits the patient information by manipulating the DOM, scrapes the response returned, and then attaches that response to the claim. We will handle this later in the chapter.

Another task that gets run on submission is verifying that the patient on the claim is, in fact, registered with that provider. If the registration is not done, the application should not allow the user to proceed with the claim and is directed back to correct the claim. The provider on the claim is linked to a paycode sheet, which determines how much each procedure code grouping will pay out to the provider. The last thing that needs to be run before the claim is reviewed is estimating the claim's amount. This is done by looking up the CPT combo in the paycode sheet and attaching an "estimated amount" to the claim. If no amount could be resolved from the paycode sheet, that indicates that the combination of CPT codes does not exist in that paycode sheet, and it must be added before the claim can be sent to the FQHC.

After the automated processes all run, the claim goes to the review team for claim review before it's sent out. The reviewer again checks all the documents on the claim and manually validates everything submitted on the claim (and the fields that the application has created and attached to the claim as well); the reviewer either approves it or deems it as needing correction, in which case the claim is sent back to the provider for corrections (with a claim status that indicates this: CORRECTION_NEEDED). There is also a notes section on the review page that the reviewer can use to enter specific notes or comments about the claim, and these notes are attached to the claim; then, the provider submitting the claim gets a notification that the claim needs attention. They can correct it and send it through again, starting the process over.

If the claim is good to go, the reviewer marks it as REVIEWER_APPROVED, and the claim is sent out to the FQHC for billing review. A billing user working at the FQHC pulls up the data associated with the claim and does a final check against the estimated amount and ensures that the amount corresponds to a valid CPT combination that is listed in that provider's respective paycode sheet. Once this is done, the biller marks the claim as BILLER_APPROVED, and three weeks later a paycheck is issued to our company on behalf of the provider. Then we distribute the money to them. Otherwise, the biller marks the claim as `BILLER_CORRECTION_NEEDED`, where it is then sent back to the provider once again for corrections (at which point the submission process starts over). Overall, the process is pretty straightforward, but there are lots of verifications and validations that go into a claim to ensure it will be accepted and paid.

What Are We Building?

Now that you have some understanding of the flow of the claim submission process, we can start rationalizing how we want to implement the features of this example. First, however, it is critical to define what it is we are building. I will walk you through setting up the project's context map and defining the bounded contexts in this application.

Keep in mind that this application is considered an "enterprise application" in that it manages multiple user types, provides authentication and authorization management, and exists in a variety of contexts. After we map out the application in terms of boundaries, domains, contexts, and subdomains (we'll get to all that in a bit), we will focus on designing and implementing a few different aspects of the system, specifically the following:

- The claim submission process, including all required checks and balances and status code changes.

- A role system that defines roles for the various user types in the system, and their respective checks when performing system tasks (i.e., authorization).

- The process of determining the amount of a claim based on the inputted CPT code combinations and their respective rows in the paycode sheet for the given provider.

- The scraper that will scrape the Medi-Cal site and return an image of the resulting check to determine a patient's eligibility to receive benefits. This process runs automatically on claim creation.

- Validation of all data points on the claim and verification of their accuracy, as well as the required documents to submit a claim.

Identifying Domains, Subdomains, and Bounded Contexts

So, where do we start? We identify the domains, subdomains, and bounded contexts involved in the system requirements; then we start building out our naive prototypes; and finally we refine the concepts until we have a valid, working model of the domain.

Table 6-2 better represents the list in the previous section, with the unknowns specified as well (you can come back and fill in the blanks as we go over them).

Table 6-2. *Claims Example Requirements*

Requirement	Description	Domain	Subdomain	BC
Claim Submit	Model claim submission process	CLAIM SUBMIT	--	--
Claim Verification	Verify submitted claims	CLAIM SUBMIT	--	--
Claim Estimate	Determine a claim's expected amount	CLAIM SUBMIT	--	--
Eligibility Scraper	Scraper for Medi-Cal's patient eligibility verification	CLAIM SUBMIT	--	--
Role System	Authorization of users on a per-user basis	AUTH	--	--

In Table 6-1, I have briefly included the requirements of the aforementioned list and have given them their core domain. Here are Eric Evan's comments on the core domain from his book, *Domain Driven Design Reference* (Dog Ear Publishing, 2014):

> *"Boil the model down. Define a core domain and provide a means from easily distinguishing it from the mass of supporting models and code. Bring the most valuable and specialized concepts into sharp relief. Make the core small."*

> —Eric Evans

Based on our understanding of what a core domain should be, it would appear that I've made the domains a little too broad in Table 6-1. Evans notes that the core domain should be small and should be easy to distinguish from other models that exist to support or facilitate the models found in the core domain. Initially, I included only two core domains for each main request: CLAIM SUBMIT and AUTH. If we think about it a little more, we find that the process of submitting a claim should be different from the process that validates the claim. However, the two concepts are intimately related (i.e., you cannot have a claim validation at all if there is no claim submission to begin with). We can even go so far as to conclude that the claim validation is part of the wholeness of what the claim submit process is. We need to be able to split up the domain in such a way that the fabric of the application is woven together from smaller pieces, each potentially having their own context, ubiquitous language, or even independent team that sees to its maintenance and release cycle.

There are valuable tools that DDD offers that give you some idea of where to draw the boundaries between core domains, subdomains, and bounded contexts. Generally speaking, there is normally one subdomain for every one bounded context in the system, with multiple subdomains/bounded contexts living together in the same core domain. Once this is done, we start getting an idea of how the modules that encapsulate the various concerns of the system look and can see the full perspective of the different domains working together to achieve a single, well-defined goal within the system.

Armed with this knowledge, let's revisit Table 6-1. At first we may have thought that the concept of a CLAIM SUBMIT application should perhaps have different core domains, such as, for example, one that handles the submission process itself and another that does the validation of the claims submitted. After realizing that they are different concerns but so related to each other that one (i.e., CLAIM VERIFICATION) cannot live without the presence of another (i.e., CLAIM SUBMIT), we conclude that it makes sense that the two should be in the same core domain.

Now, let's revisit the Claim Estimate requirement. A claim's estimated amount is a calculated value, which relies on a process that identifies each claim's particular CPT combo and establishes an amount for the combo within a given paycode sheet. To me, this implies that the process of estimating a claim cannot occur without a CPT combo and `provider_id`, and those two things are only together in the sense and context of a claim. However, one detail that comes to my mind when looking at this thing at a high level is that a claim estimate happens after a claim has been submitted successfully. Should we model this as a different core domain? I don't believe so, and here's why: the act of submitting a claim and verifying that the claim is accurate and has all required data and documents with it occurs alongside the submission process, but it actually happens to occur before the claim is considered "submitted."

It is only after this happens that an estimated amount can be calculated for that claim's payout. Collectively, these facts lead me (and I hope you too) to the understanding that they are different contexts of the same overall process. Claim submission is done by the provider, our application auto-verifies its accuracy prior to it being officially "submitted," and an estimated amount is then attached to the claim based on a different process related to CPT code combinations and paycode sheets. For now, we will model the estimating claim amount logic as another bounded context within the same core domain, CLAIM SUBMIT. The only other item on this list relative to the claim itself is the process of validating a patient's eligibility by scraping the Medi-Cal eligibility page and providing it with the patient information (including their Medi-Cal number) as well as the provider giving care and captures the result. This process is also triggered after the claim is technically "submitted." Even though this is the case, we have a number of different ways we could choose to split the application up.

1. We could leave it as is (that is, having the two core domains CLAIM SUBMIT and AUTH) and just assign different subdomains to the elements inside each.

2. We could make the core domains a little more granular, which may look something like Figure 6-2.

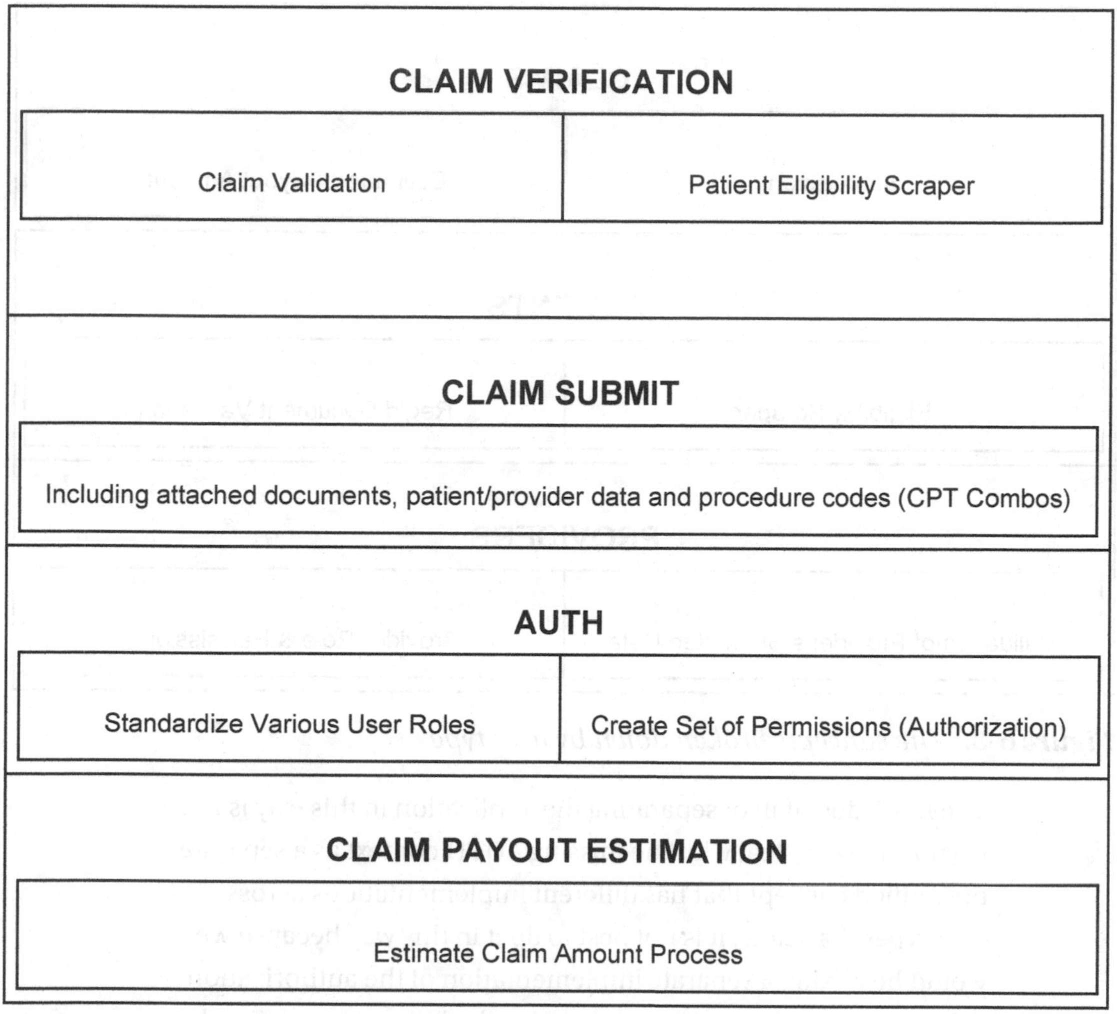

CLAIM VERIFICATION

Claim Validation	Patient Eligibility Scraper

CLAIM SUBMIT

Including attached documents, patient/provider data and procedure codes (CPT Combos)

AUTH

Standardize Various User Roles	Create Set of Permissions (Authorization)

CLAIM PAYOUT ESTIMATION

Estimate Claim Amount Process

Figure 6-2. *An initial drill-down of the concepts making up the core domain of our application*

3. We can choose to create each core domain in light of the various models existing within the system. In this regard, the AUTH bounded context would basically be absorbed by the surrounding contexts (Figure 6-3).

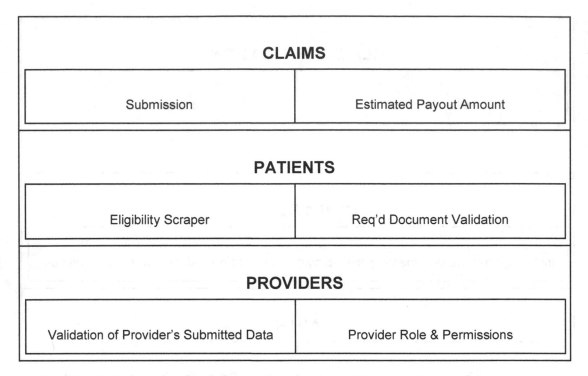

Figure 6-3. *The concepts broken down by user type*

The main downfall of separating the application in this way is that
we now have to deal with the missing AUTH context as a separate,
un-unified concept that has different implementations across
user types. Basically, it is not best to do it in this way because we
would be mixing a separate implementation of the authorization
concern into each specific user type in which they were defined,
causing a blatant violation of the separation of concerns as well as
the DRY principle (which stands for "Do Not Repeat Yourself"),
because we would have to define what each particular user can
do in each context, which wouldn't be so bad if we had a single
implementation of an AUTH service or something similar, but
that isn't the case here. Not ideal. Let's find a better structure that
makes more sense and fits into the domain model easier.

4. We can combine the idea presented in option 1 of this list with
    that in option 2 and have the core domains separated by the two
    primary concerns living within the core domain that revolves
    around a claim, while making the variations between each

concern explicit and obvious by specifying the subdomains each
of them target and then creating a bounded context for each one
of these subdomains. Figure 6-4 shows what that might look like.

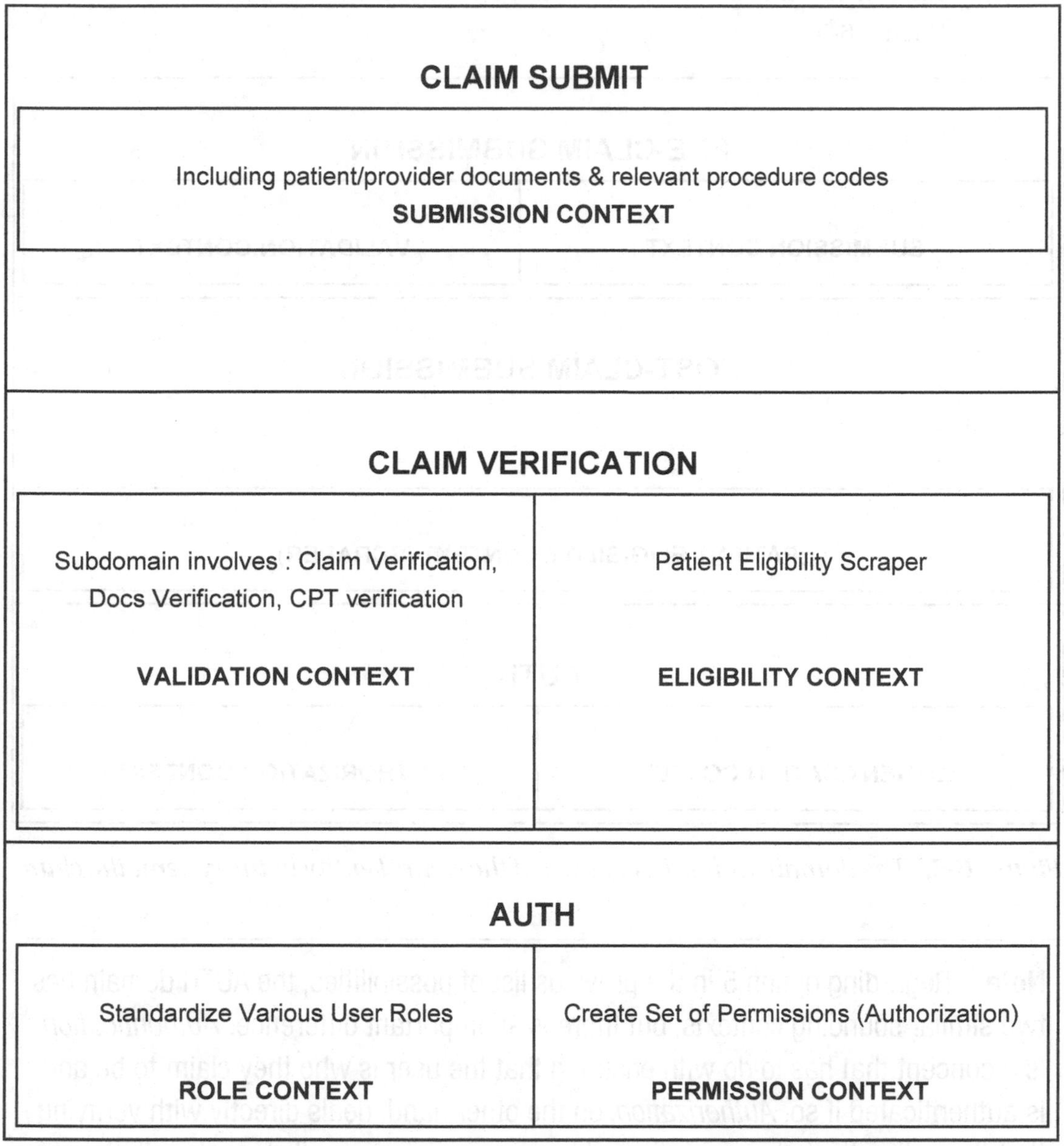

<table>
<tr><td colspan="2" align="center">CLAIM SUBMIT</td></tr>
<tr><td colspan="2" align="center">Including patient/provider documents & relevant procedure codes
SUBMISSION CONTEXT</td></tr>
<tr><td colspan="2" align="center">CLAIM VERIFICATION</td></tr>
<tr><td align="center">Subdomain involves : Claim Verification,
Docs Verification, CPT verification

VALIDATION CONTEXT</td><td align="center">Patient Eligibility Scraper

ELIGIBILITY CONTEXT</td></tr>
<tr><td colspan="2" align="center">AUTH</td></tr>
<tr><td align="center">Standardize Various User Roles

ROLE CONTEXT</td><td align="center">Create Set of Permissions (Authorization)

PERMISSION CONTEXT</td></tr>
</table>

Figure 6-4. *The separation of the concepts into three central forces (if you will)*
that are at work in the heart of the domain model

5. We could also split up the domain in terms of the central model
    existing in our feature requirements: the claim. In this case, the
    claim would be the center of attention, and different contexts
    can be created in regard to its association to a claim, particularly
    the contexts that a claim is in initially and after it's submitted
    (Figure 6-5).

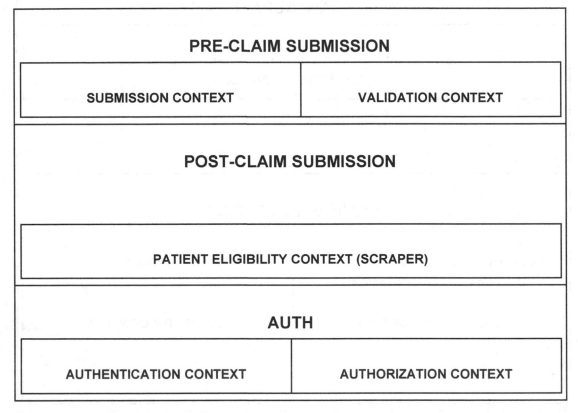

Figure 6-5. *The domain as it exists in light of the central entity in the system: the claim*

Note   Regarding option 5 in the previous list of possibilities, the AUTH domain has
two similar sounding contexts, but there is an important difference. *Authentication*
is a concept that has to do with ensuring that the user is who they claim to be and
is authenticated if so. *Authorization*, on the other hand, deals directly with verifying
that the authenticated user is allowed to do something, usually based on that
user's role in the system (this would fall under the permissions umbrella).

A valid use case can most likely be made for all items in the previous list, perhaps aside from option 3. According to Eric Evans, we should look for ways to split up the core domain from ones supporting the core domain. In our case, for this example, the core domain would be the claim itself, with various concerns surrounding a claim, that being the validation, eligibility scraper, user auth checks, and any other operations that happen on the claim as it goes through the claim submission process. When faced with an important decision that will impact the structure and modules you define in your application, it can be difficult to decide on the best scenario that will achieve the best possible outcome. In cases like these, I usually fall back to things that I know are correct such as the definitions and abstractions defined within the DDD philosophy. What comes to mind for this scenario is Evan's definition of an abstract core, shown here:

> *Even the core domain model usually has so much detail that communicating the big picture can be difficult...Therefore: Identify the most fundamental differentiating concepts in the model and factor them into distinct classes, abstract classes, or interfaces. Design this abstract model so that it expresses most of the interaction between significant components. Place this abstract overall model in its own module, while the specialized, detailed implementation classes are left in their own modules defined by subdomain.*
>
> —Eric Evans

So, for our purposes, what would be considered "the most differentiating concepts" that exist within our Medi-Cal claim domain model?

- Submitting a claim
- Validating a claim
  - Pre-submission validations
    - Check for proper documents
    - Validate CPT codes + CPT combos
    - Verify form-submitted data

- Post-submission validations

  - Patient eligibility scraper

- Estimating a claim's amount

- Authorization and authentication concerns

I think we should make the Claim be the core domain in this project, with subdomains being the Submission, Validation, and Claim Amount Estimation processes. In a different context, we have the authentication/authorization portion of the app. This is best defined as a *generic subdomain* (a concept in the business that exists to facilitate crucial business concerns but are not the business concerns themselves). These subdomains are "generic" in the sense that they are reusable, decoupled components that are called upon in many places throughout the entire codebase. Figure 6-6 shows the final structure that we will use.

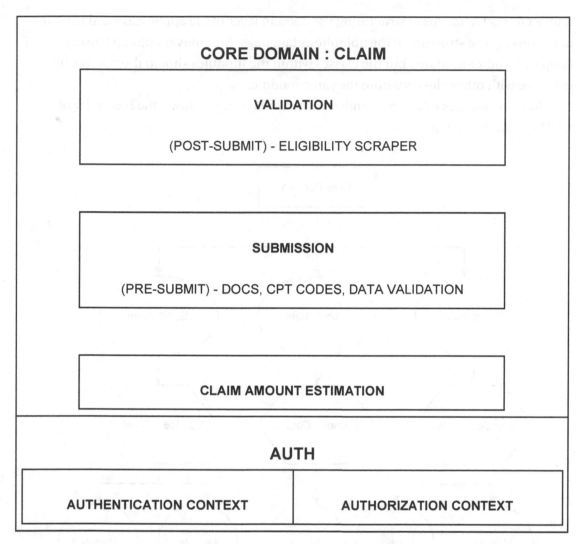

Figure 6-6. *The final separation of concerns of our application*

At this point, we have separated the application into more manageable pieces and have defined the various subdomains that are an integral part of the core domain and help facilitate the transition of a claim in the system to a paycheck for the providers.

Modules

In DDD, there is the concept of a *module*, which is a boundary around a specific set of classes logically grouped together based on the concepts in the domain and are named from the ubiquitous language. Modules correspond to the items in the domain directly and act as both a means of structuring the domain layer of the application and a means of expressing the structure of the ubiquitous language. Modules should be loosely coupled to other modules, but the classes within the modules should themselves be cohesive with other classes within the same module.

How do modules relate to bounded contexts? Figure 6-7 shows the hierarchy of DDD's strategic design.

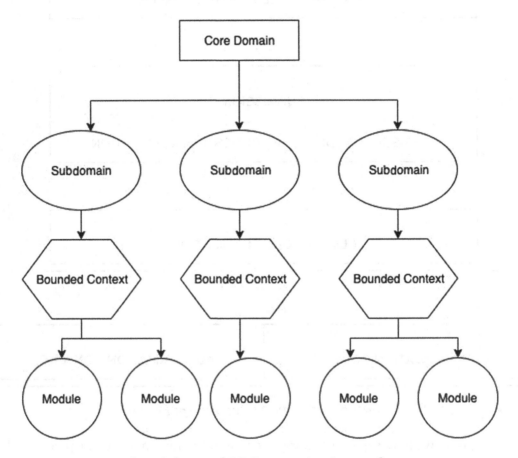

Figure 6-7. *Strategic breakdown of DDD organization and structure*

We can see that the core domain is the top-level concern, and the core domain is represented by a variety of subdomains, each of which have a corresponding bounded context. The bounded contexts themselves are broken down once again and split up into a variety of modules that, together, represent the logic that make up the ideas expressed in the subdomains. In the case of our example, Figure 6-8 shows a possible configuration for the module structure.

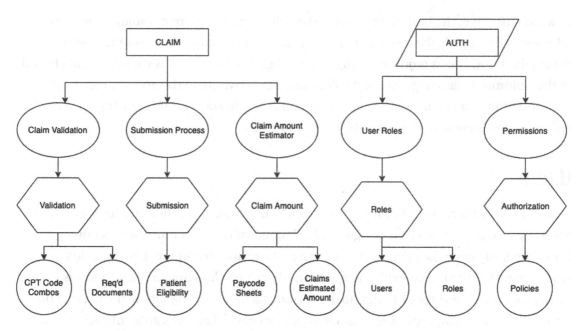

Figure 6-8. *The structure of modules, bounded contexts, subdomains, and core domains in our claims example project*

Note   The book doesn't go through an exhaustive, complete rundown of every line of code that this example project is built with but instead gives you possible ways to translate the application's various parts in Laravel. For a complete code listing of this project and all other source code in the book, please visit the Apress website.

Now that we've covered some architectural design solutions and have one that fits the needs of the application and domain model, we can start building the components themselves, using Laravel, and start to see our application take shape.

Creating the Laravel Components

Let's see if we can break this down into classes that we will employ in different modules to accomplish what we need done. To do that, we need to have a clear concept of the domain so that the model we end up creating expresses it in a literal way. In cases where you have defined the general structure of the modules and know the bounded contexts in which they live, the best place to start when defining the more granular structures (classes) is to identify the models that are needed in each context and define them within the bounds of a module, taking care to align the class names with the terms found in the ubiquitous language. Since it will be used everywhere in the app to determine authorization to a given resource in the domain, we will start out by focusing on the generic subdomains, in this case, the users and roles.

Users

Now, we know there will be different users using the system at different times, and each of those users must have a login and a defined role so that our system knows how to identify each user and what they can and cannot do and see. Laravel ships with a standard User class, which extends another User class that, in turn, extends from Eloquent's base model to define the various facilities for managing the users. The parent User class employs various traits to gain access to Laravel's authentication and authorization features.

A first thought on how to proceed might be to make additional User classes that also extend from the base (aliased as Authenticatable), which then provides each type of User class with their own subset of available methods and properties. It would look something like Figure 6-9.

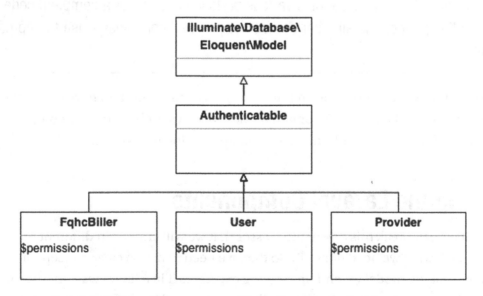

Figure 6-9. *Initial design of the various User classes needed in the app*

There are numerous problems with this design, listed here:

- There is an extra User class that appears to have no explicitly identified purpose to our application or domain. This is rather awkward and leaves room for misunderstandings.

- We are, in fact, breaking both the separation of concerns and the Law of Demeter because we are mixing the concept of a user in the system with that of permissions in the system when they are obviously different.

- We have muddled together the authentication and authorization concerns inline with the User definitions and have created two additional classes that also extend the same parent class. The problem is that the explicit concept of a "role" is lost. We should think of the user as having one or more roles as opposed to the user being one of those roles (which would imply it does belong inline to the User definitions).

- Instead of having a single User class that we can pass around and manage, we are going to constantly be juggling between the three User classes when performing authentication or permission checks. That sounds like a big pain to me!

- This design is not at all scalable. If we ever needed to add additional user types (or user roles, to be more precise), then we are forced to have to create additional classes and objects in the system, each with their own implementation and validity checks throughout the rest of the system.

The biggest problem with this design can be found in the third and fifth items of the list. The concepts of a user and a role should be separated inside the same module, not in the same class. We should decouple these concerns from each other and make explicit the two groups of classes.

All that being said, Figure 6-10 shows a better version of the previous design, taking into account our decision to split up the user and role models (no pun intended).

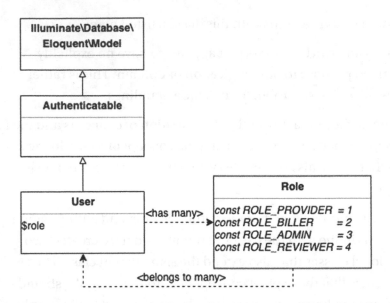

Figure 6-10. *A better approach to designing the users and their corresponding roles*

As you can see in Figure 6-10, we have now encapsulated the concept of a "user role" within the confines of its own class, and we have defined several constants that reflect the various roles used in the system. The design is flexible, because we can attach any role we want to a specific User object. It's also scalable in that we can add roles to the system without adding classes. We are able to keep up with the current and future demands of the system while also keeping our overall number of classes in the system as low as possible. We are on the right track! However, one problem remains: we don't want the concept of a role to leak into the User object, nor do we want the concept of a user to leak into the Role object. How do we accomplish such a thing? I won't give you all the details of this now, but I'll give you a hint: we can employ a pivot table that will act as the intermediary between the roles table and the users table, effectively known as the user_role table (or role_user).

THE COST OF BAD DESIGN

Good programmers are both artists and scientists. We get the requirements nailed down to a science, and we construct the various solutions to those problems using our paint (in this case, it would be DDL or PHP, depending on how you look at it). When we recognize a clarity in the design or model logic like we have here with the users and roles split, we should always try to capture that knowledge inside of what is the very canvas of our application: the design. Good design in hard; worse design is harder. Think about it: a good design has little to no overhead because you don't have to change a bunch of stuff to compensate for another single change inside a different part of the app because the programmers followed proper standards and best practices to design their software, one of which was a strict adherence to the separation of concerns. You cannot get these types of cool benefits in a poorly designed system that was not well thought out or improperly planned. The costs of fixing and maintaining that pile of junk someone calls a real web application that just happens to be hacked at enough to make it technically "work" far supersedes the cost, frustration, headaches, architectural changes, and level of maintenance you are left to deal with, until finally the day you have to (or get to, rather) rewrite it from scratch or employ an even more advanced solution, such as the anti-corruption layer, to solve the problems that the poor design left behind. Whether the cause of the poor design had to do with scope creep, misunderstandings of the domain, misrepresentations of the misunderstood domain, or a sheer lack of experience and know-how regarding the lower-level business rules and policies regulating the domain, a poorly designed system is far more complex, difficult, costly, and simply not an option for bright developers such as ourselves.

I've taken the time to craft you a witty poem that will help you remember that the main focal point of the design should be the domain and how best to model it as software (although, as Voltaire once said, "a witty saying proves nothing...").

Take the time,

nail the design,

but don't waste time,

on the issues you find,

if they're not in the domain,

for now, leave them behind.

Another point I attempted to make is that infrastructural and application layer concerns should not influence the domain layer; the domain layer should influence the infrastructure and application layers.

Modeling the Design

For us to continue the modeling process, we need to solve an issue that is caused by Laravel's default namespace and directory structures. The problem is that they are not geared toward a clean, separated architecture that fully expresses the intent of our domain model. This is something we will take a look at in the next chapter, which focuses on creating a standard component for mapping out the many user roles that are needed in our application. Our application is considered an enterprise web application, which means that we are going to have to properly track, manage, and check all users attempting to access a protected service (such as searching for a patient) or a protected entity (and its corresponding fields) to make sure they are allowed to invoke a particular service or select, modify, or delete a given entity (which in the context of an API is known as a *resource*). An example of this would be putting a policy in place that only allows the searching of patients belonging to a given practice or provider with which they are registered in the Medi-Cal system as the patient's primary physician.

Conclusion

In this chapter, we took a look at the various domain-level aspects of the example claims application used in this chapter and following ones. We discussed a real problem that medical providers have these days when completing a claim submission in the "old way" to get reimbursed for their services to eligible patients. Because of the level of scrutiny placed on the claims coming through the system, many claims were delayed a payout due to some error (or missing information). The only verification effort was done manually with human eyes.

Our application solves all that and provides a solution for the various checks and balances done on all claims entering the system so that a far fewer number of submissions get returned, with 99 percent of them being accepted on the first attempt. The application exists as an enterprise-level app, requiring such components as user roles and services such as authentication and authorization in a finely grained manner as to support all users in the system through logins and credentials. The submission process itself is made up of various smaller-sized processes that work together with one another to produce an expected result. We took a stab at a possible component (module) structure using some common best practices and, most of all, using the core concepts in the domain to craft a rough structure of a model in terms of Domain-driven design. We took a look at concepts such as bounded contexts, core domains, and generic subdomains.

CHAPTER 7

Modeling and Implementing the Domain

Now that we have some idea about the way the domain works in the real world, we can start developing the domain concerns and create some fundamental domain objects that will help us produce a solution that covers all the core requirements.

Note The directories for the domain model objects included in this chapter are going to change as the book continues with this project in Chapter 8, when we have some additional insight on better ways to represent our domain in the code.

Defining the Main Claim Model

First, let's define the main Claim model we will use throughout the rest of the system, as shown in Figure 7-1.

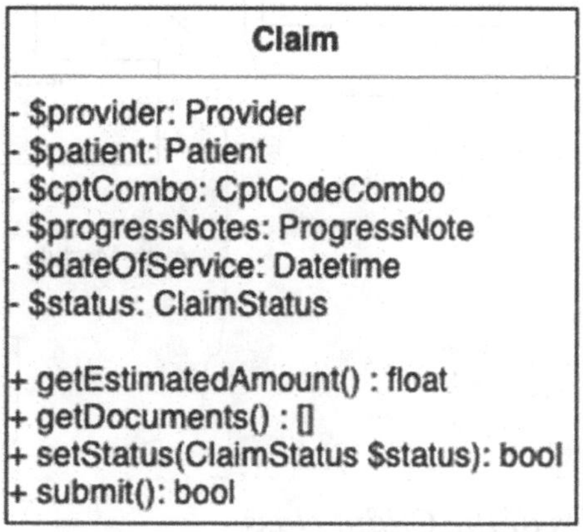

```
                  ┌─────────────────────────────────────┐
                  │              Claim                  │
                  ├─────────────────────────────────────┤
                  │ - $provider: Provider               │
                  │ - $patient: Patient                 │
                  │ - $cptCombo: CptCodeCombo           │
                  │ - $progressNotes: ProgressNote      │
                  │ - $dateOfService: Datetime          │
                  │ - $status: ClaimStatus              │
                  │                                     │
                  │ + getEstimatedAmount() : float      │
                  │ + getDocuments() : []               │
                  │ + setStatus(ClaimStatus $status): bool │
                  │ + submit(): bool                    │
                  └─────────────────────────────────────┘
```

Figure 7-1. *First attempt at prototyping the Claim model*

© Jesse Griffin 2021

J. Griffin, *Domain-Driven Laravel*, https://doi.org/10.1007/978-1-4842-6023-4_7

The `Claim` model has two sections; the one on top defines the properties of the claim. We will need to create models and migrations for the classes that the properties represent (`Provider, Patient,` etc.). For now, the properties are part of the data required by the FQHC in order to pay out money to the provider. In the bottom portion of the UML is a list of methods that do various things to the claim state or that pull in additional data that is also part of the requirements (i.e., `getDocuments()` gets all associated documents for a given claim).

There are many parts of the application that touch a claim that need to be modeled as well. Sometimes, it's better to start with a high-level view of the system so you can figure out the relationships between classes. One important distinction to make is that we have included two actual types of users in the system, `Provider` and `Patient`, which are explicitly used in the model for domain logic, not authentication or authorization (which would be in the application layer). If we were trying to model security concerns inside this class (which would be a blatant violation of the separation of concerns principle), we would have imported the `User` class instead. We need to make this inclusion explicit in our class map as well.

Figure 7-2 shows a high-level overview of what lives *inside* a claim.

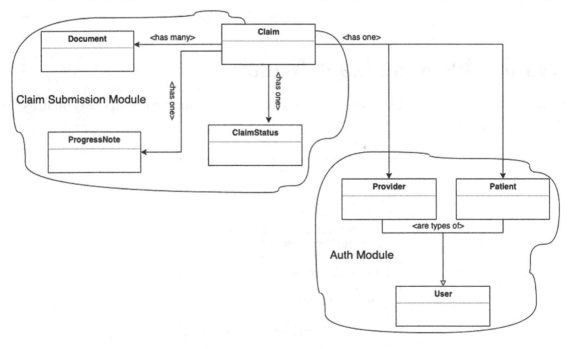

Figure 7-2. *The properties of the Claim class*

Notice that there are two groups of classes each enclosed within a border that separates the class group from the rest of the application, corresponding to two of the modules we worked out in the previous chapter: the Auth module and the Claim Submission module. The actual `Claim` *model* is found within the Claim Submission module and acts as the gatekeeper to any of the enclosed classes.

If you haven't guessed already, we are making the classes within the Claim Submission module aggregates, with the `Claim` model acting as the aggregate root. Any of the enclosed classes within the boundary of the claim aggregate can be accessed only through the claim itself. For instance, the `ProgressNote` that is submitted with the claim should be accessed only via `$claim->progressNote`. The same goes with the `ClaimStatus`; it is accessed via `$claim->status`. Now, if you look at the other module, it is represented as a regular set of classes residing under the same parent namespace. The boundary drawn around it doesn't signify an aggregate, but just a grouping of related classes. The `Claim` model explicitly uses both the `Provider` and `Patient` models, both for authentication/authorization and as a means of asserting requirements necessary for a claim's submission into the review queue. Let's flesh out the models using Artisan commands, as shown in Listing 7-1.

Listing 7-1. Artisan Commands to Create the Domain Models of Our System

```
php artisan make:model App\\Models\\Claim -a
php artisan make:model App\\Models\\Patient -a
php artisan make:model App\\Models\\Practice -a
php artisan make:model App\\Models\\Provider -a
php artisan make:model App\\Models\\ProgressNote -a
php artisan make:model App\\Models\\Document -a
php artisan make:model App\\Models\\ClaimStatus --migration
```

The commands in Listing 7-1, aside from the last one, create one of each of the following for the model they correspond to:

- A model class located in `App\Models`

- A migration class located in `database/migrations`

- A test factory in `database/factories`

- A controller in `app/Http/Controllers`

Let's start with the easiest one and define our `ClaimStatus` class and migration to support it, as shown in Listings 7-2 and 7-3.

Listing 7-2. The ClaimStatus Class

```
// ddl/app/Models/ClaimStatus
<?php
...
class ClaimStatus
{
    const PENDING_REVIEW = 1;
    const REVIEWER_APPROVED = 2;
    const CORRECTION_NEEDED = 3;
    const BILLER_CORRECTION_NEEDED = 4;
    const BILLER_APPROVED = 5;

    public $table = 'claim_status';
    protected $fillable = ['*'];
}
```

Note that we omit the code that would otherwise add `created_at` and `updated_at` timestamps to the status table, which are pretty useless considering this is a static reference (i.e., *lookup*) table.

Listing 7-3. ClaimStatus Migration File

```
// ddl/database/migrations/{YOUR_TIMESTAMP}_create_claimstatus_table
<?php
...
use App\Models\ClaimStatus;
function up()
{
    Schema::create('claim_status', function (Blueprint $table) {
            $table->bigIncrements('id');
            $table->string('name');
            $table->string('slug');
            $table->string('code');
    });
```

```php
ClaimStatus::create([
    'id' => 1,
    'name' => 'Pending Review',
    'slug' => 'pending_review',
    'code' => 'PENDING_REVIEW'
]);

ClaimStatus::create([
    'id' => 1,
    'name' => 'Reviewer Approved',
    'slug' => 'reviewer_approved',
    'code' => 'REVIEWER_APPROVED'
]);

ClaimStatus::create([
    'id' => 1,
    'name' => 'Correction Needed',
    'slug' => 'correction_needed',
    'code' => 'CORRECTION_NEEDED'
]);

ClaimStatus::create([
    'id' => 1,
    'name' => 'Biller Correction Needed',
    'slug' => 'biller_correction_needed',
    'code' => 'BILLER_CORRECTION_NEEDED'
]);

ClaimStatus::create([
    'id' => 1,
    'name' => 'Biller Approved',
    'slug' => 'biller_approved',
    'code' => 'BILLER_APPROVED'
]);
}
```

Note   We defined a set of constants inside the ClaimStatus model to easily distinguish it from the rest of the application. Now instead of having to remember that the ClaimStatus with an ID of 1 indicates a PENDING_REVIEW status, we can just reference App\Models\ClaimStatus::PENDING_REVIEW. Also important to note is the records we've added when the migration runs—they all correspond to the model constants we set at the top.

Not all of the models and migrations will be listed here in the text, but you can find all the code for this and other examples in the GitHub repo. I do not provide in-text definitions of Practice, ProgressNote, or Document because they are trivial implementations—please find the definitions for these classes online. I will, however, define the Claim, Provider, and ClaimStatus classes inline because they are unique and important to the discussion at hand.

Let's get the Provider class done and over with (please see the website for the code for the migration). Check out Listing 7-4 for that.

Listing 7-4. The Provider Eloquent Model

```php
// ddl/app/Models/Provider
<?php
...
Class Provider extends Model
{
    public $table = 'providers';

    protected $fillable = ['fname', 'lname', 'address', 'practice_id',
    'npi_number'];

    public function practice()
    {
        return $this->hasOne(Practice::class, 'practice_id', 'id');
    }
}
```

The Provider class is fairly simple. There are some standard identifiers including name and address, along with the practice they work at and a National Provider Identifier (NPI), which is an ID that every practicing physician in America has once they register with the government to practice medicine in the states. The only relation we defined here is the corresponding Practice (which we made clear with the practice_id field designated in the $fillable array).

Now we can tie the models together in the Claim model by using relationships, as shown in Listing 7-5.

Listing 7-5. The Claim Model

```php
// dll/app/Models/Claim.php
<?php
// ...
namespace App\Models;
class Claim
{
    public $table = 'claims';
    protected $fillable = ['cpt_code_combo_id', 'provider_id', 'patient_
    id', 'progress_note_id', 'date_of_service', 'status_id'];

//relations:
    public function provider()
    {
        return $this->hasOne(Provider::class);
    }

    public function patient()
    {
        return $this->hasOne(Patient::class);
    }
    public function progressNotes()
    {
        return $this->hasMany(ProviderNote::class);
    }
```

```php
    public function cptCodeCombo()
    {
        return $this->hasOne(CptCodeCombo::class);
    }
    public function status()
    {
        return $this->hasOne(ClaimStatus::class, 'status_id', 'id');
    }
}
```

Listing 7-6 shows the Claim model's migration.

Listing 7-6. Migration File for the Claim Model

```php
// dll/database/migrations/{YOUR_TIMESTAMP}/_create_claim_table.php
<?php
...
class CreateClaimsTable extends Migration
{
    Schema::create('claims', function (Blueprint $table) {
        $table->bigIncrements('id');
        $table->integer('status_id')->unsigned();
        $table->integer('provider_id')->unsigned();
        $table->integer('patient_id')->unsigned();
        $table->integer('cpt_code_combo_id')->unsigned();
        $table->integer('progress_note_id')->unsigned();
        //define foreign keys:
        $table->foreign('practice_id')
            ->references(Practice::class)
            ->on('id');
        $table->foreign('provider_id')
            ->references(Provider::class)
            ->on('id');
        $table->foreign('patient_id')
            ->references(Patient::class)
            ->on('id')
```

```
        $table->foreign('cpt_code_combo_id')
              ->references(CptCodeCombo::class)
              ->on('id');
        $table->foreign('progress_note_id')
              ->references(ProgressNote::class)
              ->on('id');
        $table->foreign('status_id')
              ->references(ClaimStatus::class)
              ->on('id');
        $table->datetime('date_of_service');
        $table->timestamps();
    });
}
```

At this point, we have the basic models sketched out that are required for a claim to *exist*. We have not yet discussed any constructs that will be needed to facilitate a claim through the submission and validation process, nor have we modeled the pipeline with all the various steps and statuses involved in the process. We will get to all that later in the book. Those problems are more advanced in terms of skill level and experience with DDD and Laravel. I promise we will get there.

Let's touch on aggregates. An *aggregate* is basically an object that is comprised of separate, individual objects grouped together using some set of components such that they can be recorded, broken down, and reconstructed and serve as a possible solution when faced with the code implementation of complex objects in the domain. Aggregates help prevent data inconsistency when persisting them by employing a number of principles that make them useful.

- Atomicity

- Consistency

- Integrity

- Durability

One way to ensure this is to use transactions to manage the persistence of a group of events or domain models when there is a requirement of the system where you would need to track the state of a given domain object at all times. An example of this is event recording. When interesting things happen in the application that other contexts want to know about, the persistence and re-creation of events becomes difficult to manage as one large chunk.

By making the object an aggregate with proper boundaries in place, you can employ techniques that will make it easier to save and load on a persistence level. It seems to me (and I hope to you as well) that an aggregate would be a good fit for the claim object in our example model; however, being as though have their own chapter in the book, I will leave the details for later.

Implementing the User and Role Design

Now that we have the design nailed down, let's code out a prototype. The first thing is the database. Database concerns in Laravel are found within the /database folder of the Laravel project directory. Inside this directory are several subfolders:

- migrations/: Incremental transitions that the database goes through to maintain consistency and access a bunch of features that Eloquent provides out of the box such that you usually don't ever have to physically touch a database directly and instead rely on the simple Artisan command php artisan migrate.

- factories/: Factories that generate dummy data for use in the application as a model and is used for unit testing.

- seeds/: Test data that can be inserted at the run of another command: php artisan db:seed.

We need to build out our models that represent the different roles in the system. Here is the command that generates the models and migrations we need so we can represent the concept of a role:

```
php artisan make:model Role --migration
```

This will produce something like the following:

```
Model created successfully.
Created Migration: 2019_10_03_033254_create_roles_table
```

Wow, check it out. We are able to generate both the model and the corresponding database table with one command. Let's modify the migration first; then we can build our domain model. Open ddl/db/migrations/*_create_roles_table, where * is whatever the timestamp is when the command was run, and find the method up(). Then modify the method to look like Listing 7-7.

Listing 7-7. Roles Migration File

```php
public function up()
 {
     Schema::create('roles', function (Blueprint $table) {
         $table->bigIncrements('id');
         $table->string('name');
         $table->string('slug');
         $table->timestamps();
     });
 }
```

Basically in Listing 7-7 we've defined our roles table, with each role corresponding to a role ID that is defined as a BIGINT data type, is autoincremented, and is set as the table's primary key. The next two fields are string types corresponding to the role's name and a slug so we can easily represent them in an HTTP query (i.e., /fqhc-biller/ billClaim). Lastly, we add the basic timestamps created_at and updated_at to the table for reference.

Before we actually run the migration command, let's define our model (I'll show you why later). Check out Listing 7-8.

Listing 7-8. Role Domain Model: Role.php

```php
// ddl/app/Role.php

<?php
namespace App;

use Illuminate\Database\Eloquent\Model;

class Role extends Model
{
    const ROLE_ADMIN = 1;
    const ROLE_PRACTICE = 2;
    const ROLE_PROVIDER = 3;
    const ROLE_BILLER = 4;

    protected $fillable = ['name', 'slug'];
}
```

When we are designing models that we know what the values are going to be ahead of time, then we should decide on an identification that the system can use to pass around different role types and that we as developers can reference with a constant defined in the Role model. These values will be consistent throughout the application. The reason we did the model before executing the database migration is because the values for the IDs and role names shown earlier need to be aligned with the ones defined in the roles table in the database. That is, the roles table must obviously hold the same values as their corresponding counterparts existing within the Role model.

The $fillable array holds a list of fields that are allowed to be auto-generated by Eloquent's various methods (for example, using create() --auto to insert data into the database in this manner will fail if we attempt to insert a value into a field that isn't in this list). Think of the $fillable as a whitelist.

First, we import the newly defined Role model in the migration class so we can use the easier-to-read syntax (Role::ROLE_ADMIN). Re-open the Role model and append this to the list of use statements at the top of the file:

```
// ddl/app/Role.php
use App\Models\Role;
```

Let's add the content in Listing 7-9 to the end of the up() method in the role's migration file.

Listing 7-9. Modified Migration to Include Standardized IDs, Names, and Slugs

```
public function up()
{
    //...
    Role::create([
         'id'   => Role::ROLE_ADMIN,
         'name' => 'Administrator',
         'slug' => 'admin'
    ]);

    Role::create([
         'id'   => Role::ROLE_PRACTICE,
         'name' => 'Practice',
         'slug' => 'practice'
    ]);
```

```
Role::create([
    'id'   => Role::ROLE_PROVIDER,
    'name' => 'Provider',
    'slug' => 'provider'
]);

Role::create([
    'id'   => Role::ROLE_BILLER,
    'name' => 'Fqhc Biller',
    'slug' => 'fqhc-biller'
]);
}
```

So, what we did here is add the predefined roles to the database, exactly how we have established them in the Role model. Now we have a documented set of roles we can attach to our users to determine authorization at various points in the application, and we have an easy way to refer to them using the constants we defined in the model. Now, when we run the php artisan migrate command, we will create the database table *and* populate it with the roles we've defined in Listing 7-9.

We also need to change the User class to include the new role, as we do in Listing 7-10.

Listing 7-10. Modifying the User Model to Support the New Roles We Defined

```
// ddl/app/User.php
//import the Role class so we can use it here:
use App\Models\Role;
// add the following as a new method on the User class:
public function roles()
{
    return $this->belongsToMany(Role::class, 'role_id', 'user_id');
}
```

We still have a lot of work to do to finish the example. Some of it requires an even deeper understanding of the more advanced topics and techniques found within DDD and within DDL as well. That's why we will cover all of them throughout the course of several chapters. We have used the knowledge of the system to sketch out the models using Eloquent as an ORM. We have our base set of domain models that we extended from Eloquent's `Model` class that give us superpowers that will allow us to more easily manage and better facilitate them, manipulate them, persist them, or destroy them.

When you couple the features of Eloquent with the techniques found in DDD, you get a rich domain model. It's rich because the model corresponds directly to the underlying business rules and policies that the business itself is based on. The model will reflect deep insight and understanding of the core domain. The models are easily distinguished from one another, like they are in the real world, and are easily identifiable by all members of the corporation or department. This is (not surprisingly) because it was well-established, iteratively refined, and fully agreed on by domain experts in the company. This is the ultimate goal of DDD.

Reality Check: Success in the Real World

Getting to this point in a project isn't easy. In my opinion, using a framework is better than not using one, and using Laravel is better than any other framework. At the least, I want to give you examples you can use in your own process. In the next few chapters, we will go deeper into our discussion about DDD processes and how we can implement them with Laravel.

Our main objective of the claim example is to build a solution that will accept incoming data, validate it on an attribute level and on an object level, and track the claim as an aggregate so that the various parts of the claim can be saved independently and so that a status can be attained from the state that the claim is in at any given time. We also should log what we are doing in some sort of transactional log both for debugging purposes and for simple information about the application or its moving parts. We need to design it in such a way that is modular and has proper boundaries in place that separate or group domain objects in an attempt to mirror their real-world structure. We need to be able to identify objects that are made up of other objects, and we should be able to reconstruct such an object in an easy manner.

That being said, we have hit somewhat of a roadblock in our design: *Laravel's default directory structure*. Laravel is set up in a monolithic structure, and because we've elected to use PSR-4 autoloading with composer, the directory structure is exactly the same as the namespaces the classes live in. We cannot possible define all the models and objects we are going to need for this claim example in a single directory... There are multiple pieces corresponding to the various components in the domain that make it function. It is essential we free ourselves of a one-directory fits all monolithic solution. Even though it will still me technically monolithic when complete, it will leave us in a good position to move toward a microservice or hexagonal architecture. Microservices make a more profound impact on separation of components because it mandates splitting the domain logic into single, self-encapsulating "services" that are spread across several servers (the traditional way) or multiple containers (with Docker & Kubernetes).

Conclusion

While the architecture laid out in this chapter is a stable one that is widely used in development today, it is very complicated to setup and requires a high level understanding and working knowledge of various dev-ops related concepts and know-how in order to properly setup things like virtual private servers (VPS), enterprise grade networks and subnets, and establishing proper firewall rules and route specifications, . We will not be going so far as to make a distributed system in this book, but what we will do is get up to the step before it...by encapsulating our business logic into natural boundaries as dictated by the domain structure (which we call bounded contexts and modules) so that they *can* be distributed across different nodes. What this ends up becoming is a domain model whose internal moving parts are all cleanly separated and can be developed independently, managed by different departments and can be independently deployed without the need to deploy the entire codebase. There are many other benefits to a microservice or service oriented architecture--too many to list here.

Back to the problem at hand--we need an easy way to restructure the namespaces and directories that Laravel ships with so that we can employ the separation of concerns in our domain model and have a solid backbone laid out to help us build out the remaining functionality needed to submit and process a claim through the pipeline we discussed in this and prior chapters, as well as manage the user types and roles--ensuring permissions, policies and protected resources within the system are setup and accessed only by the users *allowed* to consume them. The next chapter is dedicated to doing just that... By the end of the next chapter, we will have an established architecture for our various modules and classes for which to implement the more complex features on top of.

Luckily for us, Laravel has the facilities built-in to customize the behavior, structure and just about every other aspect we would need to customize in order to meet our unique project requirements and guidelines. We will explore this and more in the following chapter!

CHAPTER 8

Modularizing Laravel

In the previous chapter, I mentioned that we had hit a sort of roadblock in our development of the claims processing application example we've been slowly defining since the beginning of the book. The application we are building has a number of different bounded contexts, a generic subdomain, and a bunch of different modules that encapsulate the various features and components that we need in our application. If we were to use the standard directory structure provided out of the box with a fresh Laravel installation, we would soon find things cluttered, scattered, and almost impossible to maintain once we started building even more complexity into the application when we implement future feature requests.

We are planning for our application to have a long life, and that means it needs to be able to withstand change. Change comes in various forms on any software project. Features get added or removed, and priorities on what should be included in the initial release are constantly changing. Not to mention scope creep, which in itself can be a big pain to get a handle on, especially when working within a structured team environment. If we were to place all the logic of our application in a monolithic namespace/directory structure, we would not have a strong team dynamic or know who is working on which parts of the app at a given time. Multiple departments would spend more time fixing issues that creep up during development that would be better spent getting things done. Further, the deployment of the application would have to be done all at once, creating room for errors and also causing other unrelated parts of the application to break for no reason when a completely different part is modified. This couldn't be predicted and would cause the user-facing site to be the first appearance of the error, because the whole application had to be deployed to fix just one bug.

These are all valid possibilities that, in the real world, can happen faster than you can get a handle on at times. One thing I can recommend to prevent such things is to spend enough time thinking about the implications the features have on our system as a whole and to properly plan out the structure of the components that will satisfy those requirements. By properly segregating our code to conform to a standard derived from

© Jesse Griffin 2021
J. Griffin, *Domain-Driven Laravel*, https://doi.org/10.1007/978-1-4842-6023-4_8

the domain model, we are setting ourselves up for success because we can build the different aspects of the application independently inside their corresponding directories and namespaces as defined in the domain model. And because the modules and classes are named with the terms from the ubiquitous language, there will be no question as to which module does what.

We will spend some time in this chapter to take a look at the namespace structure that comes with Laravel so you get a good understanding of the structure before modifying it. This will also give us an idea of what needs to be modified for our own project's requirements. The claims project will be broken down into corresponding pieces that will allow us to segregate the core domain model into its various components and form a directory and namespace scheme that will meet the defined requirements of the project. This initial attempt won't be perfect but will serve as a solid stepping-stone for you to get some good knowledge regarding *how* to change Laravel's default behavior. It will also provide you with some guidelines on splitting a project up by its bounded contexts and recognizing any generic subdomains.

In the later chapters, we will refine our structure and refactor the namespaces and structure as we gain additional knowledge about both the domain itself and Laravel's internal workings and default mechanisms.

Laravel's Default Structure

I once asked the creator of the Laravel framework, Taylor Otwell, if he had written the framework with the concepts and practices of domain-driven design in mind. He replied that he had not incorporated DDD into the framework when he was building it and instead relied on his own experience and know-how to build out and architect what would eventually become the most popular PHP-based web framework in the world.

The answer wasn't all that hard to figure out after seeing the directory structure that Laravel ships with out of the box (you can see the stock root directory in Figure 8-1). This isn't anything wrong with this structure for a simple application, but for a domain-driven application, this will not work.

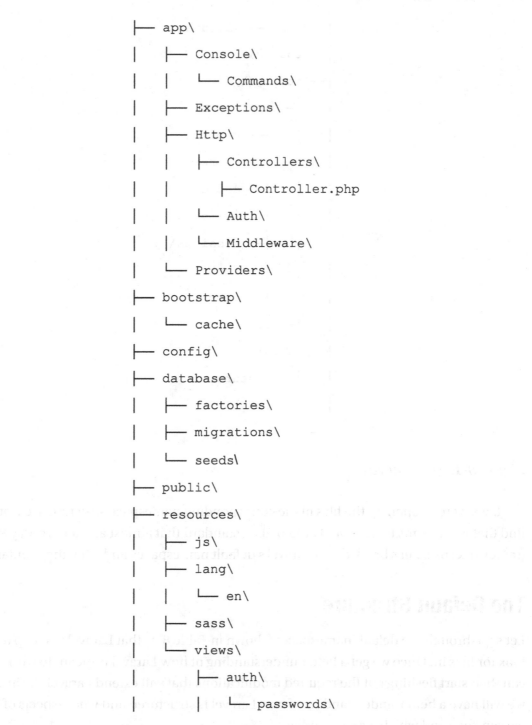

```
├── app\
│   ├── Console\
│   │   └── Commands\
│   ├── Exceptions\
│   ├── Http\
│   │   ├── Controllers\
│   │   │   ├── Controller.php
│   │   └── Auth\
│   │   └── Middleware\
│   └── Providers\
├── bootstrap\
│   └── cache\
├── config\
├── database\
│   ├── factories\
│   ├── migrations\
│   └── seeds\
├── public\
├── resources\
│   ├── js\
│   ├── lang\
│   │   └── en\
│   ├── sass\
│   └── views\
│       ├── auth\
│       │   └── passwords\
```

Figure 8-1. *Laravel's default directory structure*

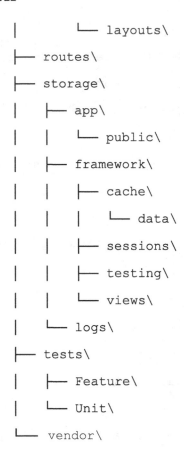

```
|              └── layouts\
├── routes\
├── storage\
|    ├── app\
|    |    └── public\
|    ├── framework\
|    |    ├── cache\
|    |    |    └── data\
|    |    ├── sessions\
|    |    ├── testing\
|    |    └── views\
|    └── logs\
├── tests\
|    ├── Feature\
|    └── Unit\
└── vendor\
```

Figure 8-1. (*continued*)

If we were to open up the files in the corresponding namespace structure, we would find that it conforms to the PSR-4 autoloading standard that almost all modern-day PHP frameworks use. Let's break down Laravel's default namespaces and what they contain.

The Default Structure

Let's go through the default namespaces (shown in Table 8-1) that Laravel is set up to look for files in. Once we get a better understanding of how Laravel is meant to work, we can then start fleshing out the required modifications that will extend Laravel. All in all, we will have a better understanding of how Laravel is structured and what aspects of it we can keep and which we can modify.

Table 8-1. *The Namespaces in Laravel and Their Corresponding Layers in the Application*

Directory	Namespace	Description
/app/Http/Controllers	App\Controllers\	All controllers in the framework
/app/Http/Requests	App\Http\ Requests\	All requests in the application
/app/Http/Middleware	App\Http\ Middleware\	All middleware
/app/Http/Jobs	App\Http\Jobs\	All jobs
/app/Policies	App\Policies\	Authorization policies (model based)
/app/Providers	App\Providers\	All service providers in the app
/app/Events	App\Events\	Generated events
/database		Infrastructure concerns (database)
/database/seeders		Houses classes that create dummy records in the database on a per-table basis
/database/factories		Factories for unit testing system models by generating fresh instances from a set of criteria
/database/migrations		An important directory containing all the changes and creation specs of the database
/resources/views		Houses blade view files
/routes		Application routes
/tests	Tests\Unit	Unit tests

It's clear now that what we are going to need is a new structure for our application, one that fulfills all the previous guidelines and one that is focused on expressing the domain effectively. The names of the directories would indicate that the majority of the code present in them more than likely relates to application layer concerns, which makes sense, as it is an application framework for a monolithic application that isn't meant to

241

be distributed, shared, or even developed by more than a single department or a couple programmers at a given time. For a domain-driven design, what we want is a directory and namespace structure that is modeled as close to the actual domain as possible, which we cannot possibly accomplish with the directories the way they are, centered around the application concerns of the system. The namespaces are simply too generic for our use cases regarding the claim application we have been building in the previous chapter.

We want to be able to look at the structure and get a good idea about what the application actually does because the directory structure corresponds to the underlying business model and because the directories are named after the terms defined in the ubiquitous language. This part is key and is worth repeating:

> *Make the namespaces of modules, classes, subdomains, domains,*
> *and all other domain-related component's names reflect the terms*
> *agreed on within the ubiquitous language.*

By following this simple practice, the project's directory and namespace structure will be realistically modeled in accordance with how the business domain is structured and therefore will be easy to understand by any member of the company that looks at the project's root folder. The application is broken down by *domain concerns*. The modules in the application represent the same format that the business itself operates on, and they are separated and named using the terms in the company's ubiquitous language.

Fortunately, Laravel is flexible enough to be able to support virtually any directory structure we can throw at it, for whatever level of complexity we may encounter in the particular domain we are working with. We can leverage Laravel's powerful extension features to rewire the namespaces to be more domain-driven, which brings up a good point.

As you will find out later in this chapter, even though Laravel wasn't necessarily built without DDD concepts and procedures in mind, it doesn't, by any means, imply that it wasn't created using best practices and SOLID standards. Specifically, the best practice that is demonstrated here is the open/closed principle. The open/closed principle basically suggests that an application, program, or framework should be closed for modification but open for extension. What this equates to is that we should be able to alter the behavior or structure of it without having to modify the core files that make up the application's internal facilities and, instead, have a predetermined means of extending the behavior of the application, usually by employing additional classes or by modifying a high-level service class or even modifying a configuration file or constant. Laravel allows you to do just that.

Service Providers

Laravel's configuration that relates to the directory and namespace structure is found deep within the bowels of the framework's source code...not exactly a good place to modify it directly because it sits within the vendor/ folder. Laravel uses facilities for configuring the various aspects of the system called *service providers*. Service providers are the central place to configure your application and are a great place to register various services, create instances of various classes that are needed in service definitions, or configure the service container, which powers the core services used in Laravel for both the application and infrastructure layers, and they are what we will use to configure the domain layer of the application as well.

Note   For more information about service providers and how they are used within Laravel, check out Chapter 4, or refer to the Laravel documentation on the subject at https://laravel.com/docs/6.0/providers.

Generally speaking, the service providers are used to define the service container's various registrations, bindings, singletons, and aliases within the service container that can be utilized to create complex, well-structured and elaborate service definitions that are available throughout the entire system. Before we get to the coding portion of these modifications, let's define how we want our structure to look for the claims project.

Structure of the Claim Application

Getting back to the claims example we've been focused on in the previous chapter, we will need a way to organize the structures of our domain layer while still keeping the other layers in mind.

Note   Although we decided to make the concept of a "claim estimate" a bounded context all on its own, we will not be focusing on modeling that portion of the domain until later in the book due to the extensive amount of supplemental information that would be way too boring to read in one sitting. We will explore the prerequisites to the claim estimation features of the application in later chapters (such as CPT code combos, pay code sheets, and how the individual CPT codes should be grouped). For now, let's focus on the claim's submission and validation concerns.

We need to devise a better structure for our application, one that is indicative of the business concerns and whose classes and modules are named intentionally, with terms defined in the ubiquitous language.

Guidelines for Structuring Namespaces and Directories

There are a set of guidelines that are described in DDD that will help to ensure we use best practices when defining the backbone structure of our application's directory and its namespaces, first formally introduced and highlighted in Eric Evan's *Blue Book*.

- Use names from the ubiquitous language for modules, classes, bounded contexts, and namespaces.

- Do not name anything in terms of a particular pattern or building block (such as entities, factories, etc.); stick with terms in the ubiquitous language. It is my opinion that these would be fine if they were contained within a folder pertaining to a concept in the ubiquitous language, as a means of separating functionality on a technical level, but only within the confines of a defined boundary drawn from the domain in its natural language.

- Create the namespaces in such a way that has very little coupling of the various classes or components in other namespaces. A good way to do this is to adhere to the separation of concerns principle, using the terminology from the domain.

- As additional insight is gained in the project's requirements or the knowledge of the domain, refactor namespaces and directory names to include the new insight, the same way we would refactor the code itself.

- Avoid using commercial product names as namespaces because they change too frequently.

Most important, the concepts and segregations that exist as foundations to a given business model (as well as its natural structure) should drive the designs of both the architecture and the domain model. The organic models and procedures that apply to the business itself within whatever domain you are working in should guide the direction and decision-making regarding the structure of the application as well as the selection of entities and the boundaries drawn between them. When the aspects of the domain are properly segregated into its various bounded contexts and modules that make up the full features offered by the application and when these features are modeled after the real-world business objects they represent, we see many benefits, as listed here:

- The code is a clear representation of the domain model that most likely involved the combined efforts of both developers and domain experts.

- It's obvious where in the code each portion of the domain lives and in what context the finer-grained pieces correspond to which coarser contexts.

- The question of where to place additional modules or classes is much more easily answered because the system has well-defined modules that are easily identified by the terms in the ubiquitous language.

- It sets us up for potentially transitioning our application to an even more segregated and clearly defined architecture in the form of microservices or hexagonal.

- We can develop each bounded context (even at the module level) independently of each other, which means they can be in different languages and can be worked on by separate groups or departments.

- Although you would still have to roll out the entire codebase when deploying, the application would be easier to manage as separate components, and you would be one step closer to converting it to a completely distributed architecture (like microservices).

Where Do Claims Fit In?

We are going to have to modify this structure to be less generic and more specific to our claim processing example. Since we do not yet have the design in a state where we can start mapping out the building block components that we will need to implement a proof of concept in code, we will use what we do know to sketch out a rough directory and namespace structure, keeping in mind that we can always, and should always, refactor the model and its implementation to reflect any gained knowledge in the domain.

What do we know about the app? We know the bounded contexts, we know the subdomains, and we have a rough understanding of the modules we need. We need to make the distinction between the bounded contexts clear and explicit by properly sectioning them off from each other and the rest of the app. This separation should be based on the contours of the domain, or the natural splitting of the concepts or departments that exists in the business domain. We also want to remember that we are using a layered architecture, and the layers themselves provide adequate means of separation as well. Let's start with our bounded contexts (note that there are more in reality but thus far in the book we will be focused on the three we described in Chapter 6). See Figure 8-2.

Figure 8-2. *Bounded contexts of our claim processor*

Just to recap, here is the process:

1. Claims enter the system through a provider's (or practice's) office and are allowed to be input only by the `Practice` and `Provider` user types.

2. After the initial form is filled out and before it's actually submitted for review by the review team, automatic processes occur to make sure the claim has all the valid criteria to be able to submit to the reviewers, at which point the claim has been "submitted." These processes include the following:

   - Verifying patient/provider registration

   - Ensuring all required documents are attached to the claim

   - Verifying patient eligibility

   - Looking up the paycode sheet and validating the CPT code combo (we cover this later in the book)

3. Although not expressed yet in this model, the review process is what happens next, following claim submission, at which point all the data on the claim is manually validated by a reviewer before being sent off to the FQHC for payment reimbursement.

Generic Subdomains

The authorization/authentication context is a generic subdomain because it stretches across all the rest of the contexts and into the hearts of the modules themselves. These are sometimes called *cross-cutting concerns* (i.e., specific portions of an application that are generic enough to be implemented as the de facto standard solution to a given software problem across all other bounded contexts). Although they are not the primary focus of the project, they play some important role in the system that is required for it to function. Concerns like these should be segregated and encapsulated into their own namespace directory.

Note   Oftentimes, generic subdomains are fulfilled using third-party, off-the-shelf solutions, ones in which the members building it or maintaining it are considered experts in whichever field the generic subdomain falls under. A good example of this is Laravel's decision to 86 the UI portion of the authorization scaffolding that the framework used to offer via the Artisan `make:auth` command, in favor of using a third-party vendor that specializes in doing just that: managing the authorization and authentication of your users, creating and managing groups, creating and performing checks against permissions, creating user roles, and doing just about any other feature supported by a modern-day authorization management system. The vendor is Auth0 (`https://auth0.com/`).

Here are some examples of cross-cutting concerns:

- *Logging*: Errors can occur inside any layer of our system. Typically, there is a single implementation of some form of logger that gets used in many places throughout the application, including in all three architectural layers for debugging and informational purposes.

- *Security*: Authentication ("signing in") is a generic subdomain on its own. The functionality encapsulated within this concern is responsible for managing users, permissions, and roles as they are used as a standard way of enforcing security policies across the system.

- *Notifications*: Our application must have notifications enabled for each delivery mechanism in our app (API endpoints, web pages, etc.) so we can communicate to the user the state and status/well-being of (or not) the app after the request.

We will from now on model the security concerns as an independent "generic subdomain," as shown in Figure 8-3.

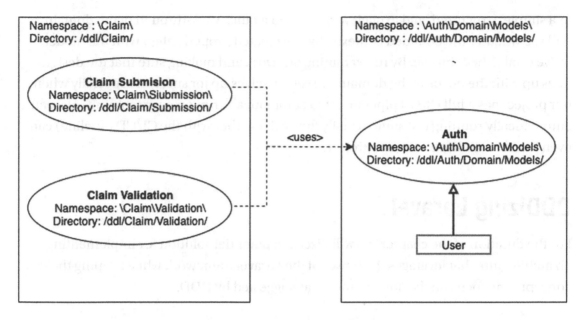

Figure 8-3. *The newly shaped bounded contexts (left) and their usage of Auth, a generic subdomain that also houses the User class that the domain implements for each user type*

Don't Lose Sight

Now that we have taken a stab at the separation of concerns on a contextual level, we have a rough draft that is, in all regards, the highest-level view of the system possible, at least for the purposes of this discussion. However, remember that your ultimate goal in creating a domain-driven design, which, in short, equates to building a model where the boundaries separate the various components such that they mirror the structure and context of their real-world counterparts. Always try to keep the domain and the model of the domain in lockstep with each other. We want to craft an application that is intention revealing, meaningful, and relevant to the policies and business rules that they exist to enforce. We want to be able to capture all the quirks of the domain in the model, eventually, by making frequent commits, narrowly focusing on a single task at a time, following coding guidelines and best practices, and employing concepts borrowed from the continuous iteration paradigm in an effort to refine the model to correspond to the real-world domain as closely as possible.

What we always need to remember to do with any rough draft or loose specification regarding architectural designs is to work backward and see whether the given design still meets the conditions and requirements of the domain and properly represents it

249

in a simple, structured, and explicit way. Let's do a quick walk-through of the domain and see whether the bounded contexts that we created properly align with the model we've established thus far. By re-examining our work and making sure that the design lines up with the needs of the domain, we set ourselves up for success, especially when our project has a full CI/CD pipeline set to automatically run on every commit. Also, an automatically running test suite (usually lumped together with the CI/CD pipeline) can even further stabilize a software project.

DDDizing Laravel

For the duration of the chapter, we will discuss a potential solution for implementing an architecture that leverages the power of the Laravel framework while keeping the concepts and focus on the domain model as suggested by DDD.

Via a Layered Architecture

To create this DDD-friendly Laravel application, we must include with it a new namespace and directory structure because the default one will not meet our needs (too monolithic). For our first attempt at it, we will employ the layered architecture pattern and attempt to divide the monolith into the various components corresponding to the three architectural layers that we should be used to seeing by now: the domain, application, and infrastructure layers.

The first step in customizing Laravel to meet our needs (in relation to DDD concepts and practices) is to run through the current, stock directories/namespaces and categorize each one into their corresponding layers. We've already started the process (see Table 8-1). Here is the outcome of doing that, but first, here's a quick recap of what each layer contains:

- **Application layer**
  - Responsible for orchestrating, organizing, and encapsulating domain behavior and controlling data access

- **Infrastructure layer**
  - Handles concerns such as persistence mechanisms and logging, by implementing the abstract interfaces defined in the domain layer (via dependency inversion)

- **Domain layer**

  - The heart and soul of any DDD project (and should be for every web development project also), containing the meat and potatoes of what makes the business actually function

Table 8-2 lists the layers presented in the default architecture that comes with Laravel.

Table 8-2. *Defining the Stock Structure in Terms of the Layer Which Each Directory Belongs*

Directory	Architectural Layer	Description
/app/Http/ Controllers	Application	Controllers accept requests entering the system and respond to different delivery mechanisms through a single, well-defined structure (this is known as an API). Controllers can be thought of as the moderator between external requests and internal domain processes.
/app/Http/ Requests	Application	Encapsulates requests and separates them from the delivery mechanism and domain/infrastructure concerns.
/app/Http/ Middleware	Application	Middleware is run at specific times during the request/response cycle and typically performs actions that live in the application layer.
/app/Jobs	Domain	Jobs can be thought of as "commands," or a narrowly defined task encapsulated within a single Job class.
/app/Policies	Application	The policies of the system control access to every model at the request level; authentication concerns are application layer concerns.
/app/ Providers	Application	Service providers are what we will use to configure our custom directory structure and also provide a means for third-party packages to be configured.

(continued)

Table 8-2. (*continued*)

Directory	Architectural Layer	Description
/app/Events	Domain	Events fire when something specific has occurred in the domain layer and will act as a record of that action that may trigger additional actions.
/database	Infrastructure	The database directory houses all database concerns and schema configurations, which operate within the infrastructure layer.
/database/ seeders	Infrastructure	Seeders are test records for the database.
/database/ factories	Infrastructure	Factories for database testing.
/database/ migrations	Infrastructure	Migrations contain a record of database schema changes on a granular, per-change basis.
/resources/ views	Application	This can also fit into a separate layer known as the "view layer" or "presentation layer" and typically just contains UI concerns
/routes	Application	Routes define what can go in and the configuration of the URI's that ultimately lead to a console command being ran or a web page being displayed
/tests	*	In a well-constructed system, it is typical to find tests that cover every layer in the application

Something to notice in Table 8-2 is that most of the directories encapsulate application concerns (i.e., belonging in the application layer). This makes sense when you consider the fact that Laravel is an "application framework." In other words, it handles as many *application-level* concerns throughout the system as are needed in a typical web development project, so it is only right that the application concerns in the default structure make up the majority of the directories and namespaces.

In fact, from Laravel's documentation, it hints that it intends to provide you with the most practical solutions to the most common problems at the *application* level so that you can focus on what matters most to any DDD application: the domain. It allows flexibility at the "joints" of the application. By this I mean the code connecting the various components together, such as the service providers and dependency injection.

That being said, I think the best approach here is to allow Laravel to do what it is good at doing, which is managing the variety of application concerns. We will restructure the layout of the namespaces to section off the various bounded contexts in our application. We will leave the root app folder that is Laravel's default project folder but leave inside it only files and directories that apply to the entire application and that don't fit into our declared bounded contexts. These include things such as service providers, policies, the console kernel, and App\Http\Kernel, which is responsible for assigning middleware groups and middleware routes.

Everything else we will do an analysis on, following these steps:

1. Analyze the component, class, or module within the project's root directory and determine its layer.

2. Determine which bounded context each component falls under (or if they are present in all contexts) or if they should stay in the generic app/ folder because they pertain to the entire system and not to a single context.

3. Move the items from their default location in the root project directory to their respective locations in one or more bounded contexts (in some cases we are going to have to replicate parts of the structure that should be included in every module, to live as independent constructs *belonging* to their corresponding context).

4. Once we iron out a stable structure, we will make the required changes in the configuration as well as the service providers to let Laravel know where to find our code corresponding to the various endpoints in our system.

5. Modify the composer.json file to include the autoloading for our new namespace structure *created in the previous step* and create the necessary providers to hook up our project's code with Laravel's internal mechanisms.

6. Revisit the core requirements constantly to ensure our design meets the needs and requirements of the system.

Let's do it.

Step 1: Analyze the Project Root Directory Structure

If we take a standard Laravel installation and go through its default directory structure, we are more than likely always going to find parts of the structure either that are not needed for a particular project or that have too rigid of a structure for what we need it for. The standard structure in Laravel is not set up to be modular and instead crams the majority of its "project code" within the /app directory. This is not ideal for those of us who want to build an application using DDD practices.

A good first step is to analyze the directory structure that comes default in Laravel and compare it to your project's requirements. This can give you ideas on how to modify the namespace structure to conform to your needs. For example, if you are building a five-page informational website with a single contact form and maybe a few inline graphics here and there, you most likely don't need the extensive components provided by Laravel, nor would you need (or want) to implement DDD for such a trivial project. On the other hand, you may find that the project's scope is fairly complex and would be better represented with a more formal namespace structure, so you may apt to break apart the app/ directory into more manageable layers (i.e., the application, domain, infrastructure, and interface layers).

Step 2: Determine Which Components Are Needed for Each Bounded Context

Seeing as though we are actually dealing with two bounded contexts as well as one generic subdomain, we will go through the default structure and determine which ones we will need in each bounded context (Claim Submission, Claim Validation) and which belong to the generic subdomain (Authorization/Authentication). It's important to note in Table 8-3 that the bounded contexts that we have identified in the second column doesn't necessarily reflect the given structure or namespace. For example, the Views component is going to be needed for the Claim Submission context (so the user can interact with the application via the browser) and the Auth subdomain (so the users can log in, log out, and register).

Table 8-3. *Components Needed in Each Bounded Context in Our Claim Example*

Laravel Component	Claim Context	Explanation
→ Http → Controllers → Requests → Middleware	• Claim Submission • Claim Validation • Auth	All web apps share the same basic process: receive request, return response. These components drive this basic need, so we need them for all contexts.
→ Jobs	• Claim Submission • Claim Validation	Jobs will encapsulate specific domain knowledge and provide a means of executing specific, one-off actions.
→ Policies	• Auth	Although policies revolve around a given model, the concern of authentication in general is an application concern, which makes sense because the application layer is the direct client to the domain layer.
→ Providers	• Generic (app/) • Claim Submission • Claim Validation • Auth	Service providers are going to be needed in all layers of the app, including the generic one residing in /app. Each BC will have their own as well, and there is one built-in for the authorization concerns: `AuthServiceProvider`.
→ Events	• Generic (app/) • Claim Submission • Claim Validation • Auth	Events will occur in all layers of the application: domain events, auth events, and system-wide events.
→ Artisan Commands	• Claim Submission • Claim Validation	Console commands are handy for a variety of one-off tasks and scheduled maintenance. We will want both our BCs to have a `Console\Command` namespace.
→ Exceptions	• Generic (app/) • Claim Submission • Claim Validation • Auth	Exceptions can happen at any time, in any layer of the application, including generic system issues and authentication errors.

(continued)

Table 8-3. (*continued*)

Laravel Component	Claim Context	Explanation
→ Views	• Claim Submission • Auth	We will initially need views for entering in the data to create a claim as well as the login/logout UI. The Validation component shouldn't need it because its functionality occurs in the backend.
→ Routes	• Claim Submission • Claim Validation • Auth	To allow access into our application from external sources, we will need routes. We also need to be able to route things to the backend, to all the BCs, and we are removing the default generic route files from the app.

→ Tests	• Claim Submission
	  o Unit
	  o Functional
	• Claim Validation
	  o Unit
	• Generic/Auth
		All BCs will have some form of tests, either unit or both unit and functional. We may or may not have tests for authorization, authentication, or other generic components. When we do, we can make room for them.

This doesn't indicate that there should be a `views/` folder in each of the corresponding contexts. We will go into details about the structure of our application later in this chapter.

Table 8-3 is a catalog so to speak of the relation that the default structure has with what we are trying to implement and will serve well as a general guideline of which components are needed for each context, which will later be used to determine a namespace and directory structure that will support it. In *The Big Blue Book* (Eric Evans), he points out that, oftentimes, frameworks force you into a particular style or confine you in their own adopted structure, making it more difficult to implement things the way we want...the way that DDD suggests.

However, it is my aim to show a possible implementation of DDD in a framework in which the two complement each other, rather than fight each other. Laravel will be used primarily for its facilities and backbone features that provide the answers to problems at the application level, in the application layer. This will allow us to laser focus on implementing the patterns and practices defined in DDD, without worrying too much about the application concerns or the places "in between the cracks" that are often the cause of much frustration and wasted time trying to develop and maintain.

Tip   The DRY principle is a big deal in the programming world. If you don't already know what the DRY principle is, it's a simple acronym meaning "Don't Repeat Yourself." It is a good piece of advice and one that we should always attempt to take when developing software.

Step 3: Reorganize the Project Directory

This section of the book was difficult to write simply because there are so many different ways to go about designing a domain-driven structure that no one answer can be the 100 percent surefire way to create the architecture of the system. So, I think it's best to document my own experience with the claims example. I wanted to first give a brief background of the claims application that inspired the example used in this text.

A BRIEF HISTORY OF THE CLAIM APPLICATION

The application that I worked on was inherited by our team and was originally developed off-shore as a means to manage the claim submission process in relation to the federally regulated Medi-Cal program, essentially increasing the number of patient visits the owning medical practice could support and allowing medical providers to focus more on what they do best: diagnose and treat patients. The off-shore team utilized the Laravel framework, but the overall architectural structure that the off-shore team initially established was poorly designed (if it was actually *designed* at all in the sense of any sort of strategic planning), and the implementation was bloated. Concerns were scattered across the entire application, there was no sense of any conformity to any sort of adoption of code or syntax standards, and more. However, as terrible as it was, it worked.

After its initial construction and proof of concept on the market as an income-producing business-to-medical-provider web application, the owner decided to hire an in-house development team to take over the project with the goal of long-term sustainability, along with the ability to roll out new business features quickly and efficiently. Because the company was

---

a startup, they faced the typical need most startups have when developing software: features needed to be added or removed at random times throughout the application's development. While this vision turned out to be a reality in the long run, initially when the first in-house team stepped into the codebase, the majority of their time was putting out fires (i.e., bug fixes).

Due to the off-shore team's lack of experience along with other problems that made working remotely with a ten-person development team a bigger challenge (such language communication barrier), some concepts got misconstrued and others misrepresented or disfigured. Oftentimes this left behind a bunch of code that bloated the repository; the "working" code all but worked correctly. Fixing the bugs usually meant the application went down and we were losing money. Drop everything, fix the application. When this happened, every developer on the team hopped on their computers and began bouncing ideas off each other after glancing at a barrage of stack traces, exception dumps, and log files as to what the issue could be and how to best fix it in the least amount of time possible.

The point I'm getting at is that the application I worked on for more than a year that served as the basis for this example was by no means constructed in a domain-driven way or even in a way that remotely resembled what any good developer would consider to be "best practices." The boundaries were often blurred around the different portions of the code addressing the concerns of the domain, so our task later became refactoring the various portions of the domain into separate, new structures that were, more or less, set up as if they were microservices (i.e., independent, domain-driven modules with well-placed barriers around each portion of the domain), which we then implemented within the same monolithic application using the anti-corruption layer pattern as a means of integrating the new self-containing context into the original codebase. The original clients were still used for the same calls, except that those calls all had to be changed to point to the new context established in our anti-corruption layer.

What I'm going to present to you with will mirror my own experience, will highlight the trials and errors that I faced, and will show the final structure that I decided on. This will best reflect the real-world experience of designing and modeling software in the shape of a particular domain and show what to expect in terms of coming up with a viable solution that is going to do more than simply "work." It will eventually provide a foundation for which to build any other future components on top of, and it can be decomposed into independent microservices fairly easy due to the level of encapsulation they were built with in regard to the core domain's natural boundaries that isolate one domain concept group from another. The goal of that project was to eventually reach a distributed system, which is a difficult thing to do; however, you reap the rewards in both the near term (such as discovering missing gaps or unknown corners of the domain) and the long term (like the ability to deploy the various components independently and to have them developed by different teams, by departments, or in different programming languages entirely).

Framework Application Concerns

Now that we have a clear means of categorizing the components in each layer, we need to come up with an equally good way to organize them in terms of their respective bounded context, which we will do via directory structure and namespace selection.

Tip   Keep in mind that this is not the finalized structure, but only a rough draft of one. Later, we will move things around and refactor this structure for better organization. This will be the case when we introduce a hexagonal approach to the project.

Let's see how the project structure looks like after the modifications to it but before we install our own bounded contexts and domain layer, as shown in Figure 8-4.

├── app\   This will be for generic items or Laravel-specific components

│   ├── Console\   The standard console component (CLI)

│   │   └── Kernel.php   The central configuration for Artisan commands

│   ├── Http\   System-wide Http concerns

│   │   ├── Controllers\   System-wide controllers (for now, only Auth)

│   │   │   └── Auth\   Handles authentication/authorization concerns

│   │   └── Middleware\   Generic middleware (stock Laravel middleware)

│   ├── Events\   System-wide events (generic)

│   ├── Exceptions\   System-wide, generic exceptions

│   └── Providers\   Core service providers (Auth-, App-, Route-, Event-) Providers

├── bootstrap\   Standard Laravel startup folder

│   └── cache\   Laravel's standard class cache

├── config\   Configuration for the entire application

│   └── claim_submission.php   Configuration for the claim submission context

│   └── claim_validation.php   Configuration for the claim validation context

│   └── auth.php   Built in auth config that we can customize

├── database\   Standard infrastructure-level (database) concerns, basic auth tables

│   ├── migrations\   Iterations of changes to the database that come stock

│   │   └── 0000_00_00_000000_create_users_table.php

│   │   └── 0000_00_00_000000_create_password_resets_table.php

│   │   └── 0000_00_00_000000_create_failed_jobs_table.php

├── public\   Default public web directory

├── resources\   Generic front-end assets or views

│   ├── js\   Standard Javascript configuration files

│   │   └── app.js   Core Javascirpt file & VueJS configuration

Figure 8-4. *The new directory and namespace structure for the claims project*

```
|    |    └── bootstrap.js    Core Javascript bootstrap file
|    ├── lang\   Language definition files
|    |    └── en\  English
|    ├── sass\    Don't you Sass me, as my co-worker Kieth would say
|    └── views\   System-wide, generic view files
|    |    ├── auth\    Blade files for the authentication interface
|    |    └── layouts\    Site-wide layouts
|    |    |       └── app.blade.php    Standard layout that our BCs extend
├── src\      This is where our domain layer will live (the BCs and claim concerns)
├── storage\    Standard Laravel storage for cache, logs and other framework metadata
└──     vendor\  Standard Composer vendor folder
```

Figure 8-4. (*continued*)

Note   For a spoiler, see the repository for this project on the book's website or at Apress.com.

In Figure 8-4, we basically laid out the revised structure of the application with respect to what we defined in Table 8-2 a few pages ago. The rearrangement presented here does a few things for us architecturally.

- We have a much clearer separation of concerns because we have kept all application-wide components that apply to the system as a whole (and not to our bounded contexts) inside the project's root directory using the setup that comes stock with Laravel...mostly.

- Laravel's default components that address application concerns are still within the default /app folder and correspond to the App\ namespace, which makes it easier for us to identify at first glance what a given class does and where it lives.

- All domain concerns are neatly encapsulated inside the /src folder, which we will need to set up in our composer.json file so it recognizes our new namespace for our domain layer: Claim.

- We have moved a few directories that come with Laravel to live within the boundaries of our domain layer (such as Jobs, Events, etc.).

261

There are cons to this structure, however, as there are in most everything else that appears to be perfect in software development. The main con that comes to mind is that the architecture seems a little scattered. The reason for this, however, may be because the developer implementing this is not used to a Laravel-style directory structure, and it may be a little overwhelming at first to try to remember all of these folders and what they do. I feel that a tad bit more experience and usage of the framework will help to mitigate this.

The structure we have designed mirrors the one that comes with Laravel. Besides the addition of the `src/` folder, it has almost all the other pieces of the components that have been there since the installation of the framework. We are simply making a few of the changes regarding folders from the project's root directory that would normally exist within a traditional Laravel application and repurposed in the name of DDD. This decision will help us keep order to our application and will allow us to focus directly on the core domain model and aspects of the application that exist within the domain layer and will pay off for us when we set out to develop a variety of pieces that will make the puzzle fit together. So, even if the overall structure appears a little busy, there is a method to the madness, which will unfold as we continue with our domain concerns.

Additional Directories

There are more directories that we need to fulfill various aspects of the system. I believe it would be best to find some middle ground between maintaining the core domain-driven focus that we rely on to build architecture with while still allowing the framework to do the heavy lifting with regard to the application concerns, which is what it does best. We will use Laravel's standard directory and namespace names, although we may relocate them or replicate them to other bounded contexts. Without creating too rigid of an initial structure, we will need to make room for such components, as described in the following bullet list:

- Console (commands): Application-wide Artisan commands.

- Exceptions: Application-wide exceptions.

- Http.

    - Controllers.

        - Auth.

- Middleware: Standard Laravel middleware.

- Requests: Not needed in the application wide context.

- Moved to the domain layer.

- Events: Global events within the application.

- Listeners: Global listeners for the global events.

- Models: The only application-wide model at this point is the User model, which we can decide to move later.

- Observers: Observers applicable to the system as a whole .

- ~~Policies~~: Policies are related to domain objects and are named in regard to a given model. Moved to the domain layer.

- Providers: Laravel standard providers that configure the system on a high level.

Notice that we are etching out a global context for the moving parts of the application that apply on a global context (or a system/application-wide context). We will use this structure as a template for our bounded contexts, but keep in mind we don't want to add folders just for the sake of maintaining conventions or adhering to framework name restrictions. As far as software development goes, simple is always better than complex, and small is always better than large, indicating that finer-grained components are generally better than larger-grained ones. However, what really matters is if the level of object and class granularity is such that it reflects that of the underlying domain. If we were building a simple single-page application that contained a form that posts to the backend on submit and another page for the confirmation message, we probably aren't going to need but a few bite-sized components (including the Form model to represent submitted form data, tracked perhaps by IP address). If, on the other hand, we were building an e-commerce platform from the ground up, we would need a pretty complex array of models to house all the logic that occurs when things happen (user views product and selects desired attributes and variations for that product; user adds product to cart, then proceeds to checkout; etc.). However coarse or fine you decide to make your models and components that operate on them, you can't go wrong if you model them as they exist in real life as business rules and underlying policies cultivated from the business domain and named after the ubiquitous language.

Domain Concerns

Let's dive into the `src/` folder and put together our initial domain structure. Keep in mind that the ultimate goal at this point is to devise a layout for which our domain-centered components can live and be developed independently. We are going to go as far as we can, with the knowledge regarding the core domain (claims) that we've so far been able to acquire. We intend to use the various practices and maintain a high degree of quality while relying on foundational principles on which to make our decisions.

Directory Structure: Claim Submission Context

Each bounded context will have a folder for each layer within the domain model: `Application`, `Infrastructure`, and `Domain`. Since we have, for the most part, left the `/app` folder intact as it is in a stock Laravel install, we can basically now think of this folder as the framework concerns. `/app` now contains Laravel-specific items, which will make it easier to add more in later when we need to. That leaves the `src/` folder being the actual "model layer" of the system in regard to the domain. However, within the umbrella of the domain as a whole needs a clear boundary around its sublevel architectural concerns, which is why I've elected to include a directory for each layer (Figure 8-5). This also will support long-term growth because it will be clear where any particular piece of code should live right off the bat.

```
src/Claim/Submission/
```

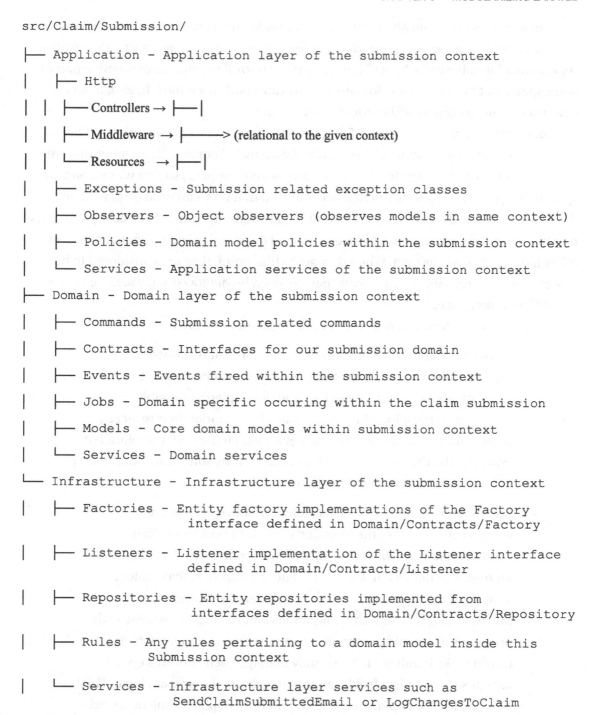

```
├── Application - Application layer of the submission context
│     ├── Http
│   │     ├── Controllers → ├──│
│   │     ├── Middleware  → ├──────> (relational to the given context)
│   │     └── Resources   → ├──│
│     ├── Exceptions - Submission related exception classes
│     ├── Observers - Object observers (observes models in same context)
│     ├── Policies - Domain model policies within the submission context
│     └── Services - Application services of the submission context
├── Domain - Domain layer of the submission context
│     ├── Commands - Submission related commands
│     ├── Contracts - Interfaces for our submission domain
│     ├── Events - Events fired within the submission context
│     ├── Jobs - Domain specific occuring within the claim submission
│     ├── Models - Core domain models within submission context
│     └── Services - Domain services
└── Infrastructure - Infrastructure layer of the submission context
      ├── Factories - Entity factory implementations of the Factory
                       interface defined in Domain/Contracts/Factory
      ├── Listeners - Listener implementation of the Listener interface
                      defined in Domain/Contracts/Listener
      ├── Repositories - Entity repositories implemented from
                          interfaces defined in Domain/Contracts/Repository
      ├── Rules - Any rules pertaining to a domain model inside this
                   Submission context
      └── Services - Infrastructure layer services such as
                     SendClaimSubmittedEmail or LogChangesToClaim
```

Figure 8-5. *The Submission bounded context structure*

Something else to note about the way we are structuring the layout of our system is that we are utilizing the terms found within the ubiquitous language, and only creating separations for patterns or "types" (i.e., factories, controllers, etc.) underneath a parent namespace that belongs to the domain directly (and pulls from the UL) and, in fact, belongs to a given context within the domain model.

So, what we've done in Figure 8-5 is split each of the standard concerns (in Laravel's terms) into their corresponding layer within the bounded context. Remember that we want each BC to be independent of the others (loosely coupled) so that we can one day split them apart into separate microservices and so that they can even be placed on different servers or developed by a different department or team. What that equates to is that the bounded context needs to incorporate all the standard components that would allow it to function on its own. When they get to that point, they are considered to be loosely coupled, reusable components that can even be deployed separately or written in a different language.

Here are a few additional notes about the structure in Figure 8-5:

- Earlier we identified policies as being an application concern; we include claim policies in the Submission context because we want our contexts to be as independent and decoupled as possible to the rest of the application. We want to place them under their respective context that is the same as the model for which the policy applies. For example, the ClaimPolicy will live in the Submission context because the `Claim` domain model lives there as well.

- I considered creating a `Database` folder that lives inside the infrastructure layer of the bounded context to house only that context's database concerns (migrations, seeders, test factories), but, for now, I've decided to leave the standard root `/database` folder intact as far as its location and house all database concerns within it. My reasoning for this is that migrations and the like are system-wide processes that could potentially span numerous contexts, which would make it difficult to separately manage each context's own `database/` folder in a feeble attempt to split up the domain logic. This is an area of the application that should *not* be split among bounded contexts but left in a global, application-wide context.

- The *Infrastructure* within the Claim Submission context contains many of the patterns that we will visit later in this book. The idea is that we define interfaces within our `Domain\Contracts` namespace (for repositories, factories, or classes that are concerned with persistence) and then implement them within the `Infrastructure\` namespace, allowing us to maintain a domain-driven approach and retain the "D" in SOLID (dependency inversion). The infrastructure supports the models and handles persistent concerns as well as provide a means for the domain layer's residents to operate across requests (due to HTTP not having a default sense of state other than the session).

- There is a `Service` directory in each layer of the bounded contexts to allow them to be self-contained and properly sectioned off from each other. For a refresher on the different services in different layers, refer to Chapter 1. Here are some examples of things you are likely to find in each:

  - `Application\Service`

    - `laimLoggingService`

    - `ProviderNotificationService`

    - `EmailNewsletterService`

  - `Domain\Service`

    - `ClaimSubmissionService`

    - `ProviderRegistrationService`

    - `PaycodeSheetVerificationService`

  - `Infrastructure\Service`

    - `FilterSpecificationService`

- Although we are naming the directories after the patterns that they contain, we are doing so within the confines of a bounded context. We are still maintaining that thread of continuity between the implementation and the underlying business domain and will continue to do so in the future by naming things after the terms expressed in the ubiquitous language.

Directory Structure: Claim Validation Context

The claim validation context will have the same core structure as the claim submission context. One obvious difference is that the validation context will not need its own set of blade views or a presentation layer at all, since it will be used for automated validation and in the event of an issue with the claim's data or violation of the pre- and post-conditions of claim submission would simply return some type of specific Exception class to the Submission context, which would then process the exception and notify the user via its presentation files.

Step 4: Updating the Configuration

To make the structure we've devised earlier actually work, we need to let Laravel know where to find the various components in our bounded contexts because the majority of the code that we write will end up living in one of these two contexts: Claim Submission or Claim Validation.

app/Providers/RouteServiceProvider.php

Because we've adopted new directories with which to store the various routes of the bounded contexts, we need to tell Laravel where to load these and how we want to structure the routes for our domain layer. We do any special routing configuration inside the app/Providers/RouteServiceProvider.php file (Listing 8-1).

Listing 8-1. Modified RouteServiceProvider, with Updates Shown in Bold:/ddl/app/Providers/RouteServiceProvider.php

```php
<?php
namespace App\Providers;
class RouteServiceProvider extends ServiceProvider
{
    /**
     * This namespace is applied to your controller routes.
     *
     * In addition, it is set as the URL generator's root namespace.
     *
     * @var string
     */
```

```php
protected $namespace = 'App\Http\Controllers';
protected $submission_namespace = 'Claim\Submission\Application\Http\
Controllers';
protected $submission_dir = 'src/Claim/Submission/Application/Routes/';

/**
 * Define your route model bindings, pattern filters, etc.
 *
 * @return void
 */
public function boot()
{
    parent::boot();
}

/**
 * Define the routes for the application.
 *
 * @return void
 */
public function map()
{
    $this->mapApiRoutes();
    $this->mapWebRoutes();
}
/**
* Define the "web" routes for the application.
*
* These routes all receive session state, CSRF protection, etc.
*
* @return void
*/
protected function mapWebRoutes()
{
    Route::middleware('web')
        ->namespace($this->namespace)
```

```
            ->group(base_path('routes/web.php'));

        Route::middleware('web')
            ->namespace($this->submission_namespace)
            ->prefix('submission')
            ->group(base_path($this->submission_dir . 'web.php'));
    }

    /**
     * Define the "api" routes for the application.
     *
     * These routes are typically stateless
     *
     * @return void
     */
    protected function mapApiRoutes()
    {
        Route::prefix('api')
                ->middleware('api')
                ->namespace($this->namespace)
                ->group(base_path('routes/api.php'));
        Route::prefix('submission/api')
                ->middleware('api')
                ->namespace($this->submission_namespace . '/Api')
                ->group(base_path($this->submission_dir . 'api.php'));
    }
}
```

Note   If you were following along, you will need to clear your route cache via the Laravel command `artisan route:clear` and can always verify your routes are being picked up by Laravel with `artisan route:list`. If running the clear cache command gives you an error you don't recognize, try running it again at the end of this chapter.

Essentially what we have done here is added support for our domain-related contexts and have stated where to find the custom routes for the application, in addition to loading the standard routes that come with Laravel (inside /routes). The mapWebRoutes() method gives a custom route namespace via the namespace() function available via the Route facade. Route namespaces define the location of a specific namespace that will be the container for which the controllers belonging to that namespace (and bounded context) will be located under. In our case, we are configuring the Submission context's routes, so we want to point this namespace setting to our main Controller namespace we defined for this bounded context: Claim\Submission\Application\Http\Controllers. We specified this to be located in the directory src/Claim/Submission/Application/Routes/. Now when we go to define our routes within a route file, like the one in the aforementioned directory under the filename web.php, we can specify this syntax to refer to controllers that make it easy to configure our application's route structure: SubmissionController@index.

This points to the class Claim\Submission\Application\Http\Controllers\SubmissionController and invokes the logic contained within the index() method, which is set up to be located in the file src/Claim/Submission/Application/Http/Controllers/SubmissionController.php.

The route prefix is simply the portion of the URI after the main URL of the application. What we have done is configured the routes defined in the route files (web.php for web routes and api.php for API routes) to start with a proceeding /submission and /submission/api, respectively. We then group together the route prefix along with the namespace we gave them via the Route facade using its group() method, passing along as its parameter a valid set of routes to which the chain-linked configuration should be applied, which we define in the corresponding routes files, web.php and api.php, like so:

```php
<?php
// configured to run SubmissionController::index() when the route
// "/submission" is hit with a GET HTTP request
Route::get('/', 'SubmissionController@index');

// configured to run SubmissionController::submit() when the route
// "/submission/submit" is hit with a POST HTTP request
Route::post('/submit', 'SubmissionController@submit');
```

app/Providers/EventServiceProvider.php

Laravel's event system uses Symfony's event component under the hood and offers an additional layer of configuration of where events and listeners are located as well as other functionality regarding events and listeners in the application. We will want to tell Laravel where the listeners to these events are located, which we can do by adding this method to the EventServiceProvider class, which overwrites its default method defined in the parent class (Listing 8-2).

Listing 8-2. Updates to the EventServiceProvider to Specify the Location of the Listeners

```
/**
    * Get listener dirs that should be used to discover Events.
    *
    * @return array
    */
   protected function discoverEventsWithin()
   {
       return [
           $this->app->path('Listeners'),
           $this->app->path(base_path(
               'src/Claim/Submission/Application/Listeners')),
           ];
   }
```

Step 5: Create a New ClaimSubmissionProvider

As we continue with this example throughout the book, we will need a place to put our more general-level configuration and customizations that are specific to a particular bounded context. I've decided to place a Providers namespace in each BC's Application directory so that each one may contain multiple providers, separated by the established needs of the business as per the domain model and named after the ubiquitous language.

Note Because we are using a completely separated namespace that we had to specify in composer.json, the Artisan command-line tool's make:* set of commands will not function properly to create components within the bounds of a domain context. To get around this, you can either issue the make:* commands without specifying the FQDN of the generated file and then move it where you need it to be and modify the namespace or simply create a new file and copy the content of a pre-existing provider and modify where needed. For simplicity, I opted for the create-paste-edit method rather than the latter.

Create a new .php file in the namespace Claim\Submission\Application\Providers\ClaimSubmissionProvider and place the code shown in Listing 8-3 in it.

Listing 8-3. The New ClaimSubmissionProvider Service Provider Class

```
// ddl/src/Claim/Submission/Application/Providers/
    ClaimSubmissionProvider.php

<?php

namespace Claim\Submission\Application\Providers;

use Illuminate\Support\ServiceProvider;

class ClaimSubmissionProvider extends ServiceProvider
{
    /**
     * Register any application services.
     *
     * @return void
     */
    public function register()
    {
        //
    }

    /**
     * Bootstrap any application services.
```

```
 *
 * @return void
 */
public function boot()
{
    $this->loadMigrationsFrom(__DIR__ .
        '/../../Infrastructure/Database/migrations');
    //$this->loadTranslationsFrom(__DIR__.'/../resources/lang',
        'domain-driven-laravel');
    // $this->loadViewsFrom(__DIR__.'/../resources/views',
        'domain-driven-laravel');
    //$this->loadMigrationsFrom(
        __DIR__.'/../database/migrations');
    // $this->loadRoutesFrom(__DIR__.'/routes.php');
}

public function register()
{
    $this->mergeConfigFrom(__DIR__.
        '/../config/claim_submission.php',
        'domain-driven-laravel');
}
}
```

So far, our service provider contains only one setting in its boot method, and that is where the migrations for the context is located. In this case, we are keeping the migrations within the Infrastructure folder, inside of the Database namespace, and using the standard Laravel naming conventions for the standard database concerns that the framework provides solutions for (one of them being the ability to roll forward and back on database schema changes by incrementally recording them into what's known as a *database migration*).

Notice also that I've included some additional methods there for reference in regard to some other ways we could tweak the default behavior of Laravel. They are commented out because we don't quite need them yet, but when, for example, we want to split up the views and translations into their separate contexts or even have different language files to support international users, all it takes is a simple change in the service provider's boot method to do so. Lastly in Listing 8-3, you will notice the register method simply loads any defined configuration values from the `config/claim_submission.php` file. For more information regarding configuration, check out Chapter 4.

UTILIZING THIRD-PARTY PACKAGES, FRAMEWORKS, TOOLS

In this day and age, it is not uncommon to see a variety of different technologies that are developed independently but that all come together in the end to provide a full working application. Companies usually have only a select few foundational technology stacks for which to base their corporation's software architecture on: Solaris, Linux/Unix, Windows, and a handful of others. Selection of the core stack should be based on the needs of the system, the support of the infrastructure, and the experience of the development team. If everyone knows PHP very well and the project calls for a web-based architecture that can be built from a framework to save time and costs, then going open source is by far the better, more practical way to go. However, if it's support that you want in a technology stack, both customer support and software maintenance/updates/features, and you are looking for something that is easy to use, then a Windows-based tech stack may be the way to go.

Startups tend to go with open source development because it's widespread, cheap, and effective. There are open sourced solution tailored to virtually all common development and Internet needs. A lot of the time a successful implementation of an architecture that supports the specific needs of a narrowly focused niche-based business strategy consists of finding prebuilt libraries, frameworks, tools, or anything else that adds business value without a lot of overhead and/or speeds up the process of development and increases the quality of its finished products. These third-party libraries' functionality is then utilized when implementing business logic and stitched together to achieve some common goal or to build out a set of features.

Although this is the cycle that basically spans the entire industry in one form or another as a means of developing out web application software, we must be careful to not muddle the intent of the domain. At the same time, many of these packages and frameworks, including Laravel, are built with high-quality standards and modern-day best practices, so utilizing them isn't necessarily a bad thing. What it boils down to in the end is how *extendable* those packages are and how easy it is to make the changes to the stock distribution of the code to make it suit your needs (that's what is so great about open source!). I chose Laravel as my standard web development framework because, among many other reasons, it is straightforward and easy to extend and customize.

Step 6: Take a Step Back

At this point, we have sketched out the boundaries of our claims example project and have a good understanding about how to break up the domain to make it more manageable. However, this architecture is far from perfect. If you've noticed, the lines between the architectural layers within each bounded context are oftentimes blurred because it's not always obvious where certain components should go. It's almost as if we are sort of fighting Laravel, forcing it to bend to our will.

Moving forward, we need to look for ways we can architect the system so that the domain is still the top priority, but using Laravel components, traits, and interfaces that our domain layer can expands on. In this manner, we maintain a domain-focused approach to crafting the application while still getting the most benefit that Laravel offers.

The problem lies in the encapsulation rules of the layered architecture. It states that the domain must not depend on anything outside of its own layer. Inherently, this would imply that, because we have some Laravel classes or interfaces that we want to extend within the boundaries of the domain layer, we would be forced to extend into our domain model from a different layer. In fact, when we take a step back and look at the entire scope of what we're dealing with, we find that there really is no proper place within the architecture we've established thus far that would house any third-party code or framework libraries existing in the /vendor folder (and not already included by default in the stock Laravel installation). But, when we try to model this in a simple UML diagram, we can see that there is indeed a dependency that must exist for every line which is pointing the wrong way (i.e., "away" from the domain layer), indicating that the domain relies on code and components located outside of the domain layer when the dependencies should point *toward* the domain layer so that the code outside of the domain relies on the classes in the domain model (Figure 8-6).

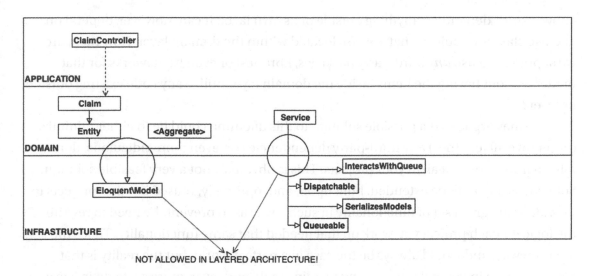

Figure 8-6. *Dependencies going in the wrong direction*

Breaking the Rules?

To form a better architecture for our application, we are going to have to break a rule that purists would put up a fight to protect. Let me explain.

We need to be flexible in the way we think and perceive the development of our applications. Laravel is a framework. That in itself goes against one of DDD's foundational opinions that frameworks are too constrictive to be used in a domain-driven project. We as developers need to understand that the nature of software and web development is such that we hardly ever build anything truly "from scratch." I myself cannot tell you the last time I wrote an entire program, not just a script or a one-off, starting from an empty directory and a single blank PHP file. The simple fact is that the purist mindset can only exist in a perfect world. Seeing as though the world is far from perfect, we need to be a little more realistic in our thought processes and our opinions.

Our first attempt at creating a new structure for the app technically will work, but it is far from being an optimized solution. The components that make Laravel valuable to us need a place to live so that our code can utilize and extend it. Obviously, this place is the /vendor folder, and the items that we reference inside the /vendor folder all have a structured namespace that reside within the different packages. However, when you consider that, in a layered architecture, the domain layer (aka the business rules and "low-level" policies that correspond to the implementation that you are working with) is supposed to be self-encapsulating. Nothing within the domain layer is supposed to know, use, or depend on anything outside of its own layer. It can, however, depend on and use classes or objects that are *also* located within the domain layer. How then, are we supposed to use *any* third-party packages, libraries, or even frameworks for that matter without having the items inside the domain layer utilize any code existing outside its layer?

One may argue that a possible solution to this dilemma could be to either minimize (or remove all together) any third-party dependencies or, even more ridiculous, don't rely on frameworks at all in your projects. This is obviously not a very feasible solution. Software is meant to be extended, built upon, and, optimally, reused in other projects to provide some given set of functionality in such a way as to prevent the need to rewrite the logic for each project you work on that needed that same functionality. That's the idea, anyway, and would always be the case in a perfect world, but the reality is that software reuse in general is a challenging thing to do and, even more so, to do in a way that is extendable, flexible, and loosely coupled to the other pieces of the application while utilizing as much outside code as you can.

In fact, this is the driving concept in an area of modern-day software development known as *rapid application development*. The idea in rapid development is to implement your features, business logic, and anything else you need the system to do functionally using as many third-party packages, libraries, and frameworks as you possibly can, thereby freeing up your time and effort to focus on the higher-level concerns and the important, required pieces vital to the system's success (take this to mean the domain model). All the third-party code is there for you to use to build out features and functionality that are common to many other applications. For example, there are a lot of libraries out there on GitHub and in open source packages for common concerns in software, including things such as logging, ORM concerns, or CRUD packages. These are meant to be easy to use and allow you to rely on third-party libraries so you don't have to reinvent the wheel for common concerns such as these.

Another possible solution is to invert the dependencies, as in the dependency inversion principle. The general concept of this principle is broken down into two separate rules.

- Abstractions should not depend on details. Details (concrete implementations) should depend on abstractions.

- High-level modules should not depend on low-level modules. Both should depend on abstractions (e.g., interfaces).

So, what this means for us is that we can use interfaces (abstractions) to make the dependencies point in the other direction (inward toward the domain model). The problem with that for our usage is that there really isn't a clear-cut way to extract abstractions out of domain models; they are meant to be self-containing and have all the knowledge relating to the domain within its layer. Also, because we want to leverage the Eloquent framework within our domain models, inverting the dependencies would still leave us with a domain model that knows about things outside of the domain layer.

Evolving Paradigms

The explosion of frameworks, libraries, packages, and tools we've witnessed just over the last two decades has made enough of an impact to completely change the way we write code; however, the way we think about code hasn't changed a whole lot since the 1980s and 1990s. Sure, we are more aware of the impact our code has and as a result are more careful about selecting the best locations for the functionality created to make the software work, and we have learned to be agile in our involvement of domain experts and stakeholders in the frequent decision-making that happens in successful projects. However, the way we think about software is basically the same as it was a long time ago. Object-oriented programming has been around since the 1960s, and that is still the most popular general paradigm in use to build most modern-day software and web applications. The design patterns debut book released in 1994 by the Gang of Four is still the driving force behind all these latest and greatest frameworks and "can't live without" packages that make our lives easier and our potential for success higher.

What has happened in the last few decades is, in my opinion, just the natural evolutionary process that web development programming has endured; we have only just recently adopted those standards that were discovered so long ago but that still hold true today in the web development industry. More recently, another example can be seen in the evolution of front-end web development practices and languages. Frameworks such as Vue.JS, Angular, and React all have foundational roots in programming paradigms discovered 70 years ago. Although it may *appear* that front-end web development has taken on a new form, really all that is happening is the same thing that happened to general web development around the year 2000: it is evolving. The number of programming languages has exploded over the last 20 or so years as well, usually with the intent of being tools to specifically cater to newly discovered business concerns that have arisen along with the web development demand.

A similar thing is happening to the thought processes surrounding web development. The purist mentality has good intentions and is by no means wrong or bad, but in my opinion, being a "purist" toward any particular technology, language, process, or architectural direction puts a mental blockade, albeit a subconscious one, between the current way we know how to do something and a new (often improved) way of accomplishing the same thing, causing our ability to evolve as developers to stagnate. Our understanding of development as we know it are (ideally) based on best practices that we had to spend time and effort to understand, and even more time and effort to use in our applications *effectively*. Oftentimes that understanding that we've worked so hard to achieve is the exact thing that ends up holding us back from utilizing the next advancement in the industry. These advancements, of course, take many different forms out in the wild, from new versions of long-loved languages (PHP 7.0, JavaScript ES6, and HTML 5 to name a few) to the introduction of completely new ways of thinking about the development process (Angular and Vue.JS), but their ending result is ultimately the same: a working piece of software, web application, API interface, or something more advanced such as a microservice architecture that is centered around Google RPC (gRPC) protocol buffers. You can find more information on protocol buffers at `https://grpc.io`.

Now, that's not to say that design patterns, SOLID principles, and other such standards and practices regarding software architecture and web development are not going to be around for much longer. On the contrary, understanding these types of universal concepts is crucial to becoming a good developer, and they will lay the path, if used correctly, to create a long-lived, high-quality piece of software. But, what we have to be careful of is our complete obedience to a single concern or paradigm in our personal web development practices. A long time ago, the world was thought to be flat. I bet if you went back to that time and made a suggestion that the world was round, you would be laughed at, ridiculed for your noneducated argument, and maybe even killed. Even though the world is indeed round, the mentality back in the day was that it was flat. It took quite a while (I would imagine) for the rest of the population to catch up and adopt the idea after it was introduced by the ancient Greeks. The same is true for web development. It takes time, many experiments, many attempted-and-faileds for the community as a whole to accept and adopt a new standard of doing it differently.

A Change in Thinking

The biggest change to our thinking we are going to have to make involves the dependency inversion principle and the domain encapsulation practice that is at the heart of domain-driven design. It is important that we encapsulate our domain model in some sort of conceptual boundary that separates the concerns of the domain from the concerns of the application or infrastructure that handles the song and dance of the domain layer objects (be it persisting them, initializing them, re-creating them, logging them, etc.).

There are various ways to handle architecting web applications. For example, in the wild (or whenever starting a new job or inheriting a legacy codebase), what tends to happen is that the project's development is directed not by best practices but by a strict adherence to the famous "just make it work!" paradigm. Oftentimes in startups what tends to happen is that whatever system they have built to make them money or serve as a proof of concept for inventors to get them to invest money into the business is built with slapped-together code that is messy, hard to maintain, and even harder to teach someone else about. The rapid application development paradigm runs parallel to this concept: start the development process with as many prebuilt things as you can, then customize what you need to in order to create the desired functionality, hack together the (at this time) "rough" business policies and practices that are indeed still being defined and established at the point of the application's inception, push it out to production, rinse and repeat.

There's nothing inherently wrong with this approach from a technical or programming perspective; after all, the name of the programming game is code reusability and abstraction. The problem usually rears its head when the codebase grows and at some point collapses under the weight of its own infrastructure, thereby rendering the application useless or increasing the time it takes to make modifications and additions to it as the business needs get more complex and involved. At that point, the company owning the software is usually forced to make a crucial decision and either refactor the system in its entirety or, the worse of the two evils, create the whole thing from scratch starting at the bottom. The latter option has been proven time and time again in the coding industry to almost always fail, because when you start from scratch, you have to solve all the problems, issues, and malfunctions with this new application that you did with the old one.

We should all be more receptive to new ideas and not allow our current understanding of how things work or our knowledge of the best way to do something interfere with new and better thought processes, tools, concepts, and practices. The very practices and standards that are constantly evolving in our digital ecosystem are what makes our industry less malleable—the industry of course being one that is constantly redefining and reshaping itself to meet the ever-growing needs of modern-day business requirements.

Getting back to our problem at hand, what we could do is break the rules and have our domain entities extend the Eloquent base `Model` class, understanding that we are simply using it as a means to allow the models and things inside the domain layer to utilize the features within the framework via extending them or including them via a trait, and nothing else. If we stick to just relying on an outside class or trait offered by the framework, we can then keep our overall structure of the application intact, still clearly and cleanly separate the various concerns into their corresponding layers, and still have our boundaries established between layers, while still leveraging the power of Laravel.

Conclusion

In worse-case scenarios, the architects and developers who aren't up to par with current standards and best practices will "determine" that the whole system is bad and that they have to rewrite it, from the ground up—basically for the sake of rewriting it. Then, although it may appear by all logical reason to be a quicker implementation on the second go-around, this next version is doomed to have the same issues and shortcomings as the last one did. The reason for this could vary.

- An overly complex domain that is hard to model

- Architects who lack the proper experience needed to design a quality system that will meet all the project's requirements

- Developers who lack general software development experience (either low level or high level)

- Developers who lack the domain experience (although you'd obviously not want to put someone new in charge of architecting the entire system or part of it)

- Company politics that are preventing progress

- "Experts" who are part of the company's engineering team preventing technological advancements and new, improved processes and standards

- Other team members who are reluctant to change their own ways in favor of learning new, oftentimes improved, development practices

- Some members (or even a single member) of a team who are reluctant to accept automation processes, even though it may save time, effort, and money

- Close-mindedness

- An inability or desire to learn

- And many, many others...

This approach to software development isn't very efficient; however, it may not actually appear to be that bad because, at the time, finding adequate packages and libraries to use in your application and then gluing them together is generally pretty fast to build (that's why it's called rapid application development). This is somewhat of a dangerous misconception that can have profound consequences when and if the business grows and becomes successful for the reasons listed earlier.

One way to mitigate this is to use good design principles and design patterns as well as abstractions and interfaces, which really equates to good architecture. We find that when we employ good principles and standards when architecting the system, we allow ourselves flexibility in the sense that we have planned for change. We leave our code open for extension but closed for modification by employing the use of interfaces and/or abstract classes to define the various parts of our application that change. In this manner, other code can interact and be used within our application by simply extending that interface and plugging it into the application. Things like this can get complex, but the proper use and understanding of Laravel's service container, including how to set up implementations that get loaded and run automatically when certain internal conditions are met. The service container is powerful and provides us with a level of flexibility that is extremely useful for managing dependencies and creating customized dependency injection configurations that operate on a contextual basis. For more information on the service container, see Chapter 4.

In this chapter, we gave our application's structure a starting point. Although the various concepts and boundaries between the layers may be slightly blurred at this point, we can utilize what we have to forge the necessary functionality together to get our application off the ground. This structure is far from perfect, and we will be modifying it as we progress through the rest of the book, when it makes sense to. Whenever it helps clarify the intent of the application and whenever we can leverage the framework for the common tasks present in all web applications, we will do so.

But we must not lose sight of the domain. Although this chapter has been a heavily involved Laravel-related chapter, we should always maintain the notion that the domain is the most important thing, and the best way we can move forward is by allowing the domain to drive the construction of the application. By allowing our models to implement Eloquent's base class and by implementing such functionality as dispatchable events, services, and Laravel jobs, we have access to all the features of Laravel without breaking too many rules. What we are going to begin to see is that the layered architecture we've presented in this book is only one way to structure an application such as ones created with DDL. There are better ways to separate things, which we will be exploring later. For now, we have a structure that will work and that will give us a foundation to build the initial functionality required by the project. Later, we will start developing a better way to structure the components by utilizing use cases and hexagonal architecture.

PART II

A Domain-Driven Approach

CHAPTER 9

A Domain-Driven Approach to Claim Submission

This chapter will hold the meat and potatoes (the "main course") of the domain-driven dinner we are cooking up. As such, I will include some additional details about the `Claim` domain so we can continue to use the example throughout the book. We will improve the application as we go on, incrementally adding value. That is the name of the game in DDD. Let's get to it!

Additional Background Knowledge

To provide solutions for the various validations we still need to perform (on an object level), you will need some additional information about how the process is structured. In the real world, you would have to do a number of things over a period of time to cultivate enough knowledge to be comfortable working on the requirements, including talking with domain experts, cultivating a ubiquitous language, and implementing that language in the code and in any other communications regarding the domain. In addition, you'd have to make prototypes, refine them, and deal with any unforeseen bugs or issues once the application goes live and is used by real users.

© Jesse Griffin 2021
J. Griffin, *Domain-Driven Laravel*, https://doi.org/10.1007/978-1-4842-6023-4_9

CPT Codes

This is where things get a little more complicated in our claim project. The medical billing and coding standards that are in effect for Medi-Cal claim submissions get very involved. Here is the definition (from MedicalBillingAndCoding.org) of a CPT code:

"CPT codes are used to describe tests, surgeries, evaluations, and any other medical procedure performed by a healthcare provider on a patient. As you might imagine, this code set is extremely large, and includes the codes for thousands upon thousands of medical procedures."

—MedicalBillingAndCoding.org

The "CPT" potion of CPT code stands for "current procedural terminology." They are not kidding about the size of the CPT code list, which contains virtually every medical procedure that a doctor could ever do on a patient. The list is maintained by the American Medical Association (`https://www.ama-assn.org/`). Table 9-1 provides the different ranges that dictate the type of CPT code.

Table 9-1. *CPT Code Procedure Category Ranges*

CPT Code Range	Category
00100 to 01999; 99100 to 99140	Anesthesia
10021 to 69990	Surgery
70010 to 79999	Radiology
80047 to 89398	Pathology and Laboratory
90281 to 99199; 99500 to 99607	Medicine
99201 to 99499	Evaluation and Management

As you can see, the CPT code ranges are broken down into six main categories of procedures. Additionally, there are CPT code categories that classify each CPT code into groups.

- *CPT Category I*: The largest body of codes consisting of those commonly used by providers to report their services and procedures

- *CPT Category II*: Supplemental tracking codes used for performance management

- *CPT Category III*: Temporary codes used to report emerging and experimental services and procedures

To give a little more context to what the categories and types actually represent, here are a few examples of some common CPT codes describing various face-to-face consultations for a few different scenarios:

- **99202**: Represents a new office patient visit for a problem-focused medical treatment

- **99213**: Represents an established patient visit for a problem-focused medical treatment

- **99221-213**: Range of codes that indicate initial hospital care for a new patient

- **99281-85**: ER visits

The other aspect of CPT codes that is important to the billing and processing of Medi-Cal claims is the amount that gets paid to the provider (which is the cost that the federal FQHC endures for treatment and medical services done for the patient). When professionals in the industry speak of this relationship, they refer to it as either a *paycode sheet* or a *fee schedule*.

The concept of a CPT code combo arises from the fact that, more often than not, a typical visit to the doctor's office entails multiple CPT codes that correspond to the variety of treatments given to the patient. It is this combination of multiple CPTs that the FQHC uses to establish the price paid to the providers giving the treatment. It's important to note that the paycode sheets (aka fee schedules) are *not* set by the same organization that maintains the CPT coding standard.

Note   To see a full list of CPT codes broken down by category of procedure, check out the Coder search tool provided at `https://coder.aapc.com/cpt-codes/?_ga=2.39310822.419811336.1574365287-1004373537.1574365287`. It will only give you limited information on any given procedure unless you spend a good chunk of money to purchase the software that looks up CPT codes for you and allows you to search for procedures codes with plain text.

Table 9-2 provides an example of a few common CPT codes used in the industry.

Table 9-2. *Sample CPT Codes and Their Fee Structure That Determines How Much the Physicians Get Paid for Services to Medi-Cal Patients*

CPT Code	Description	Ages	Rate
90654	Influenza virus vaccine, split virus, preservative free, for intradermal use	19+	$19.00
99384	Initial comprehensive preventive medicine evaluation and management of an individual including an age- and gender-appropriate history, examination, counseling/anticipatory guidance/risk factor reduction interventions, and the ordering of laboratory/diagnostic procedures; new patient; adolescent (age 12 through 17 years)	12–17	$25.00
99213	Represents an established patient visit for a problem-focused medical treatment	12–17	$50.00
2000F	Physical evaluation	12–17	$30.00

In Table 9-2, we find a few CPT codes along with their corresponding description of what the procedure is or involves, the age of the patient for which the treatment applies (or age range), and the rate paid to the provider for their services. Note that the rates for these CPT codes are for that individual CPT code. We also have instances where there are going to be multiple CPT codes (called *CPT combos*) that directly affect the amount that the provider gets paid. The following is an example of a combination in which two single CPT codes apply and describe a set of services received as the patient's treatment. CPT combos also all have specific rates paid out on a Medi-Cal claim.

Example Claim with Combinations of CPT Codes

As an example, let's say that there was a CPT combo that existed to describe a scenario where a patient who is 18 or under visits the doctor's office in preparation for going to a new school in the fall. Since the patient wants to play sports, he needs a physical exam as well as standard immunizations as required by the school.

Note   Due to the complexity involved in the underlying medical terminology used in real-world CPT code descriptors, instead of including a bunch of irrelevant medical terminology and/or an anatomy lesson to decipher what the CPT codes actually mean, I have just made up some arbitrary codes to give you some context about the purpose of the application. The codes don't really matter—what does matter is that we understand the basic concepts of this system so that we can properly solve the problems introduced in the validation context.

- The patient was given a medical evaluation as an "established" patient (one that is already registered in the system at the time of exam).

  - CPT code: 99213

- The patient was given standard vaccinations required by public schools for Hepatitis A and B.

  - CPT code: 99384

- The patient was given a physical evaluation so he can play sports next year.

  - CPT code: 2000F

If you refer to Table 9-2, you may think that a logical approach to coming up with an estimated claim amount for the claim described would be to add up the various individual rates for each given CPT code (shown in the previous list), which would yield $124 (as derived from Table 9-2). However, life isn't that simple. The paycode sheet is what dictates how much is paid out to the provider completing the services and treatment, for both single procedures or combinations. We won't worry too much about this right now, as the process of estimating a claim's amount is handled in a different context and chapter. In the context of validating the claim itself, we need to ensure the following:

- The individual CPT codes are all valid
- The CPT code combinations are valid and exist in the respective providers

Another important thing to note is that CPT codes generally have a specific age range associated with them, and claims that include these types of codes must meet the age requirements and restrictions; if they don't, the procedure will not be valid, and the claim will not be paid. We will want to include some validation check upon submission of a claim so that we can catch any errors before they hit the FQHC for final verification of the claim and payment to the provider.

Obviously, CPT codes are pretty much a pain for everyone involved, especially the receptionists at the practice or provider's office who is actually doing the billing, coding, and creating of the claim.

Note   This is a known pain point, which is the exact type of problem that software aims to automate, segregate, and alleviate.

With the background information out of the way, let's start coding the models we will use in the system as they relate to the billing and coding portions of our domain model.

Developing the Eloquent Models

We know we have to create models for the static information common to all procedures in the system. Specifically, the CPT code must include the various properties that describe the CPT code and separate it from many other CPT codes. We will also have to model the CPT code combination as a separate eloquent model to keep the static knowledge of which CPT code combinations are valid in the system.

CPT Codes and Providers

To the provider, CPT codes represent the foundational procedures that are used to treat a patient, which is of course the bloodline of their operation as medical practitioners or medical practices (pun not intended!). The federal Medi-Cal system works on a strict reimbursement structure that mandates the work performed on a patient be done before the provider is paid for their services. The "strict" structure comes in the form of CPT code combinations. The provider selects the specific CPT codes within our application during the submission of claim, and the system then validates those codes to make sure that there is a matching combination that exists in the paycode sheet for that provider.

How should we model this in our system? What could we do to account for the code combinations being multiple single CPT codes? Keep in mind that providers will want to see an estimated claim amount for the codes that were listed in the claim before the claim is actually submitted. There are a few concerns we will need to consider when we are constructing a model.

- Modeling a single CPT code
- Modeling a single CPT code combination, made up of multiple CPT codes

CPT Codes and the Claims

A submitted claim will hold all the relevant patient data, linked documents, and other important information about the procedures and treatment that they have performed on a given patient for a given day. CPT codes also must be present on the claim, but what's the best way to do that? Tack this one on to the concern list:

- Creating a way to tie multiple CPT codes to a claim

CPT Codes and Paycode Sheets

A paycode sheet holds the actual amount that the provider makes for each given CPT code combination. There is one paycode sheet for many providers; however, only one single unique provider can be specified on a given paycode sheet. We need to include this constraint in modeling the paycode sheets. How we model the CPT code and CPT code combinations within the domain model will dictate how we should design the paycode sheet. The reason for this is that the paycode sheets contain the amounts paid to providers on a per-CPT code combination basis, not at the individual CPT code level. You could even say that this is a dependency that we will have to figure out when we go to model paycode sheets.

- Creating a way to store per-provider rates on a per-CPT code combination basis

---

Note   We will go over a breakdown of the components that we would need to include in our design to meet the current needs of the system; however, I won't waste page space with a bunch of PHP source code that is already included online in this book's Git repository. We will, of course, discuss all the components in the design, how they fit into the overall architecture, and how to go about designing a model-driven and domain-focused system. To give you a better understanding of how things fit together, I include relevant source code wherever it makes sense in the hopes of simplifying the design or clarifying any blurred concepts in the domain. For a full look at the source code, please visit the GitHub repository online.

CPT Codes and CPT Code Combos

Although a CPT code can be considered a value object by all technicalities, the implications that the concept itself brings to the table from the perspective of Laravel is somewhat obfuscated. This is actually one area that a DDL doesn't have a good solution for. I discuss these implications in a later chapter.

CPT Code Structure and Translation

For now, let's continue modeling the CPT code portion of the application within the context of a Laravel application using the Eloquent ORM. We will start with modeling a basic CPT code. For this, we know that all CPT codes are different, which is signified by their code property that uniquely identifies them (such as 99213). There are different categories of code that a CPT code belongs to, along with different types of procedures (surgery, radiology, medical visits and examinations, etc.). We will want to capture this information in our model. Table 9-3 is a first attempt at a database schema. It includes an English description of the procedure, the CPT (category schedule in 1, 2, or 3), the procedure group (type), and whether or not it's a pediatric code (i.e., procedure done on a child younger than 3). The design depicted in Table 9-3 captures all of the required data regarding a single CPT code.

Table 9-3. *Sample Database Row for a Given CPT Code*

id	description	Code	category	group	is pediatric
1	Expanded, problem-focused visit either as an in-office visit or as an outpatient visit	99213	1	Evaluation & Management	0

We give it an auto-incrementing id field so we can track the code throughout the system. This field is a primary key so we can use it to create our CPT combos and allow individual CPT codes to be referenced on the claim when the providers are selecting the procedures that were completed on a given patient for that day. Figure 9-1 shows the CPT model.

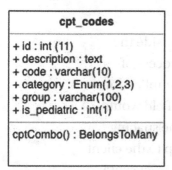
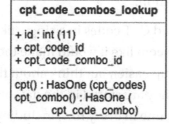

Figure 9-1. *A UML diagram of the cpt_code, cpt_code_combo, and intermediate lookup table*

The next concern we face is modeling the combinations of CPT codes.

One thing we need to keep in mind when designing this portion of the application is the way we are going to store the code combinations. We have a few options:

1. Store a comma-separated list of individual CPT codes inside a column in the cpt_code_combos table

2. Create a pivot table that will join the various CPT codes to form CPT code combos (as shown earlier)

When facing decisions such as these, it helps to take each possibility and cycle it through the would-be requirements or use cases that it impacts (touches). For example, consider the use case of when a provider goes to submit a claim. All they would see is a form field with a drop-down and an autocompleted list of the various CPT codes, listed by name. They would select one or more codes from the drop-down menu; then they would expect to see an estimated claim amount before they submit the claim. To derive the estimated claim amount, we would need a mechanism in our application that would query a paycode sheet, which ties together the CPT codes (via CPT code combos) and the providers, specifying the amount that each is worth. The estimated amount would then be the result of querying this paycode sheet with the provider's ID and CPT code combo on the claim.

Getting back to the question of how to model a CPT code combo, we are going to have to query the database to find out whether a given CPT code combo exists and then select the corresponding record in the paycode sheet for that combination of codes. Would it, then, be easier to do this with the solution described in option 1 in the previous list, or is option 2 the better way to go? Well, let's run each through the now clarified way we would use them in the application.

1. Storing a list of separated CPT codes in a single field inside the CPT code combo may seem like it would make the process of selecting them in a group easier, but think about the implications of doing this: the way they are stored in the database field would have to be exactly the same in every row, including the spacing between the CPT code IDs. This would also leave it up to the client to ensure (which isn't usually the best way to go) the exact syntax for the combination. Another consideration would be whether to list them in any particular order, again keeping in mind that the client would be responsible for keeping the order of CPT codes in the *exact* format that the database uses. However, querying the table for a combination based on the corresponding CPT codes would be quite easy, We could do it in a single database call.

2. While this solution does take away the benefit of storing the combination itself and the codes that comprise the combination living in the same model and database table, it has a number of desired benefits: it alleviates the need to maintain any kind of structure for the individual codes (if they were in one field), plus we don't have to worry about parsing out the string of CPT codes to find which combo they belong to. On the other hand, since we are given the individual CPT codes to work with, the process of figuring out which combination the codes belong to (if that

combo exists) is much more complex than just querying a single field of comma-separated CPT code IDs, mainly because CPT codes themselves may belong to more than one combination. For example, oftentimes a standard office visit is submitted alongside additional procedures that were done as part of that visit, but they are billed differently depending on which codes follow the one indicating an office visit.

There may be other considerations to think about when choosing the proper logical way to handle representing the particular elements involved in this particular use case. With the current information given, even though option 2 is much more elegant than the first solution, the simplicity offered by option 1 is a straightforward approach to solving the issue at hand. Having a comma-separated list of CPT codes will simplify saving and retrieving the CPT code combos by limiting the number of tables and cross-table (or even cross-database) queries required to calculate the estimated claim amount. However, if we chose to go this route, it would take away all the functionality we would gain in our Eloquent models, because there would be no relationships.

The answer to this problem is to use *both* solutions described. We want to have our Eloquent models set up properly with the correct relationship, which in this case would be many-to-many relations with a pivot table (lookup table). Eloquent provides an easy interface to set this up, which we describe in more detail in later chapters. We also need to have a way to find a specific CPT code combo given the individual CPT codes, which we are unable to do using only option 2. Having a single field within the CPT combo table allows us to query the combination that is referenced by the set of CPT codes.

Listing 9-1 actually shows the code for the model classes, without concern for the comma-separated CPT codes.

Listing 9-1. Initial Version of the CptCode model, with a Many-to-Many Relationship to the CptCodeCombo Model

```
// ddl/Claim/Submission/Domain/Models/CptCode.php

<?php
namespace Claim\Submission\Domain\Models;

use Illuminate\Database\Eloquent\Model;

class CptCode extends Model
```

```
{
    public $table = 'cpt_codes';

    protected $guarded = ['id'];

    public function cptCodeCombos()
    {
        return $this->belongsToMany(CptCodeCombo::class,
        'cpt_code_combo_lookup');
    }
}
```

Notice in Listing 9-1 that we have specified a many-to-many relationship to the CptCodeCombo class as well as the specified pivot table cpt_code_combo_lookup. Of course, we would still have to create the pivot table with that name, which we would do with a migration, specifying the IDs from both the CPT code and the CPT code combo. For a look at the migration, check out the online repository. For now, let's continue to model the CPT code combo, which would look like Listing 9-2.

Listing 9-2. The Inverse Relationship to the CPT Code Model

```
<?php
namespace Claim\Submission\Domain\Models;
use Claim\Submission\Domain\Models\CptCode;
use Illuminate\Database\Eloquent\Model;
class CptCodeCombo extends Model
{
    public $table = 'cpt_code_combos';
    protected $guarded = ['id'];
    public function cptCodes()
    {
        return $this->belongsToMany(CptCode::class, 'cpt_code_combo_lookup');
    }
}
```

The database schema for the CPT code combo is fairly simple because we really just need it to be a container with which to reference multiple CPT codes. All we will include at this point is an ID field along with Description and Notes columns (just to give the table a little more context), but it could even do without these fields. Table 9-4 provides the schema for a CPT code combo.

Table 9-4. *A Sample from the CPT Code Combo Table*

ID	Description	Notes
1	A problem-focused visit followed by immunizations	Some arbitrary notes

The only other thing we would need for this to work would be the pivot table that holds both table's IDs so that we could have the various CPT code IDs relate to exactly one CPT code combo, which would look like Table 9-5.

Table 9-5. *Sample Records from the Pivot Table That Links Any Number of CPT Codes to a Single CPT Code Combo*

id	cpt_code_id	cpt_code_combo_id
1	1	1
2	2	1

With the setup we have created, we could then do things like find out the individual CPT codes for a particular combo.

```
$cptCodeCombo = CptCodeCombo::find(1);
$cptCodes = $cptCodeCombo->cptCodes->toArray();
print_r($cptCodes);
```

This would give us the following as a result:

```
Array
(
    [0] => Array
        (
            [id] => 1
            [description] => Expanded, problem focused visit either as
            an in-office visit or an outpatient visit.
```

```
            [code] => 99213
            [category] => 1
            [group] => Evaluation and Management
            [is_pediatric] => 0
            [pivot] => Array
                (
                    [cpt_code_combo_id] => 1
                    [cpt_code_id] => 1
                )
        )
    [1] => Array
        (
            [id] => 2
            [description] => Immunizations for Influenza
            [code] => 90605
            [category] => 1
            [group] => Immunizations
            [is_pediatric] => 0
            [pivot] => Array
                (
                    [cpt_code_combo_id] => 1
                    [cpt_code_id] => 2
                )
        )
)
```

If you take a closer look at the resulting array shown previously, Eloquent already included the pivot table we created automatically, without specifying anything but the table name in the ManyToMany relationships inside the corresponding models. This is a powerful way to describe your entities and models in terms of the relationships they have with other models in the system. This would also allow us to find all the given CPT code combos that a particular CPT code belongs to.

```
$cptCode = CptCode::find(1);
$cptCodeCombos = $cptCode->cptCodeCombos->toArray();
print_r($cptCodeCombos);
```

This produces the following output:

```
Array
(
    [0] => Array
        (
            [id] => 1
            [notes] => In office exam + Immunization shots
            [description] => ...some description
            [pivot] => Array
                (
                    [cpt_code_id] => 2
                    [cpt_code_combo_id] => 1
                )
        )
    [1] => Array
        (
            [id] => 2
            [notes] => TEST
            [description] => fasdfasdf
            [pivot] => Array
                (
                    [cpt_code_id] => 2
                    [cpt_code_combo_id] => 2
                )
        )
)
```

As you can see, Eloquent sees that there is a pivot table for the supplied relationship, and auto-detects it without specifying anything but the table name we chose when writing the migration for the cpt_code_combo_lookup table. This is extremely beneficial because it not only allows us to query the logical relationships that are derived from that data that it represents, but it also alleviates the hassle of building an additional model in our domain layer to account for the pivot table itself. Laravel does all of this for us. Most of the time, we have to build in and manage that ourselves and create countless specific queries to get the data we need to fulfill whatever task we are working on. If there is additional data in your pivot table that you need when you pull out the corresponding database objects that they reference (in this case, the `cpt_code_id` and `cpt_code_combo_id`), you always have access to the virtual pivot table model that Eloquent creates in the background by means of a `pivot` attribute on the returned model.

```
$cptCodeCombo = CptCode::find(1);
$cptCodeCombos = $cptCode->cptCodeCombos->pivot->description;
```

In the previous table, the description is located in the pivot table, which would be used if you needed a granular way to describe something that would exist on *every* relationship, for every record in the database. A less granular approach would be to store the description inside `cptCodeCombos` itself to describe the relationship (that could be composed of several other relationships) to give meaning to a model containing relationships with multiple other models.

This is all fine and dandy, but it still doesn't exactly solve the problem of selecting a single combo from a list of CPT codes. One way to handle that problem is to adopt the solution described in option 1 a few pages back and to have the `cpt_codes` values listed from least to greatest and separated by commas; then we can use a group concat in the SQL query. We will continue this discussion in Chapter X and explore the details of this requirement.

Paycode Sheets (aka Fee Schedules)

Paycode sheets can be thought of as a per-provider set of rates for a given set of CPT codes (enter CPT code combos). In a nutshell, a paycode sheet is the amount that a provider will settle for various services described by CPT code combos. Basically, it is the provider's *value* of their services. A paycode sheet is specific to each provider and usually exists in the context of the FQHC, which in turn is composed of practices, each of them with many providers. We need to model this in software. Here are the relationships to the other models in our application:

- There are many providers on any given paycode sheet.

- There are thousands of possible CPT code combinations (the average is 2,500).

- Each provider is paid a given rate for their services based on the CPT code combination that captures the procedures given to a patient, for a particular claim.

When broken down like this, we can assume we are dealing with a good amount of data that needs to be captured and modeled. We can estimate this as follows:

```
Total # of Providers in a given FQHC Center:    800
Total # of CPT Code Combinations                2500
Total # of FQHC Centers                         5
---------------

10,000,000 (Ten Million Rows)
```

Remember, the centers each have their own paycode sheet, containing records in it for every provider, and each provider has an agreed-upon *rate* at which they were paid out for every individual procedure, which gets represented by one of or more CPT code combos. So, the CPT code combos themselves comprise multiple single CPT codes. Wow! That sounds complicated (Figure 9-2). In times like these, it never hurts to break out the dry-erase marker (or if you're like me, old-fashioned pens and Moleskine notebooks) and diagram it.

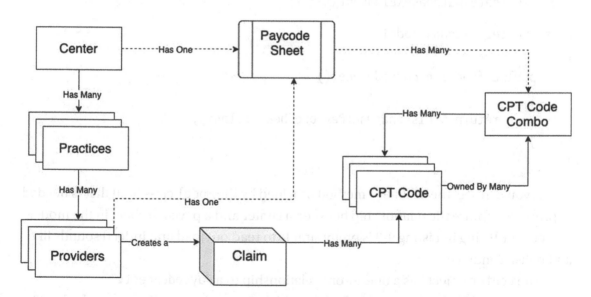

Figure 9-2. *The associations between the central components in the application and their relationship to a paycode sheet*

When you model things in terms of their relationship to other objects in the system and choose specific keywords to describe these relationships ("has many," "owned by many," etc.), it not only becomes much easier to understand the entire system model in terms of the individual pieces that comprise it, but we can use Eloquent's powerful relationship methods as the mechanism for which to describe the ones depicted earlier, in the same terminology that results in the code being written so that it makes an English sentence. The reason this is really cool is that memorizing an English sentence like "A center has one paycode sheet" is much easier to remember than a bunch of specific method calls (Listing 9-3).

Listing 9-3. An Easy-to-Read Model Class Center That Contains a "Has One" Relationship to a PaycodeSheet

```php
<?php

namespace Claim\Submission\Domain\Models;

use Illuminate\Database\Eloquent\Model;

class Center extends Model
{
    public function paycodeSheet()
    {
        return $this->hasOne(PaycodeSheet::class);
    }
}
```

As you can see, the `hasOne()` method provided by the `Model` class is all that is needed to properly capture the relationship between a center and a paycode sheet in the model. The `center` listing in Listing 9-3 is pretty simple to read out load and indeed sounds like an English sentence:

"The `Center` object has a one-to-one relationship to a `PaycodeSheet`."

However, what if you wanted to find out which centers have a given paycode sheet? You would just have to create the *inverse* relationship on the `PaycodeSheet` model (Listing 9-4).

Listing 9-4. A Sample FQHC Center Class with the Relationship to the
PaycodeSheet Class Explicitly Defined

```php
<?php

namespace Claim\Submission\Domain\Models;

use Illuminate\Database\Eloquent\Model;

class PaycodeSheet extends Model
{
    public function center()
    {
        return $this->belongsToOne(Center::class);
    }
}
```

In Listing 9-4, we simply added a new method whose name corresponds to the `Model`
class that the relationship references. This one also sounds like an English sentence:

"A `PaycodeSheet` belongs to a `center.`

For the purposes of this discussion and to cut down on the complexity, we will limit
our scope to just modeling a single paycode sheet for a single FQHC. On a high level,
without diving into the details of storing the CPT code combinations for each individual
claim, we can come up with a rough draft for the database schema.

Here are some additional considerations to make:

- How the data is coming into the system, and in what format.

- When to use data transfer objects (DTOs) to model responses
  returned to, for example, a client consuming the API.

- Document! Use tools like SwaggerHub to model your DTOs and the
  various endpoints that exist for the application.

The last item on that list has the biggest benefit to a project that has multiple
developers, such as front-end developers and backend developers, because the two can
work on the project separately without requiring that the other be complete. It basically
acts as a tool to decouple development efforts and ensure that one side of the fence
doesn't conflict with changes on the other.

In terms of paycode sheets, we aren't too concerned at this point about the storage of the CPT code combos within the claim. We simply want to model out the paycode sheet so that it can be ultimately used to assess the cost of a set of procedures for a given provider and (later) to determine a claim's estimated amount (which we will do in the Submission context; however, it actually occurs before the claim is submitted). Let's continue to model the data schema for a paycode sheet.

Tip   For the sake of brevity, I won't go through all the details and aspects of paycode sheets other than what we've discussed so far; however, when modeling real-world objects in software (which is arguably the majority of our job as developers), it is best to leave the specific data schema until the end of the modeling, when you have reached some sort of concrete, usable model that corresponds well to the domain in which it exists, including value objects, entities, services, etc. This is a better approach than attempting to flesh out the database schema first, because it is highly likely that the schema will change many times during the course of development. It is a good practice to ignore the data schema until you absolutely have to. *How* the data for our application will be stored should never be a primary focus point on a project. Keep the top priority on modeling the domain so that it corresponds as close as possible to the business model. That's not to say that the schema isn't an utterly important aspect to the application. Interestingly enough, not too long after your project is in production and has been running successfully, the team may realize that the most important thing is the data itself, because the rest of the application is just a way to manage the data in different views and formats.

Paycode Sheet Database Schema

The first clarification that must be made is how we are going to access the correct CPT code combo from a list of CPT codes. What we could do for now is add a field that will contain the comma-separated CPT codes on one of the tables. The best place would be the table that it actually pertains to the most, which would be `cpt_code_combo`.

Normally, having duplicate data in the database is a bad thing; however, in respect to domain-driven design, properly modeling the software in a manner that works for what you need it for trumps this best practice. In this instance, a case can be made for this comma-separated list because it will allow us to query it the way we need in order to extract the data that will become the estimated claim amount, which is an important concern to include in the system. Providers are always going to want to see the estimated amount paid on a claim before they submit it, so it is a must that this be an included feature.

That being said, Figure 9-3 shows a rough data schema for the paycode sheets, with the cpt_code_combo table updated to include a new field for the comma-separated list of CPT codes. Keep in mind that this may change in the future. For example, we may feel better about the contents of such a field if it were in some type of structured format (a JSON typed field could be an improvement to this design).

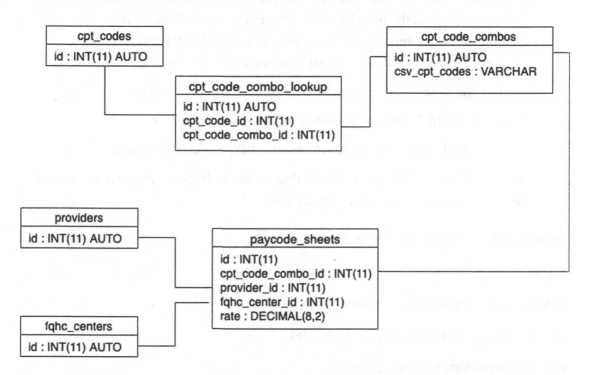

Figure 9-3. *The database schema for storing paycode sheets, including the other entities involved as well as the new csv_cpt_codes field containing a list of the CPT codes involved*

This is a pretty straightforward approach to modeling a paycode sheet in the system that allows for a clear separation of concerns between the codes, the combinations of codes, the provider, and the rate that the provider earns from completing each combo. Let's step through our notes and see whether this proposed schema addresses all the requirements of the system in regard to both paycode sheets and the application itself in terms of the interactions it has with the paycode sheets.

- The CPT codes are properly related to the claim in the form of CPT code combos.

- The paycode sheet are composed of many different cpt_code_combos values that are set up on a per-provider basis.

- We have the CPT codes saved in two places; although this is usually frowned upon, the initial draft of the architecture will utilize a comma-separated list of CPT codes within a given CPT code combo record, thereby making it possible for us to do the following:

  1. Get the CPT codes contained within a CPT code combo

  2. Get which CPT code combos include a single CPT code

  3. Get the CPT code combo from a list of specified CPT codes

Listing 9-5 shows the Eloquent models that make up the paycode sheet concept and its relation to the other models in our application.

Listing 9-5. The Paycode Sheet Model

```php
<?php

namespace Claim\Submission\Domain\Models;

use Illuminate\Database\Eloquent\Model;

class PaycodeSheet extends Model
{
    public function provider()
    {
        return $this->hasOne(Provider::class);
    }
```

```php
    public function cptCodeCombos()
    {
        return $this->hasOne(CptCodeCombo::class);
    }

    public function center()
    {
        return $this->hasOneThrough(Center::class, Provider::class);
    }
}
```

This is a pretty straightforward model and should be of no surprise. We can make the following sentence regarding paycode sheets:

"A paycode sheet belongs to one provider, who in turn is a member of an FQHC and also has a single CPT code combo that it relates to."

There is something else that we haven't yet thought about: if a paycode sheet is, in model terms, *one* of many possible combinations of procedures (CPT code combo) and the rate paid for those procedures (estimated claim amount).

After the creation of the PaycodeSheet model, we need to make the changes to the other models that it touches (the ones we added relations via class methods: Provider, CptCodeCombo, and Center). We will also add the Center class along with its relations to the other models in Listing 9-6.

Listing 9-6. The Updated Provider Model

```php
<?php

namespace Claim\Submission\Domain\Models;

use Illuminate\Database\Eloquent\Model;

class Provider extends Model
{
    public function patients()
    {
        return $this->hasMany(Patient::class);
    }
```

```php
    public function paycodeSheet()
    {
        return $this->hasOne(PaycodeSheet::class);
    }

    public function practice()
    {
        return $this->belongsTo(Practice::class);
    }
}
```

The Provider class is pretty self-explanatory. Notice that the paycodeSheet() method is what defines the relationship between a Provider and a Paycode Sheet in Listing 9-7. The only interesting thing about the Center model is the HasManyThrough relationship that it has with the Provider. Let's look at what the Center model could look like:

Listing 9-7. The New Center Model

```php
<?php

namespace Claim\Submission\Domain\Models;

use Illuminate\Database\Eloquent\Model;

class Center extends Model
{
    public function practices()
    {
        return $this->hasMany(Practice::class);
    }

    public function providers()
    {
        return $this->hasManyThrough(Provider::class, Practice::class);
    }
}
```

We will go into more details about Eloquent's relationship types and defining the inverses of those relationships. For now, all you need to recognize is the fact that there exists multiple providers belonging to a single center, and that relationship is captured as "Centers have many providers via their practices." These two statements give the same result, shown here:

```
$providersInCenter = Center::first()->providers;

//is the same as writing :
$providersInCenter Center::first()->practices()
                                ->get()
                                ->map (function(Practice $p) {
                                return $p->providers; })
                                ->all();
```

The HasManyThrough relationship is merely a shortcut way to get a relating record. It saves us the hassle of creating the SQL query to grab the rows via an INNER JOIN on the providers table and the practices tables to collect the rows we need (Listing 9-8).

Listing 9-8. The Updated Practice Class

```php
<?php

namespace Claim\Submission\Domain\Models;

use Illuminate\Database\Eloquent\Model;

class Practice extends Model
{
    public function center()
    {
        return $this->belongsTo(Center::class);
    }

    public function providers()
    {
        return $this->hasMany(Provider::class);
    }
}
```

The way we have defined the relationships here includes an inverse method on the related model. In Listing 9-8, the Practice model "has many" providers, meaning that the foreign key belongs on the farther model (providers.practice_id). On the other hand, the `Practice` model belongs to a center, so we can expect that the relational ID is on the nearer model (`practice.center_id`). When we define the inverse relationship between two models, it allows us to query in either direction.

```
$center = Practice::first()->center; //returns a Center object
```

```
$practices = Center::first()->practices //returns a Collection of
                                        //Practice objects
```

Conclusion

In this chapter, we took a look at additional details and domain-specific concepts, practices, and general knowledge about CPT codes and the healthcare billing system. When we model things in the real world, it is much easier to do so when you have a well-selected and utilized toolbelt of coding techniques (such as found in DDD); what makes these truly powerful is when they are paired up in an efficient manner with some means of implementation of the concepts into real, working code (such as what you get with Laravel). Modeling in Laravel is made simpler because of its use of fluent interfaces and well-named methods whose chains form real English sentences. What better way to describe your models and their relationships than in plain English? That way, there can be no miscommunications as to what a concept or model is or does. We will go more deeply into these topics in later chapters.

CHAPTER 10

A Domain-Driven Approach to Claim Validation

In this chapter, we will get more acquainted with the concepts and practices of domain-driven design by formally applying them, and I will explain how these practices relate to an application in the real world and to a Laravel project in particular. Most of these core strategies apply to a much broader scope than that of a framework, however. Many of them are meant to be applied to any project, regardless of the language or framework it was built with. In fact, when abstracting out a model of your domain, it is best to keep the focus on the domain itself rather than the technical concerns that come with it. The technical concerns can be deferred, which is a good thing in programming, because the longer they are deferred, the more thought you put into the project, and you can then make the best possible decision. The technical concerns are meant to give you ideas on how to solve complex problems that relate to the core of your domain so you can properly create a usable model out of it that closely mimics the business objects and practices within that domain.

I will mostly use examples derived from the claims submission project we introduced and elaborated on earlier in the book. Specifically, we will attempt to nail down the validation requirements as well as discuss the pre-conditions and post-conditions associated with the claim model and how best to implement such things in the code (spoiler alert: by keeping them contained within the entity or class for which the condition applies). We will also go over context maps: what they are, how to use them, and the various patterns used to describe the relationships within a context map. In doing so, we will gain a high-level view of the system's architecture, which will allow us to make better decisions in other contexts as well.

313

© Jesse Griffin 2021
J. Griffin, *Domain-Driven Laravel*, https://doi.org/10.1007/978-1-4842-6023-4_10

Note   The majority of the examples in this chapter will be derived from the Claim Validation context.

Where Laravel Fits In

Laravel provides you with an easy-to-use means of creating those non-domain-related portions of the app that consume, maintain, handle, or otherwise touch objects in the domain layer; these are things such as logging, caching, database to object representations, response generation, request validation, and others, the entirety of which is too long to include in the text.

Of course, in the end, the concepts of DDD are all just strategies for how to formulate a good design of your domain in such a way that can eventually be embellished in code. All the dirty work involved in doing whatever it is that you need it to do in relation to the core domain is still your responsibility to figure out. DDD does, however, make the craziness of the domain more manageable and easier to contain and describe, because the patterns apply not to any particular industry or domain but to modeling business problems in software, from a general standpoint. They are a set of tried and tested patterns and methods to bring about the best possible model of a domain. Perhaps what you are building is something that doesn't yet exist—some new, groundbreaking web application to shake the ages. That's great! That does not, however, indicate that you have to build absolutely everything from scratch—just the domain portion. We can use Laravel to tie everything together in the domain layer to provide functionality that is required for the application to be successful.

We should strive to functionally decompose the business processes, constraints, and logic regarding the relating domain and abstract all the inner workings and entities into separate portions, broken down in a manner that is the most native to the real-world operations that occur in the business. It is only then that we can come to an understanding and agreement with domain experts about the (possibly many) classes and objects of a system in a truly meaningful and refined way that best captures the intent and underlying business concepts for which the application was built to facilitate/automate/unobfuscate. Obviously, we don't wait until we get this point to start coding features. There is always a back and forth between modeling, implementation, and real-world usability (or unusability) that causes the domain and the code that handles its various aspects to be separate (this type of separation is actually bad). This separation of the model and the reality of the domain must be kept in check, which is why DDD suggests CI/CD along with refactoring to cultivate a truly meaningful representation of the model. Stay focused on the domain model and let Laravel's features and structures be the glue that ties everything together to create a fully functional and practical application that is actually of use to the business and solves the business problems (those were the reasons for the application's inception to begin with).

We will discuss how DDD presents a series of building blocks (also known as the technical aspects of DDD) including such things as entities, value objects, factories, repositories, services, and domain events. When these building blocks are used in conjunction with supple design and distillation, they can help yield a model of the domain that is a practical and realistic outline of the business objects themselves as well as the relationships between them and the processes that act on them. Tightly relating the code to the model is what gives the model meaning and also makes the model relevant. We will touch on these subjects here and go in depth into some of them later in the book. We will also discuss the impact that validation and constraints have on a domain model and what tools Laravel provides that can provide quick solutions to some of these problems.

Just to Recap

Domain-driven design, on a high level, has two primary concerns in a software development project.

- The primary focus is on the design, implementation, continuous integration, and refactoring of the model.

- Any complex domain designs are based on the model.

Because the primary focus is on the model, the benefit of a domain-driven design will start to be realized almost immediately, even before the software is actually released. How is this possible? You can start to see good things happening to your design and in the business itself by cultivating a proper ubiquitous language and gaining business-wide adoption of it, so it is used across departments and employees as a unified language to describe the domain. It will be the language spoken in that domain to refer to documentation, processes, architectural structures, classes, entities, and anything else that can be considered part of the domain.

The knowledge gained simply by coding (implementing) the design quite often is revealing in that it can point out places in the domain model where the design may have been off conceptually or maybe even not structured properly and therefore doesn't fit into the context it has been placed in. Whenever there is a gained understanding of anything in the domain that is technical or related to the domain's inner logic, this knowledge should be captured in both the design and the implementation (I say that to accommodate for this gained understanding occurring before and after the code has been written). We will go through some examples of how to do that in this chapter.

What we want to try to avoid at all times is the tempting practice of naming things after the concepts and elements found in any framework, pattern, or other such components that usually describe what something in the system *is*. We should always opt to name any and all aspects of the system, including the architecture structure and namespaces, with terms from the ubiquitous language so we can have those names actualized into the software in terms of what each thing *does*. Although it may seem like a certain object or concept in the domain fits well into one of these patterns or predefined structures, it is better to simply allow the domain and the core business logic to be the source of the ubiquitous language and to allow the objects in the domain model to be named in accordance with that ubiquitous language.

Everything looks good on paper—ideas and rough plans are a great starting point. They are potential pieces of the finished product, and they can have the appearance of a complete and well-thought-out solution. However, you really never know until you go further into the knowledge discovery phase or until you start coding the project. It is at that point where you are most likely to find things such as the following:

- Inaccurate definitions of domain models.

- Unneeded or unused domain objects.

- An infeasible combination of domain concepts or bad implementations of patterns.

- Components and concepts that are too broad (wide scope) and need to be separated.

- Components and concepts that are too narrow or that instead should be decoupled.

- A design that only partly (or not at all) represents the underlying domain.

- Scoping issues within functionally decomposed concepts.

- Classes or contexts that have too much or too little responsibility.

- Noticeable conceptual differences between the design and implementation.

- The items in the ubiquitous language were not used in the naming convention applied to other components or classes.

- The architecture doesn't express the intent and separations of the model as it should.

- Many other unclear points are present in the domain model, and/or there are misconceptions/confusion as to the extent of a given definition.

- Poorly designed models have found their way into the implementation.

- Rules and constrictions are not explicit.

If you took the reverse of this list, you would find a description of a quality, domain-driven design that encapsulates the domain knowledge in a way that represents the underlying domain in a clear and functional manner. Something like this:

- Domain models have accurate definitions that are agreed upon by the domain experts.

- Well-segmented components correspond well to the underlying business processes.

- There is a well-thought-out design with proper boundaries around the different parts.

- The scope of each component is well-suited to support itself (along with any identified dependencies)

- Processes and structures in the domain model are literal reflections of the domain.

- Services and contexts are self-encapsulating, exposing a highly cohesive set of elements that are internally coupled to other items in the same grouping but are loosely coupled to other services and contexts.

- Responsibility has been properly displaced in each class or context.

- The implementation reflects the model and represents the underlying domain in meaningful and insightful ways that clearly demonstrate intent.

- All components, classes, or anything else in the system are all be named in accordance with the agreed-upon ubiquitous language.

- The architecture is loosely coupled but still displays a highly cohesive nature.

- All prior misconceptions or indifferences have been ironed out, and their hidden details have been made explicit.

- The design of the system feeds the implementation of the system (the design and the model are intimately in tune with each other to the point where they are complements to each other as well).

- All rules and constrictions are explicitly defined.

Modeling the Problem and Solution Spaces

One way to think about the elements of a system is in terms of two "spaces" that anything in the domain can belong to:

- *Problem space*: In DDD, the problem space is represented by the various domains and subdomains involved in a domain model. This is everything in the system that needs to be solved, such as requirements. Examples from our claim project include claim submission, claim validation, and permissions for different user roles.

- *Solution space*: This is represented by bounded contexts and context maps. Examples include a custom backend to handle all the claim submission's verification requirements and the Auth generic subdomain to handle user authorization.

It may be helpful to keep a list or diagram (somewhere in the documentation so that the whole team can view it) that keeps track of these two spaces. Make a simple "T" chart, with all the problems in your domain's problem space and the associated solutions you are going to implement to solve these problems. This will help keep things in perspective and also ensure that the needs of the software are actually being met. Figure 10-1 shows an example for some (not all) of the concerns related to the claim project (note that we don't cover every concern that would exist in a real-world application), taken from the Claim Validation context.

Problem Space	Solution Space
A Patient's documents need to be included with the claim (as requirements) on submission and must be readily available for displaying on a web page or printing out on request	• Include places for file uploads on a filesystem & a naming convention • Provide a model to interface with the rest of the spplication • Include proper validations for the file as they enter the system
The CPT Combos entered on a submitted claim must be valid on a per-provider basis	• Create an interface & model to provide Paycode Sheet data for a given provider • Provide an API to expose said model • Build custom validations for CPT codes
Patient must be eligible to receive care, which is found on the MediCal website. Providers need an easy, automated solution	• Create a scraper for the website data to automate collecting the eligibility results • Create an Eligibility Model that would belong to one (and only one) provider
All documents, patient data, cpt codes and all other data items that get collected during the submission of a claim must exist and must be carefully validated to ensure acceptance by the FQHC and the provider to be paid on time	• Provide custom, field-level validation to ensure all basic data captured is present and valid • Model a process flow for a set of review procedures that aim to provide a form of manual validation of all claim data, documents, and treatment details / paycode sheet concerns

Figure 10-1. *Problem space and solution space in the claims example project for the Claim Validation context*

The diagram is pretty straightforward and includes some brief summaries about the various problems we are facing in developing this application, along with some corresponding bullet points on possible solutions to each problem.

Delivery Mechanisms

There are different ways to deliver a response in Laravel and in any other web application, depending on a few aspects of the system. One of those aspects is the delivery mechanism, which is either a single class or multiple classes working together to provide the domain's services and logic to the outside world. In a web application, this is usually done with a controller and a view that is compiled to HTML and sent to a browser as a response to client requests, but you may have or need additional mechanisms to respond to API requests (resources, resource controllers, and transformers), command-line requests (Artisan commands), or SMS text message requests with another SMS message.

No matter what the delivery mechanisms you implement for your application, they should always be separate from the domain model. Nothing in the domain layer should ever be concerned with how the responses are delivered to or how the requests enter the system; we can rely on Laravel for these things. In doing so, we can save time building the foundational code that would serve as the "plumbing" for which to manage the domain objects and the interactions with other objects in the domain layer.

Continuing the Claim Model

To get a better understanding of DDD, we will be continuing where we left off when designing the model for the claims project. Figure 10-2 provides a refresher of what we are building.

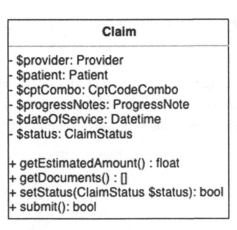

Figure 10-2. *The Claim model*

This model has some relationships with other entities and business objects in the system. A claim obviously has a provider that submitted the claim and a patient that the procedures were done on. Additionally, there are ongoing doctor progress notes for that particular patient that get saved with the claim, as well as the date the services were performed. There are also CPT codes, which describe the specific treatments given to the patient, which are used by the FQHC as what they actually pay out to the provider. Basically, this means the claim in this case *is* the deliverable. Without the claim, no one would get paid. When we think of it in these terms, we can even compare the deliverable in this case to the deliverable required by software developers in order for them to get paid: working, usable software. If we ship something out to production that's buggy, we realize it almost immediately as the barrage of hateful emails and the number of contact support tickets both rise exponentially. That's why we make sure we have tested and coded our system properly to avoid all the bugs and downtime that can come when shipping an untested or unstable product.

We need to take the same care with a claim as we do with software because, in the end, it's up to the FQHC (with the validation and sign-off of an FQHC biller user) to determine whether our claim meets the requirements defined by federal law and only then will they issue payment to the providers for their services. We need to make sure our *deliverable* is spotless to prevent delays in payments, which is what our application aims to do.

Defining the Scope

This section covers the portions of the overall architecture and design that include the concerns encompassed within the Claim Validation context. Figure 10-3 shows what that includes.

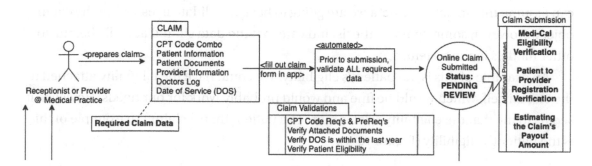

Figure 10-3. *The concerns regarding the claim project we will be covering in this chapter*

The items depicted in Figure 10-3 mostly include such things as validating all the required documents and input data, ensuring all other requirements such as the patient eligibility are correct, and verifying the CPT code combos are valid for that provider. Remember that each provider has their own paycode sheet that describes the CPT combos that they can use and the amount of money they are paid for a certain procedure. There is also the matter of estimating the claim's payout based on a calculation from the paycode sheets and CPT combos on the claim.

The overall goal here is to eliminate sources of error that would otherwise be present from mistakes made by the provider or a receptionist. We need to make sure that the required data is all there and valid before we actually submit the claim to the system (in which case the next stop for the claim would be the manual claim review process). This process involves a team member physically verifying all data is correct on the claim before submitting it to the FQHC.

Validations

Validations are an important aspect of software development; they provide some sanity in the form of constraining an otherwise infinite number of items in an even more infinite universe. Specifically, they allow us to make sure that whatever data we have is valid and accurate so that we don't have to go back and "do it over" because of user errors, typos, or any other mistakes that could cause bad things to happen down the road if not correct.

For our claim model, there are several things we need to validate so we can actually deem the claim as "valid" (at least for the automated validation checks) and move the claim onto the review process. From what we can tell, the Claim model that we devised earlier in the book has the relationships for the majority of the required data—so we can assume that most of the data we are going to have to validate lives within the claim object. However, some items on the list indicate that the data should actually belong to other models in the system.

An example of this is the patient's eligibility. We could have the eligibility attached to the claim itself, which would be fine and would probably work for our needs. However, it seems to me that the eligibility relates more to a patient than a claim. An example of this is the patient's eligibility (Figure 10-4).

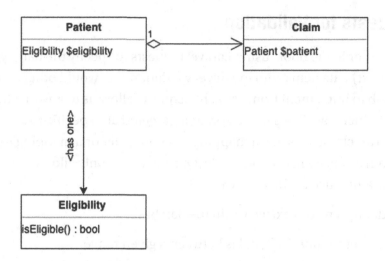

Figure 10-4. *Having the Patient object hold the eligibility data instead of Claim*

This feels more natural than putting the eligibility in the claim itself. Now, although we are verifying the claim data, all we have to do to get the eligibility and ensure that the patient is eligible to receive care is something like this:

```
if ($claim->patient->eligibility->isEligible()) {
    //patient is eligible
}
```

So, all we do is traverse the association to find the data we are looking for and then make a decision or action based on that data. Done, right?

Then, we realize that a patient's eligibility could change from one period to the next. However, this shouldn't be a problem for the design in Figure 7-4, because it's simply a matter of keeping the results of the latest eligibility check done for that patient in the system. Anytime there is an update for that patient's eligibility status, we can just update that associated record in the database. Because we are putting the eligibility inside its own encapsulated model and declaring a one-to-one relationship with it and the Patient Model, our claim will already have the data available to verify the patient is eligible to receive care.

Using Requests for Validation

As described earlier in the book, using Laravel requests to specify the data types of incoming (request) data helps with low-level validation that would otherwise be a fairly tedious job to implement from scratch. Requests allow us to abstract the delivery mechanism by which data flows into the system targeted at a specific route, which as we learned from prior chapters is just a mapping to a controller or a mapping to some logic contained within a closure in the routes file. Of course, this only allows us to validate low-level constraints such as the following:

- Validating a record exists within the database

- Validating a numerical field is between a given range

- Validating a parameter is within an acceptable list

- Validating the type of parameter that is passed in as input

To reiterate, all the validation documentation can be found at `https://laravel.com/docs/6.x/validation`. Anything you could possibly want to verify with code, Laravel has a constraint for. There is also a `Validation` component that ships with Laravel that can be customized to meet validation requirements that are not already available.

Within a request, you can specify any rules that the incoming data in the request must follow in order for the request to make it to the controller specified in the route within the `rules()` method (as we went over earlier in the book). When the rules are set up in the request, it is known as a *form request*, as they are used mainly to validate a request coming in from an HTTP form. However, you can implement either custom validation requirements or predefined validation using the `Validation` facade, which would look like this:

```
$validator = Validator::make($request->all(),
    'title' => 'required|unique:posts|max:255',
    'body' => 'required',
]);
```

Keep in mind that it doesn't have to be a `Request` object that gets passed into the `make()` method, but any key/value array. Once the validator is set up, you can check whether the validation passes with this:

```
if ($validator->fails()) {
    return redirect('/page')
        ->withErrors($validator)
        ->withInput();
}
```

If you want the errors to be flashed to the session (aka displayed to the user on the screen in the frontend while also keep the original input), tack on a `withInput()` method.

We can utilize this to form all the standard, basic validations when we are validating user input data for the claim. For example, the first line of defense for our claim submission model should be to check the data's validity. We need to be able to validate such things as the patient's details (name, date of birth, medical ID, etc.), the status and existence of the required patient documents, the existence of the progress notes included with the claim, and the date of service valid for the claim (which means that the treatment for the patient on the claim was completed within the last year). In leveraging Laravel's validation system, we will be able to handle the majority of the validation of input that is required to submit a claim.

The user interface for the claim will most likely be split among different screens to make it easier for the user to input data without clogging a single screen with all the required data needed to submit a claim. However, the frontend/UI will handle the majority of the validation on the screen that the user sees (so errors can be shot to the session and displayed to the user on the screen). The way we can handle this is by making the initial request for a claim coming into a system as a single request into our application. This will allow us to put the validation constraints within a single class and automatically invoke them by type hinting that request in the corresponding controller method. Listing 10-1 shows how that might look.

Listing 10-1. An Implementation of the Request When a Claim Is Submitted, Including the Validation Rules

ddl/Claim/Domain/Submission/App/Http/Requests/ClaimSubmissionRequest

```php
<?php

namespace Domain\Submission\App\Http\Requests;

use Illuminate\Foundation\Http\FormRequest;

class ClaimSubmissionRequest extends FormRequest
{
    /**
     * Determine if the user is authorized to make this request.
     *
     * @return bool
     */
    public function authorize()
    {
        return true;
    }
    /**
     * Get the validation rules that apply to the request.
     *
     * @return array
     */
    public function rules()
    {
        return [
        'claim.patient.first_name' => 'required|text|min:2',
        'claim.patient.last_name' => 'required|text|min:2',
         'claim.patient.dob' => 'required|date',
        'claim.patient.medical_number' => 'required|integer',
        'claim.progress_notes' => 'required|min:1',
        'claim.patient.documents.identification' =>
                'required|file',
```

```
        'claim.patient.documents.application' => 'required|file'
    ];
    }
}
```

I have purposely left out discussions on topics related to the front end. However, for the application to work properly so we can have one request to model the simple validations for each field, we would have to somehow figure out a way to display the various pages of a claim to the user and keep track of their entries into the form as they move from one screen to the next. This could be done using the session or even `LocalStorage,` but it would be pretty tedious to have to manually manage the state of every input on the form across several different pages (which may consist of textboxes for free-form responses like the progress notes, checkboxes for lists of multiselectable options, perhaps a few drop-downs, and other inputs as well). You could use what's called *prop drilling*, which basically passes properties down to the UI and back up to the back end, but that comes with problems also because you'd have to do that every time there is a change to any of the props used in the form; it can get messy quickly when you are dealing with a bunch of props. I suggest you check out the React library from Facebook (`https://reactjs.org/`) as it has special programmatic features and is made to manage application state on the front end and handle cross-page and cross-component state as well a combination of React/Redux, contexts, and hooks. I won't get into that here, but Google is your best friend.

Laravel validations provide an easy-to-use, out-of-the-box solution for simple validation checks, primitive type validation, character length, etc. The rules I defined in Listing 7-2 are there to give you an idea of the power of predefined Laravel validations. From a DDD perspective, these validations should be part of the application layer within the context of the Claim Submission domain. That is the reason the class resides in the `Domain\Submission\App\Http\Requests` namespace. The validations provide a way to abstract out what would otherwise be a whole lot of overhead code directed toward validating the simple constraints we have listed in Figure 7-3.

This one request class takes care of the majority of the *basic* validations needed during claim submission. There are additional validations that will require custom logic that is also involved in the concerns of claim submission; however, they actually belong to the Claim Validation context, and not inside the claim submission context (which handles such concerns as claim state tracking, claim change history, and following a claim through the submission process).

- CPT code combos included with a claim need to be validated in two ways.

  a. Each individual CPT code needs to be validated for existence within our system (which will rely on a static database table for lookups).

  b. Validate that the combo selected in the claim is actually a valid set of individual CPT codes *belonging* to the provider submitting the claim (which will rely on the provider's paycode sheet for verifying that the CPT combo is a valid one).

- The check that ensures the patient on a given claim actually belongs to that provider.

Adding Validation to the Claim Model

The way traditional DDD describes it, validations done on any model are best kept in the model itself (if what you care about validating are individual attributes of the model). The best place to keep constraints that are valid within a model or that apply directly to that model should be kept as close to that model as possible. For validating an object as a whole, it is best to decouple the validation logic from the model itself as they are different concerns. One concern is the business entity itself and its encapsulating logic, and the other is concerned with validating that entity.

Validating the Date of Service

For example, the constraint that a claim has to be filed within a year of the date of service (DOS) is a global validation that is important. What better place to put this strict requirement than the one place we can guarantee that it will be called every time a new instance of a claim is created? In other words: in the claim itself. Here is how that would look.

In Listing 10-2, we are explicitly stating that there is a business invariant present in the context of a claim, which is that the claim's date of service falls sometime within the last year. If not, it will throw an exception. By defining our validation inline to the Claim model, we make it explicit—what qualifies it as a "validation" mechanism is that the check is forced on the client within the constructor.

Listing 10-2. The Claim Model with the Date of Service Validation Handled Explicitly in the checkDateOfService() Method

```php
// /ddl/Claim/Submission/Domain/Models/Claim.php
<?php
namespace Claim\Submission\Domain\Models;
//use statements
class Claim extends Model
{
    const DOS_MAX_AGE = '1 year';

    public function __construct(array $attributes = [])
    {
        parent::__construct($attributes);
        $this->checkDateOfService();
    }
    private function checkDateOfService()
    {
        $dos = new \DateTIme($this->dos);
        $expiration = new \DateTime(static::DOS_MAX_AGE);
        if ($dos > $expiration) {
            throw new DateOfServiceExpiredException();
        }
    }
}
//the remaining functions describing the Claim's relationships
}
```

At first this seems to solve the problem, but we haven't yet considered that the claim model instance we have at any given time could be one that already exists and whose date of service falls more than a year behind the claim's expiration. In that case, the previous solution would actually cause problems if we were trying to instantiate older claims as models, perhaps to be included in some history aggregation to produce a detailed report. There are numerous ways to handle this problem. It does make sense to keep validations close to the thing it validates, but wouldn't that actually be pushing the architecture as a whole more toward a monolithic application? We want to be able to abstract away any details that we can so that the model itself can be a pure, rich model that captures the intent of the domain. Among those details for sure would be the validation constraints that are imposed upon a model's creation, but not necessarily if the claim already exists.

One way to handle this that lines up with the idea of the separation of concerns is to split up the model from the logic that validates the model. The reason you'd want to do that is because the code that makes up the object more than likely evolves (changes) at a different rhythm than the code that validates it. A benefit you can employ here is utilizing Eloquent's model lifecycle events that are automatically fired on every model extending Eloquent's base class. You can use these events to hook into additional logic, and because they are emitted at various points in a model's lifetime, you have a lot of flexibility in defining *when* exactly you want to execute that logic. The following are events that are automatically fired by Eloquent:

- `Retrieved`

- `Creating`

- `Created`

- `Updating`

- `Updated`

- `Saving`

- `Saved`

- `Deleting`

- `Deleted`

- `Restoring`

- `Restored`

You can hook into these events at any point during the application's lifecycle. For our use case, we could use the `Creating` event to hook into and provide logic to be run before the object is actually saved to the database. This would be the perfect place to inject our business invariant into. To encapsulate the concept that a claim has been created that the rest of the application will react to, we should create a domain event to tie everything together.

Note   It is a good idea to use Laravel's Artisan commands to build basic structures via the `make` prefix. The problem is that with our domain-driven namespaces living inside `\Claim` aren't supported by the command (to my knowledge at least). The commands will build out the component and save it in a corresponding namespace within the root `App\` only. Custom namespaces outside of the main `App\` aren't supported at this time. One work-around would be to run a `make` command and then move the resulting file to its location within the domain, which in our case would be `Claim\Submission\Domain\Events\ClaimCreated`. The command to generate this class is as follows:

```php
php artisan make:event ClaimSaved
<?php
namespace Claim\Submission\Application\Events;

class ClaimSaved
{
    use Dispatchable, InteractsWithSockets, SerializesModels;
    public $claim;
    public function __construct(Claim $claim)
    {
        $this->claim = $claim;
    }
}
```

We have made this class an event within the Claim Submission context and have indicated by its namespace that it should be regarded as an application concern, because events themselves shouldn't contain any real *business logic* but should be used strictly in the sense of "container objects" that get fired off at specified points in time, in our case being anytime there is an instance of `claim` being created.

As you can see, this is just a regular plain ol' event class that accepts a `Claim` instance as its constructor, making it available to the listeners of this class by making it publicly accessible in its declaration. We make this event fire automatically by hooking into the Eloquent event that gets fired at the correct moment in time (during a claim's creation).

```php
class Claim extends Model
{
    /**
     * The event map for the model.
     *
     * @var array
     */
    protected $dispatchesEvents = [
        'saving' => UserSaved::class,
    ];

}
```

This small change to the Claim model allows us to override the $dispatchesEvents property of Eloquent's base Model class, which is just a mapping of which Eloquent lifecycle events fires which of our domain events that the rest of the application will be set up to use and react to. In this case, the saving lifecycle event is going to fire off a UserSaved domain event.

Now that we have the event set up so that it will only run on any attempt to save it to the database, we need a place to put the actual logic of the validation for the date of service. We could use a traditional Listener; however, Laravel comes with a special type of listener known as an *observer*. By using an observer, we can attach multiple listeners that listen for changes in the underlying domain object in a single place. This is perfect for us and actually fits the DDD scheme fairly well because the observer lives in the domain layer and is focused directly on the object in the domain and the changes to it. We can make a ClaimObserver as shown in Listing 10-3.

Listing 10-3. An Example ClaimObserver Class with the Logic That Validates the Date of Service Before It Is Saved to the Database

```php
<?php
namespace Claim\Validation\Domain\Observers;

use Claim\Submission\Domain\Models\Claim;
class ClaimObserver
{
    const DOS_MAX_AGE = '1 year';

    public function saving(Claim $claim)
```

```
    {
        $dos = new \DateTIme($claim->dos);
        $expiration = new \DateTime(static::DOS_MAX_AGE);
        if ($dos > $expiration) {
            throw new DateOfServiceExpiredException();
        } else {
            return true;
        }
    }
}
/* additional class methods pertaining to the fired model event*/
    public function creating(Claim $claim)
    {
        // some other broad-scoped validation checks
        // occurring on a create + save operation
    }
}
```

The only issue with this approach is that the observer contains the constant of "1 year" as the claim's allowable range for the date of service. It doesn't feel right to put it in the observer. This setting would be better off in the .env file under a specific key so that the entire application would have access to it. Keep in mind that observers are useful only when you have something *global* that needs to occur at a specific event in the corresponding model's lifecycle. We chose to use one for the previous example because we need the global constraint of "date of service cannot exceed one year from the date of the claim's submission" to apply every time, but only before saving the record to the database. It would not apply, for example, to any models that were queried to select, indicating they already exist in the database. It is a fairly clean and straightforward solution that you could repeat for multiple validation requirements.

Additional Validations

Using observers is great if you want to be able to store any important logic that absolutely must run *every time* that model hits the particular lifecycle event specified via a method on the observer class—in our case, a validation check against a single attribute in the model, the date of service. For validation of specific attributes on the models, we can do a number of things, depending on the use case.

- If we were going to use the validator to validate a given attribute that is coming into the application via a form request, we could write the validation logic within the controller that it gets routed to, like so:

```
public function store(Request $request)
{
    $validatedData = $request->validate([
        'cptCodes' => 'required|array',
        'body' => 'required',
    ]);
    // The claim is valid
}
```

Or, as we have seen various times throughout the book, you can encapsulate these into a separate Request object and pass that into the controller function instead.

- If the validation needed to take place at a specific point in time or before/after something else had occurred or if we wanted to add some structure to the validation itself, we could instead build a validator that would handle various specifics we needed to validate in an OOP and SOLID way.

- We could go back a few ideas and revisit the one where we kept the validation constraints in the model itself and then talk our way out of a good separation of concerns by reasoning that they are too intimately connected to be separate and then add in a validation check that ensured that validator would run only on creation. A better version of this strategy would be to use Eloquent's lifecycle model events and tap into whichever point in time spanned the course of a model's life.

- We can create a validation service that would be responsible only for validating the specific object type that it is configured to support; plus, we can utilize the architecture that we are going to build in the next few pages to facilitate the service. This is the most involved idea in this list, but it also comes with the biggest benefit (and biggest chore of setting it up as well). You can set up a Service class that would hold references to these foundational objects and then write the code to utilize it efficiently and expose that functionality to the outside world by means of a well-encapsulated (and ideally well-documented) API. Because of the sophistication that this solution offers, I would only actually ever do it if I had a complex bunch of objects and I perhaps needed to validate both individual attributes as well as the entire object. Such added complexity demands a more sophisticated approach.

When faced with decision, always revisit the context that you are working with for the scope that the current issue and provided solution deals with. Keep the focus on the domain behaviors and not necessarily the technical details that they imply. What we are actually trying to do at this point is as follows:

- Validate the form input requirements for information about the patient and their submitted forms and documents (we handled this via the request we created earlier).

- Validate the CPT code combo that is specified on the incoming claim to make sure that it is valid and exists within a provider's paycode sheet.

- Validate the patient's eligibility (just the validation part, not the entire web scraper; we will build that out later).

Building an Abstract Validator

For individual attributes, validation in Laravel is best done either within a `Request` class, using Laravel's `Validator` component manually, or as simple class methods that initiate the validation from the model's constructor. What we want to do now is to be able to validate a `Claim` object in its entirety. Because a claim is made up of several other smaller pieces, each one needs to be valid for the whole claim to be considered validated. We also want to make the validator reusable so that the next time we have to employ some custom validation logic somewhere else in the application, we can utilize the same code.

To make a reusable component, it helps to break down the individual items that the component is made up of in terms of what it does. For validation, we have a few key players.

- Validator interface

- Actual validation logic (aka validation handler)

The validation interface for a validator is pretty simple. I placed this interface for `ValidationHandler` inside the `Validation\Infrastructure\Contracts` namespace because they both deal strictly with generic validation and therefore contain no actual business logic; therefore, I thought they should be placed outside the domain layer in the `Validation` context. Since it is technically an infrastructure concern, I feel that it's the best choice, but really you can put these anywhere that best fits the needs of your application and your style of architecture. Listing 10-4 shows what the `ValidationHandler` interface looks like.

Listing 10-4. ValidationHandler Interface

```php
<?php

namespace Claim\Validation\Infrastructure\Contracts;

interface ValidationHandler
{
    public function handleError($error);
    public function validate();
    public function getModel();
}
```

In the `ValidationHandler` interface, the `handleError()` method receives a primitive error (because we don't yet know the specific errors that may occur in the application yet) and will contain any actions or events that occur as a result of an error. The `validate()` method is where the meat and potatoes of the validation logic lives. Let's implement the `ValidatorInterface` contract by creating a new child class. To make the implementation's core logic available to all child classes, we will make the class abstract. This cannot be done with an interface because interfaces contain simple function signatures that must be defined by the implementing class and therefore contain no actual logic (Listing 10-5).

Listing 10-5. An Abstract Validation Class

```php
<?php

namespace Claim\Validation\Infrastructure\Validators;

use Claim\Validation\Infrastructure\Contracts\ValidationHandler;
```

```php
abstract class AbstractValidator
{
    private $validationHandler;

    public function __construct(ValidationHandler $validationHandler)
    {
        $this->validationHandler = $validationHandler;
    }

    public function handleError($error)
    {
        $this->validationHandler->handleError($error);
    }

    abstract public function validate();
    abstract public function getModel();
}
```

The abstract class shown here doesn't implement any interfaces; however, it is set up so that it technically could so that a child class that does implement the ValidationHandler interface will already have the required functions present in the abstract class, with the validate() method specified as abstract to force child implementations to define its specific validation logic. We include also an abstract getModel() method so that we can ask whichever validator which model it is validating.

Implementing a Validator for Claims

When implementing a validator, keep in mind the proper relationships between the claim and other models in the system would need to exist for this to work, as well as any additional attribute-level validation functions (isValid()). This is shown in Listing 10-6.

Listing 10-6. AbstractValidator Class

```php
<?php

namespace Claim\Validation\Infrastructure\Validators;

use Claim\Validation\Infrastructure\Validators\AbstractValidator;
use Claim\Validation\Infrastructure\Validators\Handlers\ValidationHandler;
use Claim\Submission\Domain\Models\Claim;
```

```php
class ClaimValidator extends AbstractValidator
{
    private $claim;
    private $validationHandler;

    public function __construct(Claim $claim,
                                ValidationHandler $validationHandler)
    {
        parent::__construct($validationHandler);
        $this->claim = $claim;
    }

    public function getModel()
    {
        return Claim::class;
    }

    public function validate()
    {
        if (!$this
            ->claim
            ->documents()
            ->exists()
            ){
            $this->handleError('missingDocuments');
        }

        if (!$this
            ->claim
            ->eligibility()
            ->exists()
            ){
            $this->handleError('missingEligibility');
        }

        if (!$this
            ->claim
            ->cptCodeCombo()
```

```
        ->exists()
      ||
      !$this
        ->claim
        ->cptCodeCombos()
        ->isValid()) {
        $this->handleError('invalidCptCombo');
    }
  }
}
```

Lastly, we need the actual ValidationHandler to handle the error-specific functionality (Listing 10-7).

Listing 10-7. Example ValidationHandler for Claims

```php
<?php

namespace Claim\Validation\Infrastructure\Validators\Handlers;

use Claim\Validation\Infrastructure\Validators\AbstractValidator;
use Claim\Submission\Domain\Models\Claim;

class ClaimValidationHandler implements ValidationHandler
{
    public function handleError($error) {
        $method = 'handle' . ucfirst($error) . 'Error';
        if (method_exists($this, $method)) {
            return $this->{$method};
        }
    }

    protected function handleMissingDocumentsError() {
        //handle documents missing error
    }

    protected function handleMissingEligibilityError() {
        //handle missing eligibility error
    }
```

```php
    protected function handleInvalidCptComboError() {
        //handle invalid cpt combos error
    }

    public function getModel()
    {
        return Claim::class;
    }
}
```

In Listing 10-7, the `ClaimValidationHandler` class is relieved of any other concerns or considerations besides the handling of the various errors that can come up as part of validating the claim's internal attributes or the object as a whole (which actually comes from the `ClaimValidator` object, not the `ClaimValidationHandler`). At this point, we have decoupled our `Validation` aspects and error message concerns into their own classes. In Listing 10-7, each possible error associated with the model can have its own error message that will display when (you guessed it) there is an error. The `ClaimValidator` object makes a call to the `ClaimValidationHandler` to dispatch the appropriate error, via the `handleError()` method on the `ClaimValidator`, allowing you to tailor your error messages to the very granular (or less granular) validation that you need.

For this setup to work, however, we will need to make a small addition to the `Claims` model (Listing 10-8).

Listing 10-8. Updated Claim Model to Account for the Decoupled Validation

```php
<?php

namespace Claim\Submission\Domain\Models;

// ...

class Claim extends Model
{
    public function validate(ClaimValidationHandler $validationHandler)
    {
        (new ClaimValidator($this, $validationHandler))->validate();
    }

    /* other methods */
}
```

In this previous example, I showed you a way to create a basic `Validator` that is reusable and that doesn't rely directly *on* the Laravel `Validation` component but does rely on the Eloquent models to do the sanity checks.

There is a better way to do this so that we don't necessarily have to write all the low-level plumbing that facilitates and manages which validation and validation handler to use, automatically. Those very things are already solved inside. The way you implement validation is dependent on your particular use case; however, Laravel's `Validation` component is powerful and extendable if you don't want to create an entire validation library from scratch.

A good place to start is by creating a rule, which is some type of constraint that you want to place on the validator stack to be run by the Laravel validator and error out if necessary. You can create a new `Rule` class by running the following command and then updating the files physical location and namespace:

```
php artisan make:rule CptComboExistsInPaycodeSheet
```

Listing 10-9 shows how the class looks after we make our tweaks to it.

Listing 10-9. The Rule Class for Checking If a CPT Code Combo Is a Valid Record Within That Provider's Paycode Sheet

```php
<?php

namespace Claim\Validation\Infrastructure\Rules;

use Claim\Submission\Domain\Models\Claim;
use Claim\Submission\Domain\Models\PaycodeSheet;
use Illuminate\Contracts\Validation\Rule;
class CptComboExistsInPaycodeSheet implements Rule
{
    /**
     * The Claim being validated
     * @var Claim
     */
    protected $claim;

    /**
     * Create a new rule instance.
     *
```

```php
 * @return void
 */
public function __construct(Claim $claim)
{
$this->claim = $claim;
}

/**
 * Determine if the validation rule passes.
 *
 * @param  string  $attribute
 * @param  mixed   $value
 * @return bool
 */
public function passes($attribute, $value)
{
  $cptCodeCombo = $this->claim->cptCodeCombo;
  $code = PaycodeSheet::where('provider_id', $claim->provider_id)
              ->where('cpt_code_combo_id', $cptCodeCombo->id)
              ->first();
 return $code !== null;
}

/**
 * Get the validation error message.
 *
 * @return string
 */
public function message()
{
    return 'No Entry Found In Provider\'s Paycode Sheet';
}
}
```

The CptComboExistsInPaycodeSheet class accepts a single argument in its constructor, the claim. Thanks to Laravel's Facade, available on all models in our application that extend Eloquent's Model class, we can run a query in a few lines of code (or a single line with no line breaks) to find a matching record inside the `paycode_sheets` table, made possible by the `PaycodeSheet` model. `passes()` receives the `$attribute` and `$value` arguments from the Laravel validator. `$attribute` is the field name, and `$value` is what is being validated. It also tacks on an additional `where` clause to narrow it down to a single CPT code combo, thereby giving you an affirmative that the record for that combo does in fact exist within that provider's paycode sheet for that specific procedure. This method needs to return a Boolean indicating that the supplied input has passed validation or false to indicate the opposite. All we need to check here is that it exists, so we grab the first record in the returned collection (because everything returned from an Eloquent query is wrapped in an Eloquent `Collection` object) and do a simple predicate like check on the results and return `true` or `false`.

You can have as many `Rule` objects as you want in order to validate virtually anything in your system, and the best part is that you can plug these rules directly into a `Request` object as a normal validation requirements. If you were manually creating the validator, the way to use the previously defined rule would be something like this:

```php
<?php
// ...
use Claim\Validation\Domain\Rules\CptComboExistsInPaycodeSheet;

$request->validate([
    'claim.cpt_code_combo' => [
        'required',
        new CptComboExistsInPaycodeSheet($this->claim)
    //other validation requirements for claim…
    ]
]);
```

Or, to use the new rule with the `Request` object that is arriving, you just add the validation inline within the `rules()` method to the returned array.

```php
function rules()
{
    return [
        'claim.cpt_code_combo' => [
            'required',
```

```
            new CptComboExistsInPaycodeSheet($this->claim)
        ],
        // ...
    ];
}
```

This provides a clear and concise way to define the various rules that need to be run on anything requiring validation. We have also clearly separated out the rules and validations from the domain objects they validate and have placed them inside the infrastructure layer of our application.

There are several ways to utilize the validation components provided by Laravel, depending on your particular need or context. In software development, it is common to utilize third-party code and libraries to handle the repeatable, common tasks required by an application, saving you time and energy. Right? Well, not always. Preconfigured packages are fine and dandy until you actually need to implement them. Oftentimes, it is only then when you realize that it doesn't support your particular needs so you end up extending the package and customizing the classes and the interconnections between them so that it fits the business needs required by your project. In the time it takes to do all that, you could've written the whole thing from scratch anyway!

The problem here is that libraries, packages, and frameworks all impose some restrictions and different levels of constraints that are often too constrictive for a particular use case. However, there is a way to design shared code libraries in a decoupled yet cohesive manner that greatly extend the possibilities of its usage. That's the great thing about open source, right? Get it. Change it. Redistribute it. Other people enhance it. Rinse and repeat. What I'm of course referring to has a lot to do with the open/closed principle, which is the "O" in SOLID. By keeping our code open to extension yet closed to modification, we are allowing for a maximum level of customization while still leaving the backbone of the project intact, so we can rely on it as a means for which to plug in any customized extensions. We do this by creating interfaces for the "moving parts" of the application. We will explore this in future chapters.

Conclusion

During the course of development, it is common to impose certain restrictions, validations, and rules on objects and processes required by your domain. In DDD, there is a common practice that helps clarify implicit, possibly hard to track concepts (or subprocesses or routines) within a domain model, and that is to program explicitly. That means we should try our best to not take anything for granted when performing or writing operations on a model in the domain; any validations or restrictions that exist on a particular model or within a particular context should be made an explicitly defined and easy-to-recognize class or function that is intentionally named by terms borrowed from the ubiquitous language.

Tip   As a rule of thumb, if the concept exists in the domain and in the core business logic, it should be included in the domain model; if the concept exists in the domain model, it should be included in the ubiquitous language. Anything in the ubiquitous language should be included as an explicit, intention-revealing interface in the model.

We can, of course, create a handwritten validation system from scratch that could indeed work; however, the amount of code it would require is sufficient enough to rule it out as a possible solution. To save ourselves the time and boredom of rewriting a similar library for validation by hand, we instead can rely on the Laravel `Validation` component to do the dirty work for us, leaving us with the only actual logic, which is the validation itself. You can use it throughout the application anywhere; it is completely decoupled and placed in a separate namespace within our infrastructure layer. It's explicitly named and clearly indicates what it is and what it does.

The takeaway here is that Laravel provides the backbone for the validation as part of its base features that allow us to extend and add logic in different places throughout the code. I've provided examples of possible ways to utilize the component in this chapter, some of which may not necessarily be the best approach on a realistic scale but are used to add context and demonstrate the various concepts that the concepts corresponded to. In terms of DDD, we have a start to what will become an entire claim validation context, encapsulating not just the data attribute side of things but relational contexts as well.

CHAPTER 11

Context Maps

In this chapter, we'll look at different means of communication between bounded contexts. From a high level, a *context map* is a way to identify the actual means of interconnectivity between the application's different bounded contexts.

Domain Models and ORM Entities

Although Laravel, as with most modern-day frameworks, doesn't really come with any sort of means to integrate any kind of development flow, or process, the work that it takes to get to a solid and productive development flow is well worth the effort, if you go about it in a smart way. While this is intentional of the framework so that it can be applicable to a wider audience of users, it isn't exactly ideal to just start programming if you haven't properly taken the time to model. Granted, the delicate scale of "over-engineering versus under-engineering" is fairly easy to tip in either direction for an individual; having a team offsets this touchy boundary line, because there are more people committed to solving the problem, and more heads are always better than one. From experience, I can tell you that even if you are dead-set on a particular side of a debate, it is best to still keep an open mind about your co-workers' ideas. If you put in the time to hear other people's perspectives regarding this or that, then the worst thing that could happen is that you look at the problem from another perspective, in which case you will most likely learn more about how your co-workers think, and it may even show you a way to do something that is new to you and potentially better than your old way. You just never know.

The following is an example scenario in which me and a co-worker were discussing a matter related to rich domain models and ORM entities. A rich domain model, as described in the early chapters of the book, is refined as such to represent the real-world objects that are important to the success of the application and business alike, and it is heavily focused on the behaviors of the objects in the domain that can be specified within the pseudo-global context of the actual model that they correspond to, meaning

347

J. Griffin, *Domain-Driven Laravel*, https://doi.org/10.1007/978-1-4842-6023-4_11

that the models themselves capture and encapsulate various aspects of domain logic, usually in the form of pre- and post-conditions, entity-level validation, or constraints that apply directly to the entities and models. I will note that Ruben is a respected senior Symfony developer, and I of course was the same for Laravel. However, the project we were working on at the time was written with Symfony2 and Doctrine ORM, and we were in the process of rewriting it in Symfony4 (with the new, cool Symfony Flex components).

Ruben: Hey, Jesse! I wanted to talk to you about what you mentioned in that meeting last week that you believe it is best to place business logic inside the entities themselves. Can you explain to me what you meant?

Jesse: Yes, I can. The way I understand it to be, it is best that we push the domain logic that is relevant to each entity as close as possible to it in order to couple it and give more context to the domain model. Fat model, skinny controller, right?

Ruben: Well, yes, but the thing is that the ORM is meant to abstract the data that it represents so it can be modeled as a DTO and transformed into the various structures and formats we will need for our application's APIs to function properly with the custom API framework we've implemented. This would imply that an entity, as far as the ORM is concerned, is strictly meant to be a direct mapping between the database fields and the object-oriented model in PHP.

Jesse: I can understand that. However, what that could potentially lead us to is what's called an anemic domain model…or one in which the members in it act as simple data containers, to be passed around like DTOs. We want to have any important constraints or preconditions as close to the objects in which they apply as possible.

Ruben: Right, that makes sense. However, the entities are what establishes the relationships that each one has to the others. The getters and setters are there as a means of accessing and changing the protected properties of a given entity [respectively]. Because some of the tables have quite a few fields that the ORM must map against, the entity classes can get pretty long, especially if we decide to move business logic into the entities themselves.

Jesse: Okay, so what you are saying is that the code that makes up the entity's properties as they exist in the database should pretty much match the way you have them mapped to the entity, via annotations? That almost just makes the entities the same a standard DTO, doesn't it?

Ruben: (LOL) Well, I suppose in some ways you are correct...aside from the fact that DTOs may or may not be structured the same way as the entities or even have the same fields as the entities do. Both points are making pretty good sense to me.

Jesse: Me as well!

A Closer Look at Context Maps

We can take this a step further and categorize each problem in the problem space into a domain/subdomain of the system as well as categorize each solution in the solution space as belonging to a certain bounded context. Once we have the overall solution plotted out in some form or another, we can begin to describe the design in terms of the relationships that each bounded context has to the other BCs, domains, subdomains, modules, and/or generic subdomains. This map of relationships between the subsystems of our application is known as a *context map* in DDD, which is a map of the bounded contexts and the interactions they have with other pieces of the application. The relationships that each subsystem (module/domain/subdomain/bounded context) has with the others can be classified by a number of different patterns.

Before we get into the nitty-gritty of context maps, you should first understand why they are even "a thing." Let's go over why they are used in modern-day DDD-driven development processes.

Different Bounded Context = Different Ubiquitous Language

Many large-scale applications supporting entire organizations or enterprise-grade software have such a defined separation of the many contextual aspects that make up their domain model that there exists a separate ubiquitous language for each. This means the same exact term or phrase in the UL can appear in multiple places at different times and have a different meaning depending on which bounded context you are working with at the time.

For instance, take, for example, the term *product*. A product is a pretty high-level term that doesn't really have any sense of specificity or details that would suggest which product the product in discussion is. Now imagine a product within the boundaries of a warehouse. A "product" in the warehouse can have different meanings, depending on which stage it is in at the time. When products first enter the warehouse, they arrive on a pallet off a delivery truck. In this regard, there are specific data points that would most likely be of high importance at the receiving stage of the process (if the workers are going to effectively sort and stock the products within the warehouse to be any sort of productive). The data points I'm referring to would be things like these:

- Product's pallet number (example: WSH99)

  - This is so that every pallet can be tracked.

- Product's general merchandise code (example: WOMENS_SHOES)

  - This is the internal number of the *type* of thing that the products are (respective to a larger group of products, which is captured by quantity).

- The product's received quantity and the quantity expected by the warehouse to be delivered so that accounting can ensure they got what they paid for

- Product's batch source ID (example: 399483982340)

  - This is the identification number of the batch that the product arrived in. This is matched up to an identifier of the particular *bill of lading*, which serves as a receipt for the truck's delivery to the warehouse.

In the previous list, you should take notice that the data points themselves are geared more toward a *bundle* of products rather than the physical details of a single product. This.is because, at the point that the batch (pallet) of products arrive, they need to be accounted for in a large-grained to fine-grained sort of manner. When the trucks hit the warehouse and the products hit the floor, the truck driver is only going to wait so long for you to count up the delivered amount and ensure every *large-grained* piece is accounted for (by counting the pallets and batches along with a given packing list/purchase order). If you had to sit there and count every product one after the other, the trucker would be there all day!

After the initial "check-in" of the larger-sized items are accounted for, they generally have to be broken down into smaller subparts that the warehouse can easily sell, track, and deliver. At this point, the finer-grained items of the delivery (the items on the pallets) are then verified manually and, unless a defect or anomaly is detected, the product gets added to the inventory and placed on the shelf, ready to be sold, picked, and packed (the next stage in the process). During this part of the sales process, the aspects of the products themselves are drilled down into a more granular context. These aspects might include things of the following sort:

- The individual product's physical characteristics (example: Nike Air Force 1 Low '07 Black/Black)

  - Brand, style, model, color, size, etc.

- A UPC representing the product in terms relative to the rest of the universe (example: UPC 883412741101)

  - 2D and 3D barcodes are great for conveying this information (as we have already learned previously in the book); see Figure 11-1.

Figure 11-1. *Barcode for the previously described pair of Nike Air Force Ones*

- A line number of the purchase order that the product that came with (as specified also in the initial receiving stage, detailed earlier)

  - This would also require the actual purchase order ID to refer to the line item on that purchase order that the product belongs to.

At this stage in the sales flow, the items are really only ever touched again until someone has purchased them from the online store, where they enter the next phase of the process: picking and packing. In this context, there is most likely a specialized role in any mid- to large-size warehouse that specializes in the picking and packing portion of the process. What matters the most at this point is finding the item's physical location in the warehouse (as determined by the person handling the receiving of the merchandise at the truck dock), picking the correct items off the shelf, packing them appropriately into their shipping container, and printing out shipping labels for the boxes' destination. The following aspects would apply to any given product that is at this stage of the game:

- The product's physical location in the warehouse (example: Isle 13, Section 3B, QuickPick item #98).

- A description of the product so that it can be verified by the picker that they are grabbing the correct item.

- Because shipping the item occurs only after it has been added to an order and properly invoiced (and paid for), the total amount of the purchase must reflect the total selling price of all the items, plus any added shipping fees (for example, the purchaser has opted to pay an additional fee for UPS Next Day Delivery). Important data points involved in this regard are the price, quantity, shipping company (UPS/FedEx/USPS), the method of shipping the buyer selects, and any applied taxes that are added at the end.

In respect to the shipping portion of the product's lifecycle as it travels through the various stages in the warehouse before being shipped out, the data needed in this particular process is more finely grained than that of prior stages. The data needed to facilitate this portion of the process revolves around the actual products themselves, such as UPC, physical appearance, brand/make/model, color, and things of that nature that distinguish it from other items like it. When we look at this thing from a higher level, we can clearly see the different ubiquitous languages that form around each concern of the different processes that, together, make the system work. Figure 11-2 shows a visual of this example.

As you can see from Figure 11-2, the work "product" means different things in different contexts. Each context can (and probably should) contain its own ubiquitous language. The term *product* would mean different things in each context. There are also a few concepts inside the dotted oval that indicate that they are shared among more than one component (context).

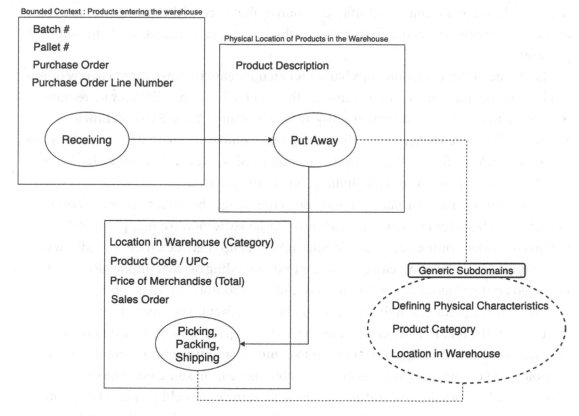

Figure 11-2. *The different contexts in a common warehouse indicate different usages of the same term in a ubiquitous language or, more specifically, the concept of a "product"*

The best approach to take when building such a system as described earlier is not always the clearest, easiest, or most obvious one to take—especially when you are architecting the system from a high level. A good starting point is to sketch everything out like we have done already, focusing on where lines can be drawn inside the domain model to section off the various concepts and components that power the application (and make up the domain model itself).

The concept of a context map is really just a series of common patterns that one could take in order to implement functionality across the various context boundaries, by limiting the code that gets shared by the different contexts. The more independent we can make the boundaries of the domain model, the better off we will be; the name of the game is pretty much limiting the dependencies that each BC has with the others while still providing the functionality that allows the components function as one application while still limiting the amount of shared resources that each of them relies on (i.e., the fewer interactions between the contexts and their relational contexts, the better off you are).

Each one of these relationships has either an upstream or downstream to any others it relates to, depending on their reliance on the other subsystems that may be required in order to function. If we have two subsystems, SubsystemA and SubsystemB, and SubsystemA was *downstream* to SubsystemB, that would indicate that the overall success of SubsystemA is affected directly by the operations of SubsystemB. Contrarily, the items in SubsystemB are not necessarily influenced by SubsystemA.

This is important information to include in the design, because to model a complex domain, we should come up with a high-level, large-scale view (or mapping) of the various bounded contexts and associations/relationships between them as indicated by the domain model so we can get a better understanding of what implications each bounded context has on the rest of the application in addition to what contexts speak with what other context and the relationship between them. The context patterns defined in DDD that I mentioned in the previous paragraph give us a reasonable set of relations that could help define context to context communications, and there isn't a whole lot of others that could really be possible, aside from some extreme cases or hyper-complex domains. We will go over these patterns in this chapter and use them to construct a basic context map that will shed light on our application's boundaries, relations to and from those boundaries, and how each context affects (upstream) or doesn't affect (downstream) the others. We will use this context map as the driving force behind the decisions regarding what points of communication there are from which boundaries and *how* we are going to build out some communication paths connecting the boundaries so we can create *real* functionality for our users from the refined domain objects that we have decomposed into their own separate layer.

In the wide-angled scope of things, this makes complete sense when you think about how the domain layer and its object, class, and interface participants even came about: functional decomposition. Once we have a rough sketch of the model (which usually indicates some degree of success in the functional decomposition process), we then need to re-compose them in some form or another to create usable functionality and features specific to the application's underlying domain. However, we need to be careful about where we are placing the different concerns in our system (and in what layer each should go) and ensure that their structure is closely associated with the domain it models.

Context maps are also used to show a breakdown of the data that's shared between each context in addition to where a given context falls in the application in respect to this global view of the system. Diagrams help convey the information within the context map, and I would suggest that you keep a context map diagram that's available for the entire team (or teams) to use, make changes to, and even help put in perspective the overall architecture and the dependencies that a single bounded context has on the rest of the bounded contexts.

Bounded Context Relations

The relation that a bounded context has with others can be categorized into a few patterns that describe the central concepts of the relationship as well as the upstream/downstream affiliation each context has on the other subsystems present in the domain model. It is a common practice to sketch out the "terrain" of a current system (if there is a current system) using these relationships as a means to catalog those aspects of the system within the domain as well as the interactions they have on the other subsystems, modules, or bounded contexts. More often than not, an automated test suite that aims to test all interfaces within each context and the points of contact between them proves to be an invaluable resource that can maintain a degree of certainty that each context is providing what the other needs, and vice versa.

In the following section, you will find the list of context mapping patterns and a brief explanation of each, and you will get an in-depth look into the Partnership pattern specifically and how that would apply to the concerns of the submission process related to patient eligibility and the means of acquiring that eligibility. Sometimes the subsystems are actually physical projects that have some type of relation between them that can also be described using these context mapping patterns.

Partnerships

This type of relationship happens between two teams, two projects, and/or two subsystems depending on each other for their individual success. If one project fails, they both fail, and vice versa. Projects that have a partnership with another project must have coordinated planning sessions as well as a well-defined workflow for handling the integration of the two projects that are agreed on by both teams. Teams should be careful to collaborate closely with each other to meet the development needs of both projects in such a way that will allow for each project to meet their specific goals and requirements so that both projects can succeed. It may not be a requirement that both teams or systems have an intimate knowledge of the details of the other, but it *is* a requirement to maintain each system in light of the other system so that the shadow of that other system can be properly integrated with the first system. That requirement is coordinating planning meetings and constantly refactoring and refining each system so that it still maintains the balance existing between the two systems as well as their own individual ones, as well as continually integrating both projects' features and code as often as needed to keep the two in step with each other.

Example Partnership in the Claims Application

In our claims project (which we will be continuing to develop in this and later chapters), there exists a partnership-type relationship between the Claim Submission context and the Patient Eligibility context. The two are dependent on each other to be successful.

The Patient Eligibility tool leverages a scraper to determine whether a given patient is eligible to receive care by a Medi-Cal provider. Without the claims context, this could still possibly be useful, but in the context of claim submission, it wouldn't provide any additional time savings or other such benefit to providers in filing a claim—partly because, without our system, providers' offices would be forced to go back to the print-and-fax method of submitting claims (which is not efficient and prone to small errors that could cause a delay in paying out the provider providing treatment for that patient, and the patient's eligibility could have changed during the time of the patient's last visit). This opens the door to the possibility of treating patients who are *not* eligible to receive treatment and therefore will not be paid anything for the visit.

On the flip side, the claim submission context cannot be completed in an automated fashion by which it was intended to support when we first set out on building the application. If providers or receptionists at a practice must stop right in the middle of doing the other claim-submission-related activities (required for a claim to be accepted by the FQHC) so that they could log into the Medi-Cal federal patient eligibility checking system and verify the patient's eligibility by hand, the full automation of one of the pain points for submitting claims in theory could never be reached. The verification that the patient is eligible could not be tested and would hence rely completely on the accuracy of the provider's office submitting the claim, which is not something we can inherently trust our users to do. However, an automated scraper that goes out and grabs the data for you and then auto-updates the claim to include that fact would be a fairly straightforward approach to resolving this pain point.

Defining the Boundaries of the Two Contexts in a Partnership

To manage the overall success of the projects from a general perspective, we need to have sufficient boundaries in place that act as guardrails for each context to provide functionality and support for. In the previous case, the boundaries already exist (as they are in different contexts, different namespaces, and different folders). Now what's left to do is design how it is that these two contexts *communicate* with each other to achieve some goal. Figure 11-3 will help to clarify these aspects of communication between the two contexts; it depicts the two systems, completely separated at this point, along with the various core aspects and elements that they will use and manipulate to provide applicable solutions for.

As we can see, although the models specific to each context are included in the diagram, both contexts have an outermost domain service that will provide a means accessibility to the context's inner-functionality. This would imply that

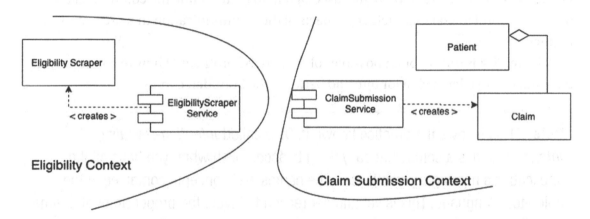

Figure 11-3. *A high-level view of the claim submission and eligibility scraper contexts and their core structures/constructs that allow them to function*

we do not have to manage the Eligibility object *directly* from within the claim submission context. Instead, the submission context could just make a call to the EligibilityScraperService, which would handle the request by scraping the Medi-Cal website's data and then returning the results in a usable format for the submission context to consume, at which point it would cause the claim to pass the required eligibility checks (as deemed as one requirement to accepting a claim in the system) and allow it to continue forth to the claim review phase.

On the data side of things, if you look ahead to Figure 11-4, you will see a possible implementation of the data portions of the patient to eligibility data structure. The eligibility of a patient's Medi-Cal status is attached to the patient directly, instead of the claim, because it is a much more native "fit" in the domain model and makes sense when saying it out loud. This is not inherently obvious in Figure 11-4. In fact, it may look like this isn't the case because the `Patient` and `Eligibility` models are separate. When you find yourself in situations like this where the data representing each model is located in a different context or setting than that model's behaviors, it may be best to review the requirements of the system so you can be sure that the separation is needed. If it is, then we can still keep the number of dependencies in each context to a minimum by having the actual model's code reside in one specific location inside one of those contexts and then create something like a DTO to be used in other contexts. By using DTOs, we can still provide the data that other bounded contexts need to know about (which arises because of the relationship they have with each other inside the context map), while still maintaining the separation of behaviors encapsulated within a given context. Figure 11-4 shows an iteration of the last diagram to better refine the communication boundaries and to make explicit any aspects of this communication that are cloudy or implicit.

Figure 11-4 is only a rough possible solution to the problem of how to communicate data and encapsulate behavior into and between the bounded contexts.

Note   This follows the practice known in DDD called *intention-revealing interfaces* and is a somewhat easy thing to accomplish when you base all the application's naming conventions on the names and concepts contained in the ubiquitous language. This is yet another reason to invest the proper amount of time in cultivating and perfecting the items and business concepts that will become the ubiquitous language.

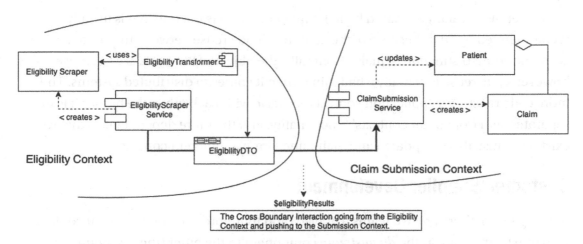

Figure 11-4. *The two contexts with the communication between the boundaries explicitly defined and made noticeable to anyone who reads the diagram*

This particular design is just one potential solution to the problem at hand, and it is in no way concrete and could change several times before the design gets implemented (at which point there's a good chance that the implementation itself would show holes or cracks in the architecture or design of the solution space for some related domain concern).

This still leaves many details up in the air regarding *how* we are going to implement the communication between the two contexts, which we address in more detail later. For now, the following sections provide a breakdown of the remaining patterns you are likely to find inside a typical context map, although they are not described in nearly the amount of detail as the Partnership pattern.

Shared Kernel

A shared kernel in a domain-driven design is a pattern in which one bounded context has some type of shared codebase with another, making the relationship between them (and any changes to either of them) happen only under strict scrutiny. Usually, these contexts can be managed by different teams. In a case like this, both teams need to agree on the exact modifications to either context; otherwise, an unexpected change could in theory break both contexts.

Generally speaking, a shared kernel implementation is not one that is usually recommended by DDD because of the amount of code reuse between the contexts. This is an important distinction to make. Generally, the object of the game *is* code reuse; however, code reuse is actually a bad thing when it comes to distributed systems. The more code reuse and application context they have with each other, the harder it is to separate them from other contexts' functionality, and the more dependencies that will exist that must also be updated and maintained for two different contexts.

Customer/Supplier Development

In this pattern, there are two teams involved (and therefore two bounded contexts), with one team acting as the *downstream* component to the other (the *upstream* component affects the downstream, but not the other way around). The upstream team can make changes to their code without affecting the downstream only through careful implementation and an automated testing suite (usually coupled to some CI/CD solution or service).

Conformist

The contexts are in an upstream-downstream relationship; however, the upstream team has no motivation to accommodate the downstream team's needs (it may be ordered as a service from a larger supplier, for example). The downstream team decides to conform to the model of the upstream team, whatever it happens to be. Changes made on the upstream most likely will affect those on the downstream, but in the end the changes to the upstream are basically "the law," and the downstream team has no option but to conform to it.

Separate Ways

This is the best-case scenario that multiple bounded contexts can be in. The interactions between them are structured and limited, and in terms of cross-functionality, there isn't a whole lot of reliance from one context to the other. Both contexts (or all) are free to go their separate ways in development and need cooperation from the opposite BC only if the code that touches the first BC (either in the request or in the response) gets modified. Other than that, each context can choose their own course of development, and decisions can be made within each without needing to consult the other. The contexts are basically considered to be independent and may even exist in the form of multiple smaller applications that connect to one another along well-defined and published means of interaction in order to form a fully functional application.

Conclusion

Different patterns can be identified using concepts known as upstream or downstream that detail in which direction the dependency between each BC actually flows. Patterns such as the shared kernel and the partnership have heavy reliance on the BC in terms of the dependencies that each one has on the others. Ideally, the BCs making up the application should exist in such a way as represented by the Separate Ways pattern. This means that the two contexts can be developed independently of each other, without worrying about breaking the other context. The only code that must be in cooperation with the opposite BC for an application whose modules can go separate ways is the actual code that does the sending or receiving of the transmission to the other BC (this includes any code that actually uses the BC directly).

PART III

Technical Aspects of DDD

CHAPTER 12

DTOs, Entities, and Value Objects

In the previous chapter, we examined DDD's idea of context maps and why it is a good thing to distribute components via their bounded contexts within your architecture, and why it is good to have as few cross-dependencies between the contexts as possible. The fewer dependencies each BC has to all others, the better off we are and the more independent our BCs (and application) become. In the real world, a large enterprise application could be split up to the extreme by having an entire team dedicated to each of its bounded contexts. In this chapter, we will focus on specific building blocks that come with DDD such as DTOs, entities, and value objects and discuss how to create and manage them in Laravel.

In the software development world, entities and value objects are common to (virtually) every application in existence today and can be considered vital aspects of the system. The way we represent entities and value objects in the system should correspond as literally as possible to the way they exist in real life. The model, then, is a sort of translated version of a business rule, constraint, entity, or value that is associated with a real concept or structure that is utilized somewhere in the business process of the domain and modeled in code that lives in our application. In a typical domain-driven application, the classes that model their real-world counterparts normally would contain the majority of the business logic in the application. These are first-class citizens in a domain model; therefore, it should not come as a surprise to you that they reflect the domain's business rules in a literal and direct way; ergo, those citizens are expected to be on the "fat" side of the scale. We will explore these ideas in this chapter but ultimately arrive at an old programming mantra that I've added a little extra on to: "Fat Model, Skinny Controller, Thin Service." Entities should arguably contain the majority of your business logic and as such reside within the domain layer. I use the terms *model* and *entity* throughout the book to mean the same thing.

© Jesse Griffin 2021
J. Griffin, *Domain-Driven Laravel*, https://doi.org/10.1007/978-1-4842-6023-4_12

Although there are a few different approaches to modeling both entities and value objects, the introduction of these concepts to a typical Laravel application causes a few inconsistencies between what are considered to be DDD's best practices and the standard way that Laravel operates out of the box, which ends up causing some issues with the suggested DDL practices. We will define these problems and explore the various choices we have to make regarding what we cannot solve with the desired outcome of "everyone wins." The two choices are simple: DDD or Laravel. The reason we cannot have both in certain contexts is because there exists an obvious inconsistency with the separation of concerns in the way that knowledge about the database is leaked into the domain layer, causing the implementation to know too many specifics about the database details to have a fully DDD-compliant application at the end. This inconsistency occurs pretty much any time we use Eloquent.

The main cause for this is that Eloquent is based on the Active Record pattern, while standard DDD practices utilize the Data Mapper pattern for ORM functionality. We will discuss this in greater depth in later chapters. The other option is to simply accept the fact that some of our classes will inherently be aware of the database details in our domain layer, which is a small sacrifice to make, given all the functionality it enables when working with Eloquent. We are going to be going with the second option, and I will justify the decision in this and future chapters.

We then explore entities and value objects in regard to how they could be implemented using Laravel and Eloquent. We'll also be discussing data transfer objects (DTOs). You can think of these objects as custom versions of our entities that are specifically made to be returned to some client (either outside of the application or internally) and are preformatted to fit the context of whatever the client is using them for. A common reason to use DTOs is because you don't want to pass around an actual entity, which for us means passing around an Eloquent model. There are numerous reasons for this that we will explore in this chapter.

We will be continuing to explore these technical DDD concepts in the context of the Laravel framework and take a look at how they can be implemented using the framework. Let's get started.

DDD and Laravel Inconsistencies

DDD is all about being *explicit*. Explicit naming conventions allow us to be able to more likely predict, with a positive affirmation, the behaviors and functionality encapsulated within a given class or object. The names should be directly derived from the concepts, business rules, and, of course, the ubiquitous language that is defined within the domain. Names given to various structures in an application should make it as obvious as possible to future developers who have to figure out what something does and why it's there.

Laravel and Eloquent both are, in my opinion, *implicit*, mainly because the design goals for each project allow users the fastest, easiest way to accomplish something and with as little code as possible. A big portion of how Laravel manages to do this can be attributed to its widespread adoption and usage of the Facade pattern. This pattern is simply a way to leverage functionality across many different classes and objects dynamically by placing it within a facade (or a single point of entry to that collective functionality). In Laravel, facades basically look like plain, static methods. However, they run much deeper than that. We won't get into the details of facades here, but we will dive into them later in the book, with a much more in-depth discussion.

One inconsistency between Laravel and DDD you can see right away is this explicitness versus implicitness. Because of the nature of the Laravel framework, a lot of functionality exists in (sometimes) not so obvious of a place. Having things operate in an implicit manner downplays the role of whatever class, object, or module's intent as it relates to the domain. It makes it much more difficult to find the purpose or meaning of a given piece of code (without diving into the code and following a bunch of object calls and stack traces.)

Eloquent is really no different. Take, for example, a typical Eloquent model, extended from the abstract Model class that Eloquent provides (Listing 12-1).

Listing 12-1. An Example Child Class of Eloquent's Abstract Model Class

```php
<?php

namespace Claim\Sumbission\Domain\Models;

use Illuminate\Database\Eloquent\Model;
class Provider extends Model
{
```

```
    public $table = 'providers';
    protected $guarded = ['npi_number', 'practice_id'];
}
```

In the code in Listing 12-1, aside from being able to identify which table the model is supposed to be representing, could you tell me which attributes the model has at first glance? No. You could tell me that the two fields npi_number and npi_number are guarded, meaning that their values cannot be auto-assigned when creating a new instance of them (which, on persistence, is equivalent to creating a new record in the database), but the actual fields that belong to the model are, from just looking at the Provider class, unknown.

To actually derive which specific fields this model includes, you could do a few different things.

- Open the table in a database GUI (or do a manual describe table query in a MySQL console

- Start a Tinker session (php artisan tinker), run the command (new Provider())->getAttributes(), and look at the result

There are probably additional means of discovering the model's attributes, but the point is that there is no way to determine them simply from looking at the Provider class. In other words, you can say that the attributes are implicit to the actual Provider class. This goes against many aspects of DDD because even if we overlook this fact, there is still the issue that Eloquent utilizes the Active Record pattern, so all of the properties that are stored within the $attributes array are all merely *fields* that exist within a table of a database.

Why is this a problem? Because we are mixing up the concerns of the domain with that of the database, which is a practice that is highly frowned upon in domain-driven design. There really isn't a clear way around this issue when we consider the options we have for improving the application or framework to be more DDD-oriented.

- We could make it a new rule for all developers to simply place *all* fields in a given model inside their respective $fillable arrays; however, that undermines the intention of the $fillable and $guarded arrays.

- We could inject all the attributes into the constructor of the model, which we could then explicitly assign to a class member variable only if they exist within a given set of fields, but that would complicate the instantiation of the models everywhere we needed to use them.

- We could make every one of the attributes a known, defined, and typed member variable on the `Model` class, but it really would do us no good because, internally, Eloquent uses this main `$attributes` array for many (if not most) of its features that we don't want to lose.

None of these solutions fits the bill, as they all have downsides that outweigh the benefits. This leaves us in an awkward position when developing an application with regard to DDL, because there really is no good solution. We are instead left with a hellish decision: do we scrap the whole project because we cannot find a good way to explicitly define all the properties a given domain object has inside its corresponding `Model` class, or do we accept the fact that by using Eloquent as our ORM with its Active Record implementation, we are technically mixing together concerns of the database and the domain layer?

If you haven't already guessed, we won't go with the first option because, if we did, I would've stopped writing the rest of the book right now. So, we are going to go with the second option—with an improvement. Now, it is true that the attributes on the model are not (and will not be) explicitly defined in our `Model` class; however, that does not mean we cannot at least document the fields in the model using comments. This approach would allow us to explicitly document (not define) the fields within that model and would provide developers with a reasonable way to decipher the meaning behind the model. On the downside, the comment block we create at the top of the class will itself need to be maintained and updated anytime there is a change to the table in the database or we add a new field. This presents a small issue because I have not known many developers who constantly keep their comments updated with every change to a given class or, in this case, database table. The best way to solve this is by placing the comments somewhere they are likely to get noticed and updated: within a PHP docblock at the top of the class. This looks something like Listing 12-2.

Listing 12-2. A Version of an Eloquent Model Class Similar to Listing 12-3, with an Added Docblock Explicitly Suggesting the Individual Attributes of the System

```php
<?php

namespace Claim\Sumbission\Domain\Models;
use Illuminate\Database\Eloquent\Model;
/**
 * Provider : A medical doctor
 * {@property array $attributes
 *     first_name varchar(50)
 *     last_name varchar(60)
 *     npi_number varchar(10)
 *     practice_id integer(11) not null
 *     paycode_sheet_id integer(11) not null
 *        ...}
 */
class Provider extends Model
{
    public $table = 'providers';

    protected $guarded = ['npi_number', 'practice_id'];

    //
}
```

I'll admit that this isn't the most desirable solution, but once we make the decision to allow a small portion of database concerns to leak into the domain layer, we can then utilize Eloquent to its fullest potential, as we will discover in a bit.

Value Objects

Eric Evans describes value objects as follows:

> *"An object that represents a descriptive aspect of the domain with no conceptual identity is called a VALUE OBJECT. VALUE OBJECTS are instantiated to represent elements of the design that we care about only for what they are, not who or which they are."*

> —Eric Evans

Value objects, as suggested by their names, are business objects whose identity relies strictly on the value of the object, rather than an explicit ID field found on an entity. That means they differ from other objects of the same type only by their values. Value objects are simple in nature, although the actual business objects that they represent may be complex, depending on the domain.

The cool thing about value objects is that they are immutable. Once instantiated, they cannot be modified. While this may sound counterproductive at first, it's actually a desirable trait to have because we can always guarantee that the object we initially instantiated will always be the same. If we want to change the object or one of its properties, we would simply replace that object with the new one. This makes value objects extremely cheap and useful when used to represent business objects in the domain. Which kinds of business concepts could be represented by value objects? I'm glad you asked! Check out Table 12-1 for some examples of everyday value objects.

Table 12-1. *Business Concepts in a Domain and Example Value Objects That Represent Them*

Related Business Concept	Example Value Objects

Measures, quantifies, or describes	`Currency`: Declaring separate value objects for the different pieces of what can be considered "money" would yield you with a clean, separated interface to describe any nominal amount of money. See `https://martinfowler.com/eaaCatalog/money.html` for more information. Classes in this pattern involve the following:
	
	`Amount (float $amount)`
	`Currency (string $isoCode)`
	`Money (Amount $amt, Currency $cur)`

Objects that cannot change unless they are replaced	`DateTimeImmutable`: Oftentimes, within a domain, a date field should be immutable in the sense that it should not change. An example is in a bank transaction; the date of the transaction should stay static. `$date = new DateTimeImmutable('now');`

(continued)

371

Table 12-1. (*continued*)

Related Business Concept	Example Value Objects

Using arrays of objects over arrays of object IDs (this gets handled for us by Eloquent, but it's worth mentioning)	Typical blog application:
	Instead of:
	`$post->comment_ids (returns array<int>)`,
	`$post->author_id (returns int)`
	Use value objects:
	`$post->comments (returns array<Comment>)`,
	`$post->author (returns Author)`

Has value equality: when equality between two value objects occurs within an equals method that compares the internal attributes of two objects or any other comparison logic	`Comparing Equality`
	`class Money {`
	`public function equals(Money $mo){`
	`if($this->currency ===`
	`$mo->currency &&`
	`$this->amount ===`
	`$mo->amount) {`
	`return true;`
	`} else {`
	`return false;`
	`}`
	`}`
	`}`

Replaceablility: value objects, being immutable, cannot have their attributes modified and instead have the entire object replaced when such a change is needed	`Replace Value Objects`
	`$string = strtoupper('hello');`
	`//returns 'HELLO'`
	The `strtoupper()` method and many other built-in PHP functions return *new* objects/data with the requested operation performed on it.

(*continued*)

Table 12-1. (*continued*)

Related Business Concept	Example Value Objects

Side-effect-free behavior: to mitigate possible side effects that a particular class or method has that isn't implied or explicit	Computations on Object Values Should Return a New Value Object
	``php
	class Money {
	public function add(Money $money){
	if ($this->currency ===
	$money->currency) {
	return new self($money->amount
	+ $this->amount,
	$this->currency);
	}
	}
	}
	``

Value Objects in Laravel/Eloquent

We have accepted the fact that Eloquent's attributes are not explicitly defined or mapped and understand that we are just going to have to deal with this characteristic of the ORM if we want to build a domain-driven design using Laravel and Eloquent. As a matter of fact, this acceptance of one of the shortcomings of the framework (in regard to a pure DDD implementation) makes creating value objects is fairly simple. We can utilize Eloquent's accessors and mutators to easily convert the calls for a specific attribute (via a Model's facade) into the proper value object. However, this has a problem of allowing the properties on the object itself to be changed, which is not how a value object is supposed to operate. Another thing to consider is that the types of attribute within a value object are not enforced, because Eloquent allows us to simply override any values of a model with any other values via setting it directly on the model instance. Both of these are issues when we are creating and utilizing value objects in our models because value objects are there to maintain a degree of consistency in our domain model. Take the following, for example, given a value object called Address and a Patient entity (model):

```php
$address = new Address('101 W. Broadway, San Diego, CA. 91977');
$patient = Patient::find(234);
```

```php
$patient->address = $address;
$patient->save();
```

In the previous code, we have instantiated a new `Address` object, defining its identity with the set of primitive string values we pass to its constructor. But then later, this happens:

```php
$patient->address = "Type Not Enforced";
```

We've successfully overwritten the `patient`'s `Address` type with a primitive string. How do we set ourselves up so that the value objects on a model class are enforced with the correct type of data? We can implement a mutator for that attribute on the `Model` and then type hint the argument in the signature of the mutator method, as shown in Listing 12-3.

Listing 12-3. A Sort of "Bumper Rail" in the Form of a Mutator Method on the Model That Enforces the Types of Value Objects When They Are Actually Set on a Patient Object

```php
<?php

class Patient
{
  // ...
    public function setAddressAttribute(
                  Address $address) {
        $this->attributes['address'] = $address;
    }
}
```

In Listing 12-3, we have created a mutator by using the following format:

```
set + Address + Attribute
 |       |          |
"set" + {attributeName} + "Attribute"
```

The logic that we include in the body of the mutator method will be run every time that attribute is set on the model. So, the code that inaccurately sets the `cptCodeCombo` attribute on a `Claim` instance would actually error out when attempted with our new mutator method shown previously.

```php
$claim->address = "This will throw an exception";
```

This code will throw an invalid type exception because the type expected to be held within the `address` attribute is the `address` type, which would not accept a string or any other data type as the `address` attribute on the `Claim` model. Looks like everything is peachy keen, right?

Well, not exactly, because the problem still exists that the attributes array that Eloquent uses to track the specific properties of a model (and bases the majority of its features on) is still relative to what's stored in the database. What that translates to for our purposes is that even though we may have set the object to be of a proper instance of `address`, whenever that same record gets retrieved from the database, the type will be a primitive PHP type because of the way that Eloquent handles type castings to and from the database. If and when the object's attribute(s) are set within the app, everything works perfectly, and those attributes get type checked against the types specified in the type hint of the mutator method; however, it's when Eloquent goes to fetch the stored row that we have this issue of the attribute being returned as a primitive value instead of a value object.

Note   The reason for this is because of the call to an internal Eloquent method that happens every time Eloquent retrieves something from the database: `setRawAttributes()`, which looks like Listing 12-4. It's used by Eloquent when fetching and returning data from the database and to the client and bypasses any mutators or accessors that may be defined on the model.

Listing 12-4. Method That Sets the Attributes to Whichever Primitive Types Were Specified in the `$attributes` Array When Fetching from the Database

```
/**
 * Set the array of model attributes. No checking is done.
 *
 * @param  array  $attributes
 * @param  bool   $sync
 * @return $this
 */
public function setRawAttributes(array $attributes, $sync=false)
{
```

```
    $this->attributes = $attributes;
    if ($sync) {
        $this->syncOriginal();
  }
    return $this;
}
```

The result of the way we have it set up in Listing 12-4 has the potential to cause some unforeseen side effects, which are extremely bad in domain-driven design because they have the potential to cause an inconsistent model state. One way I've found to get around this is by allowing only a specific type of data to be set to the attribute in question (as we did earlier with the address attribute already); however, Eloquent actually retrieves the object through that method, the results of which are primitive types, such as int or string, that were specified when calling the function. This will help ensure that the internal state of the model is kept intact and consistent.

The first thing is to create a new accessor method for that particular attribute, which would convert the attribute's primitive value (because of the setRawAttributes() call) into the value object we want to represent it, as shown in Listing 12-5.

Listing 12-5. An Accessor Method for the Address Value Object on the Patient Model

```php
<?php

//within the Patient Model

public function getAddressAttribute($address)
{
    return new Address($address);
}
```

Accessor methods in Eloquent have the same overall structure as mutators, with the difference being their signature and method bodies.

get + Address + Attribute
```
  |      |          |
"get" + {attributeName} + "Attribute"
```

We will also amend our previous version of the `setAddressAttribute()` method to include the proper checks to be able to store the value for the address property of a patient using only primitive types to do so. We are using this method strictly because we need to get around Eloquent's process when saving models to the database—specifically, the part that calls `setRawAttributes()` and forgoes any type checking via mutators on the model for all attributes. This is another one of those things that goes "against the grain" of a standard DDD-constructed application because we are modifying the domain model in a way to adhere to the standard process implemented by our application's ORM. Generally, this is frowned upon. However, given the circumstances of working with Eloquent and Laravel, I believe it is a small price to pay; plus, this has the advantage of being a straightforward, strict, and explicit way of defining the types that we want our objects to have coming out of the database. It's a way to enforce type hinting. Listing 12-6 shows what that could look like.

Listing 12-6. A Better Way of Defining an Address's Mutator on the Patient Model

```php
<?php

// In Patient model
public function setAddressAttribute(Address $address) {
    $this->attributes['address'] = (string)$address;
}
```

This is just one example of a value object in the application, and there are a lot more of them. Later in this chapter, we will identify additional objects in our claim application that would make good value objects.

Serializing Value Objects

If your value objects need to be serialized to arrays or JSON, you are going to have to include a `__toString` method and set it up with the `JsonSerializable` trait, like the class in Listing 12-7. This technically will work; however, this solution isn't ideal because we don't want to repeat all that boilerplate code to enable serializing the object for every value object that we create in the system. According to `https://www.ntaso.com/author/ntaso/`, the programmer "Chris on Code" came up with a trait that encapsulates handling the attributes in such a way that supports value objects.

Listing 12-7. A Possible Representation of a Value Object That Supports Serialization and Converting Its Value to a String

```php
<?php
class Address implements JsonSerializable
{
    private $value;

    public function __construct($address)
    {
        $this->value = $address;
    }
    public function getValue()
    {
        return $this->value;
    }

    public function __toString()
    {
        return (string)$this->value;
    }

    public function jsonSerialize()
    {
        return $this->__toString();
    ]
}
```

The trait looks similar to Listing 12-8.

Listing 12-8. A Trait for Value Objects That Enforces the Type of Attribute

```php
<?php

trait CastsValuesToObjects
{
    protected function castAttribute($key, $value)
    {
        $castToClass = $this->getValueObjectCastType($key);
```

```
        if (!$castToClass) {
            return parent::castAttribute($key, $value);
        }
        //or else create a value object:
        return $castToClass::fromNative($value);
    }

    public function setAttribute($key, $value)
    {
        $castToClass = $this->getValueObjectCastRType($key);
        if (!$castToClass) {
            return parent::setAttribute($key, $value)
        }
        //Enforce type defined in $casts
        if (! ($value instanceof $castToClass)) {
            throw new InvalidArgumentException("Attribute '$key'
            must be an instance of '$castToClass'");
        }

        return parent::setAttribute($key, $value->getNativeValue());
    }

    public function getValueObjectCastType($key)
    {
        $casts = $this->getCasts();
        $castToClass = isset($casts[$key]) ? $casts[$key] : null;
        if (class_exists($castToClasss)) {
            return $castToClass;
        }
        return null;
    }
}
```

The previous trait can be used like so:

```
class Patient extends Model {
    use CastsValueObjects;
    protected $casts = [
        'Address' => Address::class
    ];
}
```

With the previous implementation, there is no longer a need to define the mutators and accessors separately on a per-model basis. The only catch is that the value object itself needs to include a few methods that make it compatible to use with the CastsValuesToObjects trait. The interface for the value objects looks like Listing 12-9.

Listing 12-9. Interface for Value Object, Must Implement This to Be Compatible with the Aforementioned Trait

```php
<?php

interface ValueObject
{
    public static function fromNative($value);
    public function equals(ValueObject $object);
    public function __toString();
    public function getNativeValue();
}
```

This interface helps to enforce that all value objects will have these basic pieces of functionality defined, which we can use to determine the casts and native values of those objects at any given time. When using this interface, you can make the constructor of the value object protected, ensuring that the only way to instantiate an object is to use the static factory method fromNative(), which will help provide some consistency for their creation, ensuring that something cannot bypass the intended factory and instantiate the object directly.

Listing 12-10 shows an implementation of the interface for an EmailAddress value object.

Listing 12-10. An Implementation of the ValueObject Interface Defined in
Listing 12-9

```php
<?php
final class EmailAddress implements ValueObject, \JsonSerializable
{
    private $value;

    private function __construct($value)
    {
        $filteredValue = filter_var($value, FILTER_VALIDATE_EMAIL);
        if ($filteredValue === false) {
        throw new \InvalidArgumentException("Invalid argument
                $value: Not an email address.");
        }

        $this->value = $filteredValue;
    }

    public function fromNative($value)
    {
        return new static($value);
    }
    public function equals(ValueObject $obj)
    {
        if (\get_class(static) !== \get_class($obj)) {
            return false;
        }

        return $this->getNativeValue() === $obj->getNativeValue();
     }
    public function getValue()
    {
        return $this->value;
    }
```

```php
    public function __toString()
    {
        return (string)$this->value;
    }

    public function jsonSerialize()
    {
        return $this->__toString();
    }

    public function getNativeValue()
    {
        return $this->value;
    }
}
```

Notice that we made the constructor on the previous class `private`. The reason for this is because we don't want the object being instantiated from the outside. By making the constructor `public`, we are forcing clients to use the `fromNative()` method. This is commonly referred to as the Factory Method pattern.

One last thing to note about the code in Listing 12-9 is that, as is, we would have to duplicate almost every method the same way for each value object we create in the system. It would be better to throw those parts into an abstract class, which would allow us to reuse code, not repeat ourselves; plus, we get the added benefit of being able to override any of the methods on the abstract class as we see fit for the specific value object we are creating. Listing 12-11 shows a better approach.

Listing 12-11. An Abstract Class That Encapsulates Code to Facilitate Value Objects

```php
<?php
namespace App\ValueObjects;
abstract class AbstractValue implements ValueObject, \JsonSerializable
{
    public function fromNative($value)
    {
        return new static($value);
    }
```

```php
    public function equals(ValueObject $obj)
    {
        if (\get_class(static) !== \get_class($obj)) {
            return false;
        }
        return $this->getNativeValue() === $obj->getNativeValue();
    }

    public function getValue()
    {
        return $this->value;
    }

    public function __toString()
    {
        return (string)$this->value;
    }

    public function jsonSerialize()
    {
        return $this->__toString();
    }

    public function getNativeValue()
    {
        return $this->value;
    }
}
```

After pushing that logic into the abstract class, our actual value object itself is greatly simplified, and only needs to extend this single class, which in turn defines the methods to meet the contracts that it implements. The value object can now be as simple as Listing 12-12.

Listing 12-12. Simplified Value Object Extending the New Abstract Class
We Just Created

```php
<?php

use AbstractValue;

namespace App\ValueObjects;

final class EmailAddress extends AbstractValue
{
    private $value;

    public function __construct($value)
    {
        $filteredValue = filter_var($value, FILTER_VALIDATE_EMAIL);
        if ($filteredValue === false) {
            throw new \InvalidArgumentException("Invalid argument
            $value: Not an email address.");
        }

        $this->value = $filteredValue;
    }
}
```

This is all fine and dandy, but there is one last thing to point out with this
implementation. As long as we are extending Eloquent's base Model class, we are going
to always be mixing the concerns of the database persistence with the concerns of the
domain model. In the real world, such a downside can be acceptable, although on paper
and in discussion it's often frowned upon. We have to be willing to take a few hits and
make some sacrifices along the way when creating a domain-driven Laravel application,
and this is most certainly one of them. Overall, value objects are easier to maintain
and use compared to entities, mainly because they don't require a full-fledged object
lifecycle like entities do (which adds a lot of overhead in terms of complexity manifested
in the form of sometimes tedious details in the code), so employ them wherever
possible.

Entities

An entity in domain-driven design is any object that holds its own identity such that the identity can be used to determine its uniqueness from all other objects of the same type (in contrast with value objects, which use the object's value to determine uniqueness). This identity may come from one of multiple possible places, the most common being the identities of entities that we establish ourselves within our own application.

Entities are the models in the system. Entities may hold references to value objects (as we've seen before), but not the other way around (value objects cannot hold references to entities). Entities can be of a singular, independent form (such as a `Patient` object that has some references to an `Address` value object and has other entities that it references, such as the patient's primary care physician, which would be an instance of the `Provider` class). They can also be set up in such a way as to encapsulate their interdependent parts into an easy-to-recognize and use form that has only a single point of entry into the inner-objects. This is known as an *aggregate*.

An entity's identity (I'm a poet and didn't know it!) is meant to withstand the test of time as well as modifications in such a manner that no matter how much time passes or how many modifications have been done to that entity's internal state or attributes, the identity will remain the same. Entities serve as a fundamental building block of a domain-driven design. Table 12-2 provides a few examples of entities and their corresponding value objects in the claims system we've been developing throughout the course of this book.

Table 12-2. *Example Value Objects and Entities in the Claims Application*

Entities	Value Objects
Patient	Address, Medi-Cal Eligibility, Email Address
Provider	Address, NPI Number, Pay-Per-Visit Amount, Practice Address, Email Address
Practice	Address
Claim	Estimated Claim Amount, Progress Notes

In contrast to value objects, which cannot change and can be replaced only by other value objects, entities can be modified and updated many times throughout the lifecycle of the object, but the actual *identity* never changes.

Defining Entity Identity

The simplest way to generate an identity for an entity is to delegate the entire entity identification process to the persistence mechanism.

- The persistence mechanism generates an identity.

- The client generates an identity.

- The application generates an identity.

- Another bounded context provides an identity.

Persistence Mechanism Generates Identity

In the usual case of Laravel and for the purposes of this book, we will rely on the most common way to generate identities: MySQL's AUTO_INCREMENT data type on a primary key. The main drawback of this approach is that we will not have an entity's ID until we actually persist the object.

To add to this inherent problem, the fact that we are using Laravel means that we can do things like the following without any exceptions being thrown, allowing you to basically persist blank, empty objects without any type checks or constraints:

```
$patient = new Patient();
$patient->save();
```

This type of freedom can be bad and lead to a model being in an inconsistent state. There isn't a whole lot you can do to prevent this type of thing either. That also means you can pass around a nonpersisted, nonvalidated object to different parts of the application, and you wouldn't see any indication that something is awry until you actually attempted to persist the object. This is a downside of using an ORM based on the Active Record pattern (which we will discuss shortly).

Client Generates Identity

Sometimes an entity's identity will come from the client consuming the domain model. Usually this is the case for standardized identifiers that are universally unique to that entity on a broad scale. The most common example is a book, which has the convenience of coming with a universally accepted identifier known as the International Standard Book Number (ISBN). ISBNs are either 10 or 13 digits long, depending on the date of publication. An example Book entity with its corresponding ISBN can look something like Listing 12-13.

Listing 12-13. Example of the Client Providing an Identity: A Book and ISBN

```php
<?php
// use statements + namespace ...
class Book extends Model
{
    public $table = 'books';
    public $fillable = ['title'];

    public function setIsbnAttribute($isbn)
    {
        if (!strlen($isbn) == 10 || !strlen($isbn) == 13) {
            throw new InvalidIsbnLengthException();
        }
    }
}
```

Notice that I'm *not* including the ISBN in this entity's `$fillable` property because, even though it is something that already exists and all books already come with (as opposed to an identity we must generate and track ourselves), we still want to somehow enforce the length invariant when saving a book's ISBN. This can be done with a mutator function but can be basically skipped over if it's listed in the `$fillable` array.

This class will work and everything, but can you see anything we may have missed? We have overlooked a chance of adding additional consistency to the model by making the ISBN a value object that can be reused independently instead of being stuck within the confines of the Book entity as a primitive integer or string value. Check out Listing 12-14.

Listing 12-14. The ISBN Concept as a Value Object

```php
<?php
//...
use App\ValueObjects\AbstractValue;
class ISBN extends AbstractValue
{
    public function __construct($value)
    {
        if (!strlen($value) == 10 || !strlen($value) == 13) {
            throw new InvalidIsbnLengthException();
```

```php
        }
        //other ISBN validation checks
        $this->value = $value;
    }
}
```

We then can update our Book model to incorporate the new value object, as shown in Listing 12-15.

Listing 12-15. The Updated Book Model with the Included ISBN Value Object as a Relation

```php
<?php

namespace App\Models;

use App\ValueObjects\ISBN;

class Book extends Model
{
    public $table = 'books';
    public $fillable = ['title', 'isbn'];

    public function isbn()
    {
        return $this->hasOne(ISBN::class);
    }
}
```

Now that we have made the ISBN a value object, we can go ahead and include it in the Book model's `$fillable` array because we know that the object will come prevalidated by the value object's constructor. Using this setup could look something like this:

```php
$isbn = ISBN::fromNative('0123456789');
$book = Book::create([
    'title' => 'Domain Driven Laravel',
    'isbn'  => $isbn
]);
```

This code looks pretty concise and easy to follow. We've made all the validation requirements explicitly defined in the value object's constructor and can guarantee that the ISBN property set to the Book object will be either 10 or 13 characters long.

Application Generates Identity

Sometimes the decision regarding how to handle an entity's identity is left up to the application. A common approach for determining such an identity is the usage of a UUID field. UUID stands for "universally unique ID" and consists of a series of characters separated by hyphens; a UUID acts as a unique identity for any given entity in the system with the same type as per RFC 4122 (`https://tools.ietf.org/html/rfc4122`). There are different formats of the standard, which differ by the needs of the application and the requirements of the project.

- *UUID1*: Generated based on the current time

- *UUID3*: Name based + md5 hashed

- *UUID4*: Random

- *UUID5*: Name based + SHA1 hashed

Whichever method you select for your identifier, you would most likely never encounter a collision or happenstance of generating an identifier that is the same as one generated in the past if you were to generate one billion UUIDs *every second* for the next 100 years! I'd say we are pretty much covered in that regard and can basically guarantee with a high degree of certainty that it is next to impossible to generate two of the same UUID numbers for a given entity.

At any rate, once you are in a situation where UUIDs would be useful for one of your models in an application, I recommend using a tried and tested implementation of the UUID generator that's specifically for PHP: `https://github.com/ramsey/uuid`.

To add this package to Composer (and have it autoloaded and available anywhere else in your application), run the following command:

```
composer require ramsey/uuid
```

After adding this package to your application, you now have to decide where exactly to put the code that utilizes the package to generate identities for your entities. Although I've made the statement that, generally speaking, it is almost pointless to use repositories within the context of a Laravel application, this is actually one such case where a repository would come in handy and provide a clean and simple interface for which to generate these entities' identities.

We will go through an example of what that could look like in regard to a new entity to the system requiring a UUID. We will make the ID itself a separate value object to make the concept more explicit within the domain model and signify that there's something important about the identifier of the entity it resides in.

Note   Throughout this book and in real life, I've stuck with *not* creating value objects for every identifier in the system. That's because a normal model/entity (which I use interchangeably throughout the book) incorporates an ID field as required by the ORM, so it is, to me, implied. However, in the case of an application entity identifier that employs a separate package (such as a UUID), it is important enough to the domain model that the identifier be made an explicit concept by actually creating a separate class for it and incorporating it into the entity as the identifier, as we will discuss next.

For the next example, let's pretend we are building a shopping cart for use on an e-commerce site (and have completely missed that day of class or work where they learned about open source software) that sells books (i.e., a bookstore) and must establish an identity mechanism of the Cart object so that users can save carts for later and distinguish them from other users' carts. Since our application is responsible for generating the identity, we opt to use the UUID format and will rely on its structure to ensure a standard format that will provide uniqueness of the carts within the boundaries of our system. We need a place for this logic that's not within the Cart entity, as shown in Listing 12-16.

Listing 12-16. Interface for the Cart Repository

```php
<?php
namespace YarnsAndGobyl\Domain\Repositories;

use YarnsAndGobyl\Domain\Models\Cart;

interface CartRepository
```

```
{
    public function nextIdentity();
    public function add(Cart $cart);
    public function remove(Cart $cart);
}
```

This interface would really be necessary only if you were going to have different versions of an ORM or for some reason needed to support two different ORMs in your application, which isn't very likely but possible. In that case, you could implement the interface in Listing 12-15 as a DoctrineCartRepository, InMemoryCartRepository, ElasticCartRepository, etc. If this isn't the case (which it won't be for this example), to save from creating another interface, you could instead simply implement the methods directly inside a plain 'ol PHP class. The interface does add a degree of flexibility for future decisions as well and should be agreed upon by the team before making it an actual practice in a real application. As with most things in programming, things of this nature have their upsides and downsides.

At any rate, Listing 12-17 shows the implemented interface.

Listing 12-17. Partially Implemented CartRepository from the Previous Interface

```php
<?php

namespace YarnsAndGobyl\Infrastructure\Repositories;

use YarnsAndGobyl\Domain\Repositories\CartRepository;
use Ramsey\Uuid\Uuid;
use Ramsey\Uuid\Exception\UnsatisfiedDependencyException;

class EloquentCartRepository implements CartRepository
{
    public function nextIdentity()
    {
        try {
            $uuid = Uuid::uuid4();
            return $uuid->toString();
        } catch (UnsatisfiedDependencyException $e) {
            dd("Exception Occurred : " . $e->getMessage());
        }
```

```
    }

    public function add(Cart $cart)
    {
        //implement add functionality ...
    }

    public function remove(Cart $cart)
    {
        //implement remove functionality ...
    }
}
```

At any rate, we will create a separate `CartId` class that will serve as the `cart's` identifier and that will house the code that utilizes the UUID third-party package we installed via Composer. Just as we did in Listing 12-14 with the ISBN identifier for the Book model, we will make the `CartId` a value object that will be ingested by the `Book` entity as a means of establishing identity. We'll use the same strategy here as well for the constructor, specifying it to be private, as we've done in Listing 12-18.

Listing 12-18. A CartId Object Class That Will Serve as the UUID Mechanism We Established for the Cart Entity

```
<?php
namespace YarnsAndGobyl\Infrastructure\Identity\Cart;

use Ramsey\Uuid\Uuid;

class CartId extends AbstractValue
{
    private $id;

    private function __construct($id = null)
    {
        $this->id = $id ? Uuid::uuid4()->toString();
    }
```

```php
    public function create($uuid = null)
    {
        return new static($uuid);
    }
}
```

The corresponding Cart object could look like Listing 12-19.

Listing 12-19. An Example Cart Entity with a UUID Identity Generation Mechanism Incorporated via the CartId Class

```php
<?php

namespace YarnsAndGobyl\Domain\Models\Cart;

use Illuminate\Database\Eloquent\Model;
use YarnsAndGobyl\Infrastructure\Identity\Cart\CartId;

class Cart extends Model
{
    public $table = 'carts';

    public function cartId()
    {
        return $this->hasOne(CartId::class, 'id', 'uuid');
    }
}
```

Another Bounded Context Generates Identity

This is usually considered to be the riskiest and involved method of identifying an entity in the system, because it relies on the events and processes that actually live and function outside of the context that the entity lives. There are different theories on the best approach to handle such a situation.

An example of an identity that is generated by a different bounded context is in the case of an Identity service. A typical BC geared toward handling identification and management of the users and roles of a given system (or enterprise) can be contained within a separate, independent bounded context that can even be decoupled from the application and living within its own microservice.

Within this Identity context is this concept of a User, with an entity defined as such. There also exists some standard functionality that operates on or with this User model, and it exposes a limited amount of this functionality to other bounded contexts in the system.

Now let's say we have a separate bounded context, perhaps a Group context on a discussion board site that organizes its different User members together in such a way that they can easily share content, ideas, chats, and other forms of media. All of this is done on the group page, which only members of that group can see and contribute to. For each group, there are three different types of users: an Admin user who has superuser power over the group, including the content, members, bans, etc.; a Moderator user, who has the power to delete or edit content on the group site; and a regular Member user, who can only comment and participate in discussions and share media content.

From a security perspective, the Identity service should handle all the relevant authorization and authentication processes to determine the user logging in is who they claim to be and also to manage the permissions of each user based on the role that they have within the group and the site itself. However, the Group context needs to also know the different roles of each user so that it can determine who can do what on the group pages.

The question then becomes: where do we put the logic that identifies each user in the group and also checks to see whether they have permission to do whatever they are requesting to do at any given second. Do we copy the relevant data, code, and functionality to the Group context so that it can use the information that *also* resides in the Identity context so it can make decisions about user access and what not?

The short answer is, no. DRY = Don't Repeat Yourself. There is a better way to do this, and most likely an even better way that I haven't thought of and that's not included in this book. I'll leave it to you to figure out the next latest and greatest approach to handling cross-context communication and data sharing across different modules or services in the system; however, I will propose one way to handle this problem that doesn't involve repeating your code in both contexts.

The first thing is to identity the entities in this scenario. Obviously, a User can be considered an entity because it contains an ID that separates a single instance of User from any other instance of User. No matter how you look at it, a Member user belonging to a group is still a User object. The same goes for an Admin user and a Moderator user as well. They all mean different things and have different levels of access involved in regard to a particular group, but they are all technically users, or at least some constrained type of user. This gives us some indication that they may best be classified as roles and that each user should have one or more of these roles. The roles themselves don't need to be their own entities, because they really only differ by the value that they correspond to and will not require any sort of domain object lifecycle. Another way to think of these roles is that they are static in nature, and once they are initially set, they most likely will not be changed in the future. For example, it's unlikely that we will want to call an Admin role anything other than `Admin` (or root). Once we set it, we leave it alone.

Objects of this nature are best represented by value objects, similar to the way we've been attaching value objects to the entities themselves by means of a Value Object interface that allows us to easily integrate them into the entities as relational items. However, the key concept here is that the Group context is where these value objects will live, *not* the Identity context. We can think of this conceptually as in Figure 12-1, where the `User` entity resides within the Identity context and the group resides in the Group context.

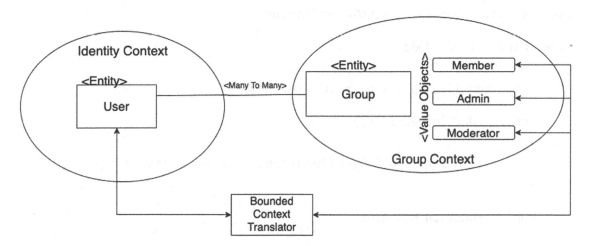

Figure 12-1. *The interaction between an Identity context and a Group context*

Among the Group context are the value objects that identify the *roles* that our application supports, as they relate to the Group context as a whole. We can establish a relationship between a `User` and `Group`, which would be a many-to-many type relationship, with the owning side of the relation on the `User` model. Many users can belong to many groups, and many groups hold many users.

Note   Even though the context I identify here is the Group context, it is actually within the root namespace `Discussion`.

This is a perfect example of how Eloquent shines. Because of its fluent nature and chainable contexts, Eloquent offers a unique and straightforward approach to specifying relationships: they can be modeled almost directly, in whole English sentences. How much more explicit can you be? Even someone who doesn't know how to program can look at these two classes and give a vague description about how they relate to each other. See what I'm referring to by looking at Listing 12-20.

Listing 12-20. Example of a User Entity

```php
<?php
namespace Identity\Domain\Models\Users;

use Discussion\Domain\Models\Groups\Group;

class User extends Model
{
    protected $fillable = ['email','username'];

    public function adminOf()
    {
        return $this->belongsToMany(Groups::class,'admins_groups');
    }

    public function memberOf()
    {
        return $this->belongsToMany(Group::class,'members_groups');
    }

    public function moderatorOf()
    {
        return $this->belongsToMany(Group::class,
            'moderators_group');
    }
}
```

```php
    public function addAsMemberOf(Group $group)
    {
        $this->memberOf[] = $group;
        $group->addMember($this);
    }

    public function addAsAdminOf(Group $group)
    {
        $this->adminOf[] = $group;
        $group->addAdmin($this);
    }

    public function addAdModeratorOf(Group $group)
    {
        $this->moderatorOf[] = $group;
        $group->addModerator($this);
    }
}
?>
```

Listing 12-21 shows the model for the group.

Listing 12-21. Example of a Group Entity and the Relation It Has to the User Entity

```php
<?php

namespace Discussion\Domain\Models\Groups;
//use statements

class Group extends Model
{
    protected $fillable = ['username','email','accountType'];

    public function admins()
    {
        return $this->belongsToMany(User::class, 'id', 'admin_of');
    }
    public function members()
    {
```

```php
        return $this->belongsToMany(User::class, 'id', 'member_of');
    }

    public function moderators()
    {
        return $this->belongsToMany(User::class, 'id', 'moderator_of');
    }

    public function addMember(User $user)
    {
        $this->members->save($user);
    }

    public function addAdmin(User $user)
    {
        $this->admins->save($user);
    }

    public function addModerator(User $user)
    {
        $this->moderators->save($user);
    }

}
```

Then there is the matter of defining the three different roles we want the system to be aware of, created as value objects: `Member`, `Admin`, and `Moderator`. To give a more explicit definition in the domain model and to lend better to the concepts that value objects represent, we should create an interface that will serve as a high-level conceptual notion of what we are actually creating in the system: roles belonging to specific users. Here is a simple interface for this new role concept:

```php
<?php
namespace Discussion\Domain\Contracts;

interface RoleInterface
{
    public function getRoleName();
}
```

Notice in Listing 12-20 that the interface for the role is actually created within the boundary of the group (discussion) and not in the Identity context. Even if you create a blank interface class, you are still setting yourself up for success down the road when new functionality and features must be added to the application regarding the way roles get defined in the system. Now, we can implement that interface for each of the three new roles shown in Listing 12-22.

Listing 12-22. A Value Object "Member" That Will Serve as a Role of a Standard Member of a Group

```php
<?php

namespace Discussion\Domain\Models\Groups;

use Discussion\Domain\Contracts\RoleInterface;
//additional use statements

class Member extends AbstractValue implements RoleInterface
{
    private $email;

    private $userId;

    private $username;

    private function __construct(Email $email, UserId $userId, Username
    $username)
    {
        //any invariant checks
        $this->email = $email;
        $this->userId = $userId;
        $this->username = $username;
    }

    public static function getRoleName()
    {
        return "Member";
    }
}
```

Notice in the previous class that we are passing a value object named `UserId` to the constructor, rather than an actual object of type `User`. This is to prevent leaking logic into the group context (`Discussion` namespace) from the Identity context, which is what we would be doing if we passed in a `User` entity instead of a value object.

You would of course implement the remaining two roles via this same approach, only modified slightly to incorporate the Admin roles and Moderator roles, respectively. The remaining code for this implementation can be found online. I didn't include it here for the sake of brevity.

The last piece of the puzzle that we can identify from Figure 12-1 is this strange `Translator` class that appears to sit between the two contexts, somehow breathing life into the value objects we have defined in the Group context. This translator class is meant to face the problem of translating between Users and instances of Members, Admins, and Moderators. We basically need a way to translate the `User` objects (which are entities) to value objects (like the three we created for the three different system roles within the Group context). This needs to happen automatically to make this work; in particular, we need this translation to happen whenever we retrieve the relationship to the `User` entity from the Group context. Because neither the `Group` entity nor the `User` entity should have this responsibility, we are going to have to create a domain service to provide the functionality we need to tie everything together.

Although we dive into services in the next few chapters, our goal here is to create a simple service that will handle the translating for us. Because we are keeping the pace of separating the concerns of the system, we will want to place this new service in the same bounded context as the `Group` entity, which, in this case, would be the `Discussion` namespace. We will access a collection of Members or Admins of a particular group called *from* within the Group context, and we want to avoid exposing the `User` entity (residing in the Identity context) within that group context as well. Avoiding this will help prevent one model's logic into another. It looks like Listing 12-23.

Listing 12-23. An Example Translator for User Objects (Entity) to Role Objects (Value)

```php
<?php
namespace Discussion\Domain\Services\Groups;

use Discussion\Domain\Models\Groups\Admin;
use Discussion\Domain\Models\Groups\Member;
use Discussion\Domain\Models\Groups\Moderator;
```

```php
use Identity\Domain\Models\Users\User;

class UserToGroupTranslator
{
    /**
    * Translates a user to a member
    */
    public function toMember(User $user)
    {
        return new Member($user->id, $user->email, $user->username);
    }

    /**
    * Translate a user to an Admin
    */
    public function toAdmin(User $user)
    {
        return new Admin($user->id, $user->email, $user->username);
    }

    /**
    * Translate a user to a moderator
    */
    public function toModerator(User $user)
    {
        return new Moderator($user->id, $user->email,
            $user->username);
    }
}
```

The code for the translator is pretty simple. Feed it a User object and get back a value object that is specific to the Group context. Once this is in place, we just need to modify our Group entity to use it, which is demonstrated in Listing 12-24.

Listing 12-24. Updated Group Entity

```php
<?php

use Discussion\Domain\Services\Groups\UserToGroupTranslator;

class Group extends Model
{
    protected $fillable = ['username','email','accountType'];

    public function __constrcut(GroupId $groupId, Name $name, Slug $slug)
    {
        $this->setId($groupId);
        $this->setName($name);
        $this->setSlug($slug);

        $this->admins = new Collection();
        $this->members = new Collection();

        $this->usersToGroupTranslator = new UserToGroupTranslator();
    }
    public function users()
    {
        return $this->hasMany(Users::class);
    }

    public function getMembersAttribute()
    {
        return $this->members->map(function($user) {
            return $this->userInGroupTranslator->toMember($user);
        });
    }

    public function getAdminsAttribute()
    {
        return $this->admins->map(function($user) {
            return $this->userInGroupTranslator->toAdmin($user);
        });
    }
```

```
    public function getModeratorsAttribute()
    {
        return $this->moderators->map(function($user) {
            return $this->userInGroupTranslator->
                toModerator($user);
        }
    }
    // ... other related methods for the Group model ...
}
```

Notice that to customize the way the class in Listing 12-23 returns the collection of admins or members or moderators via a few different accessor methods that actually take the original collection of value objects and map through the translator we've built earlier. In doing this, the outside world (client) that uses this setup won't even realize that any such translation has taken place, which is the best-case scenario.

It did take a little extra work and thought, but the concluding point here is that we can use structures from other bounded contexts (such as entities) by implementing value objects wherever possible and creating a sort of translator that can get the value objects the data they need from the entity, without crossing the boundaries of the bounded context in which they are being used. We've managed to adhere well to the separation of concerns also.

Data Transfer Objects

Data transfer objects (DTOs) are intended for exactly what they sound like—objects that are intended to be transferred to the front end or used to add structure to unstructured data throughout the application. Generally speaking, we don't want to pass around fully fledged entities in our application or to our front end, because doing that would break the encapsulation of the layers. The application layer is supposed to be the only layer that can utilize objects in the domain directly. Instead, we want to provide the front end of an application with the bare minimum data it needs to do its job. Usually, a fully instantiated entity object is overkill, and we don't want to expose functionality or behaviors of the entity to other parts of the application that don't require it. Instead, we create a watered-down, "dumb," plain ol' PHP object that contains all the data that the entity itself has and that the front end needs, but no additional behaviors or details are sent.

In terms of structured data, we refer to *unstructured data* as data expressed as a plain PHP array. It looks like the following:

```
$myArray = [
    'name' => "Jesse",
    'title' => "Web Developer",
    'dob' => "09/14/1987"
];
```

As a client of a domain service, we obviously know the data that will be in the array because it we are creating it. However, the domain service itself is left to do the various validations and `isset()` checks to verify the data inside the array is what it is expected to be.

```
class SomeController
{
    public function displayPerson($person): string
    {
        $person = $person['name']; /* we can't just use this as is
                                      Because we cannot guarantee
                                      that the 'name' key even
                                      Exists inside the array */

    }
}
```

Instead, if we used a DTO to represent a `Person` object instead of an array (which is unstructured) or a full-fledged entity, we could go about our business of displaying that person on the screen.

```
class Person
{
    public string $name;
    public string $title;
    public \DateTime $dob;
}

class SomeController
{
```

```
public function displayPerson(Person $person): string
{
    $name = $person->name;
    $title = $person->title;
    $dob = $person->dob;
    //do stuff
}
}
```

In the previous controller method, we can guarantee that there is a name property on the Person object, as well as the other attributes it has, and we can use them directly with no consequence because there is no behavior attached to the DTO, just data. Using DTOs has a number of benefits.

- They allow us to type hint objects as we've done earlier, instead of using arrays.

- By making the properties on the DTO specifically typed, we can ensure they contain the data that they should contain without the need to do additional checks or validations.

- DTOs can be statically analyzed and autocompleted, while arrays cannot.

- Structured data is easier to work with and is more explicit than arrays.

DTOs really don't change much from framework to framework, or even across languages. They are usually plain classes that just hold data that represents some entity in the database. However, I have found an extremely cool and immensely helpful package that gives you tools and a means of creating DTOs that is straightforward and adds value to the application.

Adding Spatie's Data Transfer Object Package

To install this DTO helper package on your system, issue this command:

```
composer require spatie/data-transfer-object
```

This gives us a base `DataTransferObject` class to work with, which gives your application a variety of facilities for which to create and manage your DTOs. For instance, to create a DTO using this package, you would extend the base class, which would look like the following for our `Person` object:

```
class Person extends DataTransferObject
{
    public string $name;
    public string $title;
    public string $dob;
}
```

I realize this doesn't look a whole lot different than the previous class, but what's different about this class is that to instantiate it, you can just pass in an array of keyed properties to the constructor.

```
$person = new Person([
    'name' => 'Jesse',
    'title' => 'Web Developer',
    'dob' => '09/14/1987'
]);
```

Isn't that neat? You don't even have to specify a constructor. This little baby has the power of retrieving values inside it as an array or as an object.

```
$name = $person['name'];
//is the same as
$name = $person->name;
```

The values specified in the instantiation of this object get automatically type checked against the types we've specified in the DTO. We no longer have to worry about checking types of our DTO as long as we are either type hinting the properties explicitly as shown earlier (which required PHP 7.4) or as long as they are type hinted with do blocks (for prior versions of PHP that do not support the inline typing of properties with primitive types).

There are a bunch of other features this package comes with, and I urge you to check all of them out at `https://github.com/spatie/data-transfer-object`. These features include things such as managing DTO collections, type casting nested arrays into objects, creating immutable properties on an object (or making the entire object itself immutable), and using helper functions to help you manage and facilitate your DTOs in pretty much any manner you will need to. I recommend you use this package for all your DTO-related tasks.

Conclusion

Entities and value objects are necessary building blocks to achieve a domain-driven design. Entities are more complex and come with a lifecycle that must be managed. Usually this means tracking the entity's internal state. Value objects, on the other hand, are simple objects that represent elements in a domain model that are uniquely differentiated by the *values* they contain rather than an explicit identifier (such as an ID field), which is the case with entities. We have made a trait to be used when creating value objects that makes them easier to facilitate within the application and easier to create or replace.

An entity and a model are used interchangeably in this text. Entities should hold most of the business rules and business logic in the system. A good way to remember this is to practice keeping a "Fat Model" and a "Skinny Controller," meaning that controllers should only serve as a means of facilitating the delivery mechanism (such as accepting a request object and "shaking hands" with the client), and the models should contain the business logic, not controllers.

There are numerous mechanisms used to give entities identity. Among them the client provides identity, application provides identity, persistence generates identities, and another bounded context provides identity. The last one is the most involved and sometimes requires a variety of value objects and a translator to mediate between the value objects and the entities living in the other bounded context.

DTOs are simply watered-down representations of entities that contain only data, no behaviors, and can be used to add structure to unstructured data, such as that contained within multidimensional arrays. They also provide front-end components with a specific set of data they can use to do their job. This alleviates the need for us to pass around full-fledged entities (which we want to avoid doing whenever possible) and instead provide a simple, explicitly defined object containing only the properties that are necessary for the task at hand. Spatie has published a package that helps create, facilitate, and manage DTOs, which comes with a bunch of cool helper methods and additional functionality that can save time and code when developing DTOs such as automatic type checking, nested array to object translation, and self-containing factories for which to instantiate them. It is suggested that you give this package a try in your own projects.

Overall, entities are one of the most important aspects in your domain model because they represent the actual elements of the underlying domain in a literal fashion. Therefore, care should be given when creating entities and explicitly defining the relationships they have to other entities in the same system.

CHAPTER 13

Domain Events

Things happen in applications—a lot of things. Some are more interesting than others. *Events* capture this information, package it up in a nice and clear format/structure, and rely on a broadcasting mechanism or dispatcher to dispatch the event to the rest of the application. We have already gotten a taste of events in Chapter 5. This chapter will build on that information and provide you with additional context and discussion on domain events specifically.

Which components actually get notified about a particular event is based on a subscriber or Observer or PubSub pattern (they all mean roughly the same thing). Within the context of an application, communication between all the moving parts and pieces that make the application function as a whole is critical in modern-day development. For example, if a new user registers with the system, we might dispatch a `UserHasRegistered` event, which contains a few pieces of data that are important to describe it and whatever else the dispatched event touches.

In this chapter, we will discuss events, which come in three flavors: application events, domain events, and infrastructure events. We will touch on application and infrastructure events, but the majority of this chapter will be focused on domain events. I will explain what domain events mean to Laravel and DDD and explain how we can implement domain events in a straightforward manner that abides by the general lessons of DDD and that uses Laravel. Laravel has numerous components built in that support creating and dispatching events that prove to be useful to a domain-driven design.

Lastly, we will continue our design of the claims application, adding in this notion of domain events and taking a look at where they could prove to be useful within the context of claim submission. I'll show you how and when to utilize domain events and how they can be used to integrate bounded contexts.

The examples used in the first part of this chapter are based on a more standardized and formal DDD. This is so you can get a general understanding of how events are structured and how listeners are used. Later in the chapter, we will go through some possible ways to implement domain events using Laravel's components as well as a

409

© Jesse Griffin 2021
J. Griffin, *Domain-Driven Laravel*, https://doi.org/10.1007/978-1-4842-6023-4_13

third-party package for creating and working with domain events that can be plugged into our Eloquent models, allowing you to work with the models (and therefore the database) directly. Also, we will go over event sourcing, how and why it is used, and what a possible implementation of an event-sourced architecture could look like in Laravel.

The Value of Events

The different types of events are based on the layer that they execute in. Application events get handled by Laravel's event dispatcher and are used throughout the framework to facilitate the spread of information to the various components that make up that application, located in different bounded contexts. These include framework-specific events and listeners. The last type of events are the focus of this chapter; domain events are custom to the domain in which you are working in and require setting up a custom event and listener. They convey information about the various subscribing components so that those components can react to the event in (more or less) an automated fashion. Domain events are core to your implementation of the domain model because the model facilitates and spreads specific knowledge that something interesting has happened elsewhere in the application.

Example: Accounting Software

For example, take a web-based accounting system. One of the features of this system is that it automatically reconciles a central ledger that incorporates all of the transactions in real time. Whenever a transaction is recorded in one of the account-based ledgers, a matching transaction must be recorded in the central ledger. This is beneficial for bankers to see the current assets of the bank to determine how much is available for investing, rather than waiting 24 hours for the balances and transactions to get updated in the appropriate ledger to be reconciled before the accounts get updated. Let's say that there are two bounded contexts that handle this feature.

- *The account ledger accounting context*: Handles updating the account-based ledgers in real time

- *The central ledger accounting context*: Handles the real-time posting of the matching transactions from any account-based ledger to the central ledger and reconciles the ledger after every transaction posting

These two contexts obviously need to communicate with each other so that a matching transaction can be posted in real time to the central ledger. One way to manage the communication, while still respecting the boundaries of each context, is to employ domain events that encapsulate all the transaction data for each transaction. That event would then be distributed to subscribing components interested in listening to the event (listeners are also known as *event handlers*). The event should be decoupled from any particular context that sends or receives it; this is similar to how a distributive architecture works.

One way to do this is to rely on an event dispatcher, which simply receives an event and then dispatches it to the subscribed listeners. In the previous scenario, the account ledger context would dispatch an event via the event dispatcher, which would then accept the event and propagate it throughout the rest of the system, which would include any components that have registered with the event dispatcher to listen to the event. The event dispatcher acts as the distributive hub that connects the different components of the application together in a decoupled and distributive manner. This allows you to have programmatic interactions between your components while still keeping their logic and contexts separate at the application or network level. Events are also a key component in the microservice architecture and are what more or less glues the pieces together.

Getting back to our example accounting software scenario, the account-based context would send something like a `NewTransactionWasRecorded` event to the event dispatcher. The other context (central ledger context) would have to already have been registered with the event dispatcher to listen to that particular event. So once the event has been sent from the first context, the event dispatcher would pick it up and distribute it to the subscribing components, which, among others, includes the central-account context. The central account context receives the propagated event from the event dispatcher and then acts accordingly. The context that is sending the event to the dispatcher doesn't know or care which other contexts are listening to it. It has been completely decoupled. Also, the receiving context won't necessarily know where the event actually came from, just that it has occurred.

Encapsulated in the event are things such as the accounts affected, as well as any other transaction-related data, so that any listening component has a good idea of what was involved in the event. The central accounting context will then create a matching transaction on its own ledger, thereby making that ledger update in real time with each and every transaction. In a real-world scenario, you'd probably have a bunch of different accounts to which transactions are posted most likely by the thousands or tens of thousands per day for a bank. Since there may be more than one account-based ledger that sends events to the central ledger, they can all follow the same process and simply dispatch this same event to the event dispatcher, which will handle the event and deliver it (and the attached event data) to whichever contexts are subscribed to receive them via the event dispatcher. This is a perfect example of how domain events can bridge a local bounded context with one from outside the application/service/network. Events are also key in how the hexagonal architecture functions internally.

Message Queues

An event bus or message queue is a way to incorporate bounded contexts that are on separate networks, such as asynchronous message queue such as RabbitMQ or Amazon SQS. The way this would work is you would just set up the application to fire events at the queue instead of the event dispatcher because, really, all a queue is from a high-level perspective is simply a high-end event dispatcher in the cloud that comes with a bunch of added features. However, even though you are sending the event through the queue instead of handling it locally, you will probably still want to keep a record of it in your system for analytical and historical purposes. This can be done with what's called a *projection*, where some event, after it's initially fired, sends a matching projected event to a different receiver in the system, which handles the logic via an event listener, which would include a write projection on a MySQL database to log that the event happened. Because the two events occur one after the other in a sequence (i.e., synchronously), this is known as *eventual consistency*, which, as you may have guessed, works on both sides of the operation (most likely via a persistence mechanism, queueing system, or caching server—maybe even Elasticsearch).

Naming Events

Events should always be named in accordance with, you guessed it, the ubiquitous language of the domain. Because an event is basically a record of something occurring in the past, you should strive to keep all events named in the past tense, such as the following:

- `UserHasRegistered` or `UserRegistered`

- `BlogPostWasPublished` or `BlogPostPublished`

- `PatientHasScheduledAppointment` or `PatientScheduledAppointment`

- `SomeProcessHasStarted` or `SomeProcessStarted`

- `AnotherProcessHasStopped` or `AnotherProcessStopped`

Some developers prefer the shorter syntax, which is quicker and prettier and still conveys the fact that whatever it is has already occurred. It's really up to your personal preference which to use, and it doesn't matter all that much as long as you stick with a naming convention that is from the ubiquitous language and you name things as if they already happened (which is the case). Personally speaking, I prefer the longer way to name them because it's clearer and more explicit than the other. (For example, `PatientScheduledAppointment` could very well be an entity for all we know, because it sounds like it's a thing, rather than a description.)

Domain Events: Claims

Getting back to our ongoing claim processing application, let's list some important things that *occur* within the normal process of submitting a claim through the system and create some events to describe them (Table 13-1). These are known as *domain events* because they directly correspond to domain-related concerns.

Table 13-1. Domain Concerns in the Claim Application and Their Corresponding Events

Domain Concern	Potential Events
A new patient is registered in the system and assigned a new primary provider.	`PatientWasRegistered` `PatientUpdatedPrimaryProvider` `PatientDocumentsUploaded`
A new provider is registered in the system and added to an existing paycode sheet in the system.	`ProviderWasRegistered` `ProviderAddedToPaycodeSheet` `ProviderUpdatedCptCodeGroups`
A claim was submitted.	`ClaimWasSubmitted` `ClaimWasUpdated`

(continued)

413

Table 13-1. (*continued*)

Domain Concern	Potential Events

A claim has been reviewed and approved by a claim reviewer.	`ClaimWasReviewed`
	`ClaimStatusUpdated`
	`ClaimWasApproved`

A claim has been reviewed by a claim reviewer and was marked as needing correction.	`ClaimWasReviewed`
	`ClaimStatusUpdated`
	`ClaimNeedsCorrection`

The patient was verified as eligible to receive benefits, which is saved to the claim.	`PatientEligibilityVerified` `ClaimWasUpdated`

The claim has been approved for payout, and then the estimated claim amount is paid to the provider owning the claim.	`ClaimWasReviewed`
	`ClaimStatusUpdated`
	`ClaimApproved`
	`BillerHasApprovedClaim`
	`ProviderWasPaid`
	`ClaimWasClosed`

Notice that in Table 13-1 I have chosen event names based on the entities that were affected by the event being fired and a description of what the event is about. Some events have a `Was` or `Has` in the name, and some don't, but all events describe something that happened in the past and can be directly associated with a specific piece of the application where it was fired from. The entities are all based on terms in the ubiquitous language, and generally speaking this is a good indication that we are on the right track in regard to keeping the implementation in code close to the domain itself and we are modeling it sufficiently. The opposite is also true: event names that have an unclear meaning or that don't represent items found within the ubiquitous language can be a sign that the events are not derived from the domain properly or that they model the wrong things in regard to the domain.

Services and Events

Application services are the middlemen between the outside and the domain logic. They usually accept some form of a request and transform that request into a command, which the domain layer can understand and run. Oftentimes they will operate on scalar values and transform them into business objects so that the application can process them or further utilize them within the domain layer. Using a framework like Laravel, the delivery mechanism is abstracted for you, provided you specify the incoming parameters and validations in the Request object.

An example of an application service (in the interest of the ongoing claims application) is something like a new patient registering in the system. This service may handle only one thing, registering a patient, but there may be additional logic that gets run in response to a new patient registration. Besides all the steps it takes to register a new patient before we actually emit a PatientWasCreated event, we may have logic that we can set to perform when that event is actually fired, which in this case would be when the patient is created. To start things off, you would need to define a controller that will accept an input request that is constructed specifically for that request (perhaps RegisterPatientRequest, which would then get handed off to the controller). See Listing 13-1.

Listing 13-1. Example Application Service of New Patient Being Registered in the System

```php
<?php
namespace App\User\Application\Http\Controllers;

use App\User\Application\Requests\RegisterPatientRequest;
Use App\User\Application\Services\PatientRegistrationService;
use App\Http\Controllers\Controller;
use Illuminate\Http\JsonResponse;

class PatientRegistrationController
{
    private $registrationService;

    public function __construct(PatientRegistrationService $registrationService)
    {
```

```
            $this->registrationService = $registrationService;
    }

    public function register(RegisterPatientRequest $request)
    {
        $patientDetails = $request->get('patient.details');
        $patientDocuments = $request->get('patient.documents');
        $patientEligibility =
            $request->get('patient.initial_eligibility');
        $registeredProvider = $request->get('patient.provider');
        $consentForm = $request->get('patient.consentForm');

        return new JsonResponse(
                $this->registrationService->execute(
                    $patientDetails,
                    $patientDocuments,
                    $patientEligibility,
                    $registeredProvider,
                    $consentForm
                )
        );
    }
}
```

There are a few things to note about the previous example.

- The namespaces presented are only one way of structuring the pieces
  of logic corresponding to that bounded context; however, if it makes
  it clearer for the domain and concepts within the domain model
  to have an additional category defined as a namespace, you most
  certainly could opt for things like these:

  ```
  App\User\Application\Requests\Patient\RegisterPatientRequest
  App\User\Application\Services\Patient\PatientRegistrationService
  App\User\Application\Http\Controllers\Regsitration\
  PatientRegistrationController
  ```

- A resource controller defining the actual resource in the system that encompasses what a patient is and what it does could be used instead of a plain controller, in which case you may want to employ route model binding as well.

Overall, the code in Listing 13-1 simply sets up the controller with dependency injection and automatically injects the actual service we need to use to fulfill the request. Whatever the controller needs to do its job, other than the request itself, should be type-hinted in the constructor and assigned to private member variables to be used later. Then, in the actual route method that gets called (in this case `register()`), inject the request that is specific to encapsulating all the input required for the request to be processed by the service. Notice, however, that this method only receives the request, pulls data out of the request object, and passes that data to the service type hinted in the constructor, completely delegating the logic to that service and returning to the client an instance of a response (in this case, a `JsonResponse`) that can be returned elegantly to the front end by the built-in response mechanism.

While this may sound like the controller is doing a lot of work, the actual work that it does do is very little. Its job is to do the following:

1. Accept a request (i.e., shake hands with the client)

2. Delegate the real work that needs to be done to fulfil the request to a service or job

3. Return a response (i.e., a confirmation success [200] or error message [4/500])

In Listing 13-2, you can see an implementation of one such service that can be considered a more formal DDD approach.

Listing 13-2. Service That Registers Patients

```php
<?php
namespace App\User\Application\Services;

class RegisterPatientService
{
    private PatientRepository $patientRepository;
    private DocumentUploadService $docService;
    private PatientPrimaryService $patientPrimaryService;
```

```php
    private PatientEligibilityService $patientEligibilityService;
    private EventDispatcher $eventDispatcher;
    public function __construct(
        PatientRepository $patientRepository,
        DocumentUploadService $docService,
        PatientPrimaryService $patientPrimaryService,
        PatientEligibilityService $patientEligibilityService,
        EventDispatcher $eventDispatcher,
    )
    {
        $this->patientRepository = $patientRepository;
        $this->docService = $docService;
        $this->patientPrimaryService = $patientPrimaryService;
        $this->patientEligibilityService = $patientEligibilityService;
        $this->eventDispatcher = $eventDispatcher;
    }

    public function execute( PatientDetails $patientDetails,
                             array $patientDocuments,
                             PatientEligibility $patientEligibility,
                             Provider $registeredProvider,
                             ConsentForm $consentForm)
    {
        // EX: Step 1 - Create & persist the Patient entity:
        // run any business logic required for validation:
        if ($this->validatePatientDetails($patientDetails)) {
            $nextID = $this->patientRepository->nextId();
            $patient = new Patient($nextId, $patientDetails);
            $this->patientRepository->persist($patient);

            $this->eventDispatcher->dispatch(new
            PatientWasCreated($patient));
        }
        // ... validate the rest of the inputs ...
        // ... dispatch the remaining events ...
    }
```

```
public function validatePatientDetails(PaymentDetails
$paymentDetails);
{
    //domain validations - although this could be better placed
    //within the model itself as a precondition, it still works
    if ($valid) {
        return true;
    }
    return false;
}

// similar validation methods would follow
}
```

The previous service is basically an umbrella service that incorporates additional other services under it, acting as a sort of facade in that there is a single point of entry that encapsulates a set of inner services, all of them required to be run to register a patient. This service has the services and objects it needs to do its job injected into the constructor and the data within the execute() method. The arguments for this method are merely simple DTOs that represent the various aspects of the data required for a new patient registration. It is easier to work with objects than it is arrays, and DTOs do a decent job of describing the data in the arrays in an object-oriented manner. I will show you a better version of this class that accomplishes the same thing in a more elegant manner.

For now, just understand that there are multiple services that are doing various things in the application that can be collectively considered the task of registering a new patient in the system. The first task is highlighted in Listing 13-2, which includes actually creating a new Patient entity by getting a fresh identity from the repository, persisting it to the database, and then dispatching an event to specify the successful running of that particular subtask. As the services continue to fire off in the execute method for each subtask, they all follow suit and do something with the passed-in input parameters (such as uploading a document, selecting a primary physician for a patient, etc.) and then dispatch an event to capture a history that each subtask occurred.

Listing 13-3 demonstrates what the PatientWasCreated event could look like.

Listing 13-3. Example Domain Event That Gets Fired When a New Patient Is
Created in the System

```php
<?php
namespace App\User\Domain\Events;

use Illuminate\Queue\SerializesModels;
use App\User\Domain\Models\Patient;

class PatientWasCreated extends DomainEvent
{
    use SerializesModels;
    public PatientDetails $patientDetails;

    public function __construct(PatientDetails $patientDetails)
    {
        $this->model = Patient::class;
    }

    public class getEventBody()
    {
        return (string)$this->patientDetails;
    }
}
```

The event is pretty bare-bones. This event extends the DomainEvent parent class,
which will abstract away how the events get persisted from the event. We tuck the logic
into an abstract parent class that gives us a means of persisting events to a database
table or message queue. The event is stored in a sequential fashion via some mechanism
that works with the event store to persist it. The abstract class DomainEvent houses this
mechanism, which I will give you an example of in the "Events in DDL" section of this
chapter. The event body is set to be whatever is returned from the getEventBody()
method, which, in the previous case, must have a DTO named PatientDetails, and that
DTO must support a __toString() method that properly translates the event's body to a
string that gets stored within the event_body field in the database table. This field should
contain all the relevant data from the event itself, including any other relating entities or
row IDs of the impacted database rows that are related to the event.

Of course, as we learned in a previous chapter, we do not need to create these classes from scratch. Instead, we can put the events and their listeners into the $listen array of the EventServiceProvider class and then run the Artisan command php artisan events:generate. This will create the basic class structures for our defined events and their corresponding listeners that we have included in the array. Even better, we can make all of our events autodiscoverable by setting the shouldDiscoverEvents method of your application's EventServiceProvider. See Chapter 5 for details on how to do this.

There is a better way to do this that is slightly less secure in terms of object access, because it involves leaving the properties of the event publicly accessible. This is so that the mechanism handling the persistence of the event can run a simple get_object_vars() on the object, json_encode the results, and persist that JSON-encoded data within an event_body field on the database table, along with the ID of that object. Over the course of days or months, there will be numerous rows referencing the same eventId and a different event_body.

Event Listeners

The other events are the associated event listeners that act because of the events dispatched from the event dispatcher. An *event listener* is a fairly simple concept, although the logic that event listeners contain may be complex, depending on the nature of the event. The same basic format applies to listeners as well: inject whatever dependencies you need to complete the task at hand and then place the logic that actually does stuff inside a handle() method, which is provided by the parent class and overwritten in the listener.

Listing 13-4 shows an example of a listener that listens to the PatientWasCreated event that we dispatched previously in the example. Notice that we have named the listener in terms of what it *does*, and not what it *is*. This particular listener will add the patient to an Elasticsearch cluster. This would allow admin users, providers, and reviewers to be able to search through all the patient records quickly, perhaps via an autocomplete feature.

Listing 13-4. Event Listener Triggered by the PatientWasCreated Event

```php
<?php
namespace App\User\Domain\Listeners;
use App\User\Domain\Events\PatientWasCreated;

class AddPatientToElasticsearch
{
    private EsRepository $esRepository;
    public function __construct(ESRepository $esRepository)
    {
        $this->esRepository = $esRepository;
    }

    public function handle(PatientWasCreated $event)
    {
        //get data to event store (database)
        $patientDetails = $event->getEventBody();
        //store them in Elasticsearch via a call to its repository
        $this->esRepository>addToIndex('patients',$patientDetails);
        //reindex the patient index
        $this->esRepository::reindex('patients');
    }
}
```

This is a simple example of an event listener that could be listening to the
PatientWasCreated event dispatched from an application service that gets run every
time a new patient gets created in the system. This is specific for each event based on the
return value that the events define in their respective handle() methods.

All in all, this example gave you a general understanding of events and event
handlers, but they are lacking some Laravel syntax sugar and some cool features in
Laravel and Eloquent that can be used to create easy, understandable code that is
modeled after the true intentions and processes of the domain. But this example looks
prettier than the previous code and appropriately models the domain correctly.

Events in DDL

Now that you have some foundational knowledge about domain events and event listeners, we can go over a possible implementation with Laravel and Eloquent, which is, in my opinion, simpler and more robust. Further, it is still explicit enough to rely on for type checking and follows the important aspects of DDD regarding separation of concerns and domain-driven design. It is my opinion that a bunch of added code, classes, or components can easily complicate the design of the domain model, causing the focus to switch off the domain and on to maintaining the bloated codebase, which is not what we want. We want a way to develop code that is readable, that is robust, and (most importantly) that represents the underlying domain concepts sufficiently.

If we think about it, the majority of events that get dispatched are due to (or come with) some update or change to a model in the system. Instead of manually placing the logic to dispatch events, we can employ the Eloquent lifecycle events that are baked into every model class in our system (all model classes are expected to extend Eloquent's parent Model class). This way, we already have a set of events that we can observe to hook into any additional logic we need to run when an event gets fired. You should recall the discussion from a previous chapter regarding the events in an Eloquent model, but just to refresh, here is a list of the available events that occur within every model:

- retrieved
- creating
- created
- updating
- updated
- saving
- saved
- deleting
- deleted
- restoring
- restored

We can hook in our additional logic to run on the occurrence of any of these events using an observer (we went through an example of one earlier in the book). Observers are good when you want to group the events you are listening to within the same model. Another way we can use these events is by telling Laravel that we want a custom event to be run *whenever* one of these events fire. You do this within the model itself, through a property named $dispatchesEvents, as shown in Listing 13-5.

Listing 13-5. Listening to an Eloquent Lifecycle Event

```php
<?php
namespace App\User\Domain\Models;
use App\User\Domain\Events\PatientWasCreated;
use Illuminate\Foundation\Auth\User as Authenticatable;
class Patient extends Authenticatable
{
    protected $dispatchedEvents = [
        'created' => PatientWasCreated::class,
        'updated' => PatientWasUpdated::class
    ];
}
```

After we have made this link between the Eloquent event we want to listen to and our custom event we want dispatched, we can proceed to attach logic to the application *when* the event actually happens via a standard listener, as we have done in Listing 13-4. In the previous example, we are telling Laravel that whenever the Eloquent event "created" is fired with a relation to the Patient object, we want the PatientWasCreated event to be fired along with it. This would allow us to use the same listener as in Listing 13-4, because the listener doesn't care what is causing the event to fire; it only cares that the event fired. All listener logic for implementing something like this wouldn't change.

However, in the context of domain-driven design, technically speaking, these events are coupled tightly to the framework and occur at the application level, and they are synchronous. That being said, these lifecycle events are *not* domain events. However, Laravel allows you to basically "forward" a lifecycle event to a custom event that we define, which will then be fired along with the lifecycle event. We can set up this custom event to be a domain event, and we can attach the same domain event listener that would normally be included with a custom domain event. What actually gets abstracted is *how* and *when* the event was fired, neither of which should have anything to do with the listener. Therefore, I'd make the argument that relying on Eloquent lifecycle events is fine because all they do is fire events in accordance with the changes to a given model. The model is certainly part of the domain layer, and the events associated with the model can be listened to with a listener that lives within the domain layer as well. As long as the mechanism you choose to use to facilitate domain knowledge throughout the rest of the application is directly modeled after its domain-related counterparts and you name your events and listeners in correspondence with the ubiquitous language, you can still achieve a domain-driven design.

Persisting Domain Events

Domain events are useful only if they are saved to an event store so they can act as a sort of a history of changes to a particular domain object. Event sourcing takes this a step further and allows you to replay every action taken on an event from the beginning of the entity's life to its BBC current state. The played-back events are a direct representation of the entity's internal state and any changes made to this state throughout the lifetime of the object.

Persisting domain events to an event store is essential. As stated earlier, domain events usually extend an abstract class that hides the logic to handle persistence through some type of event store. When implementing domain events in Laravel, there are a number of built-in contracts (interfaces) and traits that we can specify on the corresponding models that can help us better facilitate them. They include the following:

- `Illuminate\Contracts\Broadcasting\ShouldBroadcast`: Enables the ability for us to push events to a message queue or event bus. This contract requires one additional method to be defined on any implementing classes, `broadcastOn()`, which should return the channel that the event in question will be dispatched to.

- `Illuminate\Support\Facades\Broadcast\InteractsWithSockets`: Allows you to implement broadcasting events over a socket connection (such as `Pusher`).

- `Illuminate\Queue\SerializesModels`: Allows for serializing/ deserializing Eloquent models easily.

- `Illuminate\Support\Arr\Queueable`: Includes functionality that dispatches events to a queue.

To start things off, let's define a base class that all events will extend from. Unlike the more widely used approach of persisting events to an event store, which includes the parent class having the code needed to persist the event within it so that the child classes can just call `$this->save()`, we are going to use traits to handle the persistence tasks so we can hide these details somewhere that is easy to access and use by other classes. We will also employ a base class, but it will be for identity purposes only and will not include anything but a helper method that formats the name of the class. That way, the rest of the application can use this class as a type hint to specify some type of a domain event. Listing 13-6 is a pretty simple abstract class that all domain events will extend from.

Listing 13-6. Abstract Domain Event Class

```php
<?php
namespace App\Common\Domain\Events;
abstract class DomainEvent
{
    /** The model which the event corresponds to */
    public Model $entity;

    /** The user that initiated the event */
    public User $user;

    /**
    * Returns the result of string replace of '_' to '.'.
    * @return string
    */
    public function getName(): string
    {
        return str_replace('_', '.', snake_case((new
            \ReflectionClass($this))->getShortName());
    }
}
```

The fields on the abstract class are both public and represent the only two things required to be considered a domain event: the entity being persisted and the user who initiated the event. Additionally, there is a `getName()` method, which formats the event's name to be used as an identifier later when we collect the events. Specifically, we will group by the name field for a faster lookup than decoding the entity—also called the *event body*—which will be JSON encoded in the database. We would have to decode the JSON and pull the ID out of it before we did any queries on it, which would be too much of a hassle to have to worry about on the fly. Instead, we rely on the abstract class to hold the entity and then add the ID field to the class as a public member variable.

Thinking ahead a little bit, since we aren't going to put the persistence mechanism inside the base parent class, we need to decide where to put it. I recommend throwing things like this into a trait that the events can use to save themselves (no pun intended). We can rely on a Laravel job to hold the actual save logic. Utilizing a trait here is just an easy way to incorporate persistence into the events and is reusable for any other classes or components that may need it. The fact that we pulled out the functionality to store an event is a logical approach to separating concerns. Take, for example, Listing 13-7.

Listing 13-7. Trait Used to Persist Events to the Database

```php
<?php

namespace App\Common\Domain\Traits;

use App\Common\Jobs\SaveDomainEvent;
use App\Common\Domain\Events\DomainEvent;

trait Saveable
{
    public function save()
    {
        dispatch(new SaveDomainEvent(DomainEvent $this));
    }
}
```

The trait in Listing 13-7 is fairly simple: whenever the `save()` method is called on it, it will dispatch a `SaveDomainEvent` job to handle the persistence functionality. The only interesting part of this trait is the fact that I'm passing `$this` as an argument, which would end up being whatever class the trait is used in. To enforce the fact that this trait should only be used in an event class, we type hint the `DomainEvent` class inside the `SaveDomainEvent` job, which you will see next.

Listing 13-8 shows you an example event that gets fired when a provider and patient have been linked in the system (the provider being that patient's new primary care physician).

Listing 13-8. Job That Houses the Functionality Used to Persist Domain Events

```php
<?php
namespace App\Common\Domain\Events;
use App\Common\Jobs\SaveDomainEvent;
use App\Jobs\Job;
use App\Common\Traits\Saveable;
use App\Common\Infrastructure\Repositories\DomainEventRepository;
use Illuminate\Queue\InteractsWithQueue;
use Illuminate\Contracts\Queue\ShouldQueue;
use Illuminate\Queue\SerializesModels;

class SaveDomainEvent extends Job implements ShouldQueue
{
    use InteractsWithQueue, Saveable;

    private DomainEvent $event;

    private Model $entity;

    public function __construct(DomainEvent $event)
    {
        $this->event = $event;

        if (property_exists($event, 'entity')) {
            $this->entity = $this->event->entity;
        }
    }
    public function handle(DomainEventRepository $eventRepository)
    {
    return $eventRepository->createFromData([
        'event_id' => Uuid::uuid4()->toString(),
        'event_body' => json_encode(array_filter(array_except(
            get_object_vars($this->event),['entity'])
        )),
        'eventable_type' => $this->entity ?
            get_class($this->entity) : null,
```

```
        'eventable_id' => $this->entity ?
            $this->entity->getKey() : null,
        'event_type' => $this->event->getName(),
        'user_id' => $this->event->user ?
            $this->event->user->getKey() : null
    ]);
}
}
```

From the interfaces that the previous job implements, we can reasonably deduce that this job supports a queueable messaging system and contains the name of the channel to broadcast the events that are emitted on. The constructor accepts an instance of a domain event, which is what gets saved via the event store. The handle() method accepts any dependencies that must be injected to do its job, which in the previous case includes setting up the array of events that will be persisted to the database. It uses a standard UUID format for the application-generated key to differentiate between any other events.

For our purposes, that event store is a relational database table (most likely MySQL). However, there are other options available, such as Redis, Elasticsearch, Firebase, and a handful of others. No matter which event store you end up using for your application, keep in mind this fact: the event store (table, index, etc.) is going to get fairly large in comparison to the other tables (or indexes or whatever). What this means to you as a developer is that you should make sure that, no matter where or how you store the event data, it should be segregated from the rest of the application's data.

Tip   The best place for storing the domain events is on a separate server instance (or by some other means of segregating the domain event data from the rest of the application). the domain events table can grow large, especially a in courser-grained event system, and can eventually cause severe slowness and even cause application or database server failures. Save you and your team the hassle of troubleshooting this issue when it happens down the road.

The array containing the event data has the following fields:

- event_id: Primary key in domain_events, in UUID format.

- eventable_id: The ID corresponding to the designated $entity property on the Event class, which is also the ID within the model described by the eventable_type field.

- event_body: The actual event data that is stored within the table to describe the data that is in addition to the subject of the event (entity). We can do this because we are setting all the properties to public.

- eventable_type: The polymorphic relationship key that pertains to the entity's class.

- event_type: The name of the event.

- user_id: The ID of the user instigating the event.

Breaking Down the Process

To give you a better idea of how this mechanism actually works, Listing 13-9 shows an example event from the domain_events table that will be the result of the mechanism encapsulated within the DomainEventRepository::createFromData() method. This is a better approach to designing domain events that works with the previous SaveDomainEvent class. It is modeled after an event named ClaimWasSubmitted and is emitted when, you guessed it, a claim is verified and submitted within the application.

Listing 13-9. An Event Fired Whenever There Is a New Claim Submission

```php
<?php
namespace Claim\Submission\Domain\Events;

use App\Events\Event;
use App\Common\Domain\Events\SaveDomainEvent;
use App\Common\Domain\Traits\Saveable;
use Claim\Submission\Domain\Models\Claim;
use Illuminate\Queue\SerializesModels;
use Illuminate\Contracts\Broadcasting\ShouldBroadcast;
```

```
class ClaimWasSubmitted extends DomainEvent implements ShouldBroadcast
{
    use SerializesModels, Saveable;

    public Claim $claim;

    public User $user;

    /**
     * Create Event
     */
    public function __construct(Claim $claim): void
    {
        $this->claim = $claim;
        $this->user = $user;
        $this->entity = $claim;
    }

    /**
     * Broadcast on channel 'domain_events'
     */
    public function broadcastOn()
    {
        return ['domain_events'];
    }
}
```

In Listing 13-9, we define a fairly simple class with some public properties and a defined broadcasting channel to communicate with other services or applications. We have a defined entity property set to be whatever the subject of the event is, in this case, a claim, so it is set to $claim. The public $user property is the user who submitted the claim and is fundamental to the event itself, but is not the direct subject of the event. If there was an event that fired named UserUpdatedPassword, then the $entity property would be set to $user instead. A NewProviderCreated event would have the $provider property as the $entity. You get the picture.

The main thing to take away here is *how* the event is stored. Because of the abstract class DomainEvent, any property that we make public will be parsed, JSON encoded, and stored in the event_body field in the database. The subject of the event (the $entity property) has the class name saved in the eventable_type field and the corresponding ID of that entity stored in the $eventable_id field. The ID fields in the domain_events table are all integers (big ints) except for event_id, which is the primary key of the table and is a string with a formatted UUID. Table 13-2 shows what a row in that table may look like.

Table 13-2. *Sample Database Row from domain_events Table*

Field Name	Field Value
Id	ED7BA470-8E54-465E-825C-99712043E01C
event_body	{"id":91977,"fname":"Jesse","lname":"Griffin", "role_id":3,"address":"3230 Sweetwater Springs Blvd.","city":"Spring Valley","zip":"91977", "state":"CA","created_at":"2020-01-20 16:20:00", "updated_at":"2020-01-20 16:20:20"}
eventable_type	Claim\Submission\Domain\Models\Claim
eventable_id	9140202
user_id	426
event_type	Claim\Submission\Domain\Events\ClaimWasSubmitted

In Table 13-2, you can see the results of persisting the event described by the ClaimWasSubmitted event from Listing 13-8. As promised, the event_type class describes the subject of the event, a claim, along with the corresponding ID of that type stored in the eventable_id field. The event_body class contains the extra data associated with the event (defined by the public properties in the event class), which in the previous case is a json_encoded string of the user who initiated the event. To describe which event actually created that data, we can look at the event_type field, which in this case is the class from Listing 13-8. It may seem redundant, but the user_id field contains the user_ id value of that same user; however, it won't always be a User model that is referenced by the event_type field, but there is always a user tied to the event.

DTOs

A *data transfer object* (DTO) is a simple object, usually with public properties accessed and set with getters and setters. Their main goal is simply to provide structure to unstructured data. *Unstructured data* includes things such as multidimensional arrays, such as the following:

```
$data = [
        'id' => 91977,
        'fname' => 'Jesse',
        'lname' => 'Griffin',
        'role_id' => 3,
        'address' => '3230 Sweetwater Springs Blvd.',
        'city' => 'Spring Valley',
        'zip' => '91977',
        'state' => 'CA',
        'created_at' => '2020-01-20 16:20:00',
        'updated_at' => '2020-01-20 16:20:20'
];
```

This array has a standard set of data in it that could be used as an argument to some method or function. This is fine and will work, but it's not exactly ideal in a domain-driven design because there's no way tell what's in the array at first glance, without doing an print_r() or dumping it out.

```
public function doSomeThingCool(array $data)
{
    $this->data = $data;

    // OR
    foreach ($data as $d) {
        //what now?
    }
}
```

Without iterating through the array or using array_keys or something similar, you have no way to logically deduce its contents. An easier and more explicit way to define such a data structure is to turn it into a DTO, which can be found in Listing 13-10.

433

Listing 13-10. Example DTO Created in Place of an Unstructured Array

```
class Data
{
    private $id;
    private $fname;
    private $lname;
    private $role_id;
    private $address;
    private $city;
    private $state;
    private $zip;
    private $created_at;
    private $updated_at;

    public function getId(): int
    {
        return $this->id;
    }
    public function setId(int $id): self
    {
        $this->id = $id;
        return $this;
    }

    public function getFname(): string
    {
        return $this->fname;
    }
public function setFname($fname): self
    {
        $this->fname = $fname;
        return $this;
    }
    /* remaining getters and setters */
}
```

This DTO is pretty basic and doesn't have any other features than being just a container to hold data and methods to access and modify it, both of which we get for free with Eloquent's Model class. The only difference between a model and a DTO is that the model is directly associated with the database table, because Eloquent uses an Active Record pattern.

There is a package available from Spatie (https://spatie.be/open-source) called Data Transfer Objects for Laravel (https://github.com/spatie/data-transfer-object). It makes creating DTOs easy; however, it does come with a price: what you gain in convenience, you give up in being explicit when it comes to object and property definitions. Listing 13-11 shows an example of how to create a DTO object with this package. Note that Listing 13-11 makes it prettier than the DTO class in Listing 13-10, because you don't have to write all those boring and long getter and setter methods.

Listing 13-11. A DTO Extending Spatie's Abstract DataTransferObject Class

```php
<?php
//some namespace
use Spatie\DataTransferObject;

class Data extends DataTransferObject
{
    public $id;
    public $fname;
    public $lname;
    public $role_id;
    public $address;
    public $city;
    public $state;
    public $zip;
    public $created_at;
    public $updated_at;
}
```

The example in Listing 13-11 gives you the ability to set and get each of the public properties defined on the child class as if they each had a getter method and a setter method. An instance of this class can be constructed like so:

```
$data = new Data([
        'id' => 91977,
        'fname' => 'Jesse',
        'lname' => 'Griffin',
        'role_id' => 3,
        'address' => '3230 Sweetwater Springs Blvd.',
        'city' => 'Spring Valley',
        'zip' => '91977',
        'state' => 'CA',
        'created_at' => '2020-01-20 16:20:00',
        'updated_at' => '2020-01-20 16:20:20'
]);
```

You can then use the data like so:

```
echo $data->fname;
echo $data->role_id;
echo %data->state;
...
```

You can also add static creation methods to the class, making it fast and easy to instantiate.

```
class Data
{
    // ...
    public static function fromRequest(Request $request)
    {
        return new self([
            'fname' => $request->fname,
            'lname' => $request->lname,
            'State' => $request->state,
            // ...
        ]);
    }
}
```

There is also support for collections of DTOs that give you the added ability to create multiple DTOs when you are dealing with multiple DTOs. For more information and examples on using this package in your own code, see the documentation online.

Conclusion

Domain events are a mandatory part of any long-lived and well-distributed application and are a central part of any modern-day web application. They also allow for communication between bounded contexts and are a vital key to a distributive architecture and microservices as well. In Laravel, events are handled natively in the codebase and can be fired from any location in the code using the event() helper method. This makes it easier to manage and add events to any system, new or legacy, because you don't have to worry about passing around an event dispatcher (or using dependency to inject a separate event repository). In DDL, we can set up an abstract class, as we've done earlier in the chapter, and use an independent Laravel job as the saving mechanism. This creates a universal foundation for events, and the code is reusable for any event you may need to add to the system later. The persistence of domain events makes it possible to audit your application's data or keep track of any and all changes made to a given model over the course of its lifetime. DTOs can be useful for keeping your data structured and can be made much simpler with the Spatie package, which I suggest you try.

CHAPTER 14

Repositories

Laravel is a fairly unique framework because it abstracts away many of the details that a new application would normally require, such as routing, event management, and database access, so that we can focus on the more important tasks—the ones that actually set our application apart from others of its kind. This same principle exists in DDD, only it presents itself differently. In DDD, the patterns and building blocks are the foundational components of almost any system and are all concentrated on the core domain itself, instead of being bogged down in the (sometimes) overwhelming sea of details. This similarity between Laravel and DDD is, in part, what makes the combination of the two so powerful: they both set out to abstract away the monotonous, repetitive tasks that have already been built, rebuilt, and reinvented a bazillion times to allow you to focus your efforts on developing the domain.

In this chapter, we will explore one such abstraction that has proven to be a helpful patterns in terms of separating out the responsibility of managing how domain objects are stored and retrieved as well as providing a structure that allows clients to work with collections of the same type of object. There are two main types of repositories (at least in the context of web development and DDL).

- *Collection-based repository*: Repository that serves as a means of working with collections of the same object

- *Query-based repository*: Repository that deals with complex, custom queries that are related to a specific domain object

The way we will implement repositories is using a somewhat different approach than the "normal" way that is common in programming. This is also where the principles of DDD and DDL differ somewhat, because in Laravel, there is this notion of *collections*. A collection in Laravel is like an array on steroids. There are two types of collections, regular Laravel collections and Eloquent collections, and the latter offers a few additional methods and mechanisms related to the Eloquent models in the application.

© Jesse Griffin 2021

J. Griffin, *Domain-Driven Laravel*, https://doi.org/10.1007/978-1-4842-6023-4_14

The reason they are worth mentioning in this discussion is because Eloquent collections can basically act as a replacement for the majority of the SELECT queries you would really ever need to run on a model. There are prebuilt methods for all kinds of various functionality offered that allow you to use stock in every Eloquent object that extends the parent Model class. Collections provide a clean and elegant way to sift through a stack of like objects that have been returned from an Eloquent method (and corresponding database query). The only difference is that when you query Eloquent using one of the many methods inherited from the Model class, you receive an Eloquent collection in response. This collection will hold your results returned from database queries on the child Eloquent class, making it easy to chain together different methods to query your database via the model classes and database abstractions that Eloquent provides out of the box. There basically is no need to create separate Repository classes for each object in your domain model for the sake of being able to treat a collection of those objects in a clean and uniform way—with a powerful, fluent interface. We will go into more depth regarding collections and their usefulness next, but a key point to make here is that I will not advocate repositories to handle any such "collection" of objects, because there is no need—Laravel provides that for you. The only thing that needs to be done to tap into this power is a small learning curve that isn't very steep because of the fluent interface that collections offer.

Collections

Collections have many benefits over plain PHP arrays, and Laravel provides a nice, clean, and fluent interface that allows collections to be filtered, mapped, created, combined, and all sorts of other neat stuff, all thanks to the Illuminate\Support\Collection class (or the Illuminate\Database\Eloquent\Collection class for Eloquent collections). Best of all, every collection method will *always* return another collection object. This makes the chaining in collections a powerful and dynamic approach to dealing with lists of objects (which would normally be accomplished by implementing a collection-based repository for every model in the system (sounds like a lot of work, doesn't it?).

The really great thing about Eloquent collections is the ability to traverse relational objects (or *collections* of objects) in such an easy, straightforward way. You may have already noticed this from earlier examples in this book, but here is one way to gather all individual CPT codes from a claim model, without relying on raw SQL queries and iteration/traversal of PHP arrays. For example, we can use such collection methods as each() to loop through all objects in the collection returned by querying the relationship that a CPT combo has to a CPT code. To reference any particular relationship that one model has to another one, we merely have to reference the name of the method that we set up in the model class, without actually calling the method. Here is an example:

```
$claim = Claim::findOrFail($id);
$cptCodes = $claim->cptCodeCombo->cptCfodes;
$cptCodes->each(function($cptCode) {
    echo $cptCode->description;
});
```

The items in bold indicate that a relationship traversal is taking place. This makes traversing relational objects easy and powerful.

Querying relationships is also extremely easy with this interface. If I wanted to get all claims in the system for a given patient, I could do something like the following:

```
$claims = Claim::where('patient_id', $patientId);
```

If I wanted to iterate through those claims and print out the CPT combos that each had on the screen, it would merely be a small matter of tacking on another collection method.

```
$claims = Claim::where('patient_id', $patientId)
            ->each(function($claim) {
                echo $claim->cptCodeCombo;
        });
```

As another example, if I needed to get a list (Collection) of all descriptions in *every* CPT code in the system, I could use the map() method on the collection returned from a call to the all() method (thanks to the chaining power of Laravel collections), which will loop through all objects in a collection and make a *new* collection out of whatever you return as a result of a simple callback, which accepts a single object of the collection for a specific model.

```
$descriptions = CptCode::all()->map(function($cptCode) {
    return $cptCode->description;
});
```

441

This code basically says, "Give me a list of all descriptions of each CptCode in the system." There are many collection methods available to you to use as you want—too many to describe in this book. For a complete reference of all methods available to you on a collection instance, visit https://laravel.com/docs/6.x/eloquent-collections.

Also extremely useful, you can do inline querying of any traversed collections of a given object on the fly. For a more advanced example, let's say I'm building a report for the FQHC containing a claim amount that is going to be paid but has not already been paid to the provider to determine the cost associated with that patient's medical needs for a given period of time (say, within the last four weeks). We would need all the claims in the system, for a specific patient, that currently have the status of PENDING_REVIEW (which we built into this system in our claim state machine in the previous chapter). Then we would add up the total estimated amount of each claim only if it the claim falls on a given date range of the last four weeks. Using the Carbon package included with Laravel to handle the date range, Listing 14-1 shows what that could look like.

Listing 14-1. An Example of Chained Method Calls Using Laravel's Collection Component

```php
<?php

use Carbon\Carbon;

$startDate = Carbon::parse('-4weeks')->toDateTimeString();
$endDate = Carbon::parse('today')->toDateTimeString();

$totalAmountOfPatientsClaims = Claim::where('patient_id', $patientId)
            ->where('claim.state', PendingReview::class)
            ->whereBetween('submitted_at', [$startDate, $endDate])
            ->pluck('estimated_claim_amount')
            ->get()
            ->sum();
```

This line of code is saying, "Give me all claims belonging to the patient with an ID of patientId and in the PendingReview state that were submitted within the last month; then grab the corresponding estimated_amount value of each, add them up, and return the result." We accomplished the task of gathering the proper data needed for the report in a *single line of code*! That is extremely powerful.

Many other methods are available to you that ship with Laravel that help with the filtering, sorting, pagination, and other means of traversing relationships and associations, reducing them until you find what you are looking for. There is a tendency to place hyper-specific query methods inside the repositories. The only problem with this is that, as the application grows in size and complexity, so will the repositories, until what you are left with are classes that don't really abstract anything but act as mere SQL containers and/or specific object queries. There is a better approach that uses a `Criterion` object to describe what exactly you are looking for, by using a combination of the Repository and Specification patterns.

For example, the code in Listing 14-1 could be placed inside a repository named `ClaimRepository`, with a method named `getPendingReviewClaimsForPatient()`; however, look what we have just done. We've started a trend to place hyper-specific methods in the repository, and the trend will just continue until we have ridiculously long and complex names to represent the various combinations of different criteria that are needed to fulfill the needs of some specific query that needs to be run on a given domain model. If this trend continues, there will be more of these hyper-focused methods that will basically hard-code the SQL and filtering mechanisms that the application relies on right inside of a `Repository` class. Since a repository is usually focused on a single entity or model, its repository will pretty much house all the specific query logic that's related to that entity. This can easily get out of control and cause a typical repository written in this manner to grow far too large because of all the specific query logic that's needed to fulfill the various operations and concerns of the application.

The benefit that repositories offer is that they allow for a clear separation between the data mapping layer and the domain layer. They basically allow for a more object-oriented view of the persistence layer. They are not to be confused with data access objects (DAOs), which are simply plain data storage containers that do nothing but hold bits of data related to a single entity in the system and provide access to those properties via getters and setters. DTOs are similar. They are pretty much the most boring objects in all of programming.

Table 14-1 compares a traditional repository implementation of some functionality that we would come to expect an application like the claim application to need to implement at one point or another and compare it to the way Laravel and Eloquent can be used to solve the same problem.

Table 14-1. *Laravel and Eloquent Aspects That Replace Their Corresponding Concepts Usually Found in a Typical Repository*

Functionality/ Description	Repository Method	Laravel/Eloquent Inline Equivalent
Find a record by its ID.	`findBy($id) or ofId($id)`	`Model::find($id)`
Save a single instance of an entity or model (UPDATE and CREATE).	`$model = new Model();` `$model->setField(` `'field','value');` `$repository->save(` `$model) or saveAll( $model)`	`$model = new Model();` `$model->field = $x;` `$model->save();`
Remove a record by ID or remove many records by multiple IDs.	`$ids = []; //ids` `foreach($ids as $id){` `$repository->remove(` `$id) or removeAll($ids)`	`$model = Model::find($id);` `$model->delete();` `Model::whereId('id', $ids)` `->get()-` `>each(function($model) {` `$model->delete(); })`
Sift through data or perform aggregate computations, perhaps as part of some calculation Example: Create a list of patients belonging to a given set of providers that are no longer eligible to receive Medi-Cal benefits.	Call a hyper-specific method, passing in only an ID and a sort clause: `$result = $claimRepository->` `findAllIneligible` `PatientsFromListOf` `Providers($providers)` The actual repository method called previously would either construct a raw query or resort to calling multiple subroutines to extrapolate the needed data.	Perform an inline operation via a facade on the corresponding model and then chain on a filter by passing in a closure returning the results of a truth test: `$result = Claims::where` `('patient_id',` `$patientId)->` `whereIn('provider_id',` `$providerIds)->` `get()->filter(` `function($claim) {` `return $claim->patient->` `isEligible();` `})`

(*continued*)

Table 14-1. (*continued*)

Functionality/ Description	Repository Method	Laravel/Eloquent Inline Equivalent

Find all CPT codes for claims with a given patient (on a per-provider basis) that has been submitted within the last year.	`$providers = $claimRepository->findAllProviderClaimsForPatientWithinLastYear($patientId)`
	
	It's the same thing here: either construct raw SQL or use a query builder to join data together or call multiple methods:
	
	`$claims = $claimRepository`
	`->findBy('patient_id'`
	`, $patientId)`
	`->addWhere('submitted`
	`_at', 'BETWEEN",`
	`[Carbon::parse(`
	`"today -1 year")->`
	`toDateTimeString(),`
	`Carbon::parse(`
	`"today")->`
	`toDateTimeString()])`
	`->getResults();`
	`foreach ($claims as $claim) {`
	`$cptCodeCombos[] = $cptComboRepository`
	`->find($claim->`
	`getId())`
	`->getResults()); }`
	`foreach ($cptCodeCombos as`
	`$cptCode) {`
	`$cptCodeRepository`
	`->find($cptCode`
	`->getId())`
	`->getResults(); }`
		Same as earlier: use Eloquent's awesome features to describe the data you want; then instead of explicitly telling it how to go about retrieving that data, it will figure out the dirty work and hand you back your result set in a nice collection that can be further processed, reduced, mapped, or anything else you can possible use collections for:
		
		`Claim::where("patient_id"`
		`,$patientId)->`
		`whereBetween(`
		`"submitted_at",[`
		`Carbon::parse("today`
		`- 1 year")->`
		`toDateTimeString(),`
		`Carbon::parse`
		`("today")->`
		`toDateTimeString()`
		`])->get()->cptCodeCombo`
		`->cptCodes;`

(*continued*)

Table 14-1. (*continued*)

Functionality/ Description	Repository Method	Laravel/Eloquent Inline Equivalent
Find aggregated data that consists of the results of queries spread across different model relationships iterated over to produce some sort of query-intensive mechanism.	Too much code to put in this little box, but the solution would consist of calling more and more narrowly focused method calls on the repository as time went on, ultimately becoming too granular to be reusable or useful outside of its originally established context.	Create a complex query with Laravel's query builder that abstracts the details of the query, allowing you to focus only on what matters (the parameter's values).

Table 14-1 shows that many of the benefits that a traditional repository offers come in the form of tacking on more and more specific, granular methods that drill the data down to a precise format or structure to meet the ever-growing complexities of the application. Eventually, these repositories will be rendered completely not reusable and simply not the best solution to accommodate the heavy demands of the database data required by the application, because at some point or another, you could end up with method names such as `GetCountOfProvidersWithRegisteredPatientsWithinLastYear()` or `findMost OftenUsedCptCodesForPracticeWithinDateRange($sdate, $edate)`.

Eloquent, on the other hand, has many common, reusable methods within its `Collection` class to, more often than not, reduce the headache of manually extracting the data you need and creating long method names that will uglify your `Repository` class (not to mention throw a bunch of linting errors/warnings regarding an excessive number of characters on a line) to nothing more than a one-line, oftentimes inline solution that gives you the power to instead describe your result set in terms of common English operations that are conveniently placed behind a well-defined fluent interface. It is able to do that by abstracting out the inner workings of what would normally be a manually constructed, raw query living inside a repository.

What repositories also do well is hide the underlying persistence layer from the code that uses it. A common use for this would be to allow multiple persistence layers to implement a single repository interface, as shown in Figure 14-1.

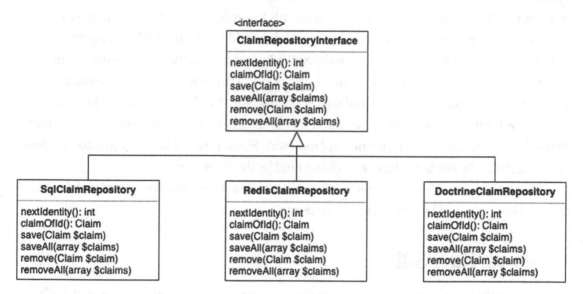

Figure 14-1. *An example of some different persistence methods of the same type of model*

In Figure 14-1, the UML diagram shows us three implementations of an imaginary `ClaimRepositoryInterface` contract, all focused on expressing each required method in that interface within the context of their own persistence layer. This is a widely taught approach when it comes to repositories and could possibly be needed in some specific use cases; however, for the majority of the time in web development, this usually overkill. If you are using Laravel and Eloquent to manage your database objects, most of the functionality encapsulated in the previous classes you get for free anyway. If you did want to implement a Redis cache of your objects for faster lookups and a better user experience, it most likely wouldn't use the same methods as the mechanism that actually saves the object. Various things need to happen to an object when it gets persisted in Eloquent such as generating the next available ID for the record in the database (which I assume is a relational database) or ensuring no foreign keys have been violated, but this process happens *once* in a domain object's lifecycle at the time it is created.

In Redis, there is no need to do any of that because it is a simple key-value object store. We wouldn't really need but one or two of the methods in `ClaimRepositoryInterface`, perhaps `save()` and `claimOfId($id)`, for us to implement a Redis caching mechanism. In fact, this would arguably be a better fit for an infrastructure service, perhaps in the form of a Laravel job (which we will explore in Chapter X). The only real logic that we need would occur *after* we have added a newly persisted record to a relational database. An Observer or Eloquent `Model` event would work great for this because we could simply listen for (or observe) the `creating` event on the `Claim` model, provided that the logic simply took the database representation of the new model and adapted it (or translated it) into something that Redis could understand. This would be the `save()` method for storing the data in Redis, which would in turn consist of an `HSET` command. Implementing a full `Repository` child class for the Redis database wouldn't be necessary, and we would end up providing definitions for methods that we wouldn't use (with blank method bodies), just so the class would technically abide by the contract required by the interface.

That being said, I have a better use for repositories within the context of a web application powered by Laravel and Eloquent.

ORMs vs. Raw SQL

At first, an ORM may seem to be an undesirable restriction on what you can and can't do with data powered by the Eloquent ORM, but in my opinion, that is not the case. Performing loads of raw SQL queries against a relational database and shoving those queries into a class you name with `Repository` at the end is *not* a good idea. For one, a repository created in this way will lack any real benefit that the Repository pattern was meant to provide and instead become more of a "logic box"—a simple-minded class that just holds things. For another, it is far easier to leave yourself and your application open to such attacks as SQL injection, session hijacking, SQL data mining, schema mapping, and other malicious attacks because you forgot to manually inspect the user's input and determine that it has no malicious intentions before allowing the query to execute for every query that you run in your application. A third reason to use ORMs over raw SQL is simply to allow your application the freedom of representing the various models and entities in the system as objects rather than data. The goal of object-oriented programming is to allow for abstraction and extension of the behaviors of an object of a class or interface in a polymorphic and practical way so that the code itself becomes rich. We discuss rich domain models next.

Even if you are in some position where you simply do not want to utilize the features and power of a full ORM, you can still use Laravel's plain DB facade to (at the least) add adequate security measures to your infrastructure to prevent such malicious attacks on your data like the ones I listed earlier. See Listing 14-2 for how to sanitize user input before sending it to the database; in an effort to prevent SQL injection attacks, you can do things like this (without Eloquent's help).

Listing 14-2. Securing Queries

```php
<?php

//somewhere in an infrastructure or domain service class definition

protected $argument;

public function __construct(string $argument)
{
    $this->argument = $argument;
}

protected function doSomeStuff()
{
    $argument = $this->argument;
    $results = DB::select(
        DB::raw(
            "SELECT * FROM some_table WHERE some_col = :argument"
        ),[ 'argument' => $argument])
    );
}
```

Rich Domain vs. Anemic Domain

Although I've mentioned it before in the book, it's worth remembering what a rich domain model is and why it should be the eventual goal of any domain model. As opposed to an anemic domain model, which ends up with the components and models becoming mere data containers with a bunch of defined getters and setters, a rich domain model is one that describes the domain in a clear and elegant manner that truly represents the concepts and behaviors that each model expresses within the domain and explicitly states its purpose, relationships, and impacts on the rest of the system, as well as defines the possible means of accessing the functionality in terms of the way that it interfaces with the established methods of communication that exist in the application (perhaps via a route definition or domain service interface).

When we have defined a "rich" domain model, we have successfully created a means of expressing a given domain in the form of software describing the very essence of the underlying domain. Behaviors are clearly defined, concerns are properly separated, and the correct usage of granularity has been applied to the domain model objects so that they may represent the domain sufficiently and elegantly. You can always use this as a sort of "rubric" to critique the structure, design, and implementation of your model of a given domain due to, of course, the reliance on the defined ubiquitous language (which, after rounds and rounds of back and forths with domain experts and developers, should even act as the basic guideline for how to structure and separate the architecture of the system you are building). Always refer to the concepts and terminology defined in the UL as a means of checking that your implementation is actually following that which is demanded by the core aspects of the domain.

Specifications

Repositories are well-established DDD patterns that provide an application with a way to separate the domain logic involved in a single model (entity) from the filtering, querying, and traversal concerns that exist when managing a relational database and a powerful abstraction in the form of reusable, object-oriented code that retrieves data and returns the result in a structured and powerful way that you can make open for extension and closed for modification.

With Laravel, we get all the collection methods for free that can (for the most part) take the place of any such traditional collection-oriented repositories common to the software development world. That's not to say that repositories themselves are useless, because they can serve a far more beneficial purpose when used in conjunction with the specification pattern. Combining the concept of a repository with the specification pattern is a much more adequate use of repositories in Laravel applications than using them for the purposes of managing a collection of a given object type or creating many long-named queries that simply return different granular database records specific to the needs of a single request (or format) of the data needed to fulfill it.

Instead, it would be great if we could specify which data we needed to gather by simply describing the results that we wanted, which would automatically be converted into the correct query and executed on the database, returning a resulting data set in a nice encapsulating object that we could then pass around without the need to transform it or adapt it. It would also be great if we could reuse these components in a "stacked" manner so that we could simply tack on additional constraints as additional methods to an explicit and fluent interface. One way to accomplish such awesome things in your applications is by utilizing the power and ease that the `Collection` component provides in conjunction with using a beloved feature of Eloquent models, something known in the Laravel/Eloquent world as *model scopes*. Model scopes can be used to wire up the specifications provided to that model to allow the execution of that logic through the interface of a repository. If all that sounds confusing, we will go over it in more detail next.

Specifications Defined

Let's quickly review what we want our application to be able to do. Instead of using repositories directly for querying the database and having many specific, finely grained methods that encapsulate the logic to query the database and then traversing those results to find the specific data, we want the ability to *describe* our data in such a way that makes it possible to query a model via a repository that accepts a specification interface and then uses the child classes implementing that interface to conduct the various queries and SQL we need to run. We will still use repositories, but in a more elegant and less static way than they are presented in software development.

A *specification* is basically a criterion object—a defined predicate check run against a single domain model class (type) or even across multiple models that encapsulate the exact criteria involved in specifying some particular data set, allowing them to be reusable if we need that same data set, for example, in such times that we are looking for the same structure, format, or set of data, but need the set to reflect the current data from the database, perhaps so that it can refresh the UI and show the user the latest information. A predicate is simply some function that returns a Boolean response. What the repository will do is accept an instance of a specification interface and then query the database based on the results of the specification's predicate, handling the persistence layer details and performing the operation described by the specification. It may translate the specification into SQL or specific ORM queries or even iterate over an in-memory collection of objects before returning the results, but the important thing to note is how the repository is being used.

Why Use Specifications?

By encapsulating the business rule inside a class and providing an easy-to-use API to expose the class's behavior for the application to consume, we see a number of benefits.

- It improves code reusability because we can use the same specification whenever we want the same data.

- The application does not need to know how the business rule is enforced because it is contained within the specification object.

- If the business rules themselves change, you only have to modify it in a single place.

- It allows "stacking" multiple different specifications for creating more customized complex queries.

The fourth item in the previous list is the most important. We want to be able to use two or more specifications together by passing them into a repository method and receiving a resulting collection that satisfies all specifications.

Specifications and Repositories

Let's say that we want to define a specification to find all the claims that have been submitted to the application for a given date range and that also have a status of Reviewer Approved. Figure 14-2 shows a diagram of a possible solution.

Note The example illustrated here to describe specifications shouldn't be used for date range queries as they are best handled when the query actually runs to avoid having to hit the database more than once. The example here is meant for demonstration purposes, but we will resolve the issue that it brings up in a "real-world" scenario later—just so you're not left hanging.

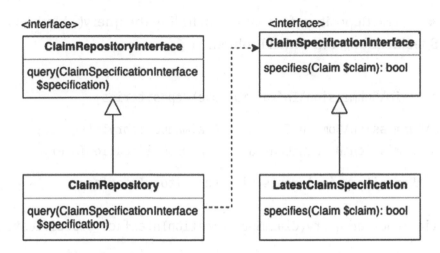

Figure 14-2. *A repository featuring an implementation of the specification pattern*

The Repository method query() accepts an instance of a
ClaimSpecificationInterface interface. LatestClaimSpecification is the class
implementing this interface and is geared for operations on a Claim model. The interface
requires only a single method, specifies(), which accepts a Claim object as an
argument and returns a Boolean, which serves as the predicate check to decide whether
the passed-in object (in this case, a claim) actually meets the predicate constraint
located in the specification. This particular specification contains the logic to determine
whether a claim has a submitted date within a given range. See Listings 14-3 and 14-4 for
an example of how the code would look for the previous architecture.

Listing 14-3. The Interface for the Repository Class

```php
<?php

namespace Claim\Submission\Domain\Contracts;
use Claim\Submission\Domain\Models\Claim;
use ClaimSpecificationInterface;

interface ClaimRepositoryInterface
{
    public function query(ClaimSpecificationInterface $specification);
}
```

Listing 14-4. The Repository for Claims, Including the query() Method to
Support Specifications, but with a Problem

```php
<?php
namespace Claim\Submission\Infrastructure\Repositories;

use Claim\Submission\Domain\Contracts\ClaimRepositoryInterface;
use Claim\Submission\Domain\Contracts\ClaimSpecificationInterface;

class ClaimRepository implements ClaimRepositoryInterface
{
    public function query(ClaimSpecificationInterface $specification)
    {
        return Claim::get()->filter(
            function (Claim $claim) use ($specification) {
                return $specification->specifies($claim);
            }
        );
    }
}
```

In Listing 14-4, we define the query() method in our repository that accepts a claim-
specific specification and filters through *all* the claims in the system, performing the
predicate check that is included with the specification on *every* Claim model until it has
filtered out any that do not meet the requirements set by the specification. Can you see
an issue with the previous code? Obviously, if there were more than a million or more
records in the claim table, the previous code would have to sift through all of them to
find the ones that match the specification, which isn't ideal. As the claims table grows,
the performance impact of running all of them through a filter will be noticeable.

Although the possible solutions around this problem vary by the situation
surrounding it, one way to make a lesser impact on the system would be to limit the
number of records you are actually filtering through, before they are run through the
predicate check in the specification. We will discuss this in more depth later.

Let's say that we wanted to find all claims in the system that have been submitted
within a certain date range. We built something that could do this for us using Eloquent,
using an inline statement like the code in Listing 14-5.

Listing 14-5. Sample Inline Mechanism to Retrieve Claims Submitted Within the Last Year

```php
<?php

$claimsSubmittedLastYear = Claim::whereBetween(
    "submitted_at", [
    Carbon::parse("today-1 year")->toDateTimeString(),
    Carbon::parse("today")->toDateTimeString()
    ]
)->get();
```

Although this code is perfectly fine in terms of it actually working, it is not exactly the most reusable piece of logic because doing things "inline" often equates to a one-off, one-time, ad hoc piece of functionality that is convenient simply because we can execute it and get results right away without breaking the boundaries of encapsulation.

A Better Approach

A better way to implement such a thing is to create a predicate function that can be run, which will return a Boolean value, and then feed it to the repository to do the handling of that logic within the proper persistence layer. In this way, the logic can be reused anywhere that it is needed by simply referring to the specification containing that predicate. Listing 14-6 is what the rest of the classes in Figure 14-2 look like in code.

Listing 14-6. Specification Interface for Claim Specifications

```php
<?php

namespace Claim\Submission\Domain\Contracts;

use Claim\Submission\Domain\Models\Claim;

interface ClaimSpecificationInterface
{
    public function specifies(Claim $claim);
}
```

Because we want our specifications to be reusable, we will want to restrict each specification to a single predicate check. We have two obligations to fulfill in this example: selecting the records submitted since a given date *and* filtering those records by status. Therefore, we should make two separate specifications: one for the date range and one for the status. Listing 14-7 shows a more reusable version of the code for finding the latest claims, which consists of a class implementing this specification interface.

Listing 14-7. The Concrete Claim Specification Class, Containing the Logic to Determine If a Claim Has Been Submitted Within a Given Range

```php
<?php
namespace Claim\Submission\Infrastructure\Specifications;

use Claim\Submission\Domain\Contracts\ClaimSpecificationInterface;

class LatestClaimSpecification implements ClaimSpecificationInterface
{
    private $since;

    public function __construct(\DateTimeImmutable $since)
    {
        $this->since = $since;
    }

    public function specifies(Claim $claim)
    {
        return $claim->submitted_at > $this->since;
    }
}
```

The specification in Listing 14-7 is meant to receive an argument of $since, which is an instance of DateTimeImmutable, because in this context we are using the $since date only to do the check, so it doesn't need to be modified.

Listing 14-8 shows how you would use the previous code in a real project.

Listing 14-8. The Client Code for the Previous Implementation

```php
<?php
use Claim\Submission\Infrastructure\Repositories\ClaimRepository;
$claimRepository = new ClaimRepository();
```

```
$latestClaims = $claimRepository->query(
    new LatestClaimSpecification(
        new \DateTimeImmutable('-30 days')
    )
);
```

The code in Listing 14-8 would perform the actual operation defined in the specification within the `ClaimRepository`'s query method; this in turn performs the actual filtering of the collection of claims, returning a Boolean value for each, which was the value that we provided to the `LatestClaimSpeceification`'s constructor (in this case, it was exactly 30 days ago). This process can be repeated for any other predicate checks to create a specific collection of claims.

Queries and Performance

There is still a problem with this implementation: if there are a significant number of records in the database for that model, it could make the system run slow. The way we have it set up, the `Claim` facade is grabbing *all* the records via the `get()` method, which loads every claim in the database into memory before operating on them. This could take a *lot* of time for a large data set.

Your initial thoughts on a solution to this problem might be to scrap the entire specification idea and simply go with the first thing that worked, such as the inline approach in Listing 14-5. I recommend you resist this urge for the sake of the benefits of using a specification implementation (which I listed in "Why Use Specifications?"). Of course, if you are working for a startup and want to get something out the door quickly, you may prefer to take the shorter, more direct route and simply keep chaining on different collection methods to the end of the model facade. However, such an approach comes with its share of tech debt in the form of repeated code that duplicates the logic offered in the specification in other places in the application as well as muddles the domain model due to the lack of separating concerns and not explicitly defining the concepts. Depending on the project, this may or may not be acceptable for your particular need or situation, but, in my opinion, when you have the time to do something the right way the first time, why not? Tech debt can become a fairly expensive beast to tame in terms of time, money, and resources.

Continuing to Refactor the Code

Because we know that there is no perfect piece of software and that good software comes only after many refactorings of the code and the domain model itself, let's take another look at the previous example. Let's consider another possible way to solve the issue described earlier. Currently, the code is set up to run a query in the repository by providing selection criteria in the form of a specification class. The problem is in the way I'm implementing the repository. More specifically, Eloquent's get() method is being improperly used here, because that is the method that actually runs the query *before* filtering the data. We need a way to limit the number of results returned before we iterate over them. We could do this with an additional repository method like submittedWithin Range($startDate, $endDate). Listing 14-9 shows how you would limit the result set to one much smaller.

Listing 14-9. Adding a Method to the Repository That Can Be Extended Further

```php
<?php
//ClaimRepository
public function submittedWithinRange($startDate, $endDate)
{
    Return Claim::whereBetween(
        "submitted_at", [
            Carbon::parse("today-1 year")->toDateTimeString(),
            Carbon::parse("today")->toDateTimeString()
        ]
    );
}
```

The main difference in the previous code is that instead of returning the results of the query using the get() method, we return an object of type QueryBuilder, which is an intermediate object that has been configured but has not been run. The idea here is to keep tacking on constraints, filters, or additional collection-related methods after calling get(), which always returns an Eloquent Collection object. That is worth repeating

---

Tip   Eloquent models used via a direct facade (which appears to be a static method, but it's not), or even any queries ran via the query builder, will always return an Eloquent collection after the call to get().

This is a powerful feature because it allows us to chain together all the conditions of our query for a given model (as well as any relationships that model may have) at any given point (or points) in the application, in an incremental fashion, and then (when are ready) run the fully constructed query via get() and have the resulting data set returned as a collection, which can then be processed, sorted, or filtered, all within a single *line* of code.

Advanced Usage of the Query Builder

For example, let's say we were compiling a report that had to be run monthly that provided (for whatever reason) a list of addresses of active users who are male, at least *x* years old, and have at least one published post in some imaginary blog application. Listing 14-10 demonstrates how that might look.

Listing 14-10. Complex Query Using a Facade Inherited from Eloquent's Abstract Model Class

```
$usersAddr = User::with('address') //join on address relation
        ->where('is_active', true) //returns QueryBuilder object
        ->where('age', '>', $startingAge)
        ->where('gender', $gender)
        ->where(function ($query) use ($request) {
            $query->whereHas('posts', function ($query) use
                ($request) {
                    $query->where('is_published', $published);
            });
        })
        ->get()     //fetches result and returns a Collection
        ->address; //grabs the 'address' relation--included via
                    //the call to with() in the first line
```

The query in Listing 14-10 is saying "Query the list of active male users, including their address, that are at least *x* years old and whom have at least one published post in the system and return the results in a collection object containing only the address of each, and store that in a variable named $usersAddr." All within a single line of PHP code! This may be a tempting approach that can be utilized directly in line with whatever functionality you are building at the time, and it is most certainly a convenient, fast, and expressive approach. However, keep this in mind: with great power comes great responsibility.

We have pretty much inappropriately mixed a few different concerns together: the database concern (represented by the query, which includes anything before the call to get()—the selection criteria), the means of traversing the resulting model objects to navigate through them and pull out each matched user their address, and the transformation of that resulting collection into a plain ol' PHP array. We have created an unreusable piece of one-off code that will probably get stuck in a repository method, along with the hundreds of others one such application includes. If this is what you've intended, excellent—you're done!

If not, then maybe it's time to realize that the mix of concerns would be better off separated into smaller pieces of functionality, increasing the likelihood of reuse and creating a better architecture for which to build additional functionality from. Another benefit you gain with this approach is that nine times out of ten, the code will be easier to read and understand by other developers because queries created in this manner can get long and complex, decreasing code readability.

One solution that would create a clearer separation of concerns and better code reusability makes use of Eloquent scopes, which we haven't yet converted but will describe in detail in future chapters. For now just know that a scope is a method that can be added to any Eloquent model that accepts a `QueryBuilder` object and any optional parameters, adds the specific constraints to that `QueryBuilder` object, and returns the object directly so that it can be further appended to before the resulting SQL is executed. A `QueryBuilder` object is an Eloquent kind of all-purpose SQL abstraction layer that powers Eloquent's querying capabilities and database abstractions.

→ Add a new scope to the `User` model named `scopeIsActive()` and define the constraint that indicates an active user.

→ Add two new scopes to the `User` model named `scopeIsMale()` and `scopeIsFemale()`, defining within them the constraint that indicates each, respectively.

→ Add a new scope in the `User` model named `scopeHasPublished()` that accepts a user's ID and returns the results of a subquery statement indicating if there are any posts by that user in the system that are "published."

→ Add a new scope in the `User` model named `scopeIsAtLeastAge()` that accepts an `$age` argument of type `DateTimeImmutable`, which will constrain the query based on each user's age.

→ Encapsulate the new behavior inside a new repository method, but name the method in accordance with the ubiquitous language so as to fully capture the purpose and intent that the new behavior offers.

We will take a look at the code used to create scopes later in the book. Using the solution provided earlier, the new function in the UserRepository would look like the code in Listing 14-11. It contains our core query but does not actually execute it yet, allowing further additions to the resulting SQL. It is common also to include the call to get() so that the repositories return actual data instead of a QueryBuilder object.

Listing 14-11. Repository Method Containing Our Core Query

```
// in UserRepository

public function getPublishedMales(\DateTimeImmutable $isAtLeastAge)
                                  : QueryBuilder
{
    $users = User::with('address')
            ->isActive()
            ->isMale()
            ->isAtLeastAge($age)
            ->hasPublished();
}
```

In Listing 14-11, you can see that we have a number of improvements over the static, one-liner described earlier.

- Our code is decoupled, allowing us to build up the proper query incrementally by calling methods whose names are domain-driven (ubiquitous language).

- We can clearly understand at first glance what the code actually does without digging into the details of the implementation.

- We have model-specific, meaningful constraints that we have placed in the proper place: the User model itself (fat model!).

- We have reusable scopes that are indicative of its use in the domain. If we wanted to see whether a user has a published post elsewhere in the application, we could just tack on `hasPublished()` to a query builder method or the `User` facade. If we needed to check whether a user is active (which presumably would happen all the time), we could make the `isActive()` method a global scope instead and have it applied all the time unless we specified otherwise using a call to `withoutGlobalScopes()`.

- Our new implementation is easier to unit test because we can simply call each new scope method we added to the `Claim` model with a set of known, predetermined data and verify the results instead of trying to test that one-liner super query in Listing 14-10.

- Last but not least, because every defined scope in Eloquent returns a new `QueryBuilder` object and we specified that the resulting call to the `getPublishedMales()` method will be a `QueryBuilder` object, we *still* haven't actually run our query, allowing us to add additional constraints to the query before it is executed. Another common approach is to have the repository query call `get()` for you and return an actual collection of data, which is perfectly fine as well (we would just need to modify the return type hint to be of type `Collection`).

Simply put, the main point that I'm trying to make with all of this is that the best, most efficient way to gather and process results from the database is to include everything you can within the context of the query itself (aka the code before the call to `get()`). When properly constructed, SQL runs much faster than a traversal of model objects within a collection in PHP—lightspeeds faster, in fact.

A good approach to use is to start with a one-line, direct query (if possible) using the model's facade, like the one demonstrated in Listing 14-10. Once you have it functional, break down any portions of the code that could possibly be used again elsewhere in the application and put them into a scope, global scope, or other such method on the corresponding model so that they may be simply appended to `QueryBuilder` objects to add constraints before execution. Be sure to name all classes, methods, and anything else in the application after the proper terms in the ubiquitous language. For more complicated queries that need to be performed across a variety of services, protocols, or classes, try breaking the functionality into smaller pieces, being especially careful to implement business rules and concepts found in the domain itself in an explicit and direct way. If something doesn't feel right about a particular piece of functionality, look at the means for which you have them split up and make sure you haven't either misjudged the boundary of a domain context or made it (them) too granular or not granular enough so that it may be reused and extended upon later.

After you have established the constraints and specifics for the query itself and placed the logic into suitable components or methods that can be reused, the next step is where you would focus on the actual filtering of the returned data set, which doesn't require the database and instead usually involves iterating through a `Collection` object to either make a new collection object or augment the data inside the collection, perhaps then converting it to an array or JSON.

As I said earlier, the more you can utilize the query (via the query builder or Eloquent), the better off you will be in terms of performance. Specifications provide an alternate means of "selecting" or "filtering" data and are the most beneficial for use *after* the query has been run (after the call to `get()`) so as to not impact performance. Figure 14-3 shows a diagram of the involved players in this approach.

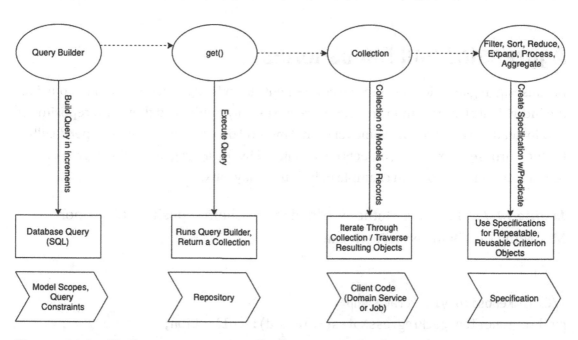

Figure 14-3. *Various processes involved in a typical solution for querying and processing data retrieved from the database regarding a given model*

This diagram indicates which portion of functionality belongs to which component as well as the order that the components are used in. First, we setup the query via the Eloquent model's facade, which generates a corresponding database SQL query that is run when the `get()` method is called. This can be done in a repository that returns a resulting `Collection` object, or anywhere else for that matter.... Eloquent will always return a collection after the call to `get()`. From there, the client code, perhaps a job or domain service or even a component within the application layer, will have that collection returned to them, which can then be filtered further via specifications.

The diagram does have one implication, and that is that it assumes you are, for whatever reason, unable to gather everything you need from a single query because of the level of complexity relating to the interactions between the domain objects themselves and/or where their boundaries are drawn in the model in relation to those objects. However, whenever possible, make an attempt to incorporate as much filtering, sorting, and selection logic as within the database query instead of querying the repository directly. More specifically, grab some collected set of intermediate results from the database and iterate over them in PHP, but only if deemed necessary by the domain.

Aggregates and Repositories

Because aggregates hide the internal components from being accessed from the outside, the individual classes composing the aggregate usually don't need their own repositories and instead are accessed via some relational method on a repository, made specifically for the purpose of extracting objects encapsulated by the aggregate via the aggregate root. Listing 14-12 shows an example of how that may look.

Listing 14-12. Example Methods Added to the ClaimRepository to Support Managing the Claim as an Aggregate

```php
<?php

//ClaimRepositoryInterface.php
public function getProgressNotes($claimId): Collection;

public function formatDateOfService($format='Y-m-d h:i:s'):
                                    \DateTimeImmutable;

public function getEstimatedClaimAmount($claimId): float;
```

This is fine and could work in a real-world implementation, but, really, I don't see anything special in the previous interface that Eloquent couldn't handle right out of the box via traversing the relationship objects associated with that model in a direct manner. Listing 14-13 shows an example of this.

Listing 14-13. Corresponding Eloquent Methods Matching the Repository Interface

```php
<?php
$claim = Claim::find(123);
$progressNotes = $claim->progressNotes->toArray();
$dateOfService = \DateTime::format($claim->dateOfService, 'm-d-Y');
$estimatedClaimAmount = $claim->estimated_claim_amount;
```

Once again, it seems like a repository implementation that includes the methods identified in Listing 14-12 that do the same thing as the three lines in Listing 14-13 is unnecessary. We could make the argument that these methods should be placed in the same class so as to group related functionality; however, each of them already exists and is available via Eloquent's abstract `Model` class that our domain objects extend from. Accessing relationships on a model is as easy as calling the name of the relationship as if it were a property on that model. If you wanted to traverse an association and then perform additional logic on the results of that association (such as persisting additional items on one-to-many relationships), you could simply call the association as if it were a method on the model and then treat the result as a means to chain together additional functionality, such as in Listing 14-14.

Listing 14-14. Example Operations Involving Relations to the Claim Object

```php
<?php
//Saving relations to a Claim model

$claim = Claim::find(123)
        ->cptCodes()
        ->save([22,45,47]);

//Query relations of Claim model
//find a Claim's progress notes and chain additional query operations
```

```
$claim = Claim::where(function ($query) use ($provider) {
    $query->whereHas('progress_notes', function ($query) use
        ($provider) {
            $query->where('provider_id', $provider->id);
    });
});
```

Are Repositories Useless with Eloquent?

The example blog application in this chapter was used to create a means of compiling a specific set of data regarding users of an imaginary system. Specifically, we needed a list of addresses belonging to all users who are male, of a certain age, have at least one post, and currently have a status of "active." To mitigate any performance bugs or bottlenecks that we encountered in the first solution, we want to try to incorporate all the constraints we can within the query itself (via the QueryBuilder) so as to offload the heavy lifting of the operation onto the database server, which we've pretty much already taken care of in Listing 14-1 using scopes and an additional repository method.

All in all, with regard to using traditional repositories in Laravel, you could live without them, for the most part, thanks to a combination of the built-in collections (which get returned from every query made using Eloquent), local and global *scopes* (which we discuss in depth over the next few chapters), and the facades that get included with the models themselves (which are inherited from the abstract Model class). The facade offers a quick, realistic, and straightforward approach to doing pretty much anything you can do with SQL and a properly set-up relational database like MySQL or MariaSQL. What's more is that scoped constraints of a given model *stay* with the model—as they should because what a scope does is accept a QueryBuilder object, which in itself may contain one or more constraints that have been tacked onto the query builder (so as to have at least some of the records preloaded). Scopes are usually extremely fast and convenient to set up and use. Specifications shouldn't be created to handle iterations through the database itself. Leave that to something that's specifically created to handle iterations and does so with a much higher rate of performance than PHP could possibly give you. However, they do serve a purpose in domain-driven design because it makes explicit the purpose of the criteria that it specifies, which can prove to be useful when we name the specifications with names that correspond directly to their domain-related counterparts.

Repositories aren't completely useless, however. They can be beneficial to use when your application actually does utilize multiple database management systems (i.e., persistence layers) that all need to be accommodated for the application to function properly. This would be fairly straightforward to set up using a variety of repository interfaces that would be implemented by each one of the persistence layers needed to interact with the application (i.e., for a `Claim` model). There could potentially be several repositories such as `SqlClaimsRepository`, `RedisClaimsRepository`, `ElasticClaimsRepository`, and/or `InMemoryClaimsRepository`, etc. You would want to have separate repositories for each interface that you define in this manner and keep them separated by model, not only for the sake of separating concerns but, from an object-oriented perspective, because what would end up happening if we mixed repository functionality across more than one model is that some repository classes would inevitably end up implementing methods demanded by the interface that aren't needed for that given model.

To sum things up for repositories: unless the domain has a demand for multilayered persistence mechanisms that must be run simultaneously, there really is no need for a conventional repository by any standard implementation, whether it's collection- or persistence-oriented. See the basic, common repository interface used in many modern web and nonweb applications shown in Listing 14-15.

Listing 14-15. A Common Repository Interface

```php
<?php

interface RepositoryInterface
{
    public function all();
    public function create(array $data);
    public function update(array $data, $id);
    public function delete($id);
    public function show($id);
}
```

Let's compare the methods required by this interface to their implementation using Eloquent, providing the same funct ionality; see Table 14-2.

Table 14-2. *A Common Repository Interface Compared to Its Corresponding Eloquent Representation*

Method on RepositoryInterface	Eloquent Counterpart
`$repository->all();`	`Model::all()` or `Model::get()`

`$repository->create(`
`$repository->getNextId(),`
`$data=[])`
	`Model::create($data=[])`
	or
	`$model->fill($data=[])`
	or
	`$model = new Model($data=[])`

`$repository->update($id, $data=[])`	`Model::update($data=[])`
	or
	`$model->association = $x;`
	`$model->save();`
	or
	`$model->someAssociation()`
	`->save($someAssociation)`

`$repository->delete($id)`
or
`$repository->delete`
	`Model::delete($id)`
	or
	`Model::destroy($ids=[])`

`$repository->findAllBy($ids=[])`
or
`$rows=$repository->where('id', 'IN',`
`[1,2,3]);`
`if (!empty($rows)) {$row=$rows[0];}`
	`Model::find($id=[])`
	or
	`$row=$model->whereIn('id',[1,2,3])`
	`->get()->findOrFail()`

It is true that most of the functionality provided in the right Eloquent column is already built into the abstract Model class and available to every Eloquent model (usually via the facades offered by its abstract Model class that our domain models implement).

I started making a list of the possible reasons to have repository implementations within a Laravel application, but as I was going along, I realized that most of these reasons could easily be invalidated with one or more of Eloquent's features. For example, here is a list of some mostly acceptable reasons to utilize repositories:

- Holding custom, overly complex queries on a specific model. On the other hand, these types of queries are perhaps better placed within the entity (model) itself to have them as close to the code that they correspond to (grouping related functionality is an excellent way to design software as long as you keep together the logic that changes at the same pace).

- Using them as a means of accessing an internal object within an aggregate grouping that could not otherwise be acquired using conventional Eloquent techniques. On the other hand, traversing associations in Eloquent is extremely easy and effective, so much so that it has the potential to replace this need of selecting/retrieving inner-aggregate objects, which you could then reconsruct using a model factory, if necessary (we dive into factories in the next chapter).

- When you have multiple persistence mechanisms using more than one storage technology (i.e., Redis, Elasticsearch, MySQL, etc.), you can create a single `RepositoryInterface` for each model, per-storage mechanism, that will help abstract away any differences in their implementations while at the same time allowing their similarities to be defined and properly encapsulated in a parent interface.

- To implement some sort of customized caching mechanism, within the context of an individual domain model, a repository could be used.

Conclusion

The repository pattern is one that has been used extensively throughout many software projects. In a traditional, pure-PHP application (which I haven't seen for about four or five years now), there was a reason to use a repository as it provided an easy means of encapsulating complex queries or traversing a domain model's relationships with other domain models. Nowadays, we have tools and frameworks like Eloquent and Laravel that come with many features aimed at providing easy methods of traversing domain models and their relationships.

However, just like with anything else in software development, it has its ups and downs. The downside of using the powerful features offered by Eloquent is that it is far too easy to use without regard for separating concerns or properly encapsulating similar parts of logic in an explicit and clear manner. Over time, these types of things can muddle the concepts in the domain model and make the classes' purpose less obvious, neither of which is desirable. One way to mitigate this is to implement explicitly defined (and ubiquitously named) criteria objects via a specification pattern involving a predicate to determine whether a given object meets the criteria held in the specification, although this approach comes with its share of issues, namely, performance.

We went over some possible use cases and examples of the functionality that Eloquent provides. We went through a few different comparisons of the methods commonly found in a model repository and possible Eloquent solutions offering the same result. Because every query in Eloquent returns an instance of type `Collection`, we are able to chain together various conditions and constraints to our queries that have the potential to replace repositories with custom inline Eloquent method chains. Although we deep dive into Eloquent a little later in the book, it is worth going through a few examples to whet your appetite.

To conclude, are repositories useless in an application leveraging Eloquent? Well, I can't (and won't) say for sure because the answer really depends on the situation you are in and the project's requirements and needs. However, between you and me, it is rare that I myself implement a repository for anything other than a way to separate out logic related to multiple persistence layers with similar methods in the same application. You can most likely replace utilizing repositories altogether using Eloquent if you are careful where you place this logic and refrain from the temptation to just do inline Eloquent queries via facade methods on a given model anywhere we need to traverse or constrain a collection of objects in the database. How to do this depends on the situation but can be best accomplished by sticking to the concepts, naming conventions, and separations implied by the project's ubiquitous language.

CHAPTER 15

Factories and Aggregates

In this chapter, we will be going over factories, factory methods, and aggregates and what purpose they serve in an application. There are some prerequisites you should understand before diving into aggregates that will give you a better core understanding of what they do and why they are one of the hardest concepts to get right in the technical portion of domain-driven design. We will explore the value that factories and factory methods have in regard to an aggregate design and explore some cool things we can do in Laravel and Eloquent to make the code easier to understand and more concise.

Before we get to that, let's go into a bit of core knowledge that will benefit you to know while you are learning about aggregates. The main concepts that I'm referring to include the following:

- Transactions

- Characteristics of transactions

  - ACID

  - Atomicity

  - Consistency

  - Isolation

  - Durability

- Data inconsistency

- Factories

- Aggregates

- Forcing invariants

© Jesse Griffin 2021
J. Griffin, *Domain-Driven Laravel*, https://doi.org/10.1007/978-1-4842-6023-4_15

Some Brain Food

I cannot stress this point enough: a modern-day web application is composed of a number of different software technologies, each splintered off into its intended niche. As is always the case, today's software technology is always getting better and more specialized. The components that businesses used to spend tens of thousands of dollars creating can now be done for a fraction of that. The reason this is possible is because of the open source movement. As it turns out (and who would've thought it), open source software in general has made a lasting impact on the way we do business, and even the way we live. We can utilize open source software to achieve our business needs, and we can use it directly in our app without paying a dime for license or subscription fees, which saves time and money because you're no longer forced to reinvent the wheel. I mean, you most likely will have to pay someone to hook it up to your system or application stack for you, unless of course you're a developer, but the true "development" time can be focused on getting the domain model right. Go open source!

Improving PHP Statelessness

If you were going to save a user's settings and configuration to load the application faster next time (or maybe you wanted to implement some sort of tracking feature to gauge what countries your visitors are in), you may choose to create a cookie that can be saved on the client computer and then loaded whenever the user hits the site. Or if you had some data that was time-sensitive, such as a JWT token that allowed users of your application to access certain specified areas of the application, you may want to instead save that token in an HTTP header (such as a Bearer token), perhaps included in every request within the Authorization header. Or if you had some data that was good only for that particular visit, such as an online order form, you could save that data in the session. The point is, PHP itself is stateless, and so is the Web in general (thanks to the client-server model), but we can create elegant means of improvising with the basic facilities of a modern-day web application with a little finesse and some well-thought-out code.

Applications Are Cheap, Data Is Expensive

We have a database that holds the data that gives our site or application its content and, most of the time, its value. You see, an application is (basically) just housing around a typical data structure (defined by a database schema, index, or if you are using a NoSQL means of persistence, document). We can change the application a thousand times, and it would still work, as long as we took the database structure/schema into consideration when developing.

The following example isn't a scenario or a "Let's say..." type of fabricated discussion, but is very much reality. Take the website `http://Slashdot.org`. Slashdot is a very old, very famous, and very popular news-bulletin-board type of website that publishes discussions, comments, and feeds from its users regarding (mostly) technology and things related to technology (although it has many categories spanning a plethora of interests nowadays). As the (new) lead developer of Slashdot, let me tell you that I came into a *mess*. I found out that the site was actually built in Perl. Not just that, it was actually some offshoot of Perl that (for some reason) got compiled into the website `http://Slashdot.org`. I had never in my life heard of such a thing. Compiled Perl? What is that?

The kicker was that the "compiled" part meant a separate, proprietary programming syntax that reminded me of some type of 4GL that actually determines what gets compiled and is the main driver for the compilation process of the entire application. Of course, my first thought was, "Let's rebuild the damn thing, start from scratch, and do it right." Then I looked at the code. Holy frijole, it was crazy complex and came with next to no documentation regarding its current implementation or deployment of a site that literally had upward of three million visitors per month. The original developers of the application were long, long gone by the time I was hired and started working with it. In fact, it had been bought and sold several times before it ended up in the hands of the company I work for now. There were few people whom I could ask a question regarding how the site worked, which function you are supposed to call for thing X to happen, or hardly anything else, for that matter. After being briefed further on the project, I came to understand that the longtime users of the site, the ones responsible for its success and popularity in the first place, insisted that the website's core appearance, look, feel, and features remained the same or similar to what they are now. Interestingly enough, they wanted the look, feel, and functionality of the site to stay the same as it had been for the last 18+ years. The reality and truth on the matter is that what the users wanted on the site, the users got on the site, because the users *are the site*!

What Slashdot was, is, and ever will be—much to the same degree as other sites similar in size and active users—are those users. This is indeed true of any public ·application. It was honestly the first time in my career that I had witnessed a scenario where the users of a popular website called the shots! Our company had purchased the site from another company that owned it for years before they themselves purchased it from yet another company; we really were at the mercy of the thousands upon thousands of loyal users visiting our site every day. One such person is Elon Musk, who has been known to directly reference articles and discussions from Slashdot on his Twitter feed. If we angered them (like Microsoft has done and still does to its users on a regular basis), they would certainly bounce out and join our competitor's site, most likely for good; afterward, the ratings would go south, and the company could even lose its investment in the site, which was substantial, to say the least. To some me degree, this devastated me, and I started to not look forward to going to work for a while.

One day, it occurred to me that an application was just a "housing" around what was essentially the only real thing that matters to a website, application, or almost any other type of software in existence today. The compiled Perl code that was powering the Slashdot.org website was doing exactly what it was designed to do: taking the data from the database and systematically turning it into something its users could digest and respond to (via comments). However, because of the complexity of the source code (and the initial lack of understanding about how it worked), maintenance of the site was a nightmare (particularly for me). Changes often took weeks at a time, and it became hard to predict with any certainty how long it would take for any change on the site to be pushed to production.

This understanding led to a break-through in the plan for the future of the site. The high cost of maintenance and updates could not be tolerated, and we decided to simply rebuild the site in something that was more easily kept up in the long run. We wanted a site that was sure to be long-lived, easily updated and maintained as the years went on. We opted for the Laravel framework. We took the existing HTML, CSS, and JavaScript that the site was running on currently and refactored it into our new backend. And yes, I suggested we go with the Laravel framework because it is well-known, well-documented, well-supported, and (most importantly), and well-maintained. Most important of all, we kept the original data from the database, and although we refactored the schema over time to be much reliable and maintainable, we migrated all the data that had been in the database since the site was first opened to the public. This migration included all the user's settings, posts, comments, and anything else for that matter. We translated the old vanilla JavaScript + HTML 4 into a highly scalable and more flexible front end built with React, which spoke to the backend Laravel implementation. The template, functionality, and look and feel of the site remained intact because we just "ported" the old look into the new code, and the users of the site never knew that they were using a completely new and refactored system at all. To them, it was the same ol' site.

How did we do it? We relied on what we knew to be quality, open source software and source code in the form of Laravel packages to do our bidding, in other words, to handle the common, frequent, and often painstaking mechanisms and components common to virtually every other application on the Web. We relied on Laravel to provide a guiding framework, supporting tools, a community of help, and well-written documentation to make the framework work for us the way we needed it to, thus making it our own.

The central point to take from this story is that no matter how or what you decide to build an application in or with, the most important aspect of any system is the data. If anything is to be set up correctly and properly, the database schema should be at the top of the list. It is worth investing enough time in the database structure (schema) to get it right, because you never know when the day will come when you want to change the backend without the long-term members knowing that anything changed at all. You can always replace, rebuild, or refactor an application. These tasks are cheap compared to the data that those applications generate and use. We want to take proper measures to ensure our data stays in a consistent state. Transactions are one way to help ensure that.

Transactions

In the book *Domain-Driven Design in PHP*, the authors define the general concept of a transaction in the following words:

> *"Transactions are a fundamental concept of all database systems. The essential point of a transaction is that it bundles multiple steps into a single, all-or-nothing operation. The intermediate states between the steps are not visible to other concurrent transactions, and if some failure occurs that prevents the transaction from completing, then none of the steps affect the database at all."*

—Buenosvinos, Soronellas, and Akbary, *Domain-Driven Design in PHP*

So, we have a set of operations that we need to either all succeed or all fail, but not some of each. The reason for this is database consistency. Database consistency can be thought of as a measure of how intact your database is in relation to it being accurate and up-to-date with the rest of the system. The application, database, server, and browser (and a whole bunch of other stuff) work on a delicate balancing act. Since PHP is stateless, measures have to be taken to ensure you can persist the state of the application's data across requests. We have a variety of tools at our disposal that may be beneficial to use in certain individual situations.

The most common demonstration of a transaction out there is the bank account. In every transaction for every account, there are a few rules, so to speak, that must be followed to actually be posted to any accounts. We'll now go through some of the common characteristics central to transactions.

Atomicity

Atomicity is a way of describing that, even though there are different queries that may be involved in a single transaction, they either all succeed or all fail, guaranteeing that the database stays in a consistent state even when there are errors.

For instance, let's say we have two accounts, Account_A and Account_B, that have the same value of currency in them, say $500.

Account_A	$500
Account_B	$500

Then, let's say we wanted to move $100 from Account_A to Account_B, which would inherently create two opposing actions in the system: one to decrease Account_A by $100.00 and another to increase Account_B by $100.

Transaction 1: Decrease Account_A by $100

Account_A	$500 - $100 = $400 (PENDING)
Account_B	$500

Transaction 2: Increase Account_B by $100

Account_A	$500 - $100 = $400 (PENDING)
Account_B	$500 - $100 = $600 (PENDING)

Note how after each transaction, there is a pending transaction that has not yet been executed. At the point when the second transaction event is set, both transactions are still in pending mode. It is only when each account has been verified to have the corresponding amounts of money in their account and that there is enough to fund the second account that each transaction will be executed, at the same time.

This is done to ensure that you don't have one transaction that actually did execute and another that didn't. For instance, if only the first transaction executed but not the second, there would be some angry phone calls and emails the next day because there would be $100 that wouldn't have been accounted for at all in the system. This is a data discrepancy, which is a form of data inconsistency, because Account_A would have been deducted by $100, but Account_B would stay the same at $500. This is what is meant by *atomicity*: either they are all executed, or none of them is. In the event that one of the transactions fails, the database will undergo a mechanism to prevent data loss from such problems known as a *rollback* (a step back in time during the database's lifetime).

Consistency

By using transactions, we keep the database in a constant state all the time, even in the middle of a transaction or a rollback. The data will either be all old values or be all new values, but not a mix of both. Either all, or none. Consistency also must exist in the code and the operations that live within the domain model. That is why domain-driven design is so important: it reflects, in an almost exact manner, the processes that are in the domain that it models, and the database should be modeled in a manner that's easy for the application to talk to, use, and command.

However, it is not just on a database level that transactions are important. A typical business operation on a domain object could span several transactions, each perhaps relating to a different table or database altogether.

The nature of the internet in respect to requests, responses, and the client-server model is stateless. To create a good user experience, it is our job as developers to manage the state of things necessary to make the functionality of the site work and seem as if it were stateful. As described earlier in "Improving PHP Statelessness," we have numerous tools at our disposal that we can employ to manage the state of our application and the data that it surrounds.

So, there are two forces at work at all times: the application itself and the data on which it operates. We can employ database transactions easily in pretty much any framework or PHP script, because there are tools such as Laravel's Eloquent, Symfony's Doctrine, and the entire PDO library for PHP that is the foundation of these and other similar tools, which is great! However, consider the following.

A database transaction is basically the running of a set of multiple queries across different tables executed in such a way that the resulting changes to the database from those queries either all happen or none of them happens. However, what this implies is that a database transaction is really an approach for saving a single transaction described by multiple queries. The reason this is relevant is because, in the real world, a company could have business processes in place that could span the entirety of many transactions, all of them in need of the same "all or none" rule that gets applied in database transactions. The problem here is that we can specify only a single transaction at a time using the database alone. How are we going to ensure that a transaction group of multiple database transactions be handled in an atomic way? Using the database alone, we really can't—not efficiently anyway.

Digging Deeper: Application- and Database-Level Consistency

The answer is the application. The application is responsible for managing the multitude of transactions that a business problem actually encapsulates in the real world, relying on the database to perform (perhaps many) database transactions to be able to fully express whatever the process is within the context of the application and data store. Depending on the situation, we may use the database to handle the majority of the work because we absolutely do need database transaction atomicity; however, the database transactions themselves are created, managed, and fired by the application, which implies the need for transactions on an application level.

In the grand scheme of things, this means a web application is both code *and* data. They are both needed for a website or application to be of any use to anyone. Granted, there are some exceptions to the rule, such as static websites, scripts that utilize an API through a REST interface as their "database"-type component, perhaps websites that simply publish a directory listing of all companies within a given niche with the intent of having those companies purchase licenses to be at the top of the list. This website could be composed of templates for the UI, and the data making up the application's content could be fetched ad hoc via a sort of one-off, on-demand service that would be called by the user once one stumbles upon (pun not intended) the landing page for that specific category of sites. In a case like this, you could actually grab the data you needed, maybe store it for caching purposes, and display it on demand via the web application. This is just an example but is a feasible and low-cost solution for an online marketing or SEO-based company.

Most of the applications that I've seen in my career use a database to hold their data, which, depending on the business needs, could be employed using any number of modern-day database technologies (most of them open source): Elasticsearch, MySQL, Postgres, MSSQL, Redis, Firebase, Mongo DB, Propel...you get my point.

So, there are two things that need to be right for us to get a usable piece of software at the end of the tunnel: the application and the database. This is why consistency in terms of the database is important; also important is consistency within the application's core functionality, logic, and processes, as well as consistency with the underlying domain when modeling the real-world situations in software. If we are to succeed in the long run, we should be mindful of both concerns in any project we work on.

Isolation

Isolation in terms of database consistency and ACID refers to transactions that state that any query or individual operation performed within the transaction itself must not affect any other query in that same transaction. For instance, when a transaction gets recorded that transfers money between two accounts, there are two queries that run: an increase to one account and an exact opposite decrease to the other. When these two queries are in the scope of a database transaction, we can be sure that they will occur at the same time, while not affecting the other until the transaction has been completed and committed to the database. This is being atomic and isolated and helps to keep our data consistent. In addition to the queries within a transaction being isolated from each other, transactions operate in the same way: as independent and completely separate operations that modify the database in a predictable, atomic matter.

Now, let's say we chose to implement the same scenario without a transaction, and just running the two queries back to back. Well, the first query that *increases* the first account will run successfully, because there is no upward limit on how much any given account can have. There is, however, a business rule implemented in this accounting system (and all accounting systems) regarding restrictions on how much the balance of an account can fall below $0 (if it is allowed to at all anyway, but let's just say this rule is not explicitly defined within the domain model). So, the second query is executed and attempts to decrease the second account by the amount the first account was increased by, which executes properly and performs the balance modification on the second account. Can you see any potential problems with the scenario I've described?

The problem lies in the possibility that the second account doesn't have enough money to cover the amount of the transfer to the first account. Because the queries were performed outside of the scope of a safe and guaranteed transaction, the first account was credited with an amount that the second account could not provide. So now, there is a negative balance on the second account. Let's say that the application somehow detects this anomaly and a minute later attempts to do the reverse of the transaction to make the balance correct in the books. As it turns out, Johnny Gambler just lost all his moolah that day and is watching his phone with anticipation for his government check to hit his account, which it does, causing him to withdrawal that same amount from his account (in this case, the first account), so that amount is deducted from his account. Generally speaking, the issue here is that the second account now has a deficit balance that cannot be reversed without creating another deficit balance on the first account.

Let's say they've fixed the business logic in the software that will check to make sure that the balance is available in the second account before it does the transfer to the first, but still refuses to implement simple database transaction to ensure the atomicity of the transactions is being respected. So, the next time, the same situation happens, and the request entails transferring some amount of money between accounts. Everything is going well, and the first transaction is executed successfully, increasing the first account by whatever amount is specified in the transaction. However, as luck would have it, the power to the server that runs the transactions goes out right after the first query is executed, and the process halts and is forgotten about by the system. In this case, the problem is that we now have a database in an *inconsistent state*, which we wouldn't even know about until we run a monthly report that indicates the numbers don't add up or until someone calls and complains that they haven't received their money.

All this could be prevented with a simple database transaction, because the separate queries inside the transaction are all guaranteed to be run separately, not affecting the others and, at the same time, to run all at once or not at all. This is the way we can ensure consistency in our data. Transactions are used in many applications but should not be overused because they have a tendency to slow down the system or create locking problems when concurrent requests are sent to the same server to be executed.

Durability

The last part of the ACID acronym stands for durability and is the characteristic of transactions corresponding to the way that, once the transactions are run (including all queries therein), the data itself is protected from power failures and system crashes. What this means on an infrastructure level is that the data has been persisted to a hard disk, and some type of redundancy has been established to ensure a higher chance of recovery in the event of a hard drive crash or hardware errors at the persistence level.

Use Third-Party Code for Common Tasks

Understand that we would all like to build some great software from the ground up, architecting it as we see fit and being able to ultimately help drive the results of a successful new product made from the latest and greatest code out there. But that's hardly the reality in the world. In everyday life, there's pressure from bosses, project managers breathing down your neck, people standing over you tapping their foot, and expense reports that loss prevention and accounting departments are always trying to "minimize." We don't always come into a situation where we can start designing a new system from the ground up. So, what do we have to do to set ourselves up for success, not reinvent the wheel, and still come out with a quality, maintainable, and long-lived piece of software? The best way to do this, in my opinion, is to rely on the best practices and standards that you know work, keep focused on the core domain and the application features, stick to the ubiquitous language, and rely on the shoulders of others who've traveled the same path. When we choose high-quality libraries, packages, and open source code that we utilize, customize, and "make ours," we gain a significant amount of time and productivity, because those third-party tools will be aimed at the common, nondomain, trivial things required by all modern-day web applications—things like cache management, database layers, ORMs, application frameworks, logging facilities, file storage management, a plug-and-play WYSIWYG interface, or an entire prebuilt application and blog that you can make your own in a matter of minutes. (I'm speaking of WordPress or Drupal, of course.) The next project you take may very well need some or all of these things, and that's okay. As long as we make wise decisions about the quality of all third-party code we integrate into our application, we can benefit from them.

The main benefit, of course, would be to alleviate the need to have to rebuild some of these systems ourselves or reinvent the wheel (or re-iterate it). When we "outsource" these common tasks to other open source code, we are allowed to focus longer and harder on the most important aspect of any software application: the domain. We will be exploiting useful third-party libraries and packages for Laravel often in this book.

Factories

Factories, like repositories, are part of the domain layer, but not part of the model representing the underlying business. While repositories encapsulate the way we persist our models, factories encapsulate the logic to build or instantiate an object, a group of objects, or aggregates. Aggregates especially cannot be weighted down with the concern of how to create themselves, just as they shouldn't know how to persist themselves. The tools in DDD to solve these problems are factories and repositories, respectively.

Figure 15-1 provides a visual on what a factory does.

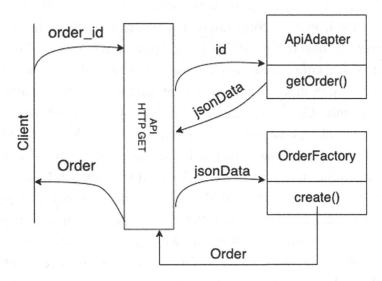

Figure 15-1. *Example order factory*

Here, the client sends a request to an API endpoint (with an HTTP GET verb) with an `id` parameter, which gets forwarded to an `ApiAdapter` class's `getOrder()` method, returning some JSON-encoded data to the API controller, which then calls the `OrderFactory::create()` method, which is what actually builds the `Order` object and finally returns it to the client. There may be more than just one `ApiAdapter` that would have to be called to get the correct data back. For instance, in an aggregate where relationships were not possible or not originally included (perhaps on a legacy application), the `OrderFactory` class would include them in the creation of the `Order` object.

A stand-alone factory like the one earlier, in my opinion, is necessary only in the following cases:

- Multiple models are involved.

- Relationships are not available for some strange reason.

The majority of the logic that is involved within a full-fledged `Factory` object can usually fit within a constructor method of the aggregate root, but may also be implemented as a factory method living on the aggregate root. The biggest concern when creating domain objects is that the true business invariants are modeled properly and in line with the domain in a way that gives the implementation of the domain value. In almost any business or domain model, there are pre-conditions, post-conditions, and invariants that need to be protected. Factories can help with that; however, the majority of the factories that I employ in real-world projects are that of the Factory Method pattern. I haven't personally used the Abstract Factory pattern too much when working with Laravel as a framework.

Aggregates in DDL

The fact that we are working with Laravel makes creating and using aggregates fairly easy, if we weren't also attempting DDD. But, that is the case, and attempting to model aggregates within the normal circumstances and practices described by DDD causes the overall process to have a few drawbacks. Just like with anything else, there is a trade-off to having an Active Record pattern, because in one instance you can use relationships and all the cool stuff Eloquent has to offer, but in the other we will never actually be able to decouple the model from the infrastructure. I am trying to prove to you that it is worth this coupling during real-world development, because oftentimes we have a fuse lit under us with the "just get it done" mentality. We will still be designing aggregates, but our version will be slightly different in numerous ways, which allows a better "flow" or progression within Laravel and Eloquent because a backbone will prove to be very useful.

When Designing Aggregates

There are a few simple rules you can adopt that will make the design and implementation of aggregates in the system easier and more streamlined.

Design Aggregates Around True Business Invariants

Aggregates are useful only if they help solve a particular business problem in the domain model, which usually involves protecting some invariant of a domain model object. On a purchase order aggregate, there may be an underlying business rule that dictates that a PO should have at least one line item in it to be able to be approved by the accounting department. This would be a business invariant that should be modeled somewhere within the aggregate as an explicit concept, which we will see an example of in this chapter. Another possible invariant that must be modeled within the Purchase Order aggregate is perhaps a maximum allowable amount that the sum of the line items within the PO must stay under if it is to be approved. The invariants in a system are needed to keep the objects in a valid, consistent order within the database and the application as well.

Design Small Aggregates

Smaller aggregates are favored over bigger ones, mostly because of the level of increased complexity that objects within a larger object spanning a bigger context come with. What makes it even more difficult is the persistence of such an object. Because aggregates are usually persisted within the context of a transaction, the complexity of the persistence process increases with the more queries that are involved in the execution of the transaction. If database locking is in place to guard against inconsistencies within the data, multiple users of a system all doing the same thing on the application could cause a performance impact as well as inconsistencies or unexpected behavior of the system.

Example Aggregate

Let's take, for example, an e-commerce application that has this concept of an `Order`, which is a model in the system that holds a number of `OrderLines`. If we were to design a model for something like this (keeping in mind the basic rules of aggregate design), we could start by listing the true business invariants.

- An Order must contain at least a single OrderLine instance in order
  (no pun intended) for it to proceed to the next stage of the checkout
  process (which in this example would be the calculation of sales tax
  and the operation needed to add it to the total amount of the order).

- The Order model tracks the total amount, which is the sum of all
  the OrderLine instances in that order plus sales tax, and uses it for
  numerous things (such as displaying the total to the user as they shop
  and conducting financial transactions at the end of the checkout
  process). This in itself isn't an invariant but is a factor of the model's
  design that gives rise to one: an Order must track the total amount,
  which entails being updated at all times, since the user will be
  looking at this number as they shop. Thus, to keep the order total
  consistent and constantly up-to-date, we must have a mechanism
  in place that performs the recalculation every time an OrderLine is
  added, removed, or updated.

- Another part of the previous invariant includes the sales tax,
  which gets added to the order total and also gets updated on every
  OrderLine update, removal, or creation because it is based on a
  percentage of the totals of the OrderLine instances. While similar
  to the previous one, for a better separation of concerns, we should
  model this as an independent invariant on the Order object.

Creating an Order Model as an Aggregate

Let's flesh out a simple rough draft of this example. We'll start with the Order model,
since it is the most important object in the aggregate. For now, we will just model the
order without the invariants we listed earlier (Listing 15-1).

Listing 15-1. An Example Entity Representing an Online E-commerce Order

```php
<?php

namespace Ecommerce\Domain\Models\Orders\Order;

use Illuminate\Database\Eloquent\Model;
use Ecommerce\Domain\Models\{Payment\PaymentId,Shipping\ShippingId, Cart\
CartId, Billing\BillingId};
```

```php
class Order extends Model
{
    protected float $total=0.00;

    protected ShopperId $shopper;
    protected CartId $cartId;
    protected ShippingId $shippingId;
    protected PaymentId $paymentId;

    protected $fillable = ['shopper_id','cart_id','payment_id', 'shipping_id'];

    public function __construct(Shopper $shopper, CartId $cartId, Payment
    $paymentId=null, ShippingId $shippingId=null)
    {
        parent::__construct();
        $this->shopperId = $shopperId;
        $this->cartId = $cartId;
        $this->billingId = $billingId;
        $this->shippingId = $shippingId;
    }

    public function orderLines()
    {
        return $this->hasMany(OrderLine::class);
    }
}
```

In the previous example, we have a basic, standard class extending Eloquent's abstract Model class. It has numerous value objects inside its constructor that correspond to the different data points of an online Order: the ID of the shopper who is ordering, the ID of the billing data for the order, the ID of the shipping model corresponding to the Order's destination address, and the ID of the cart object used to create the order. We have default values for the billingId and shippingId, because we won't know them until the last part of the checkout, when the user enters them into the web payment form. Additionally, we have a related OrderLines object defined with a hasMany() relationship to the Order model. We do not yet have any invariants inside the class. We've also made use of group use statements, which has been a feature of PHP since version 7. Now, let's create our OrderLine model in a similar fashion (Listing 15-2).

Listing 15-2. An Example Entity Representing a Single Line Item on the Order Entity

```php
<?php

namespace Ecommerce\Domain\Models\Orders\Order;

use Illuminate\Database\Eloquent\Model;
use Ecommerce\Domain\Models\{Product\ProductId, Order\OrderId};

class OrderLine extends Model
{
    protected Order $order;
    protected Product $product;
    protected int $quantity;

    protected $fillable = ['product_id', 'orderLineAmount', 'order_id',
    'quantity'];

    public function __construct(Product $product, int $quantity, Order $order)
    {
        parent::__construct();
        $this->product = $product;
        $this->quantity = $quantity;
    }

    public function order()
    {
        return $this->belongsTo(Order::class);
    }

    public function product()
    {
        return $this->hasOne(Product::class);
    }
}
```

The example `OrderLine` class has within it a defined relation to the `Product` model, the `Order` model, and the `quantity` corresponding to the amount of a particular `product` that exists on the order. If we were to use the classes as they are right now, it may look something like this:

```
//create order object
$order = new Order($shopperId, $cartId);
//create product object & quantity of that product
$product = Product::find(420);
$quantity = 3;

$orderLine = OrderLine::create($product, $quantity);
$order->orderLine->associate($orderLine);
$order->save();
```

If you have been paying attention to the characteristics of aggregates described in this chapter, then you may already see a problem with the previous implementation. We are accessing an inner object of the aggregate directly, which isn't the way we should be creating aggregate objects. We do not want to instantiate any objects within the boundary of the aggregate directly, which we are definitely doing in the previous code.

A nice and easy way around this is to use a named factory method on the aggregate root that will accept parameters needed to properly define the `OrderLine` object and then relate it to the `Order` itself. However, in regard to DDL and Eloquent specifically, every model extending the abstract `Model` class will have a facade allowing the developer to call it statically, thereby passing any attempt to prevent such direct instantiations (for example, `OrderLine::create()` can always be called as long as we are extended model). The best we can do, then, is to make a named factory, document it properly, and leave comments for the developer indicating that it should be used in any and all situations as the means of instantiating the `OrderLine` objects. It's called a *named factory* because the name of the method corresponds to the entity that's being instantiated. We cannot use the `$order->orderLine()` method because it already exists in Eloquent to allow for queries on a class *relating to* the one where it is defined. Instead, we went with `addOrderLine()`. See Listing 15-3 for an example.

Listing 15-3. Updated Order Class with a Named Factory Method,
addOrderLine()

```php
<?php

//namespace & use cases

class Order extends Model
{
    //methods and property definitions

    public function addOrderLine(Product $product, int $qty)
    {
        $orderLine = OrderLine::create($product, $qty);
        $this->orderLines()->associate($orderLine);
        $this->save();
    }
}
```

Now we can use the aggregate root class to instantiate the internal objects of our
aggregate.

```php
$order = new Order($shopperId, $cartId);
$order->addOrderLine($product, $qty);
```

This approach is better suited for aggregates and follows the basic rules of aggregate
design because we are no longer concerned with instantiating an `OrderLine` object,
filling it with data, and then associating it with the `Order` in our client cod. Instead, we
just need to call the named factory on the `Order` class, letting it handle the setting and
persisting of its order lines. However, there is another violation of basic aggregate design
in our implementation: the persistence. An aggregate object should be persisted by a
database transaction, in an "all or none" type of deal. That way, we can ensure the `Order`
object and its internal objects are consistent, even in the event of a power outage or
unrelated system failure. This isn't such a big deal here because all we have to do to fix
the problem is to delay the `save()` method on the `Order` model (which is done right after
associating the `OrderLine` to the `Order` object) and defer it until the step right before
checkout. Without overloading ourselves with requirements in this simplified example,
let's say that, within our domain model, an `Order` is ready for payment and shipping only
once the user is satisfied with the order lines in their order and clicks the designated

Checkout button somewhere on the page. Once that button is hit, an event gets fired telling the event listeners and the application that an order is ready for checkout (we could even model this as a state, but not here). This will continue the process by recalculating the total amount with the added sales tax and shipping fees.

Then, there are also the invariants to consider, which we have not yet done. To save trees (or eyes if you are reading the electronic format of this book), Listing 15-4 shows the potential ways to solve the invariants and address the transactional persistence concern for the `Order` aggregate.

Listing 15-4. Updated Order Class, with Invariant Protection Included

```php
<?php

//use cases & namespaces
use Ecommerce\Domain\Models\Orders\OrderStatus;
use Illuminate\Support\Facades\DB;

class Order extends Model
{
    //methods and property definitions
    public $orderLines = [];
    const  TAX_RATE = .10;

    private $status = OrderStatus::ORDER_STARTED;

    /**
     * Invariant #2 & #3 are protected here
     */
    public function addOrderLine(Product $product, int $qty=1)
    {
        $orderLine = new OrderLine($product, $qty);
        $price = $product->price;

        foreach ($qty as $q) {
            $this->total += ($price +
                (static::TAX_RATE * $price));
        }
```

```
        $this->orderLines[] = $orderLine;
    }

    /**
     * Invariant #1 is protected here
     */
    public function startCheckout()
    {
        if (!empty($this->orderLines) &&
                (count($this->orderLines) > 0)) {
            //save the order lines within a transaction so we can
            //guarantee the state of the order stays consistent
            DB::transaction(function() {
                    foreach ($this->orderLines as $orderLine) {
                        $this->associate($orderLine);
                    }
                    $this->save();
            });
            /*start checkout process with a job or service.
            In theory, this would also change the status of the
            Order to something like OrderStatus::CHECKOUT_STARTED*/
            }

            return new JsonResponse("Order must have at least one Order
            Line before Checkout can begin", 500);
    }
}
```

In the example in Listing 15-4, we have a fairly simple class that has a TAX_RATE variable declared as a static constant on the class, which is the amount, in decimal form, of the tax we are going to have to add to the total of the order whenever there's a new OrderLine added to it. Instead of creating and persisting a new OrderLine object when we add a product to the order (which is what the facade method orderLines on the OrderLine object does), we simply store them in an array to be processed later. This simple change is going to allow us to hold off on actually writing the separate orders to the table until the very end, when the user is done shopping and the Order proceeds to the Checkout portion of the application. It is then and only then that we actually push the `OrderLine` instance to the `Order` object using the Eloquent facade method `associate()`, which handles the persistence of a many-to-many relationship. It is only at this point that we make the call to the save method, officially writing the records to the `orders` and `order_lines` tables and concluding the ordering portion of the application. This part is done within the `startCheckout()` method of the class, which checks to make sure that there is at least one item in the `orderLines` array before moving forward. There is also a `$status` class member variable that serves to track the proper status on an `Order` object. Upon the start of the checkout process, this status would presumably change to indicate that the state transition occurred, and there would most likely be some event that gets raised in the process, if needed to tell the rest of the application that this has occurred (perhaps to store the order in some sort of cache in case the user decides to leave the page, which would then reload the order whenever the user returns to the site later). We make the call to store `orderLines` and the order itself within a transaction so we can keep the integrity of the database intact.

We could have chosen to do this calculation in some service in the domain layer, but these operations are so close to the root model (aggregate root), which in this case is the `Order` model, that it makes sense to have the operations within the model. This is partly because if we stuck the logic inside a service, we would make an implicit dependency for the process to occur because developers would always have to remember to call that service instead of just doing it manually with Eloquent (which is extremely easy using Eloquent's facades). By having the constraints and protecting the invariants on the model, we make it just as easy to persist the order lines within the confines of a transaction, making sure that nothing is persisted to the database outside it and things are only ever executed during the start of the checkout phase of the order.

This version is slicker and has a better separation of concerns. For instance, we no longer have to concern the client code with the notion of an `OrderLine` object. All we have to do is pass the arguments that the constructor of the `OrderLine` class needs, but the client code is unaware of this as well! It just has to provide the data it already has available (i.e., the product and the quantity). Another thing to note is that we've stripped any notion of sales tax out of the product to have it completely handled in the `Order` class, which is easy to change by just modifying the value of the `TAX_RATE` constant. This creates less data in the `OrderLine` objects. One upgrade we could make to this code is to further split up this functionality from the rest of the logic inside the `startCheckout()` method, but this is not required.

Listing 15-5 provides a possible usage example.

Listing 15-5. Usage Example (Client Code) for the Previous Implementation

```php
<?php

//create order object
$order = new Order($shopperId, $cartId);

//create product object & quantity of that product
$product = Product::find(420);
$quantity = 3;

//we no longer have to worry about the orderLine object at all!
//instead, we just pass in the data we already have...
$order->addOrderLine($product, $qty);
$order->addOrderLine($product2, $qty2);
$order->addOrderLine($product3, $qty3);

//user clicks on the "Checkout" button:
if ($order->startCheckout()) {
    dispatch(new RunCheckout($order));
} else {
    //return some response indicating to the frontend the issue,
    //which would presumably display a notification to the user
}
```

Something else to note is that because we are encapsulating the concept of an
OrderLine within an aggregate, any access to an OrderLine object *must* be done through
the Order aggregate root. If we think about it, it makes perfect sense because there
would be no need or requirement to modify an OrderLine outside of an Order class. All
OrderLine instances will pertain to an Order, which is why we've made the Order class
the aggregate root. Understanding this, we would need to add methods on that aggregate
root if we wanted the ability to do things such as update the quantity of an OrderLine,
replace an OrderLine, or remove it altogether. This would mean additional code like in
Listing 15-6.

Listing 15-6. Additional Methods for the Order Class Needed to Modify Existing OrderLines

```php
<?php
//namespace & use statements

class Order extends Model
{
    //properties and method definitions

    /**
    * @param $sequence : The location of the order line in the array
    */
    public function removeOrderLine($sequence)
    {
        if (isset($this->orderLines[$sequence])) {
            unset ($this->orderLines[$sequence]);
        }
    }

    public function updateQuantity($sequence, $newQuantity)
    {
        if (isset($this->orderLines[$sequence])) {
            //get the product that corresponds to that order line:
            $product = $this->orderLines[$sequence]->product;
            //remove the orderLine completely from the array:
            unset($this->orderLines[$sequence]);
            //add the new orderLine to the array:
            $this->addOrderLine($product, $newQuantity);
        }
    }
}
```

In Listing 15-6, we have two additional methods, one to update the quantity of an order line and another to remove an order line. This looks pretty good; however, it is missing an important piece to it that would make the whole system unusable. Can you identify what it is that we forgot to include?

The total amount! By changing the quantity of an order line or removing one, we essentially need to update the total amount of the order (including the tax added for each one). Remember that for the invariants listed for this example state, the amount of an order needs be updated at all times, so we will need to modify the Order class again to include that logic (Listing 15-7).

Listing 15-7. Additional Methods for the Order Class Needed to Modify Existing OrderLines

```php
<?php

//namespace & use statements

class Order extends Model
{
    //properties and method definitions

    /**
    * @param $sequence : The location of the order line in the array
    */
    public function removeOrderLine($sequence)
    {
        if (isset($this->orderLines[$sequence])) {
            $orderLine = $this->orderLines[$sequence];
            $totalAmountDelta = $orderLine->product->price +
                ($orderLine->product->price * static::TAX_RATE);
            $this->total -= $totalAmountDelta;
            unset ($this->orderLines[$sequence]));
        }
    }

    public function updateQuantity($sequence, $newQuantity)
    {
        if (isset($this->orderLines[$sequence])) {
            //get the product that corresponds to that order line:
            $orderLine = $this->orderLines[$sequence];
            $product = $orderLine->product;
            //remove the orderLine completely from the array:
```

```
        $totalAmountDelta = $product->price + ($product->price
            * static::TAX_RATE);
        $this->amount -= $totalAmountDelta;
        unset($this->orderLines[$sequence]);
        //we dont have to worry about adding the product's
        //tax because that logic is already in addOrderLine():
        $this->addOrderLine($product, $newQuantity);
    }
}
}
```

That looks better! We now have the total amount updating every time there is a change to an OrderLine using the Order as the aggregate root, as well as the invariant regarding the sales tax to be included with each product, within an OrderLine.

There's still an oversight here. Aggregate roots should have a globally accessible identity—which they do—and have a boundary drawn around other models. Also, each of them should be accessible only from the aggregate root, and not from a global context, which is hard to stop, but is made obvious by a named factory method on the aggregate root, which is what we originally were doing in Listing 15-3. We utilized a factory method on the Order class to create the various LineOrder objects that are needed to represent the various aspects of a real-life Order (which is the definition of modeling). However, we soon found that this approach lacked something we had to have to ensure data consistency within the Order aggregate: transactions. We removed the calls to associate() and save() from the addOrderLine() method and used a primitive array to hold the nonpersisted OrderLine objects (and unassociated to the Order). Then, on checkout, we put the actual code that persists the entities to the database inside the startCheckout() method, using a transaction to ensure the consistency of the records with different target tables to write the transformed models to.

Event Sourcing

Event sourcing is a large and in-depth topic that I won't discuss in this chapter in any depth, but later in the book we will walk through a simple scenario modeled using event sourcing with a package for Laravel known as EventSauce (https://eventsauce.io/). It is highly customizable and offers you the flexibility to customize virtually every aspect of the way it behaves to suit your needs. Event sourcing, in general, is an extremely complex ordeal and is not recommended for most web application projects simply because of the raw overhead and technical know-how it takes to add event sourcing to an existing application or start a fresh one based on event sourcing. As with anything in life, event sourcing comes with trade-offs. Most applications don't need the level of complexity that event sourcing offers. It should be used when you are faced with concerns such as the following:

- The requirement to track an entity's every change during its lifetime in the domain model

- Need to perform auditing on your models

- Need an asynchronous solution to handle perhaps an overwhelming number of requests across a variety of data and services

- When transactions need to be employed in an aggregate system to keep its data consistent in the database and the application

Conclusion

At the start of the chapter, we went through some basic theory of transactions, how they are used, and how they help keep the data in a database consistent and also ensure that updates to the database are done in an atomic way. Transactions are the basic concept involved in persisting aggregates. The characteristics of transactions can be remembered with the acronym ACID, which stands for atomicity, concurrency, isolation, and durability.

We discussed the characteristics of on aggregate objects and object factories. Most of the time, a factory method is really all that is needed to make an aggregate design work with all its invariant checks and balances. An aggregate is basically a boundary that contains within it several different model classes encapsulated behind what's called the aggregate root. The aggregate root is the "up-front" model that any requests made that access the internal objects within the aggregate must go through. We need to be careful that the internal objects aren't accessed directly, although in practice this really cannot be prevented. We can mitigate this by offering convenient methods on the aggregate root that will handle accessing or modifying the internal objects for us, thus keeping the invariants and business rules contained within the aggregate root. This makes sense on a high level because we shouldn't need to access the internal parts of the aggregate directly and instead rely on operations within the aggregate root model.

We looked at an example of one possible aggregate, the `Order` aggregate, which had an internal `OrderLine` object inside its aggregate boundary and an `Order` object acting as the aggregate root. Factories help us keep the boundary intact, and oftentimes aggregates should be used only where necessary, as they can cause an increase in the overhead and maintenance of the code used to model the domain, as well as add unnecessary complexity, which can take the focus off the domain model and put it on making the aggregate work throughout the rest of the application or even persisting the aggregate in the database. Complex applications are what merit the use of aggregates and event sourcing.

CHAPTER 16

Services

I saved this chapter for this spot in the book because of the raw knowledge you need to fully make use of services. Creating services should be done with caution and precision, because the service layer has a tendency to become anemic, which is a fairly common occurrence that happens when too much business logic is placed in them, usually resulting in the core value objects and entities (the most important thing to get correct) being stripped of all the behavior that is symmetrically aligned with the very concerns and business logic that exists in the real-life domain. This isn't a good thing because it basically makes our value objects and entities act as mere data containers rather than what they were meant to actually be: objects with behavior and data encapsulated within them so that they might model and represent the domain better.

In this chapter, we will go over examples of the three types of services I introduced in Chapter 1 of this book. We will then explore the surrounding issues that occur when the service layer gets overused and how we can avoid heading toward an anemic domain model. The answer lies partly in getting into the habit of not modeling the data first, which is something that many developers seem to do naturally because that's the way they originally learned. It's not good practice, because when we think of things in terms of data, we are basically adding concrete structures that would be boring static structures or properties on a class had it not been for the behaviors of other objects acting on that data to make it interesting. Instead, when modeling a domain, try to think of how the model's behavior is going to function and what operations it needs to perform to fulfil the domain concern that was intended of it. Name these behaviors in accordance with the ubiquitous language and place such behaviors in services only when they truly do not fit the bill of an entity or value object.

We will also explore the characteristics of Laravel jobs that make them straightforward implementations of what might be defined as a "service." A job can be dispatched from anywhere in the application, placed on a stack of jobs, scheduled to run at a certain time, and sent out to a queue worker that processes the independent logic

© Jesse Griffin 2021
J. Griffin, *Domain-Driven Laravel*, https://doi.org/10.1007/978-1-4842-6023-4_16

encapsulated within it (also included with Laravel). That type of job can very well serve as a service. We will discuss the possibility of using a few different traits on a `Job` class as a replacement for services within the context of DDL.

Services Primer

To me, a service might need to be defined across multiple classes or objects that take part in establishing the input or modifications needed to make the service function. It's not always straightforward where to draw the boundaries between the portions of logic that make up the application as a whole, whether it be application, infrastructure, UI, or domain concerns—just as one could say that their "application service" in Laravel actually turns out to be a request with specific validation requirements together with a controller that delivers that request to a service or component within the domain. Or, an application service could be a stand-alone service that pertains to a single class, for example, `SignupService`.

Services can be useful to capture business processes that don't fit the usual responsibilities of an entity or value object. However, I believe services are often overused to compensate for novice design or an approach taken by an inexperienced developer or team. That's not to say that services don't have their place in the real world. Look at microservices, for example. They are pretty much the de facto standard in the industry today for many different tech-related companies. But we are not talking about services from this vantage point. Microservices are different because they operate on a different scale, so to speak. They are broader concepts than we are going to cover in this book, because they encapsulate many other nested components and logic. The services I'm referring to fall into one of the three categories (as I mentioned at the beginning of the book).

- *Application services*: These are services that operate on primitive values delivered via some kind of request, turning them into domain instructions that get dispatched to a domain service, or other component that operates on domain objects. Think of a Laravel request, which abstracts this sort of delivery mechanism needed to accept input from outside the application. Together with a controller, they accomplish exactly what a "standard" application could or would, making interaction between the application and the outside world possible.

- *Infrastructure services*: Typically, these services handle infrastructure concerns such as logging or sending out an email. In the case of DDL, infrastructure concerns could be considered any interactions with the Laravel framework, as well as the persistence mechanisms.

- *Domain services*: These services operate only on domain objects such as value objects or entities as required by the domain. In terms of DDD, domain services consist mainly of business logic that operate on the Eloquent models that we established to represent the entities in our application.

Again, the key is to create a light, thin service that is stateless and create it only when the job doesn't quite fit into an entity or a value object. In the following example, we are going to build the service needed to take a `Claim` object and officially submit it into the system. We will employ a service to do handle this operation, because the concept of "submitting a claim" doesn't fit well into an entity or value object. We will make the service a stateless operation and include in it only the things that are needed for submitting a claim. What's important to note here is that the validations and checks have already been done to the `Claim` object to make sure it is 100 percent valid and ready to be submitted. We are going to focus only on the portion of the application that will submit the claim into the system. We will be using domain events to notify the rest of the application about the submission, so other bounded contexts can react in their own way.

Just to refresh your memory, a claim is submitted by a provider and has multiple validations that must be run against it to qualify it with a status of `PENDING_REVIEW`. We covered the majority of the validations earlier in the book when we went over the validation context of our application. We verified such things as the following:

- The claim was submitted within the last year.

- The provider submitting the claim has been properly linked to the patient on the claim.

- There were procedure codes attached to the claim.

- Those procedure codes were valid and belonged to a valid paycode sheet for that provider.

For a more detailed look at the validations required for a claim to enter into the system, review Chapter 8. Now, we need to build out a service that will actually handle the submission of a claim. We will put this example into the context of DDL. This means we will be utilizing a Laravel job to do our dirty work. Remember that a job can be used as a service, mainly because of the traits that it uses. Those traits are Dispatchable, InteractsWithQueue, Queueable, and SerializesModels. They are what allow a job in Laravel to be queued by the queue worker. The Dispatchable trait is what allows the job to be dispatched via the helper function dispatch(). We can call this helper from anywhere in the application. The InteractsWithQueue trait and the Queueable trait allow the job to be pushed onto the queue, as well as provide a means for checking on the job's status. The SerializesModels trait allows the ability for us to pass in an Eloquent model directly to the constructor of our job, which will be serialized and unsterilized gracefully when it is actually placed onto the queue worker's stack. We will use the Job component of Laravel as the basis for our service classes. The best thing about this approach is that any type of service can be made out of a job.

The first service we will build is the SubmitsClaims job. The only concern this job will have is to run the validations that we've set up previously in the ClaimValidationHandler, which is not too difficult seeing as though we incorporated the handler into the Claim model already, under the method validate(). So, all we have to do is receive our already created request, ClaimSubmissionRequest, which houses all the requirements down to a granular level. You can specify all kinds of validation constraints using Laravel's Request component along with its Validation component.

This is an important concept to consider. We have an opportunity here to tie in virtually all the constraints and requirements of the data that the delivery mechanisms facilitate to the controllers or callbacks (whichever is specified in the route file). The delivery mechanism itself will handle running the incoming data though the constraints we've specified in the request. Once it hits the controller method, it already validated. All the validation that you cannot or don't want to place in the context of the request (such as domain validation), can be handled in the controller, which can be as simple as Listing 16-1.

Listing 16-1. Example Usage of Laravel Rules

```php
<?php

use Claim\Validation\Domain\Rules\ClaimHasProviderAttached;
use Claim\Validation\Domain\Models\ClaimDateOfServiceIsValid;

$request->validate([
    new ClaimHasProviderAttached(),
    new ClaimDateOfServiceIsValid()
]);
```

Notice that in Listing 16-1, instead of naming our rule something like `ClaimWasSubmittedWithinOneYear`, which would have forced us to run the constraint with only a one-year allowable date of service, we chose the name `ClaimDateOfServiceValid`, which aligns nicely to our domain-driven design focus and is named after it. If we ever wanted to change the date range for which the claim would be considered valid, we would have to create another rule in the `Validation` context, which is more code and more work to maintain and creates more places to change. Instead, we kept things consistent with the domain and the ubiquitous language by naming the rule after a rudimentary concept in the domain.

Application Services

Let's create an application service that will accept a request of type `ClaimSubmissionRequest`, run any validations against it, and then forward the actual work that handles the submission and persistence of the claim to a domain service. To create this application service, we will be using a standard Laravel controller that will receive the input request (abstracted by `ClaimSubmissionRequest`, which serves as our delivery mechanism), handle running the validation, dispatch a domain service (which will be a Laravel job), and return a response. A simple DTO can be used to abstract the transmission of the data in question (the claim) when we send it to our service (which in this case equates to dispatching a job). See an example of this in Listing 16-2.

Listing 16-2. Example Application Service Calling Our Domain Service

```php
<?php

namespace Claim\Submission\Application\Http\Controllers;

use Claim\Validation\Domain\Rules\ClaimHasProviderAttached;
use Claim\Validation\Domain\Models\ClaimDateOfServiceIsValid;

class SubmitClaimController
{
    public function submit(ClaimSubmissionRequest $request)
    {
        $request->validate([
            new ClaimHasProviderAttached(),
```

```
            new ClaimDateOfServiceIsValid()
    ]);

    $claimDto = new ClaimDTO($request->all());

    $response = $this->dispatch(new SubmitClaim($claimDto));

    return new JsonResponse($response, 200);
    }
}
```

If you don't recall what exactly ClaimSubmissionRequest looks like, review Listing 16-3.

Listing 16-3. A Request Object for Submitting the Claim

```php
<?php

namespace Domain\Submission\App\Http\Requests;

use Illuminate\Foundation\Http\FormRequest;

class ClaimSubmissionRequest extends FormRequest
{
    public function authorize()
    {
        return true;
    }

    public function rules()
    {
        return [
          'claim.patient.first_name' => 'required|text|min:2',
          'claim.patient.last_name' => 'required|text|min:2',
          'claim.patient.dob' => 'required|date',
          'claim.patient.medical_number' => 'required|integer',
          'claim.progress_notes' => 'required|min:1',
```

```
        'claim.patient.documents.identification' => 'required|file',
        'claim.patient.documents.application' =>  'required|file'
    ];
    }
}
```

The previous request object encapsulates the required fields and detailed constraints for the data needed to submit a claim. In this case, the controller along with the request makes up what can be considered an application service. It abstracts the delivery mechanism so that we can focus on handling the request. What that equates to in our case is instantiating a simple DTO, which is just a data container that holds all the data we pulled from the (valid) request and then dispatches a domain service from the controller that will handle the dirty work for us. I'm not going to bother to actually make a code listing of the ClaimDTO object, as it is just a plain ol' PHP object with getters and setters for every field on the claim object.

Note   Something to consider is that since we have chosen to utilize Laravel's HTTP request/response cycle as the frame for our application service, we are left with a *multitude* of objects that work together to do what we need it to do. It is possible that some applications (simple applications, for example) could be better off taking a more unifying approach and place the core logic of the service, and all the various concerns surrounding it, inside a single class, which would be easier to find and debug. However, if the application ever grows in size (which is the case 90 percent of the time), maintenance and updates to that service will become more cumbersome as more and more concerns are mixed together. In general, I'd say it's better to have concerns separated out inline with the organization of the domain (which reflects the terms in the ubiquitous language, which should always be used as a reference point when developing software).

However, doing it this way, we have taken care of many concerns that are absolutely necessary to facilitate such an application. We have our delivery mechanism for the requests coming into the application, the routing of such requests handled by the router, the security of the request maintained by the ClaimPolicy class that I introduced earlier in the book, and a clean and clear separation of concerns. Also, at the point where this application service is called, we can guarantee that the claim data being passed to it is validated and verified by our Validation Bounded context. I'd say we're doing pretty well. We are naming things directly after concepts in the domain, derived from the ubiquitous language, which is also important to truly capture.

That's one way to create an application service—by using Laravel's built-in facilities and processes to abstract the delivery mechanism away from the code that acts on it. If you instead wanted to create a more of a stand-alone application service, you could employ a separate class, outside of the application's normal HTTP process, that can handle whatever application concern you need to implement. A good way to do this is to employ the Command pattern. This pattern allows you to write your application services against an interface to allow for easy decoration later (which can be useful when dealing with transactions) and forces a good separation of concerns among the other services of the same type. You can think of each service made in this manner as a command, which may come with their own handler (since it is best practice to separate the data in the request from the code that executes that request). Or, you may instead feel like you want to separate these things out and have a different Command object that holds the data (with no behavior), writes a handler class that will accept a Command object, and executes the given functionality specific to that Command, using the data in the command to do so (the actually running of the command takes place within the handler class).

You can use many open source packages to lay the foundation of your command/ handler pattern, such as Tactician, made by the League of Extraordinary Packages (https://tactician.thephpleague.com/). The packages and libraries made by ThePhpLeague folks are guaranteed to be tried and tested and have a lot of developer support and usage in many software projects. You can trust these packages will serve their purpose, and I highly recommend using them whenever needed.

Commands are run from a command line (not to be confused with Artisan commands). They can be useful in capturing the intent of the user. They can be thought of as actions that come from outside the application and directly express the true intentions of the user. A command shouldn't contain business logic per se, but should just hold the instructions regarding the "what" while the command handler holds the "how." Listing 16-4 shows an example application service using the Tactician library. Notice that this service lines up almost exactly to the way things are done in Laravel's HTTP cycle (using a custom Laravel response, the details are tailored to our specific use case, together with a controller).

Listing 16-4. Stand-Alone Command

```php
<?php

namespace App\User\Services;

class SignupUserCommand
{
    protected $username;

    protected $password;

    protected $role;

    public function __construct(Username $username, Password $password,
    Role $role)
    {
        $this->username = $username;
        $this->password = $password;
        $this->role = $role;
    }
}
```

Notice that the previous command doesn't have any functionality but is only a basic storage container for the data needed to handle the command. Listing 16-5 shows the actual handler, along with its invocation code.

Listing 16-5. A Command Handler

```php
<?php

namespace App\Services\Users;

class SignupUserHandler
{
    public function handleSignup(SignupUserCommand $command)
    {
        //core application logic goes here
```

```
            echo "User " . $command->username . " was signed
                up!";
        }
}

//somewhere in the code

use League\Container\Container;
use League\Tactician\Handler\Mapping\ClassName\Suffix;
use League\Tactician\Handler\Mapping\MapByNamingConvention;
use League\Tactician\Handler\Mapping\MethodName\
    HandleLastPartOfClassName;

//configure Tactician's middleware to support the naming
//convention derived from the project's Ubiquitous Language
$container = new Container();
$container->add(SignupUserCommand::class);
$handleMiddleware = new League\Tactician\Handler\
    CommandHandlerMiddleware(
        $container,
        new MapByNamingConvention(
            new Suffix('Handler'),
            new HandleLastPartOfClassName()
    )
);

$commandBus = new \League\Tactician\CommandBus
    ($handlerMiddleware);

//in a controller
$command = new SignupUser();
$command->username = $request->username;
$command->password = $request->password;
$command->role = Role\Moderator::class;

$command->handle($command);
```

The way Tactician works is via middleware "plugins" for everything, including its configuration. This is to allow for maximum extensibility when writing commands and handlers for your own projects. In the previous listing, we have initiated Tactician with a custom naming convention to support the ubiquitous language present in the domain model. In the previous listing, we have configured Tactician to look for handlers corresponding to the last part of the command name. It will then autolocate the correct handler for whichever command you instantiate. For additional information on this package, visit their website.

No matter how you choose to implement application services, take the approach that has the best separation of concerns and the method that fits into your domain model the best, so as to provide the best outcome for your domain. Keep all services stateless, thin, and focused on either a single task or a group of tasks, related to the same entity or concern.

The domain service itself, freed of the concern of validating the data making up the claim, can focus on the creation of the claim and can dispatch the functionality in the infrastructure layer to persist the object (which either can be done inline using Eloquent's facades or may be in a separate class or object or could be handled by a repository, depending on the needs of your application).

Infrastructure Services

These services pertain to concerns at the infrastructure level of the application that have to do with things such as logging, persistence, and things of that nature. An infrastructure service is one that supports the other services and concerns outside of its layer. As an example, consider the application service we created earlier to sign a new user up in the system given a username and password. Let's say that we wanted to include a password hashing mechanism that gets run during the sign-up process. Let's also say that we wanted to implement a few different mechanisms for password hashing, and we wanted the ability to choose which implementation to use at runtime. What's the best way to go about creating this?

We may decide to implement a Separated Interface pattern or a Strategy pattern for the password hashing mechanism. The first step would be to define some sort of interface that expresses the general concept of what a password hashing mechanism is. Here is a naive interface:

```php
<?php
namespace App\Contracts;
interface PasswordHash
{
    public function hash(): string;
    public function setPlainPassword(string $plain) : void;
}
```

To prevent all the child classes from having to implement the setPlainPassword() method, we could create an abstract class that will actually implement the interface and then leave the child classes to extend it.

```php
<?php
use App\Contracts\PasswordHash;
class AbstractPasswordHash implements PasswordHash
{
    public string $plain;

    abstract public function hash(): string;

    public function setPlainPassword(string $plain): void
    {
        $this->plain = $plain;
    }
}
```

Here is a possible implementation of the previous interface, with an MD5 hashing mechanism:

```php
<?php
use App\Contracts\PasswordHash;

class Md5PasswordHash extends AbstractPasswordHash
{
```

```
    public function hash(string $plainPassword): string
    {
        return md5($plainPassword);
    }
}
```

And here is another for a bcrypt mechanism:

```
<?php
use App\Contracts\PasswordHash;
class BcryptPasswordHash extend AbstractPasswordHash
{
    public function hash(string $plainPassword): string
    {
        return bcrypt($plainPassword);
    }
}
```

We could wire these all up using Laravel's service container easily and then configure the application to use a specific one before we call the hashing mechanism. This can be done either in configuration, which would be easy to change because the setting is located in one place and one place only. Another way would be to configure which mechanism to do on the fly, and keep the setting closer to the code that uses it, which is inline with the user signup procedure (possibly in a controller that would pass the decision to the service that does the hashing, so as to keep the service unaware of which hashing strategy we decided to use). Listing 16-6 shows what the service container configuration could look like for such a strategy.

Listing 16-6. Binding the Hashing Mechanism to the Service Container

```
//inside the AppServiceProvider's boot() method:
$this->app->bind('HashingMechanism', function() {
    switch (config('hash.password')) {
        case 'md5':
            return new Md5PasswordHash();
            break;
```

```
        case 'bcrypt':
            return new BcryptPasswordHash();
            break;
    }
});
```

In the previous listing, we bind an implementation, defined in a closure, to the service container based on the configuration value placed inside the respective config file, which in turn either returns the value specified in the .env file under the HASHING_ MECHANISM key or else sets a static default value.

```
//inside the /config directory, in a "hash.php" config file
'password_hash' => env('PASSWORD_HASH', 'md5'),
```

Doing so gives us the ability to change the type of mechanism we want to hash the passwords with by simply modifying the .env file, and *not* any code in the repository. This goes along with the open for extension/closed for modification SOLID principle. However, this exact case can be taken with a grain of salt: it serves a good purpose as a reference, but implementing something like this would probably not be necessary in the context of a Laravel application, because we can just use the Hash facade and utilize the make method directly. This approach does promote a good separation of concerns in an obvious, nonintrusive manner.

Domain Services

Domain services operate mostly on domain objects and facilitate business processes that are crucial to implement the core functionality required by the domain to support the model. Getting back to the claim example, domain services could exist for things such as validating that a claim is ready to be submitted (which would live inside the Validation context), checking that a patient is registered with a primary provider, submitting a claim, and initiating a screen scraper to verify eligibility. One-off scripts work well as services, which can arise from the need to backfill data or run custom modifications to a database in order to amend its data. We will build out a possible solution to the problem of submitting the claim, as shown in Listing 16-7.

Listing 16-7. Example SubmitClaim Domain Service

```php
<?php

namespace Claim\Submission\Domain\Claim\Services;

use Claim\Validation\Domain\Services\
    PatientEligibilityScraper;
use Claim\Validation\Infrastructure\
    Validators\ClaimValidationHandler;
use Claim\Submission\Domain\Services\Estimate\ClaimEstimator;
use Claim\Submission\Domain\Models\Claim;
use Claim\Submission\Domain\ValueObjects\Signature;
use Claim\Submission\Domain\Events\ClaimWasSubmitted;
class SubmitClaim extends Job implements ShouldQueue
{
    use Queueable, InteractsWithQueue, SerializesModels, DispatchesJobs;

    protected Claim $claim;

    protected Signature $signature;

    protected PatientEligibilityScraper
        $patientEligibilityScraper;

    protected ClaimEstimator $claimEstimator;

    protected ClaimValidator $claimValidator;

    public function __construct(Claim $claim,
        Signature $signature,
        PatientEligibilityValidator
            $patientEligibilityValidator,
         PatientEligibilityScraper
            $patientEligibilityScraper,
        ClaimEstimator $claimEstimator)
    {
        $this->claim = $claim;
        $this->signature = $signature;
```

```
        $this->patientEligibilityScraper =
            $patientEligibilityScraper;
        $this->claimEstimator = $claimEstimator;
        $this->claimValidationHandler =
            app()->makeWith(ClaimValidationHandler::class, $claim);
    }

    public function handle(): void
    {
        //run standard validations (see Chapter 8)
        $this->validate();

        $claim = $this->claim;

        if (!is_null($claim->progressNotes) &&
            $claim->checkDateOfService() &&
            $claim->userCanSubmitClaim(auth()->user())) {
            //claim is now considered validated
            $provider = $claim->primaryPhysician;
            $cptCodes = $claim->cptCodeCombos
                            ->cptCodes
                            ->toArray();

            //get the estimated amount of claim
            $claim->estimatedAmount = $this->claimEstimator
                ->estimate($provider, $cptCodes);

            //delegate scrape operation for eligibility
            $patient = $claim->patient;
            $claim->patientEligibility = $this->patientEligibilityScraper
                    ->scrape($patient);
            $claim->signature = $signature;
            $claim->state->transitionTo(PendingReview:: class);
            $claim->save();
```

```
            //send an event notifying listeners that a
            //new claim has been entered into the system
            event(new ClaimWasSubmitted($claim));
        }
    }

    private function validate(): void
    {
        try {
            $this->claim
                ->validate(
                    $this->claimValidationHandler);
        } catch (MissingDocumentsException $e) {
            //log & throw error
        } catch (InvalidCptCodeException $e) {
            //log & throw error
        } catch (MissingEligibilityError $e) {
            //log & throw error
        } catch (PatientNotRegisteredWithProvider $e) {
            //log & throw error
        }
    }
}
```

The claimValidator as used previously is the result of a call to makeWith() to the service container, indicating that there is a dependency within that service's constructor that cannot be resolved by the container automatically and that needs to be provided manually. In most of these cases, it means that the class or service in question has runtime dependency. We've accounted for this by passing in the required $claim object to the ClaimValidator, which looks like this (if you forgotten):

```
class ClaimValidator extends AbstractValidator
{
    private $claim;
    private $validationHandler;

    public function __construct(Claim $claim, ValidationHandler
    $validationHandler)
```

```
    {
        parent::__construct($validationHandler);
        $this->claim = $claim;
    }

    /** see the end of chapter 8 for a full listing */
}
```

However, we opted to place the call to the logic that validates the claim itself inside the `Claim` object so it is as close to the code that uses it as possible. After we have run the validations contained within `ClaimValidationHandler`, we ensure that the other requirements for a claim to be submitted into the system are met. This includes checking that the progress notes field is present, checking that the date of service is within the acceptable range, and checking that the user submitting the claim is actually authorized to do so. After these checks, we can assume that the claim is valid and continue with the process.

We use another service, `ClaimEstimator`, to determine the estimated amount that the claim will pay out to the provider (if accepted by the FQHC). This service takes the provider and the CPT codes that are present on the claim, does some calculations, and returns an amount, in dollars, that we then store in the claim. After this, we delegate to another service, `ClaimEligibilityScraper`, that will run the logic that will scrape the site and return a screenshot of the eligibility check that will determine that the patient present on the claim is eligible to receive care. The screenshot will be another thing that the human reviewer is going to have to check in the manual review phase, which is the next step of the claim process. Claims also all need to have an authorized signature, which we have encapsulated within a `Signature` value object and attached to the claim (which will also be reviewed). Last but not least, we transition the claim's status (which we set up earlier in the book) to be `PENDING_REVIEW`, and then we emit an event to the rest of the application so listeners can respond to the fact that a new claim has entered the system.

The cool part is that we don't even have to worry about or care what is listening to that event. We just have to emit the event with the corresponding event data attached to it, in this case being the claim, and the framework will handle the dispatching.

Testing Services

We covered this scenario in Chapter 9 when we wrote the tests regarding the states that a claim could be in, and I've demonstrated the basic requirements for a solid test that ensures the transition from having no status (or a DRAFT status) to having a status of PENDING_REVIEW. Considering this, I will not include any code within the text, but you can always look on the repository online and view the tests written for the classes and objects in the domain model and also refer to Chapter 9. I do want to leave you with a few additional thoughts on the possible tests you can perform on your code to ensure it's doing what it is supposed to be doing (and not messing up anything else in the process). Laravel comes with PHPUnit, which provides lots of cool helper classes and components for testing your application. It also comes with classes that allow you to test your application on the front end, not to the extent of something as intricate as Selenium coupled with Google WebDriver, but it still serves a good purpose. Consider what a test for a service could look like. For example, the application service described at the start of the chapter (the one utilizing Laravel's HTTP components) could be tested in a number of different ways, such as creating a functional test to test a specific class as a whole (such as the SubmitClaim service) or a unit test that can be as finely grained as writing one test method for every project method, but this is overkill for testing. In fact, you will be so bogged down with writing the tests (and their intricacies) that you will get very little use out of them. Instead, focus on writing tests that adequately provide coverage for main concerns in the application. Integration tests work great for this purpose as they are aimed at testing the result of a combination of different outcomes of various domain-related code—the parts that are crucial to the application's well-being and are important to the overall functionality of the core domain.

Conclusion

Services have a place when developing an application, with or without a framework. They are best used in place of something that would otherwise not be or could not be considered an entity or value object. Create a thin service layer for these such items in your application, which are grouped based on the layer that each one belongs to. Remember, though, that the more actual business logic you include in your services, the easier it will be to move toward an anemic service layer, which is a bad thing. The easiest way to avoid this is to express the majority of the business-related functionality in entities and value objects.

There are three different types of services, application, domain, and infrastructure, and they all have a specific use. Application services are used to abstract the delivery mechanism and are responsible for converting an incoming request into something the application can understand. Domain services deal directly with domain objects and facilitate the processes in the system that do not fit into value objects and entities. Infrastructure services are tasked with handling such concerns as logging, persistence, and even password hashing mechanisms.

PART IV

DDD via Laravel

CHAPTER 17

Hexagonal-Driven Development

Hexagonal architecture is basically another way to think about, organize, and model your applications (as opposed to a traditional MVC pattern architecture). In hexagonal architecture, we have the domain model itself contained within the heart of the application (as it should be), with the layers that handle the facilitation and management of objects in the domain model surrounding it (the application layer). Finally, there is an interface layer that wraps the whole thing and provides a means for requests to enter and interact with the application's internals by using ports to establish interfaces that will need to be satisfied by the client. Those implementations that satisfy the port contracts are called *adapters*.

The Git-Down

Eric Evans equated the way a hexagonal architecture works by relating it to the way our cell's membranes allow passage of various molecules in and out of the cell. These molecules flow in either direction by means of gates, or channels within the membrane that allow their passage. Similarly, in a hexagonal architecture, each of the sides of the hexagon can be thought of as channels of a cell membrane representing various ports that restrict what can go in or out of the cell (or application). The molecules in this case represent the adapters (concretions) that fulfill some purpose (which in this case would be requests and responses). You can think of the ports as "abstractions" and adapters as "concretions." The ports basically define an interface that the adapters implement for the various facilities of the application. The interfaces ensure that particular methods are available for our application to use, regardless of the decided implementation of that interface. The way that each request enters the system depends on the type of request it is. We can abstract the delivery mechanism needed to handle the request

© Jesse Griffin 2021
J. Griffin, *Domain-Driven Laravel*, https://doi.org/10.1007/978-1-4842-6023-4_17

by using an easy-to-use Laravel request (which is automatically constructed from the PHP superglobals existing on that machine/instance at that given time). Relating this back to hexagonal equates to placing a sort of main "input" side of the however-many-agon shape that's specific to your project's needs. There could be only three or four sides corresponding to the various "central" concerns of the system, which most likely wouldn't benefit from the added complexity that surrounds a hexagonal architecture and implementation. On the flip side, it could even be more complex and require additional sides to the shape.

Note   The name *hexa*gonal doesn't actually imply that there are six sides for which ports can exist. This hexagon-like structure actually holds no reference to the number six at all but is instead meant to be thought of as more of a circle (rather than a hierarchical structure like that of a layered architecture); it represents "outside" and "inside" rather than "above" or "below."

An adapter can represent an unlimited number of concrete implementations of the interfaces defined within the ports. Generally, they travel either inbound toward the center (domain model) or outward away from it (responses). Figure 17-1 contains the same concepts as a hexagonal architecture, only represented within a circle.

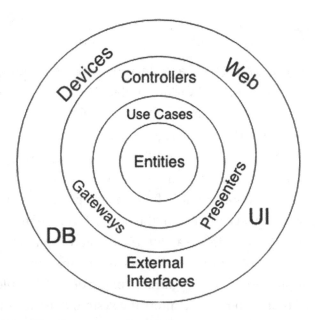

Figure 17-1. *The circular hexagonal architecture*

If this figure looks familiar, there is a good reason. I included an image similar to this one in the first chapter. This is simply a more advanced modeling architecture that allows for greater flexibility and is easier to test than layered architectures. Because the ports are basically interfaces that traffic requests/responses in and out of the system, you can create as many adapters that implement the port interface as you need. This allows for pretty much any part of the application code (outside the domain model) to be swapped out for other implementations of the same port interface without having to change the client code that utilizes the interfaces within the application. Another benefit to hexagonal is that it allows you to defer architectural design decisions until you have a better understanding of its core and more insight into the true needs of the application.

Note   A port can also be a command or query bus. In this case, a driving adapter could just be an implementation of the actual `Command` or `Query` being used and that gets injected into a controller, which constructs the concrete command or query and passes it to the relevant bus.

By the way, if you're wondering why the previous shape is not a hexagon but rather a circle, it's because of the fact that the actual shape or number of sides is completely arbitrary.

By having this loosely coupled setup, we can easily isolate the domain concerns from all other aspects of the system, which is also a central focus point in domain-driven design, allowing us to focus on what matters most—the business logic. This isolation makes the domain model the center of attention and puts the inputs and outputs on the system on the edge of the overall system architecture.

The outside edges of the hexagon are simply a set of specified means of inputs and outputs (requests and responses) that are defined by ports via interfaces (aka abstractions) and that are implemented by adapters (concrete implementations), in an effort to facilitate interaction with the internals of the application located in the deeper levels of the model. A single side on the hexagon (or point within the circumference of the circle) pertains to a single point of entry of communication from the outside world into our application (i.e., each side has one reason to talk to the outside).

Next up we will discuss another possible layer of an application that would exist on the very outside of the hexagon or circle and would be comprised of the ports (and adapters) responsible for accepting a request from the outside and routing that request to where it needs to go inside. It is called the *infrastructure layer* and is not always needed to be defined as an independent layer in addition to the other three, but, as complexity in the codebase grows as time goes on, the proper establishment of such a layer can prove to be valuable later when we add complexity.

In terms of a hexagonal architecture, the outermost region depicted in Figure 17-1 would correspond to the layer responsible for accepting requests. This makes sense because, in Laravel, one might achieve a set of access points into the application by defining specific endpoints pertaining to the type of request entering the system.

- `routes/web.php`: Endpoints corresponding to requests from a browser

- `routes/console.php`: Endpoints corresponding to the CLI (Artisan commands)

- `routes/broadcast.php`: Endpoints corresponding to a broadcast request

- `routes/api.php`: Endpoints corresponding to an API request, internal or external

What a Hexagonal Architecture Brings with It

The hexagonal approach, when executed properly, brings along with it such positive benefits as the following:

- Maintainability

- Reduced technical debt

- Easier advances

- Changes to code not affecting other code

- Easier and faster to add features, requiring less code to make them function

- More separated components

- Very little repeated code

Technical Debt

Technical debt is some arbitrary amount of work (in the form of development time) that accumulates in a project when decisions are made too fast and with too little care for disrupting any of the already existing features in the application. Every time we are forced to make an "emergency" fix for that old, disgusting piece of legacy software (which, naturally, the business completely relies on it as the majority of its income stream) and which almost always includes tacking on the same low-quality style of code in random parts of the application, we are contributing to the overall tech debt of the project and ultimately leading toward the ultimate demise of the software. This is because as new features continue to be added to the existing code, the core foundation that holds everything together at the infrastructure level will eventually collapse under its own weight.

One reason that tech debt accumulates in the codebase is an improper architecture foundation, which can quickly grind the progress of rolling out features to a halt. The reason for this is the same as the aforementioned scenario with a legacy system: we would in theory be stacking decent code on top of bad code, and because not all of the bugs were properly worked out during the testing of the software, many such issues would most likely be caught only during a live session (probably from one of your users).

There are a few tactics and techniques you can employ to prevent such tech debt from infecting the system. Most of them are the same best practices that govern most (good) modern-day web development projects and applications.

- *Foundation*: This is extremely important to get right before you start piling additional classes and components on top of it. Not that it has to be *perfect*, but enough discussions, meetings, and trials (which most likely resulted in failure) should take place as needed to create a starting point of the application's core foundation and structure. Properly identifying the application's organic points of separation (in the form of domains, core domains, subdomains, bounded contexts, and modules) would fall in this category (if I may borrow the terms directly from the context of domain-driven design).

- *Maintainability*: The ease of maintaining a domain model is important to domain-driven design as well as hexagonal architecture, because it's something that cannot be avoided. Refactorings to the core model are at some point going to be needed, regardless of the domain you are working in. There's a small chance that you are going to be able to get the domain model correct on the first attempt. Where maintainability comes into play is how easy it is to change that code and make it adapt to new requirements of the system without adversely affecting the other components making up that system. In a bit, we will discuss how to keep your application maintainable for the long term, but the short answer is that we need it to be able to change easily. Maintainability should be (or must be, for that matter) a longer-term goal that will increase in complexity as time moves forward.

- *Encapsulating change*: Expanding on the previous item, change is destined to occur in any system. This could include changing the text on a header template of a web page to completely revamping an old, outdated process (while continuing to build new features on top of it) existing from previous additions to the codebase. The important thing is how we actually go about making these changes. The best way is to not only draw the boundaries between the components/ classes/aggregates/namespaces but to keep the things that change together in the same module or component with the other thing that changed. We can even take it a step further and go so far as keeping together the various pieces of the puzzle that change at the same time tucked away from pieces that change at different times.

Ease of Modification

Applications and software in general have a tendency to change. If you've never worked on legacy systems before, then you probably don't know the horrors that can arise from modifying or extending old and outdated code written years and years ago. For up-to-date software, however, you should strive to maintain clearly separated and properly structured code that is encapsulated via their corresponding place in the domain.

By that, I mean separating out the parts that change from those that don't and making an even specific distinction between the pieces that change at the same rate when compared to the rest of the code. Separate out constants into their own module or class so that we don't have more than one reason to change the code. By keeping things organized via proper namespaces and directory hierarchies, we make the code easier to read, easier to modify, and easier to fix when and if something goes wrong in production.

Not to mention, there is an increased ability to test the individual working parts of the system on a granular level. To achieve such a level in your codebase, interfaces help tremendously.

Abstractions and Concretions

When we are discussing abstractions and concretions in regard to hexagonal design, we are referring to ports and adapters, respectfully. Abstractions are the interfaces that exist in between the layers of code making up the application. Their place on the hexagon is arbitrary and doesn't matter much. The important thing is defining the right interface to allow interaction with the application from the outside world. Figure 17-2 shows this model with a diagram starting from this outside/inside perspective.

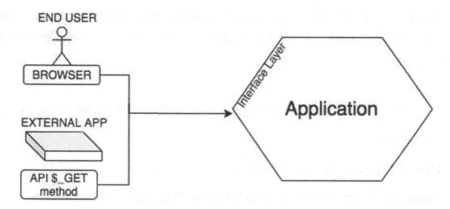

***Figure 17-2.** Basic scheme of hexagonal, including some input requests (browser and API)*

In Figure 17-2, I decided to use a hexagon to represent the application, along with two different types of input (requests): a regular user accessing the application from a web browser and an external app or external script accessing it via an API $_GET request. The first point of interaction they have with the application occurs at the outermost level, what we are calling the *interface layer*.

As it relates to Laravel, this layer will consist of the various routes, controllers, requests, and middleware found in what we were calling the application layer. The reason for this layer is to not only accept and route the input request, but to somehow transform it into something that the application can understand and pass the request along to its receiver as specified in the route. For example, the web request in Figure 17-2 could be the result of a click on a page in our app or even a direct request.

GET /index.php HTTP/1.1

User-Agent: Mozilla/5.0 (Macintosh; Intel Mac OS X 10_12.6) Applewebkit...

HOST: www.blog.continuousiteration.com

Accept-Language : en-us

Accept-Encoding : gzip, deflate

Connection : Keep-Alive

This is a stand-alone request; it does not need a body portion because it is a simple GET call and does not have a query string on the end of it. This is raw HTTP, which is the language spoken by the Internet, and almost all communications to or from it, but our application doesn't speak raw HTTP. The situation gets even more complex with the call via an API request.

GET {/api/v1/events/message?campaigns=110001_10001&event=click}

HTTP/1.1

Host: https://api.sparkpost.com

Authorization: 6302cb8bd662d5189e051cea48ae35153c366326

Accept: application/json

Content-Type:multipart/form-data;boundary=----WebKitFor mBoundary7MA4YWxkTrZu0gW

----WebKitFormBoundary7MA4YWxkTrZu0gW

Luckily for us, we are using the Laravel framework, which includes the proper abstractions and implementations that do speak HTTP and autoconverts everything specified in the incoming request to something we can use that can be passed around as a standard dependency and in the form of a plain ol' PHP object (POPO), which is Laravel's request component. What we also get out of this component is the ability to add validation to our routes, our requests, or both. The route component handles validation at the outermost level, which gets converted into a request object and checked against validations specified in the request, and then it forwards the (now validated) Laravel request to a controller object.

We have gone over this request cycle a few times in previous pages, but there is something important to take away from this: it doesn't matter how the request comes in to the inner layers of the application (the domain layer and core business logic). This is because, after the raw request hits the router and it is validated by Laravel, it is already in a usable form across the rest of the application's code. In short, it is translated into PHP objects. Under the hood, Symfony's HTTP Foundation component has been wrapped with Laravel-specific helper methods that offer additional functionality and capabilities for the framework. A bunch of other classes, traits, and interfaces make up the portion of the framework that handles raw HTTP requests, transforming them into a set of data that the rest of the code can operate on/with.

Getting back to interfaces and concretions, Listing 17-1 shows an example of how a port could look, which can be found in the `Illuminate\Foundation\Http\Kernel` interface.

Listing 17-1. A Possible Port-Like Interface That Could Be Implemented with an Adapter

```php
<?php
namespace Illuminate\Contracts\Http;
interface Kernel{
    /**
     * Bootstrap the application for HTTP requests.
     *
     * @return void
     */
    public function bootstrap();
    /**
     * Handle an incoming HTTP request.
     *
     * @param  \Symfony\Component\HttpFoundation\Request
       $request
     * @return \Symfony\Component\HttpFoundation\Response
     */
```

```
    public function handle($request);
    /**
     * Perform any final actions for the request lifecycle.
     *
     * @param  \Symfony\Component\HttpFoundation\Request
       $request
     * @param  \Symfony\Component\HttpFoundation\Response
       $response
     * @return void
     */
    public function terminate($request, $response);
    /**
     * Get the Laravel application instance.
     *
     * @return \Illuminate\Contracts\Foundation\Application
     */
    public function getApplication();
}
```

This basically defines an interface that must be implemented to use the framework at all. It is a rehash of the foundational HTTP component originally developed by Symfony that basically powers most modern frameworks in the industry (Drupal, PrestaShop, Laravel, Symfony) by establishing a clear means of interaction within the code and transforming the raw HTTP request into something the framework can identify and use. Using this interface, we can code anything we want, provided it meets the required methods and type hints. We could even code features of the application right away (even without a fully working database) by sticking to the specifications in the interface, and it would all work (provided our implementations were correct). This is known as coding to an interface, not to an implementation. Listing 17-2 shows Laravel's adapter for this port. Note that it's not the functionality we are trying to understand but the higher-level concepts related to the application as a whole (i.e., interfaces and implementations). Also, this is only a portion of the real class; the full implementation can be found at https://github.com/laravel/framework/blob/6.x/src/Illuminate/Foundation/ Http/Kernel.php.

Listing 17-2. A Portion of Laravel's Core Kernel Implementation (Adapter) for the Interface in Listing 17-1 (Port)

```php
<?php
namespace Illuminate\Foundation\Http;
use Exception;
use Illuminate\Contracts\Debug\ExceptionHandler;
use Illuminate\Contracts\Foundation\Application;
use Illuminate\Contracts\Http\Kernel as KernelContract;
use Illuminate\Foundation\Http\Events\RequestHandled;
use Illuminate\Routing\Pipeline;
use Illuminate\Routing\Router;
use Illuminate\Support\Facades\Facade;
use InvalidArgumentException;
use Symfony\Component\Debug\Exception\FatalThrowableError;
use Throwable;
class Kernel implements KernelContract
{
    /**
     * The application implementation.      *
     * @var \Illuminate\Contracts\Foundation\Application
     */
    protected $app;
    /**
     * The router instance.
     *
     * @var \Illuminate\Routing\Router
     */
    protected $router;
    /**
     * The bootstrap classes for the application.
     *
     * @var array
     */
    protected $bootstrappers = [/* … */]
    ...See full code listing on Laravel's website or API Docs
```

This is only a small section of the implementing class, but we can still see what's going on here. On a high level, the constructor accepts an instance of the current running application (the App class) and an instance of Router. I've included the first method in the class handle() to show you how a response is being generated by a request. That is the entire goal of any web framework: you receive a request and return a response. Whatever happens during the time in between the two is the actual part of the application that we have to build. What the framework offers us in order to develop software are interfaces and implementations that can be hooked into, extended, and so forth.

What Use Is It to Design and Implement Contracts?

I'm glad you asked! By using interfaces (ports) as the core structure in the whole schematic, we are adding flexibility to the system's design. We are adding pivotal points in our application so that the components we implement along the way can be replaced, relatively easily, with a different implementation (adapters). Here is a good way to think about it:

- A *contract* defines an application need that may be replaced in the future so as to promote code flexibility and/or which multiple implementations may exist within the application at one time. A contract is a port.

- *Concrete implementations* are solutions that satisfy the given contract's requirements. These solutions are adapters.

So, in theory, if you wanted your application to be reusable, or perhaps you are writing an API or even a package to be used by other applications, you could make liberal use of ports (interfaces), which would allow communication between the layers of the application (as the request moves toward the middle of the hexagon and back out again to the client). This brings up another characteristic of the hexagonal approach: the "out" ports, or the ports that exist for our application to make requests to, such as a database port. We could, in theory, divide up our hexagon into two hemispheres: one for handling the user interaction (aka incoming requests) made from external clients and the other for handling the outgoing requests made to external services by the application (Figure 17-3).

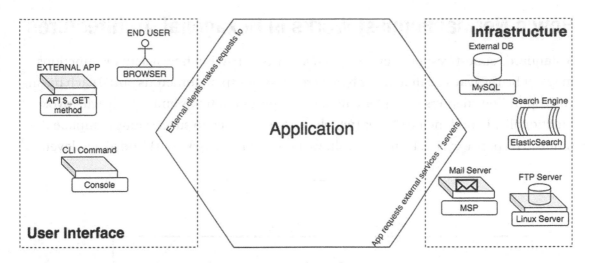

Figure 17-3. *The hexagon as split into two core hemispheres: the UI and the infrastructure*

It may surprise you to see Figure 17-3 displayed with an entire hemisphere dedicated to the infrastructure portion of the application. When we were talking about DDD, we learned that infrastructure concerns can be encapsulated into its own layer, but in hexagonal, it encompasses pretty much half of the area outside the hexagon. That's the main difference between DDD and HA: DDD relates segments making up the application to the code in terms of a specific layer, each layer having a straightforward inclination of what type of code lives in it, like its specialty; hexagonal, however, simply relates the components making up the app in terms of outside versus inside. When we think of the way the different devices, services, browsers, or other inputs that enter the application as requests, we should also consider the other side (infrastructure), which involves the application calling out to external systems outside itself.

How is this separation made in code, and how does that code establish such boundaries as described in Figure 17-3? The answer, of course, is interfaces. We can place interfaces wherever needed alongside the infrastructure layer for all types of input we are expecting to enter our application (these would be the ports) and then implement that interface for each different type (i.e., browser, CGI, etc.), which would be the adapters. On the other side of the hexagon, we would follow suit and create a port for the type of request we are making to the outside world and then implement the port's interface as adapters that can plug into the framework easily.

How a Normal Request Works in Hexagonal Architectures

A standard request/response cycle of course exists in HA, but how it actually functions may not be the way you thought. A typical request can span numerous ports, each having corresponding adapters as implemented by the port's contracts and usually will invoke functionality in both hemispheres (which needs to happen to successfully complete the request/response cycle). Figure 17-4 shows how a request looks in HA on a high level.

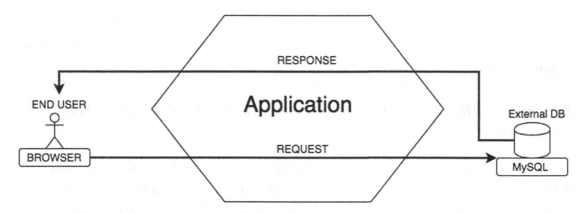

Figure 17-4. *The "flow" of a request/response cycle in hexagonal architecture*

Ports

The main concept that can derived from Figure 17-4 is that requests first hit the code in the UI (interface layer), go through the application's core, hit the infrastructure code in the backend (in this example, it's making a call to an external MySQL database) that runs the logic that has been translated into SQL queries by the infrastructure code, and returns the result to the application where it is transformed yet again into something that the browser can render and the user can see. All the working parts are not included in the diagram, but the flow of control of such a request is represented by the thick lines.

There are multiple ports involved in this request that can be found at the boundaries of each layer of logic within the hexagon. In PHP, ports are generally interfaces created inside the business logic but can also be a group of several interfaces and/or DTOs.

Adapters

Adapters come in two flavors: primary (driving) adapters and secondary (driven) adapters. In Laravel, the adapters are generally controllers, command buses, or queries that are passed along to the command bus. The adapters satisfy the interfaces made by the ports. For example, a controller would type hint the port's interface, along with any dependencies required in order to fully implement the contract. Then, the controller injects the resulting code and dependencies deeper into the application layer, where the logic is actually delegated to the domain layer (business logic) and a response returned to the client making the request.

An Example in Code

For an example of an implementation of an adapter using a controller to handle the delegation and the dance of the domain objects by utilizing a command bus as the backbone of the operation, check out the code in Listing 17-3.

Listing 17-3. Example of a "Driven" Adapter

```php
<?php

//use statements & namespace
class HomeController extends BaseController {
    /**
     * @var App\Adapters\CommandBus\CommandBus
     */
    private $bus;

    public function __construct(CommandBus $bus)
    {
        $this->bus = $bus;
    }
    public function createTicket()
    {
        $command = new CreateTicketCommand( Input::all() );

        try {
            $this->bus->execute($command);
```

```
      } catch(ValidationException $e) {
          return Redirect::to('/tickets/new')->withErrors(
          $e->getErrors() );
      } catch(\DomainException $e) {
          return Redirect::to('/tickets/new')->withErrors(
          $e->getErrors() );
  }
  return Redirect::to('/tickets')->with(['message' =>
      'success!']);
  }
}
```

Additionally, I wanted to include a diagram of a high-level perspective of a simple operation involving an external client making a request to the app, the app then making a request to the database, and the results returned to the client.

In Figure 17-5, we have an end user making some kind of request to our application, which hits the router as the initial point of contact.

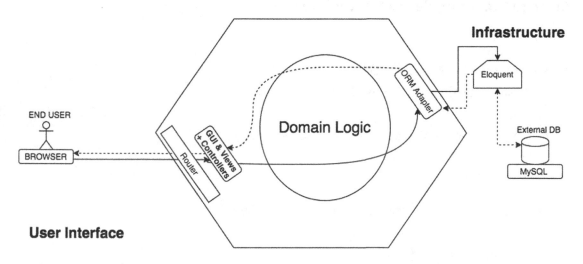

Figure 17-5. *A request operation utilizing hexagonal architecture to acquire data from the database by implementing an ORM adapter that satisfies the requirements described by the port (port not shown)*

The router routes the request (using the endpoint) to the controller specified in the route file (in our case, it would most likely be routes/web.php for Laravel). The controller is actually an adapter and is used alongside the Request component in Laravel to validate the incoming data against a set of rules, and then it sends the validated data to the controller in a form that our application can see and use. It is adapting the outside request into an internal object that can be passed around to whichever class or function we wanted. The controller, and most of the driving adapters in general, actually wraps around a port's interface rather than implementing it. The controller would be instantiated with an object in its constructor that implemented the contract of the corresponding port. This is not the case with driven adapters (on the infrastructure side), as they actually implement the port's interface directly rather than wrap around it.

In Figure 17-5, we can see that there is another adapter on the opposite side (a secondary adapter), which is an implementation of a port defined at the boundary of the infrastructure. Whatever implemented the interface described by this port would be the adapter for that port. In this instance, we created an ORM adapter that adhered to that port's interface (the port isn't shown in the diagram, but implied), which hooks up to the Eloquent ORM and allows the application access to the database, which is shown in Figure 17-5.

Here's a possible solution in code. Let's start with the few ports that we will need to make everything work properly. We will define a general interface that could handle any ORM, provided that all the interfaces and points of connection with the application have been properly established, as shown in Listing 17-4.

Listing 17-4. General Port for Establishing an ORM Connection in the Application

```php
<?php
namespace App\Domain\Contracts\Persistence\Ports;
use QueryCapabilities;
interface ExternalOrmConnection
{
    public function connect();
    public function defineQueryCapabilities(
        QueryCapabilities $query)
}
```

Using this approach, we can create an adapter that satisfies the interface described by the port, allowing us to (in theory) hook up any ORM to our application. This is a start but isn't all we need to implement the actual functionality we desire: a way to query the database through Eloquent. We have a connect() method that does any configuration logic and includes the code needed to establish a connection with the intended ORM. There is also a defineQueryCapabilities() method that accepts an instance of QueryCapabilities to describe what is possible with the ORM connection. It can be argued that we would actually want to decouple the capabilities from the connection, but they are so related that I've included one as a dependency in the other. Let's create an interface that encapsulates basic queries that we know we are going to need (or the capabilities of any such implementation). See Listing 17-5.

Listing 17-5. Example QueryCapabilities Port

```php
namespace App\Concerns\Infrastructure\Persistence\Ports;
interface QueryCapabilities
{
    public function select($statement);
    public function delete($statement);
}
```

In theory, at this point all I would have to do to connect virtually any ORM to the system would be to implement the interface defined in Figure 17-5. As long as we basically proxy the methods in the interface to the specific implementation we are working with (Doctrine, Eloquent, Propel, etc.) so that those methods are just forwarded along to the ORM, we are free to use any ORM we want.

This is, of course, extremely limited and is here only for an example. Listing 17-6 demonstrates a few possible adapters that conform to the previous two ports.

Listing 17-6. Example Implementations of the Two Port Interfaces Described Earlier

```php
<?php
class EloquentOrm implements QueryCapabilities,
    ExternalOrmConnection
{
    public function select($statement) {
        return DB::select($statement)->all();
    }
    public function delete($statement)
    {
```

```php
        return DB::delete($statement);
    }

    public function connect()
    {
        //connection logic
    }
}

class DoctrineDbalOrm implements QueryCapabilities,
    ExternalOrmConnection
{
    public function delete($statement)
    {
        $stmt = $this->connect()->delete($statement);
        return $stmt->execute();
    }

    public function select($statement)
    {
        $stmt = $this->connect()->prepare($statement);
        return $stmt->fetchAll();
    }
    public function connect()
    {
        return $this->getConnection('default');
    }
}
```

This example, of course, only takes into consideration a single concern corresponding to a single edge of the hexagon, in this case, the persistence edge. However, the general process of adding implementations of the defined port's interface remains basically the same: create an interface in the domain layer of the application that will define the general structure of whatever the edge that it's located on is focused on. Once you have defined your high-level interface, you can (and should) use the type hint of that interface anywhere in the application that you need it injected. Remember, code to an interface, not to an implementation. By doing this, you can then add specific portions of functionality that exists in a clear, easy-to-understand way because all that is required for a child of that interface is to satisfy the contract (consisting of the method names and signatures). Do this by creating adapters that encapsulate specific implementations of the given port. The beauty of this setup is that you don't have to change the surrounding code that deals with the child classes. Because we've decided to code to an interface, all the type hinting will work perfectly with any new adapter created for the purpose, which is defined within the port. Remember to have the ports define interfaces for entry points and exit points throughout the application. They should not have any knowledge of specific implementations at all. This is what allows you so much flexibility in the way you structure and form your objects.

Use Cases

Use cases are the foundational element in a hexagonal architecture that relates to (and fully describes) a feature to be developed. Use cases are simply statements of scenarios that describe the particular reason or motive to use that particular piece of functionality (it can also describe the context).

Use cases belong in the application layer, often in the form of an application service that contains the use case and has other dependencies injected into it as well so that it can perform whatever function dictated by the use case. Typically, use cases are written as English sentences before they are translated into code and follow some basic format. Here is a common approach to the formatting of a use case:

> *As a {ROLE/USER_TYPE}, I want to {DESCRIPTION}.*

Here are some examples:

> *As a Medical Provider, I want to be able to look up patients quickly via their name or birthday.*

> *As a Medical Biller, I want to be able to run reports on segmented data and have a cumulative total run for all medical bills in a given segment.*

> *As an Admin, I want the ability to log in and out of different user accounts easily.*

This format makes it clear who is requesting the work and what is entailed in the task. Obviously, additional details are more than not required before coding begins, but this format offers an easy way to describe new features to developers and nondevelopers alike.

Implementing Hexagonal in Laravel

In Laravel, the same basic principles apply that exist in non-Laravel applications: separation of concerns on an architectural level with interfaces at the boundaries that encapsulate the logic of each layer. Dependencies point inward, and the ports (interfaces) are left to define the low-level requirements for the context of the logic within its boundary. Oftentimes, we can use a Laravel contract to implement such a boundary, which works well because you can simply autowire up a given interface to a specific implementation of that interface using Laravel's service container (which involves configuring the dependencies inside a service provider). This will inject a specific child instance (fully instantiated and ready to roll and whose configuration can also be determined by the service container as a separate object in the system) into anywhere that the parent interface is type hinted. It will all happen automatically.

Listing 17-7 shows a nice, clean example of how it would look to implement events in an application (assuming you wanted your own custom solution for events across the application). It is located at the Event side of the hexagon and can be considered a "doer" adapter because, at its core, it is a dispatcher.

Listing 17-7. An Example Solution That Fits the Event Side of the Hexagon

```php
<?php
namespace App\Events;
use Illuminate\Events\Dispatcher as DispatcherInterface;
class Dispatcher implements DispatcherInterface {

    /**
     * @var \Illuminate\Events\DispatcherInterface
     */
    private $dispatcher;
    public function __construct(LaravelDispatcher $dispatcher)
    {
        $this->dispatcher = $dispatcher;
    }

    public function dispatch(Array $events)
    {
        foreach($events as $event)
```

```php
        {
            $this->dispatcher->fire($event->name(), [$event]);
        }
    }
}
?>

<?php
namespace App\Events;
interface EventInterface {
    /**
     * Return the event name
     * @return string=
     */
    public function name();
}

?>

<?php namespace App\Events;
trait Eventable {
    protected $queuedEvents;
    public function flushEvents()
    {
        $events = $this->queuedEvents;
        $this->queuedEvents = [];

        return $events;
    }
    public function raise($event)
    {
        $this->queuedEvents[] = $event;
    }
}
```

With the setup described in Listing 17-7, one would simply have to implement the EventInterface located in the App\Events namespace and can easily add behavior to any class needing to dispatch events (perhaps to a message queue or command bus) by using the Eventable trait. Listing 17-8 is an example of one such event.

Listing 17-8. An Implementation of an Event as Defined by the Interface (Port) Described in the EventInterface Interface

```php
<?php
namespace Hex\Tickets\Events;
use App\Models\Ticket;
use App\Events\EventInterface;
class TicketCreatedEvent implements EventInterface {
    /**
     * @var \Hex\Tickets\Ticket
     */
    private $ticket;
    public function __construct(Ticket $ticket)
    {
        $this->ticket = $ticket;
    }
    /**
     * Return the event name
     * @return string
     */
    public function name()
    {
        return 'ticket.created';
    }
}
```

Conclusion

Although we didn't get too far into the nuts and bolts of the hexagonal architecture, if this idea sparks an interest in you, then I encourage you to do additional research on hexagonal architecture and start experimenting with this paradigm, as it is incredibly useful. Hexagonal focuses more on "in" versus "out" rather than the traditional "top" to "bottom" approach (as found in hierarchies). It describes a set of boundaries that encapsulate core knowledge expressed as ports (which are basically just interfaces) located at the boundaries of each layer within the hexagon (or circle). The term *hexagonal* does not imply there are only six sides involved in describing all the concerns of a given application. There can be many more or fewer, depending on the context of the application. Adapters are the objects implementing the interfaces and, as such, can be created with little thought because of their required structure as deemed by the interface that they're implementing. Hexagonal in Laravel has the positive benefit of being able to use Laravel's core Contracts library and can achieve great things when used in parallel with Laravel's service container (bindings). If you'd like to dive deeper into hexagonal architecture, check out `https://fideloper.com/hexagonal-architecture` and `https://madewithlove.com/hexagonal-architecture-demystified`.

CHAPTER 18

Applying DDL in the Real World

We've gone over quite a lot of information about developing a Laravel application following the principles of domain-driven design. In this chapter, we will put that knowledge to use as we walk through various real-world problems that I have faced (whether it be alone or on a team) and look at possible solutions for these problems. We will go about them in a domain-driven manner that will recap the concepts we've learned throughout the book. We'll put these concepts into context so you can gain the most out of using Laravel and DDD. By providing interfaces at the boundary points of each layer (a concept borrowed from hexagonal architecture), we can use strict object structures to define the generalities of our application's behavior and capabilities in terms of broader concepts belonging to the same category. Examples of these categories include the following:

- *Events*: Broadcasting custom events from anywhere in the system. Events are implemented as driving adapters because they need to be dispatched, but they can have a driven portion that handles receiving these events from the proper recipients, which is more of a passive process.

- *Database*: Accessing a datastore to acquire the data necessary to run the application. This falls alongside the persistence edge of the hexagon.

- *User interface*: To be usable from a graphical interface via a browser.

- *Commands, controllers, and other "driving" concerns*: Input requests that come from outside the application and act on the application as a driving force in its execution.

© Jesse Griffin 2021
J. Griffin, *Domain-Driven Laravel*, https://doi.org/10.1007/978-1-4842-6023-4_18

In this chapter, we will go through a simple scenario and carve out a rough solution; then we'll go refactor it to add more depth and to revisit the details involved when crafting APIs in Laravel.

Real-World Example: Estimating Claims

If you recall, patients have appointments with providers for free or reduced payment (assuming they are eligible to receive care), and providers must submit claims in a specific manner before they are compensated by the Medi-Cal department of the federal government for their services. Our system provides an easy way to submit claims and has built-in verification and validation checks that are guaranteed to meet the requirements for compensation.

The amount paid to the provider depends partly on the services performed on the patient—which are captured and documented with CPT codes—as well as on the provider's specific paycode sheet. The estimated claim amount is a dollar amount that must be calculated before the claim is submitted to the system so that the provider (or receptionist) can look at it and make sure that the amount makes sense. We are going to build out this functionality in a manner that best suits the domain and application in terms of applied concepts (not necessarily just code).

First, we need a class to represent what a claim estimate is because the value of a claim is basically immutable. (This means the amount of an estimate does not change, although the calculated amount itself can change with varying inputs such as changing CPT codes.) Because of this, a claim estimate is a value object. Listing 18-1 a simple class capturing this knowledge, as represented by a DTO.

Listing 18-1. Basic Class Representing a Claim Estimate

```php
<?php

namespace Claim\Submission\Domain\ValueObjects\Estimates;

class Estimate
{
    private float $amount;
    private $codes = [];

    public function __construct(float $amount, array $codes=[])
```

```php
    {
        $this->amount = $amount;
        $this->codes = $codes;
    }

    public function create($amount, array $codes=[]): Estimate
    {
        return new self($amount, $codes);
    }

    public function setAmount(float $amount)
    {
        $this->amount = $amount;
        return $this;
    }

    public function setCodes(array $codes): Estimate
    {
        $this->codes = $codes;
    }

    public function amount(): array
    {
        return is_null($this->amount) ? null : (float)
            $this->amount;
    }

    public function codes(): float
    {
        return $this->codes;
    }
}
```

In Listing 18-1, we basically have a simple DTO that contains within it a static helper method that returns a ready-to-go instance of a claim estimate. There's nothing special about this really, although take note of the namespace: we are being consistent with the domain and aligning things in terms of the way the domain is structured. That sounds like domain-driven design to me! The previous $codes member variable is an array with the specific, individual CPT codes that were completed during the visit. The `$amount` variable will hold the computed value and will be a primitive float. Keep in mind that the `Estimated` class is only a record of the actual inputs used to calculate the amount and does not include any sort of behavior—just data.

Additional Requirements

Earlier in the book, I touched on the possibility of having potentially two payment "types" that a provider can be set to that determines what they are paid.

- *Pay per visit*: This is a fixed amount paid to a provider for each visit, no matter what procedures were completed during the visit.

- *Pay per procedure*: This type of payment requires a lookup on the provider's `PaycodeSheet` for the CPT codes present on the claim.

How might we add this aspect into the calculations for the estimated amount of a claim? Obviously, we could assume that the payment type is recorded somewhere in the database (like a `payment_type_id` field in the `providers` table or something similar). If it's not, we would have to write a migration for this field and populate it most likely upon creation of the `Provider` account, leaving us with the added hassle of having to backfill the current `Provider` account records with a value for the new `payment_type_id` field. We would also need to create a migration to create the lookup table required for `payment_type_id` to even work. We could throw the actual values into that same migration (the table would be named `payment_types`).

Let's say that we've gotten past all the minute details of implementing this payment type concept in our application and all that needs to occur now is properly calculating the estimated amount of the claim. Since we are mindful about the separation of concerns, we decide to put any input validation inside a Laravel request, which gets passed into a controller method. We decide also that this operation needs its own endpoint, so we decide to give it its own namespace, `Claim\Submission\Domain\Models\Estimate`, which will house any value objects pertaining to the estimates themselves. A claim's estimate, therefore, can be thought of as simply an array of CPT codes coupled with a dollar amount and is such what represents the final estimate for a given claim. It has no knowledge of the calculation that actually determines the cost (which may be fairly complicated). We can and should encapsulate the knowledge of a `PaymentType` as a model.

```php
<?php

namespace Claim\Billing\Domain\Models\Payment;

use Illuminate\Database\Eloquent\Model;

class PaymentType extends Model
{
    const PER_VISIT = 1;
    const PER_PROCEDURE = 2;
    /* ... */
}
```

This serves as a good point of reference for the rest of the application code because developer won't have to rely on memory and recall that a per-visit payment type actually corresponds to an ID of 1. We can simply refer to it as PaymentType::PER_VISIT.

Claim Estimate Service

We are now left with the task of creating the logic that calculates the estimated claim amount. Figuring out the best place for that logic should be the first consideration. Since it is a domain-specific task, we can choose to put our code inside a domain service. Domain services operate exclusively at the domain level and should be void of any and all concerns not relating directly to the domain. Application concerns such as facilitating the request and response cycle to run the calculation should be separated from the service, allowing it to focus on doing the one particular task for which it was made to do.

Domain Layer

The domain layer, if you recall, is the place within any software application that contains the core business logic for the particular underlying domain model for which the application was built to represent. In terms of the claim project, an example of a "domain service" would be the portion of the application that calculates the expected amount of payment from the FQHC to the provider submitting the claim. Check out Listing 18-2 for an example implementation of such a service.

Listing 18-2. The Domain Service That Will Handle the Calculation of the Claim Estimate

```php
//Claim\Submission\Domain\Services\ClaimEstimator.php

<?php

namespace Claim\Submission\Domain\Services;

use Claim\Submission\Domain\Models\Providers\Provider;
use Claim\Submission\Domain\Models\PaycodeSheets\PaycodeSheet;
use Claim\Submission\Domain\Models\Payment\PaymentType;
use Claim\Submission\Domain\Models\Payment\PaymentData;
use Claim\Submission\Domain\Models\CptCodes\CptCodeCombo;
use Claim\Submission\Domain\ValueObjects\Estimate\Estimate;
use Claim\Submission\Domain\Services\Payment\ClaimPaymentService;
Use Claim\Submission\Domain\Exceptions\
    ComboNotFoundInPaycodeSheetException;

class ClaimEstimator
{
    protected Provider $provider;

    protected CptCodeCombo $cptCodeComboRepository;

    protected PaycodeSheet $paycodeSheetRepository;

    protected ClaimPaymentService $claimPaymentService;

    public function __construct(
        PaycodeSheetRepository $paycodeSheetRepository,
        CptCodeComboRepository $cptCodeComboRepository,
        ClaimPaymentService $claimPaymentService}
    {
        $this->paycodeSheetRepository = $paycodeSheetRepository;
        $this->cptCodeComboRepository = $cptCodeComboRepository;
        $this->claimPaymentServices = $claimPaymentServices;
    }
```

```php
public function estimate(Claim $claim, array $codes): float
{
    $provider = $claim->primaryProvider();
    $estimateDate = $claim->estimateDate()->toDateTimeString();

    //we need to take into account the two different payment
    //types described above : Per-Procedure and Per-Visit
    $paymentType = $this->findPaymentData($provider);

    if ($paymentType === PaymentType::PER_VISIT) {
        return $provider->fee_per_visit * $provider->bonus;
    } else {
        return $this->calculatePerProcedureEstimate(
            $provider, $claim, $codes);
    }
}

public function findPaymentData(Provider $provider): PaymentData
{
    //this way we can add additional payment types with ease:
        return PaymentType::fromRequest ($provider->paymentType);
}

public function calculatePerProcedureEstimate(
    Provider $provider, Claim $claim, $codes=[])
{
    if (!empty($codes)) {
        $cptCodeCombo = $this->cptCodeComboRepository
                                ->findComboFromCodes($codes);

        $paycodeSheet = $this->paycodeSheetRepository
                                ->byProvider($provider->id);

        $estimatedAmount = $this->claimPaymentService
        ->lookupPriceForCombo(
                $paycodeSheet, $provider, $cptCodeCombo);
        if (!is_float($estimatedAMount)) {
            throw new \ComboNotFoundInPaycodeSheetException;
        }
```

```
                return new Estimate($estimatedAmount, $codes);
        }
    }
}
```

This would imply making an additional method on the PaymentType model that would return an instance of itself when supplied with the proper constructs. Essentially, the signature of this method would be the same as its constructor method, as demonstrated in Listing 18-3.

Listing 18-3. PaymentType Entity in the System, Allowing Us to Call a Static Method on the Class and Return a Fully Instantiated Object of Itself

```php
<?php

//inside the Estimate value object (Listing 18-1)
use Claim\Submission\Domain\Models\Payment\PaymentType;

class PaymentType extends Model
{
    const PER_VISIT = 1;
    const PER_PROCEDURE = 2;

    public static function fromRequest(int $payType): PaymentType
    {
        return new self($payType);
    }
}
```

This has the added benefit of using easy-to-remember constant variables (immutable) as arguments to the constructor of the PaymentType class and has the benefit of being referred to by a name rather than a number (PER_VISIT is easier to remember than just 1). Notice that we have properly type hinted everything in Listing 18-2. In addition to other nonobvious benefits gained by employing this style of programming, there are benefits such as reducing the number of errors both in terms of developer oversight and at runtime as well as improved performance from being specific because the just-in-time compiler (the PHP engine) has less guesswork when deducing the type and value of the arguments and variables. It may not seem like you're saving much computing power at first; however, the fewer CPU cycles required to make the thing work, the better off overall you will be.

In Listing 18-2, we have a few things going on that are interesting. First, we have the dependencies nicely listed as constructor arguments, which can be automatically injected with the correct instances of each by Laravel's service container (via its dependency injection mechanism). Inside the `estimate()` method, we are delegating to another method to get the proper `PaymentType` the given provider is set up with, which uses the nice helper method we have included in Listing 18-3 as a means of instantiating the rather static value inline, sort of like an ad hoc shortcut in a way.

Once the payment type is determined, the service will either calculate the estimated value right then in the case of a per-visit rate type or, in the case of the provider being assigned the per-procedure payment type, require additional computation and logic to come up with an estimate. `CptCodeCombo` need to be queried using the passed-in, individual CPT codes so that the `PaycodeSheet` model can be queried and so the specified amount can be derived when given the provider present on the incoming claim. The member method `calculatePerProcedureEstimate()` handles the per-procedure calculations; however, if you noticed, all that method really does is delegate certain tasks away from itself and toward one of the dependencies injected in the constructor (another domain service named `ClaimPaymentService`). This cleanly separates the actual concern of calculating the amount of the claim based on the different variables that impact it: the paycode sheets, the provider, and the codes themselves, which could potentially change and/or grow in terms of complexity and lines of code. Should another `PaymentType` be needed in the future, the cost of integrating it into the current system will be minimal because we've built in that flexibility into our domain-level components.

Meanwhile, the `ClaimPaymentService` domain logic would encapsulate the procedure that would handle the dirty work involved in estimating the claim. What's important to note is that even though we seem to be just "passing the buck" in terms of delegating the tasks we need done to other objects, we are supporting our longer-term, higher-level goal of building and maintaining an application whose logic and domain processes is easy to reason about. The code itself is a direct reflection of the level of understanding about the domain that the developer who wrote it had. By splitting off chunks of the process into smaller components, we give ourselves a better chance of code reusability and make it easier to understand for future developers.

> **Caution**   There is most definitely such a thing as over-engineering, and it can happen without you noticing it until later. There are several principles you can employ to mitigate this from happening, such as You Aren't Going to Need It (YAGNI) or Do the Simplest Thing That Works (DTSTTCPW), but the real key to preventing it is to allow the domain to guide your architectural and programming decisions. Base your decision-making as relevant as possible to the domain, and always attempt to maintain a thread of relevance between your code and the business problems that it solves.

The actual implementation that handles the lookup to determine the estimated payout amount of the claim is arbitrary at this point, so I won't be including it specifically in the text; you can see it on the online repository for this book.

Application Layer

Now that we've addressed the domain concerns of claim estimates (and have formalized their corresponding meaning in the domain model itself through domain services), we are still left to consider the application-level details. More specifically, we will go over the mechanisms for delivering the external request to our application's code (incoming request) and also creating the means for it to be returned to the requesting party (outgoing response). DTOs can help ensure that the delivery mechanism (both ways) are encapsulated into a structure that stays consistent with that particular functionality.

HTTP Request

Let's define a simple request to start off the domain processes we have defined previously, which we do in Listing 18-4.

Listing 18-4. Request to Get a Claim's Estimated Value

```php
//Claim\Submission\Application\Http\Requests\Estimates\
//EstimateRequest.php

<?php

namespace Claim\Submission\Application\Http\Requests\Estimates;
```

```php
use App\Http\Requests\Request;

class EstimateRequest extends Request
{
    public function authorize()
    {
        return true;
    }

    public function rules()
    {
        return [
            'claim' => 'exists:claims,id'
        ];
    }
}
```

The request in Listing 18-4 is fairly simple and should come as no surprise to you as we have gone over similar classes earlier in the book. Inside the request's `rules()` method, we have only one required argument: the claim.

Remember that at this point, all the information has been entered into the claim, and it is complete except for the estimated amount payable to the provider on the claim, which we are setting up now. We can pull out any relevant information needed to figure out the cost from the claim itself, so we don't have to include, for example, the provider or individual CPT codes. In fact, it would be repetitive to include additional requirements for such things because we should be able to safely assume that the CPT codes that exist on the claim are valid and have already been verified somewhere else in the code before reaching this point. The `$claim` variable will have everything we need inside it, and because it's already in the database, we can rely on its status to determine what stage of the process the claim is in (luckily, we already set up claim statuses in Chapter 9).

Did that last part sound convincing? It did to me, and that's exactly what I initially thought when I sat down to map out this system at my then-current place of work in beautiful El Cajon, California. It wasn't until later that I had an epiphany about the situation. I wasn't thinking in terms of functionality when I originally put together the previous paragraph. I was considering the problem from a purely technical perspective in that I based the design heavily on the fact that a fully instantiated `Claim` object can and would contain all the relevant data required in creating a claim estimate. However, if I had instead maintained my focus on the functionality of what needed to be accomplished, I would have come to understand that what we were trying to do was *get an estimate* for a claim. This was an operation that did not require the claim itself, but just a few select pieces of data from the claim. By coupling the claim itself to the claim estimation request, I had in fact coupled the mechanism responsible for estimating a claim's value to the claim itself, rather than properly specifying the minimal dependencies needed for that component to run (constructor injection).

This created a small issue that wasn't caught until later in the system's maturity, when the request came in to allow all professional users in the system (nonpatients) the ability to run a claim estimate against a set of arbitrary, user-supplied parameters. However, because we've essentially coupled the whole estimation enchilada directly to a claim, we've made it impossible to have a compatibility with such a context where a `Claim` object is not present. At this point, we can't possibly decide to force the front end to somehow establish a complete `Claim` object when hitting the claim estimation endpoint, so that's out. We really must refactor the code and make it so that it suits situations outside of the current context from which we are building it; that's not an easy thing to do, and it rarely is. Practice makes better. Best practices make best.

Long story short, I should have stuck with the functional aspect of the design, which in this case would have involved breaking down what was required in the request to properly derive the result returned in the response. In the end, all I needed to do was calculate an estimated amount, and that would have required properly injecting the following dependencies required for such a thing:

- A provider

- A paycode sheet

- A CPT code combo

  - Derived from an array of CPT codes

The following section goes into more detail about modeling the design of the system in terms of its various contexts.

MODELING CONTEXTS

I wanted to include a brief tangent discussion that exists in real-life development and is a frequent concern of any sort of real-time or almost-real-time application. That is, contexts. Domain-driven design is based on the concept of *building blocks*, or patterns that can be used to derive a working model or architecture that captures the full intent of the domain it was made to represent. For example, here is a hypothetical scenario.

Let's say we wanted additional functionality that allowed us to overwrite the original CPT code combo present on the claim—perhaps in the event where you wanted the capability to do a "quick edit" type of change that was separate from the claim submission form that allowed you to overwrite the original codes entered on a claim. This could be useful for a reviewer to do fast one-off updates to the claim after they have verified that the original values were of some erroneous origin, most likely by contacting the provider's office directly. In such a case, we could have the claim in question be passed in as parameters to the request, along with the array of new codes they want to update that claim with.

However, the context in the regard of this "one-off" CPT code update is different than if we were modifying the entire `Claim` object directly from the Claim Submission context. So, that begs the question: should these two contexts have their own separate implementations within the system, even though they are indeed modifying the same data?

What is cool about Laravel is how simple it would be to configure validation for such a request as `PatchClaimRequest`, or even `UpdateChangeRequest`. The `rules()` method of the request that facilitated that task could look like this and would meet basically all of our validation requirements. See Listing 18-5 for details.

Listing 18-5. A Would-Be Rules Configuration That Could Be Used to Validate the Patching of an Already Created Claim

```php
<?php
public function rules()
{
    return [
        'claim'     => 'exists:claims,id',
        'cptCodes'    => 'array',
        'cptCodes.*' => 'exists:cpt_codes,id'
    ];
}
```

557

That's of course assuming that the desired functionality is to be treated as separate pieces of code in the system. This approach has the benefit of being isolated from its "full-update" counterpart on the Claim Submission screen, which, if you recall, has a rather long list of requirements and validations that are run against the incoming claim for it to even get to this stage of the process.

At some point, it may appear that having this request separate from the one that deals with patching the entire claim equates to having to maintain the same code in multiple locations. However, when we consider that the backend code would basically be the same, and we could actually house the task of modifying the claim (`PatchClaim`) inside a job that could then be dispatched to a worker queue, we find that we aren't really repeating code in a sense of breaking the DRY principle. We are actually modeling this inline ability to modify the CPT codes present on a claim as a different *context* than when the claim is being created for the first time.

In this scenario, I would argue that it would be best to have different requests to represent the two contexts in which CPT codes can be modified, added, or removed to or from a given claim because at some point, we may need to know where these edits are actually being made, which would be indestructible if we incorporated both contexts in to the same request (not to mention making the validation a complete nightmare due to having to readjust everything around the new scenario of "A CPT code can be updated on a screen separate from the claim submission form"). The same mechanism that handles the creation of a claim via a POST request will most likely not be the same one handling the PATCH request to update it. This is by design. Many if not most of the validation required in the POST request creating the claim will not be needed in the PATCH request when updating a claim. I would consider these two separate use cases altogether and therefore would make the argument that the additional context should be modeled separately.

Controller

Let's get back to considering the aspect of calculating the estimate for a given claim.

The controller mediating the previous domain logic would be fairly straightforward and could look something like Listing 18-6 (a rough draft).

Listing 18-6. Basic Estimate Controller Following the Same Standards We've Been Employing Throughout the Book

```php
//Claim\Submission\Application\Http\Controllers\EstimateController.php

<?php

namespace Claim\Submission\Application\Http\Controllers\Estimates;

use App\Http\Controllers\Controller;
use Claim\Submission\Application\Http\Requests\Estimates\
    EstimateRequest;
use Claim\Submission\Domain\Models\Claims\Claim;
use Claim\Submission\Domain\Services\ClaimEstimator;
use Claim\Submission\Application\Exceptions\MissingProcedureException;
use Claim\Submission\Application\Responses\EstimateResponse;

class EstimateController extends Controller
{
    protected Claim $claim;

    public function estimate(EstimateRequest $request,
        ClaimEstimator $claimEstimator, Claim $claim)
    {
        $this->claim = $claim;
        $this->authorize('view', $claim);

        try {
            $amount = $claimService->estimate(
                $claim, $request->cptCodes);
        } catch (MissingProcedureException $exception) {
            logger()->error("Could not estimate given claim");
            return $this->handleMissingProcedure();
        }

        return EstimateResponse::createFromEstimate(
            Estimate::create(
                $this->estimatedAmount($amount),
                $request->cptCodes
```

```
        );
    }

    public function handleMissingProcedure()
    {
        return response()->json(['errors' => [
            "Unknown CPTCode Combo present for Claim or Paycode
                Sheet not defined for Provider on Claim: " .
            $this->claim->id
        ]], 422);
    }
}
```

This controller does what it is supposed to do: accepts a request and returns a response. It will most likely (technically) work, but it does have room for improvement from its current form. When reviewing this code, for example in a pull request, the first things I would include in the review comments are the following:

- Controllers don't usually have member variables that pertain to a single method in the class (i.e., the $claim member variable that was added toward the top of the class and injected into the estimate() method). If anything, member variables should be reserved for things such as services or other dependencies needed for the controller do its work. Anything else could potentially be a code smell that signifies that there is too much business logic happening in the controller (or any at all for that matter).

- The estimate() itself contains too much logic in the function body. A controller is meant to do two simple things: accept a request and return a response.

- The logic involved in calculating an estimate would be better expressed as a job that can be queued.

Taking the previous three comments into consideration, we decide to pull out all business logic that resides in the controller currently and end up with a clean controller with clear intentions expressed by dispatching specific capsules of business logic in the form of jobs. Listing 18-7 shows our refactored controller and the new jobs.

Listing 18-7. The Refactored Version of the Controller in Listing 18-6

```php
//Claim\Submission\Application\Http\Controllers\EstimateController.php
<?php

namespace Claim\Submission\Application\Http\Controllers\Estimates;

use App\Http\Controllers\Controller;
use Claim\Submission\Application\Http\Requests\Estimates\
    EstimateRequest;
use Claim\Submission\Domain\Models\Claims\Claim;
use Claim\Submission\Domain\Services\ClaimEstimator;
use Claim\Submission\Domain\Jobs\Claims\EstimateClaimAmount;
use Claim\Submission\Application\Responses\EstimateResponse;

class EstimateController extends Controller
{
    protected ClaimEstimator $claimEstimator;

    public function __construct(ClaimEstimator $claimEstimator)
    {
        $this->claimEstimator = $claimEstimator;
    }

    public function estimate(EstimateRequest $request, Claim $claim)
    {
        $claim = $this->claim;
        $cptCodes = $this->cptCodes;

        $this->authorize('view', $claim);

        dispatch(new EstimateClaimAmount($claim, $this->cptCodes);

        //refresh the Claim since we dispatched it to the queue
        $claim = $claim->fresh();

        //create a response by fetching the new estimate from DB
        return (!is_null($claim->estimate_id)) ?
            EstimateResponse::createFromEstimate(
```

```
                    Estimate::find($claim->estimate_id))
        : response()->make(['success' => 'false'], 500);
    }
}
```

The new EstimateClaimAmount job that was called from the previous code sample could look like Listing 18-8.

Listing 18-8. The New Job Encapsulating the Details of Creating an Estimated Amount for the Given Claim

```php
//Claim\Submission\Domain\Jobs\Claims\EstimateClaimAmount.php

<?php

namespace Claim\Submission\Domain\Jobs\Claims;

use Claim\Submission\Domain\Models\Claims\Claim;
use Claim\Submission\Domain\Services\ClaimEstimator;
use Illuminate\Bus\Queueable;
use Illuminate\Contracts\Queue\ShouldQueue;
use Illuminate\Foundation\Bus\Dispatchable;
use Illuminate\Queue\InteractsWithQueue;
use Illuminate\Queue\SerializesModels;

class EstimateClaimAmount extends ShouldQueue
{
    protected Claim $claim;

    protected $cptCodes = [];

    protected ClaimEstimator $claimEstimatorService;

    public function __construct(,
        Claim $claim, $cptCodes=[])
    {
        $this->claim = $claim;
        $this->cptCodes = $cptCodes;
    }
```

```php
    public function handle(ClaimEstimator $claimEstimator)
    {
        $claim = $this->claim;
        $cptCodes = $this->cptCodes;

        try {
            $amount = $claimEstimator->estimate(
                $claim, $cptCodes);
        } catch (MissingProcedureException $exception) {
            logger()->error("Could not estimate given claim");
            throw new MissingProcedureException("ERROR MSG");
        }

        $estimate = Estimate::create(
            $amount,
            $this->cptCodes
        );

        $claim->estimate_id = $estimate->id;
        $claim->save();
    ]
}
```

Tip   Whenever you need some Laravel component, be it a job, controller, request, etc., you should always start with the provided Artisan command to generate a blank stub for your component rather than typing out the whole thing by hand each time. In the previous case, we could have generated this job using the following:

```
php artisan make:job \\Claims\\Submission\\Domain\\Jobs\\
Claims\\EstimateClaimAmount
```

The code in Listing 18-8 should be fairly straightforward. We created a job to encapsulate the process around the claim's calculation to derive its estimate. We have injected the main dependency (ClaimEstimator) inside the handle() method of this job, which gets resolved automatically by the service container. If the object required additional logic to be instantiated, you could use the container's bindMethod() to customize how the job gets built. You could throw something like this in a service provider of your choice:

```
$this->app->bindMethod(::class.'@handle', function
    ($job, $app) {
        //custom instantiation logic goes here...
        return $job->handle($app->make(EstimateClaimAmount::class));
});
```

Notice also that we have injected the actual runtime data objects into the constructor. This is essentially setting up the job for the queue. The handle() method is what actually accepts it.

What Happened to the Infrastructure Layer?

It seems as though we have omitted an entire layer from the claim estimation procedure. Why is that? The way Laravel works and the natural order of things with regard to a web application make it so that the infrastructure related to a certain portion of code actually exists *inline* with its surrounding code, rather than separated into its own specific layer. This is often the case in Laravel applications because Laravel provides the means of performing routine database queries in an on-the-fly manner.

That's not to say that the infrastructure layer wouldn't hold standard things such as repositories or query builders to support the models present in the application. Those types of things are best placed within a dedicated infrastructure layer; I just wanted you to make a note that the infrastructure layer in Laravel can almost be thought of as Laravel itself. Because of this, there is infrastructure code scattered throughout much of the application, particularly within classes that actually *do* something (such as the driving adapters in hexagonal architecture), such as jobs. It is ingrained into the other levels in a nonintrusive, convenient manner that doesn't always fit the bill of a domain-driven design. DDD takes more of a structured, formal approach to solving business problems. Because we've decided early on to use a framework, we must be careful not to abuse its power and, for the sake of getting the domain model correct, let the decisions that you make within the code rely heavily (if not completely) on the needs and functional aspects of the domain you are crafting the model for.

Some Notes on Architecture

The previous example would need to have gone through a few cycles of rewrites, testing, refactoring, and more testing to get it to the high level it is right now. Nothing good comes easy! Take, for example, the way we are storing the estimates. Instead of saving the estimate within the claim itself (as a float or decimal value corresponding the amount of the estimate), we are storing the estimate separately in a different model and then saving the ID of that model inside the claim. This may seem a little unorthodox. However, when we step back and look at the scenario from a functional perspective, we find that this approach aligns well with the domain requirement of being able to calculate an estimate *without* a reference to a specific claim. This would mean separating the claim and estimated amount of the claim completely in terms of the data; therefore, we've created a separate model class to encapsulate the concept of a claim estimate.

Let's take into consideration only the data points that are needed to be derived for an estimate to be calculated, which would be the corresponding CPT codes that reflect the procedures done on a patient. Interestingly enough, even though the title of this functionality is Claim Estimates, the "Claim" part of it doesn't have much to do with the actual calculation of the estimate's amount. The estimate is really calculated from a paycode sheet (which it needs to look up via the provider's ID), the provider's ID (as just mentioned), and the CPT codes (procedures) completed during the visit. None of those things is the actual claim itself. They are all objects related to the claim.

If we had created a job that accepted a `Claim` object and then took out the values in that object needed to run the estimation, we definitely would have saved ourselves a little bit of typing in that we would've made the job's `handle()` method require only a single argument to do its job (this makes for easy recollection as well).

```
class EstimateClaim extends ShouldQueue
{
    // ...
    public function handle(Claim $claim)
    {
        //do the work...
    }
}
```

The issue that we have now created for ourselves lies in the coupling of the `Claim` model to the claim estimation logic. Why is that a bad thing? `Claim` is a fairly large object and is, for the most part, the most important object in the system. It contains many other objects, aggregates, values, and data inside of it and requires quite a bit of work before it can even get to a "valid" state as far as our Validation context is concerned.

This coupling obviously forces us to always have a ready-to-roll `Claim` object that we pass into the `Estimator` service to get an estimate. You can see now how this approach ends up being completely reusable elsewhere in the application. Such is the case with the hypothetical feature discussed earlier where a `Biller` user or `Provider` user could retrieve a Claim Estimate value without actually passing in a `Claim` object, or where an accounting user wants to double-check that the payment made for a particular CPT code combo that was relatively new to the system was actually set to retrieve the correct value for the estimate. They may not have a `Claim` object to pass in, because there simply isn't one in this context. There are just the CPT code combos, the provider, and the corresponding `PaycodeSheet` for that provider that are involved in creating this estimation. If you boil this down even further, you arrive at a point where you understand that the only real inputs of this function are the provider and the involved CPT codes (the `PaycodeSheet` can be looked up by the `ClaimEstimator` service, as can the CPT code combo given the array of CPT codes). The following sample shows this small but impactful change in our `handle()` method:

```
class EstimateClaim extends Job extends ShouldQueue
{
    // ...
    public function handle(Provider $provider, $codes)
    {
        $cptCodeCombo = CptCodeCombo::fromCodes($codes);
        $paycodeSheet = PaycodeSheet::byProvider($provider);
    }
}
```

The `byProvider()` and `fromCodes()` methods are simple convenience methods on the `Model` classes, but they could have just as easily (although less elegantly) been a raw query builder chain or even a call to a predefined repository method.

What Are We Missing? Events!

When an estimate is actually created in the system, other parts of it may need to know that this has occurred. For instance, perhaps the accounting department relies on these estimates in order to project sales and expenses for the coming months. There may also be real-time reporting in place, where front-end read projections are made to reflect the backend write projections using a job queue such as Laravel's or a third-party package.

Since this is the case, what should come to mind first are events! Events are made for exactly this purpose: to notify any listeners of the event that something interesting has occurred in the application and therefore give any listening components the ability to add additional logic or react to the event with custom domain or application logic. They are extremely simple to make and should reflect only the minimum amount of data needed to properly express that a particular action has been performed within the system. You can use Artisan to create a simple event stub, as we have done in the past.

```
php artisan make:event \\Claims\\Submission\\Domain\\Events\\Claims\\
ClaimWasEstimated
```

For a more in-depth look at creating events in Laravel, particularly for domain events, review Chapter 11.

Conclusion

Instead of starting from scratch and showing you a naive solution with no external dependencies, we will remind ourselves that we are using a framework and our jobs as developers depend on the utilization of functionality encapsulated within Laravel's processes and helper utilities. The following are among the most heavily used and beloved instruments in the entire framework:

- *Collections*: Eloquent and Laravel have common ground as far as supporting collections goes, meaning that they are built with what essentially is the same low-level collection abstraction so that every call to a collection method returns a new collection method with the desired permutations pre-applied. This makes passing around collections of objects extremely simple and will be useful for us to build out the specifications.

- *Eloquent scopes*: Scopes are basically just syntactic sugar built on top of Eloquent's `QueryBuilder` class. They can be thought of as sort of "mini-specifications" in that they describe a particular set of data either starting from scratch or starting from a pre-filtered `QueryBuilder` object and then adding constraints (filtering) logic to it, but within the same model's context. The way it does this is by tracking all filtering and querying details within a `QueryBuilder` object. It makes sense to use the `QueryBuilder` object to contain the criteria to query that model in the database. The specifications themselves will consume the `Criteria` objects to produce a result.

- *Eloquent model*: The abstract `Model` class used by Eloquent has a mountain of functionality and features within; I advise you to check it out for yourself (`https://github.com/illuminate/database/blob/master/Eloquent/Model.php`).

- *The query builder*: This is the low-level infrastructure that Eloquent was built on. It offers a full abstraction to work with MySQL and can handle complex queries without writing raw SQL. However, for situations that cannot be done with the abstraction methods available on the query builder, you are always free to resort to raw SQL queries using the `DB::raw()` facade call.

- *Helper methods*: The most widely used helper methods when building an API-driven application are `event()`, `dispatch()`, and `app()`. Be sure to use the `request()` and `response()` helper methods as less frequently as you can, as they tend to signify a code smell regarding the lack of encapsulating value objects properly in the system or having on-the-fly (rouge) responses and requests that should instead be encapsulated into a Laravel request or response signifying some sort of uniform way of treating requests and responses and thereby promoting consistency throughout the system.

CHAPTER 19

Conclusion and Additional Thoughts

We've covered quite a bit of information throughout this book. I've attempted to give you a working knowledge of how to develop software in a domain-driven design way that is implemented with Laravel. I walked you through many scenarios and went over some possible solutions to them, and possible failure points as well. All of the examples I've presented in the book were taken directly from experiences that I've had developing software for the Web. In this chapter, I will go over some concepts that we haven't yet covered or that we touched on only briefly.

Among these areas of interest, you will find the following:

- *Architecture*: A few alternative strategies to build out the core backbone of a system in a domain-driven way. We will use an example application I built from the ground up as the supporting structure to showcase a pseudo-hypothetical scenario relating to portions of the core implementation that tracked and managed all order, sales, tracking, and transaction processes typical of a common warehouse management system.

- *Embracing Laravel*: Leveraging Laravel at the domain level using custom-made `Collections` and `QueryBuilder` objects (rather than having them "inline" with the model using Eloquent scopes, which couples the scope to the model directly and is not reusable). There are shortcuts that you can use to employ these things seamlessly in the model, but we must be sure that we are careful not to damage the integrity of the model itself or create new models that obscure the underlying domain when using such shortcuts.

© Jesse Griffin 2021
J. Griffin, *Domain-Driven Laravel*, https://doi.org/10.1007/978-1-4842-6023-4_19

I will then share additional thoughts regarding the implementation of a domain-driven Laravel application. That will lead us into a few concluding thoughts that summarize what we've been able to do with Laravel and domain-driven design and how the choices and implementations we made to initially solve the domain problem affect the future construction and refactoring of the application.

Architectural Considerations

There are many ways to architect a system, but only a few ways to do it correctly to ensure the domain model properly reflects the underlying core domain and what's contained in it. That's much easier said than done!

In this section, we will sketch out a possible architecture that, when implemented, will satisfy the needs and requirements that a system has. We will identify certain aspects of this architecture in terms of domain-driven design concepts. We will define the system spaces to properly scope the different aspects of the domain, which we can use to start piecing together an overall architecture for the system. We will focus on the architecture and relationships the components of the system have with each other and will not actually be writing the low-level code to implement the design we've devised. Specifically, we will go through an example application that is used to manage all aspects typical of a warehouse, including accepting the orders, fulfilling them, and shipping the orders; receiving merchandise in inventory; and tracking the product's location at every step in the typical business flow (more details coming up soon—stay tuned)!

A Warehouse Management System

In Chapter 3, we used something similar to a warehouse management system, only within the context of a specific one (an online shoe retailer's warehouse). This example will be more high level and will cover a much broader area. It is based on a project that I completed within the last few years. It is extremely relevant, and there's a lot to take away from this example.

Let's imagine that you are hired as a lead developer of a freelance project to construct an all-inclusive warehouse management system. This means it can handle many (if not most) aspects of what a warehouse does, sells, and tracks (see the "Title" section for the high-level functionality).

From the perspective of the data that makes up the core of each individual warehouse in our system, the functionality must be stored in such a way to allow ease of access to it across all objects in the system—so that the data can be shared across components in a clear and manageable way. From the point of view of the application, you need a way to break down these features into smaller pieces so they can be independently worked on, yet so they come together in a cohesive manner to provide a rich set of functionality across the application seamlessly.

You meet with the project manager to go over all the different groups of functionality to properly define what will be included as part of the application's domain model. From this meeting, you come up with a list of desired functionality described at a high level that the application is to include, which looks like the following process:

- Acceptance of an order by a third-party order management system, which should get translated to a sales order on our end

- Fulfilment of an incoming order, from picking the items off the shelf to packing the boxes

- Shipment of the orders to the buyer listed on a sales order (which is outgoing from the warehouse)

- Receiving incoming merchandise from vendors, including tracking stock levels and product location management

To add some clarity to the project's requirements, you come up with the high-level diagram that's shown in Figure 19-1.

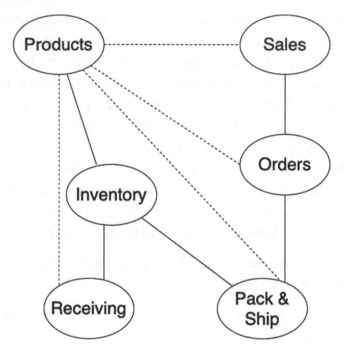

Figure 19-1. *Rough diagram of the required feature sets involved in completing the warehouse management application*

The solid lines in the diagram represent hard relationships, while the dotted lines represent implied relationships. These are high-level categories of functionality that you will need to account for when constructing a model design. Through further discussion, you were able to identify several core contexts that would be needed in this system, as well as some subitems describing the breakdown of these contexts.

- Order fulfillment

    - Sales orders

    - Inventory adjustments (temporarily "locks" a quantity of a certain product)

    - Pick, pack

- Receiving merchandise (purchasing merchandise)

    - Purchase orders

    - Inventory adjustments

- Storing merchandise
    - Product management
    - Warehouse location tracking
    - Put away
- Shipping merchandise
    - Packaging
    - Inventory adjustments (the "locks" are released and the quantity decreased)

This is a little more specific with regard to the requirements this system has. The three black bullet points describe the central concerns that the warehouse has. Order fulfillment includes this concept of a sales order that gets created on every sale (this could be determined by a successful transaction by a payment gateway). The order is then fulfilled, which includes picking the merchandise from the shelf, packing the boxes, and shipping them out. There also needs to be a means of tracking the merchandise that comes in, which it does so through purchase orders and, as we go along, must be adequately tracked and counted for in the master inventory list. The last consideration is how to properly store the merchandise in the warehouse in a manner that promotes efficiency, a process known as *put away*. Each product would have to be tracked, accounted for in inventory, and then placed on the storage shelf according to some standard system for tracking their movement while in the warehouse system.

From this list, you can determine the core contexts that need to be present in the system to capture the business model inside the new domain model. Since you are well versed in domain-driven design, you know that the organizational structure of the domain model should itself be modeled as literally as possible to the real business process it represents. Taking this into consideration, you identify the four core contexts of this system to be as follows:

- Orders (incoming)
- Receiving (incoming)
- Storing (internal)
- Shipping (outgoing/deliverable)

Note   An argument can be made that the Storing context is technically part of Receiving. I've added it here as its own because storing the items in a manageable and intuitive manner is challenging and can encompass a big chunk of logic in order to run.

Certain key aspects of the system exist to support the core domains listed previously. These aspects can be considered to be generic subdomains, as they apply to more than one context (i.e., shared across components) and are more or less supporting structures for the previous core domains. The following are examples of some of the generic subdomains we need to account for in this system:

- Inventory Management (used by the Orders, Receiving, and Shipping contexts)

- Product Management (used by all other bounded contexts)

- Location Tracking (used by Storing and Receiving, as well as Picking & Packing)

- External Order System that we will receive sales orders through

Knowing how well graphical representations of concepts make them easier understand, you are quick to devise a diagram that displays the bounded context, as well as the generic subdomains and how they are applicable to each context, which looks like Figure 19-2.

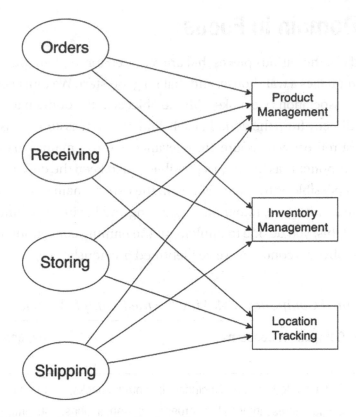

Figure 19-2. *The breakdown of relations between the core contexts and subdomains*

We can deduce that the Order context will need to have knowledge of both the Product Management and Inventory Management subdomains. The Receiving context will have similar knowledge (aka dependencies) as the Order context. The Storing context relies on the Product Management and Location Tracking subdomains, while the Shipping context has a dependency on all three subdomains. Being the awesome lead developer that you are, you have an urge to encapsulate the terms and their definitions that will be later used as identifiers for the various components themselves, commonly referred to as the *ubiquitous language* of the system. This can be used to help clarify the bounded contexts and the various interactions between them and can be thought of as a sort of "rough draft" of a context map.

Keep the Domain in Focus

We have mapped out the various pieces that are required for implementing an application that manages a warehouse, and that's a good start. We must continue to be mindful of the associations we make with the objects in the domain to be sure that they are coming directly from the domain itself, and not from assumptions made about it. One clear and surefire way to assure this relevance to the domain is to name the corresponding components as literally as possible and to keep the definitions of each model as literal as possible as they are defined in the core domain. Allow the domain to be what drives the architecture, rather than assuming and having inaccurate information.

Knowing all of this, you decide to implement the naming convention listed in Table 19-1 for the obvious concerns we've identified previously.

Table 19-1. *Named Components Making Up the Example Warehouse Application*

Component Name and Context	Component Concerns	Dependencies
Orders	Order-related concerns including inventory checks, billing/address information, order lines, transactions, and creating sales orders (for products leaving the warehouse).	Product Management, Inventory Management
Receiving	All logic that is relative to tracking products *entering* the warehouse, including in-warehouse location placement, inventory adjustments, as well as interactions with the product management component.	Product Management, Inventory Management, Location Tracking
Storing	All logic required to create and maintain some kind of in-warehouse tracking system to allow for rapid re-stocking and quick fulfillment of orders.	Product Management, Location Tracking
Shipping	Logic involved in the final stages of order fulfillment. Includes picking products off the shelf according to the order specifics, packing the products into a box, and printing out shipping labels. Inventory changes must also be accounted for.	Product Management, Inventory Management, Location Tracking

Notice how we are naming these components (using terms identified in the ubiquitous language that we ideally have been keeping up-to-date with the project). The terms here are identical to the ones found in the domain and mean literally the same thing as they do within the context of warehouse management. This method is what is meant by intentional and literal design.

Tip   To cultivate a meaningful ubiquitous language, you need to have many discussions with the people who best understand the domain—domain experts. As you are progressing on a project, you can (and should) refactor your definitions of the terms as new insight is gained in the domain or domain model.

At this point, we have the core concepts that are going to act as the backbone of the application, so to speak. They are the main sections of functionality offered by the application and, as such, require additional supporting mechanisms to function. These come in the form of various specialized supporting subdomains that are utilized across the components (and therefore must be developed in a way that allows for easy integration or delegation of work to the other components in the system). Because these are actually not regular subdomains but are considered generic subdomains, we should always strive for loose coupling between the core components of the system and the facilities that operate on them and, at the same time, promote cohesive mechanisms that are required for such operations as maintaining the stock levels in the inventory, updating order statuses, or picking and packing an order in preparation for shipment.

The ability for our system to be flexible enough to handle the various interactions between the components (the internal object interactions between domain-specific components) is essential. We will hash out a rough draft of a possible directory structure soon, but it is worth noting how simple it would be to migrate a domain-driven architecture to a more distributed one (such as microservices), as opposed to starting with a monolithic application and moving toward a microservice or even hexagonal architecture. It's not impossible, but the conversion itself can get rather complicated, because concepts have to be rethought, boundaries have to be redrawn, and concerns need to be combined or separated so that it makes the most sense.

Namespace and Directory

One last breakdown that we need to make to split the application's concerns is perhaps the most important one of all: the breakdown of the domain on a modular level that corresponds directly (and as literally as possible) to the concepts, relationships, and structures present within the underlying business domain. Now that we have our bounded contexts properly defined, we can decide on which modules to break the domain into (including its directory and namespace structure). Generally speaking, but not always, it is best practice to align each subdomain with a domain module, and that module should be named directly from the ubiquitous language of the project.

From our current perspective (without taking the infrastructure into concern just yet), we will create the App\ and Domain\ namespaces that will serve as the highest-level parent classes of the system. App\ is where we will place the logic we need to facilitate and direct the domain layer. For now, however, let's focus on the domain layer itself.

We start out with creating subnamespaces in accordance with the bounded context we've identified previously (keep in mind that we would also have to modify our composer.json file to add the new Domain root namespace).

In the structure listed in Table 19-2, we can consider the content of each parent namespace as a container that houses everything specific to its corresponding bounded context (i.e., the logic involved in creating a new sales order would happen in the Order module, while the action of stocking a product on the shelf so it can be quickly found later exists within the Storage module).

Table 19-2. *Initial Namespace/Directory Structure*

Namespace	Directory	Module
Domain\Receiving (or Receivements)	/src/Warehouse/Domain/Receiving (or Receivements)	Receiving (incoming)
Domain\Ordering (or Orders)	/src/Warehouse/Domain/Ordering (Orders)	Orders (incoming)
Domain\Storing (or Storage)	/src/Warehouse/Domain/Storage (or Storage)	Storage (internal)
Domain\Shipping (or Shipments)	/src/Warehouse/Domain/Shipping/ (or Shipments)	Shipping (outgoing)

So, where does that leave us with regard to where to put the generic subdomains that our system relies on to operate? Well, they are still part of the domain, so we can keep them within the `Domain\` root namespace, either separated by component type or within an additional layer (with a prefix of something like `Domain\Support\`).

Here is one possible namespace structure for the application thus far:

```
Warehouse
└── Domain
     ├── Ordering
     ├── Receiving
     ├── Shipping
     ├── Storing
     └── Support
          ├── InventoryManager
          ├── LocationManager
          └── ProductManager
```

In this structure, we have a clear collection of parent namespaces that corresponds to the underlying business's structure. There is an easy way to, at any given time, verify that you are on the right path in planning out the outline of the domain layer. If your original design of the domain model correlates to the underlying business structure at a near literal level and the names that you have chosen are derived directly from the ubiquitous language of the system, you are on the right track.

Because Laravel operates in a certain way (by organizing the different portions of the application into the various components that allow the domain layer to integrate with the rest of the functionality provided by Laravel's default mechanisms), we will stick with the default components used across the application and framework. This includes things like jobs (which can dispatched a queue and run asynchronously), policies (to protect the security of the model by managing access to who can see, modify, or create an instance of that model), Eloquent models (to encapsulate the specific behaviors and properties of a model), and various other components that come with Laravel. However, we will only use any specific component if we first determine that it is necessary. I advise against you creating any sort of default directory/namespace structure for the domain layer of your application, for multiple reasons (the main one involving adherence to YAGNI—you're not gonna need it). It is counterproductive to add classes and interfaces to the project that aren't 100 percent necessary, because it adds lines of code to the application that need to be maintained and kept up-to-date. Extra files and folders in the project directory will only add to the overall complexity of the application, so try to avoid putting anything in the project directory that isn't going to be needed.

Reviewing the Layers

Before we get too deep into exploring our options, let's take a few minutes to review the different layers of the architecture and which types of logic should belong in each. Figure 19-3 shows a breakdown of these layers as they exist in our DDD-based application.

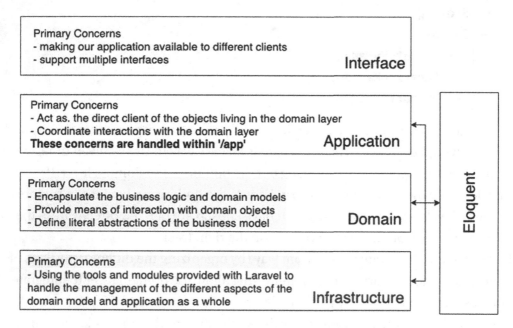

Figure 19-3. *Each layer of the application and their respective concerns*

Figure 19-3 breaks down the application in terms of the layers that it is made of and the primary concerns (focus points) of each layer. There's nothing new here, but do consider that Eloquent runs alongside each of the central layers of the application and can be thought of as its own independent layer (while previously you may have considered the functionality within Eloquent as residing within the infrastructure layer).

Mapping the Architecture

We will now start mapping out the things we know we are going to need for each module we identified earlier. For instance, we can assume (but won't actually create code for unless it is deemed necessary later) that most of the modules are going to require, at minimum, the following things:

- `Models/`: Domain models (business objects)

  a. Entities

  b. Value objects

- `Repositories/`: Access to / `Management` of those models

- `Factories/`: A logical location to abstract the building of more complex domain objects

- `Aggregates/`: A place for the combination of entities and value objects that act as an independent unit within the application

- `Services/`: The functions and processes that occur as part of the business logic and that cannot otherwise be contained within an entity or value object

Figure 19-4 represents this graphically.

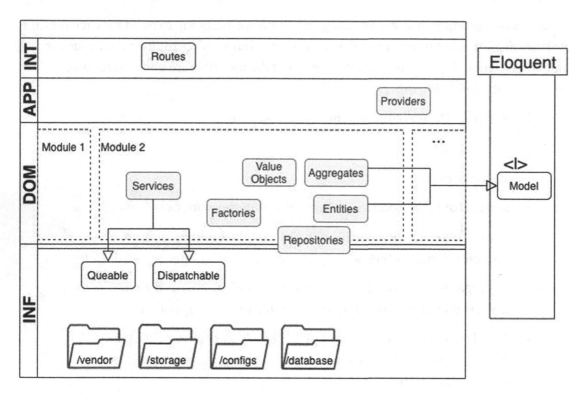

Figure 19-4. *A visual representation of the application and its layers, along with some common components we are likely to find in each*

Figure 19-4 shows a view of the application from a high level, with the various layers involved in it separated into their own swimlanes. The items in the diagram with no shade represent interfaces or abstractions, and the shaded items represent implementations to such interfaces. I've included middleware as a special item because it is not a class in itself, but more of an underlying concept. Starting at the top, the interface layer is what will support the various types of requests that enter our system, be them API requests or requests from a browser. We will discuss the interface layer and application layer in more depth soon.

For the most part, the map focuses on the domain-layer aspects of the system and, as such, indicates which types of objects are likely to be found within the context of a single module living in the domain layer. More often than not, we are going to need models to base our entities and aggregates on (so as to tap into the features offered by Eloquent), value objects and aggregates to form the base objects existing in the business domain, and services used to model processes or procedures that don't fit the normal shape of an entity or value object.

Because we are building our application using Laravel, it makes sense to model such services as either a Laravel job or some other type of domain-level construct that implements the `Queueable` and `Dispatchable` contracts so that they can be pushed to an asynchronous queue, which can provide a high level of responsiveness throughout the application in general. The easiest way to do that in Laravel is by creating a `Job` class (or `Command` class) that implements the `ShouldQueue`, `InteractsWithQueue`, and/or `SerializesModels` traits and then to make sure your configuration is set up properly to support one of many supported queues, and, *poof*, you're ready to go.

Tip   When building jobs to encapsulate the business logic within your system, remember that once they are pushed onto the asynchronous stack, they will not return any values. This means that any changes done to an entity within the context of a job or command run via the worker queue would be detectable only on a refresh of the model's properties from the database. This also implies that any data or dependencies required for the job to function must be passed within its constructor so that it has it before the job-specific logic is run.

Also in Figure 19-4, notice that the `Repository` component was placed between the domain and infrastructure layers and is represented by an implementation rather than an interface (as indicated by the shaded region). The reason for this is because, in a typical project, you would define the interface of a given repository within the domain layer of the application, which could be named something like `Warehouse\Domain\Orders\Contracts\OrderRepositoryInterface`.

This would be implemented by a class within the infrastructure layer, perhaps called `Warehouse\Infrastructure\Orders\Repositories\InMemoryOrderRepository`.

It can be argued that the implementation of a repository interface defined in the domain layer should actually live inside the application layer instead of the infrastructure layer, because the repository itself has a close connection with the model so it can be considered an app service (residing in the app layer) while at the same time could possibly belong outside the domain layer. It is also why the abstract `Repository` interface is defined within the domain layer. (This is up to you and is probably not worth spending a lot of time discussing.)

At the bottom of the diagram, the four folders that reside in the infrastructure layer that I've included in Figure 19-4 are meant to represent the various places that hold important data required for the application to run. The reason they are listed within the context of the infrastructure layer is because we've chosen Laravel as the underlying framework for the rest of the system to be built on top of. Mostly these folders store some type of cached data used by various portions of the application and framework.

Keep in mind that Figure 19-4 is there to give you a possible architecture that you can use to build your application. It is okay (and recommended) to follow the principles and best practices of software, which can be rolled together as a sort of architecture. However, what we want is something more deliberate. Let's see how our warehouse application fits into this architecture and what modifications to the architecture are needed to allow the domain to fully thrive as the underlying ingredient in the system, which is done only by letting the domain "drive" so to speak (pun intended). We will focus on only one particular module in the system, the Order module. Figure 19-5 shows an example of how this could look.

Caution   Diagrams are great, and UMLs can relay a ton of information in an easy-to-read format. However, don't make the mistake of attempting to diagram *everything* in the system. You will be overwhelmed by the amount of upkeep it takes to keep all those diagrams current. If they aren't current, then they are useless to us. Leave diagramming as an item in your toolbox you can use to inculcate more advanced or complex concerns and processes. Fight the urge to diagram everything.

In Figure 19-5, we have a high-level sketch of what the architecture for a warehouse management application could look like, with respect to the Orders domain module. Starting from the top of the (INT = interface), we have collapsed the interface layer altogether and have a few application-level services for which to facilitate the application concerns existing between the domain layer and the application layer.

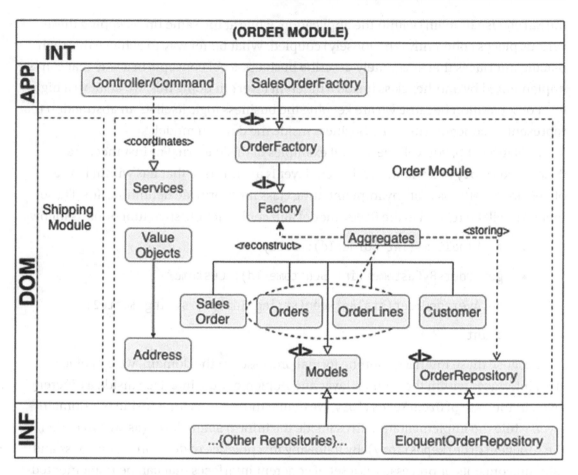

Figure 19-5. *An example of an applied module using the loosely coupled design we devised earlier. Notice that all dependencies are pointing inward toward the domain layer and there are interfaces at every boundary crossing*

If you remember correctly, the application layer is there to handle the elements in the domain layer directly. Application services, for instance, are usually the direct clients of domain model objects. In Figure 19-5, we can consider any controllers and commands that utilize the domain objects to complete some task as part of the application layer. If you noticed, we are still conforming to the dependency rule and have all the arrows representing dependencies pointing toward, not away from, the domain layer.

These commands (or controller) methods will most likely dispatch any jobs and services or delegate any other logic needed to be run to other components. It is through these constructs that the outside world can communicate with the internals of our application. We want to achieve a strong separation of concerns (in accordance with the Warehouse domain) within the application, while at the same time keeping these various pieces coherently (and loosely) coupled. What better way to achieve this than placing interfaces that adequately describe business-level concepts in a way that can be implemented by another class inside a different layer? In doing this, we achieve a high level of separation because we are keeping the business logic itself as an abstraction that represents a concept within the business inside the domain model.

In Figure 19-5, you will see several examples of this pattern. For instance, the OrderRepository box within the domain layer is an interface that has within it a set of declared methods that any implementing class must provide definitions for. These methods will be related to the Order model and could include such functions as follows:

- `getLineItems(int $orderId): array`

- `getOrdersByCustomer(int $customerId): Customer`

- `getAverageOrderTotalBetween(string $date1, string $date2)`

- `: int`

Because these interfaces outline formal processes in the domain, we can place such interfaces within the domain layer and implement the interface inside a different layer. In the case of OrderRepository, we define the contract for it inside our domain layer, while the implementation lives inside the infrastructure layer (as shown earlier, the EloquentOrderRepository). By following this practice of developing business and domain concepts or processes as a set of coherent interfaces that can be implemented by any number of clients, each client will have its own custom logic or concerns, which our design supports out of the box because we can guarantee that all clients of that given interface (such as the EloquentOrderRepository implementation of the OrderRepository interface) will have the specified methods defined within it. This is basic OO programming stuff.

The last thing to note in Figure 19-5 is the aggregate's location and the corresponding elements it connects with. It is well-known in domain-driven design that aggregates represent a sort of boundary line between themselves and the classes within the boundary from anything outside. This adds complexity to the model, but usually it's much less than when attempting to model them without an aggregate root. Because of this added complexity, it is normal for aggregates not to have any built-in logic that is concerned with saving or retrieving these objects from a data store. Instead, the "building" aspect of an aggregate is often placed within a dedicated factory class, as in Figure 19-5.

Tip   The `Factory` interface in Figure 19-5 is located in the domain layer, with its implementation living within the application layer. The reason I made it this way is because the classes and objects present in the application layer are intended to be direct clients of the domain objects themselves, and a factory whose only dedicated purpose for existence is putting together a single aggregate object would certainly fall under this category. In the real world, you are likely to find implementations that exist within the infrastructure layer instead of the application layer. This is due to preference and doesn't matter too much, as long as you are consistent and stick with your decision.

A typical factory class should reconstitute an aggregate by respecting the boundaries of the aggregate. The factory instantiates all the required parts of the aggregate (the objects located within the boundary line of the aggregate root) and, for lack of better words, packages it up into the aggregate object requested and returns it. In this manner, we essentially have transformed the data from the database to a full-fledged PHP object that we can utilize within the application so that we can interface with them in an object-oriented way. We are then left with the concern of saving and retrieving aggregate data from the database, which is best left up to a repository (which we have gone over rather intensely throughout the course of the book).

Enter the Application Layer

From a DDD standpoint, it is common to include an application-layer module for every domain-layer module existing in your system. For the previous example, we can create a namespace under the `Application` namespace, with the name being the same as its domain layer counterpart: `Orders`.

In Figure 19-6, we have devised an architecture that our system will be based on that takes into account that we are utilizing the Laravel framework as the backbone of the system, while still keeping the most important rule of the system intact (that is, to allow the domain itself to drive the development of the application). The diagram is slightly different in that it embraces the framework in more of a literal and direct way than a traditional architecture created with DDD.

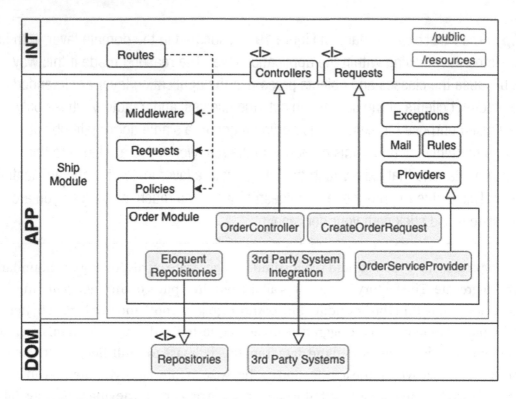

Figure 19-6. *Focused perspective of the application layer of our warehouse project. The infrastructure layer is not shown*

Just like we have a dedicated domain module named Orders, we too should provide a matching module within the application layer. As you can see, the more or less "standard" components included with Laravel are shown as being on the outside of the actual Order module (and also within the infrastructure layer, not shown here). More than likely, we are going to require a controller to handle the incoming requests resulting in the creation, selection, update, or deletion of an order in the system. Also included are Eloquent repositories (which could very well be better located within the infrastructure layer, not shown in Figure 19-6), whose implementations ultimately live within the domain layer, as well as any third-party systems that we may be utilizing to support various aspects of the application.

Take, for example, the possibility of the team deciding that they do not want to manage authentication into the application from within, but they instead want to delegate the process of signing into and creating new users in the system. Say we decide that a SaaS would be the best bet. After doing a little research on the Web, we find something called Auth0, a completely integrated system for handling all aspects of your users (or just the login portion) in a clear way that supports state-of-the-art encryption-at-rest technology so we can rest assured (no pun intended) that the user's data is as safe as possible at all times. To build this service into our system, we would need to modify the default `LoginController` to utilize a custom repository class (maybe an `Auth0Repository`?) that encapsulates the bit of logic needed to integrate with the Auth0 backend (via an API). An additional requirement is that you must include a method on the `LoginController` that will act as a "listener"-type callback for Auth0 to hit once the authentication is complete (be it a pass or fail). In a case such as this, the `Auth0Repository` would best be located within the application layer as it is an application concern. If, however, we were dealing with a repository that managed the saving/retrieving of, say, an aggregate object, the proper place to implement that would be in the infrastructure layer, which we will highlight next.

The Infrastructure Layer

Last but not least, we have the infrastructure layer, which houses most of the Laravel default objects, configuration, and other such objects inside what we are going to identify as the infrastructure layer. Just as we have done with the application and domain layers, we will create a new namespace within the infrastructure layer named `Orders` that will house any order-related code that doesn't fit the bill of an application or domain layer concern. See Figure 19-7 for an example of how this could look.

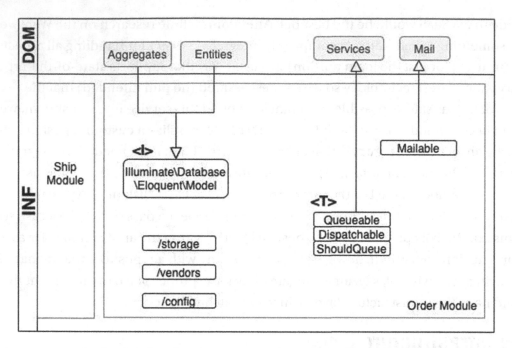

Figure 19-7. *The highlighted infrastructure layer of the warehouse application*

The infrastructure layer is pretty simple, but it will grow as we add functionality. It may also include repositories, as mentioned earlier, that encapsulate storing/retrieval knowledge of a specific model or aggregate inside our domain layer. As usual, we would create an interface for the object. Let's pretend we (for whatever reason) needed a repository that only handled data and objects that existed in memory (RAM). We could employ an `InMemoryOrderRepository`, which would implement the `OrderRepository` interface living in the domain layer. The implementation itself would exist within the interface layer, as shown in Figure 19-7. Can you notice anything strange about Figure 19-7? If not, Figure 19-8 provides a hint.

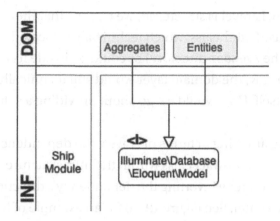

FIgure 19-8. *The problem area for the architecture depicted in Figure 19-8*

There are elements within the domain layer that have an outward-pointing dependency on another element in the infrastructure, which should strike you as problematic if we remember where the domain logic lives (toward the middle) and which way dependencies are supposed to point (inward) toward the domain layer. Let's revisit this concept by checking out Figure 19-9.

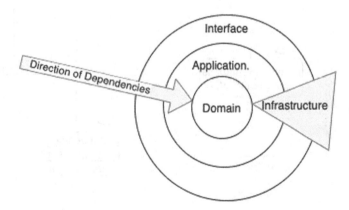

Figure 19-9. *A refresher of the different layers in a layered architecture*

Because we have chosen the Web as our median of programmatic expression and the canvas for which to cleverly paint art in the form of beautiful code that represents the science behind it, certain considerations must be made to implement a standard domain-driven design. That being the case, there are certain aspects of a DDD such as the domain layer depending on anything outside of itself, which is normally a strict no-no in the context of DDD but seems to be acceptable to an extent within one of the most powerful and popular frameworks in the world.

591

If we look at the way Laravel is structured, we can see that the Model classes, for example, extend the base Model class, which technically is located in the infrastructure layer (residing within the /vendor directory) or could be inside its own layer (see Figure 19-4), but either way, the domain layer would still technically depend on something outside of itself. How would we go about providing a solution that satisfies the dependency rule?

If you were thinking anything in terms of "invert the dependencies," you are correct! What we can do is create an abstract class within the infrastructure layer that would implement an interface, thereby inverting the dependency's direction to point toward the domain layer in the center. See Figure 19-10 for an example of how this might look.

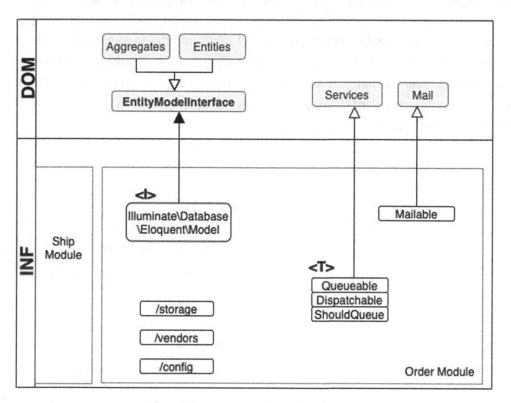

Figure 19-10. *Inverting the dependency for Model classes*

Embracing Laravel

For this last section of the chapter, we will be using previous examples (such as the medical claims application) as a reference point when going through some of these concluding topics.

On Validating Objects as a Whole

If, on the other hand, you needed additional customized logic to be run as part of the validation process (which is exactly what we need in the Claim Validator), the context of validating a composition of objects (or aggregates) could be solved implementing a custom `Validation` service that would utilize the reusable `Validator` component that we just created. Then, to make it easily accessible to the other components in your application, you can use Laravel's service container to bind aliases to your service.

Creating a Validator Service for Object Composition Validation

To create a service, there are a few things you will want to think about, model, and architect.

1. Is the service really needed? Would some sort of value object or entity suffice?

   → If what you are building doesn't fit the context of an entity or object, a service may be the way to go.

2. What exactly is this service supposed to accomplish?

   → It helps keep the scope narrow when you clearly identify the goals of the service and what it is supposed to accomplish for the application as a whole.

3. Which components, classes, services, objects, entities, and data will be needed for the service to do its job?

   → It is beneficial to define any relationships, dependencies, or other associations to code living outside of the scope of the service.

4. Where is the best place for this service? In what context or module?

→ Besides figuring out where to physically place the file, it helps give context to the service by defining what layer the service will live in.

5. How can the service be tested?

→ Always aim to create unit tests and (wherever possible) a complete automated testing suite.

For our particular context regarding claim validation, we will assume that the service is needed because of its complexity, although in reality this would probably be overkill (step 1). The service will handle the validation of the CPT code combos, verifying that the combination is available for the provider to use on their paycode sheets, establishing the proper documents were submitted with the claim, and validating that the patient is eligible to receive care (step 2). We will need access to the claim itself, along with anything that touches the claim (attributes and relations), as well as the CPT code models, paycode sheets (which we still have to define), and the patient eligibility service, which we won't be building, just validating that it has been run for the patient on the claim (step 3). In general, validation is an infrastructure concern, because it doesn't necessarily have anything to do with the domain itself and instead is concerned with ensuring that a given model (in our case, the `Claim` model) is in a valid state (step 4). This is clearly a good separation of concerns, so it belongs in the infrastructure layer. As far as testing goes, a simple unit test covering the majority of the code involved in the service should suffice (step 5).

Now that we have a little more detail into what we are actually building, we can start by creating a new file named `ClaimsValidationService.php` inside the namespace corresponding to its bounded context and module. This service will handle any complex validation logic for validating the rest of the claim. At this point, most of the validation needs to be run on a claim submission we've already handled by implementing the rules we specified in the `ClaimSubmissionRequest` class. The one we haven't covered yet is validating that the given CPT code combo exists and is listed in the provider's paycode sheet.

Within our service, we can build out the validator using the `Validation` classes we defined in this chapter. We could've even used the validators we previously built to handle another validation for the CPT code combos and the paycode sheets; however,

I chose to model this using a service instead so you can see how to go about validation when there are complex structures and/or multiple pre-conditions/post-conditions that span a variety of checks to ensure consistency. Complex validation such as that should belong in a dedicated service. To save ourselves the hassle of creating the low-level components to wire up such a service properly (that is, with the correct dependencies and located in the proper context/module), we could instead rely on Laravel's `Validation` component and even make an extension of it to better suit our needs. Therefore, we will utilize Laravel's `Validation` component.

On Web Development as an Inconsistent Practice...

I'll be the one to admit it that web development specifically is choppy, to say the least. There really aren't lots of shared resources, especially back in the day. Admittingly, things have gotten better over the last few decades as the principles and practices of software engineering have slowly found their way into the web development community. As true as this is, the reality is that HTTP is still the same. The underlying technology that web programming languages such as PHP was built on top of is a choppy, low-level architecture stemming from one of the oldest discovered protocols in the world: the client-server model. Sessions were added to mitigate the problem, and HTTP 2.0 offers a much needed refactoring of the original implementation; however, in my opinion, sessions were just a Band-Aid fix to solve the (much bigger) problem of sharing state between page hops, and HTTP 2.0 is not very widespread nor does it seem to be gaining popularity as much as everyone·thought it would. Adopting the HTTP 2.0 specification in a global context is for sure happening, but as it stands, it's a slow road.

Most Importantly, Stick to Standards and Best Practices

As complexity grows within an application as time goes on, it becomes harder to maintain a large-scale codebase no matter which framework you use, if one at all. Separating concerns becomes more challenging of a task with regard to where to draw the lines acting as boundaries between the logical segments within the code. Always remember to let the domain be the driver of the application's development and strive to name things after the ubiquitous language set in for that context. Express the domain as literally as possible.

Previously in the book, I've made the argument that repositories are not really needed unless you plan on having multiple database platforms and you must maintain access to all of them at any given time. One instance where this is not the case is specifying a qualifying set of objects of a particular model described by criteria, which employs conditions and restraints against the database data for that model. A repository can be useful here as a means of abstracting the way the criteria itself is described.

It's one thing to say all of this, but let's put some context around the idea of describing sets of data in terms of criteria. Because we all know that interfaces are the way to encapsulate change and the specific details of its various implementations, we decide it best to first describe the entire concept of criteria using a set of interfaces (which works well for documenting the idea in code, making it easier for newcomers to quickly understand what the contract is and what it's used for). Let's build a basic interface for the concept of "criteria" in respect to the way we can use it to filter and constrain our data. We will be using our good ol' friend the claim processing application as an underlying platform in Listing 19-1.

Listing 19-1. Example Interface to Manage Criteria

```php
<?php

namespace Claim\Submission\Domain\Contracts;

interface CriteriaHandler
{
    /** Skip any applied criteria during processing */
     public function skipCriteria(bool $status=true): Criteria;

    /** Return the currently configured criteria */
     public function getCriteria() : array;

    /** Immediately run the passed in criteria and return results */
    public function getByCriteria(Criteria $criteria): array;

    /** Add some criteria to the set of criteria to be applied */
     public function pushCriteria() : array;

    /** Apply any pushed criteria */
     public function applyCriteria();
}
```

In this first listing we have a few required methods for implementations of the Criteria interface that include functionality to skip any pushed criteria for the current iteration, add one or more criteria objects to the stack, and add a helper method to immediately run the criteria passed into the getByCriteria() method and return the results (without dealing with the stack). There is also the method to run the entire stack of criteria at once (what has been pushed to the stack), applyCriteria. This nicely describes what it means to our application to be a Criteria-enabled object. Take note of the responsibilities.

Because we want to include a set of rich functionality to our criteria implementation and because we can't put anything inside the interface except for the methods and signatures, we can create an abstract class to house the common functionality across child classes. Instead of doing this in another set of classes (or traits) that would be required to be attached to the implementation of repository anyway, what we could do for the sake of conservation of class types is implement the Criteria interface inside the base repository class. It would then be a matter of creating a child class that extended this base repository for any such model we wanted to be able to query the data under that model via specifying Criteria. Before we do that, let's be sure to define an interface for a basic Repository class within our system. Just to be clear on what capabilities a standard repository should have in the general sense, we will create the interface as if we did not have Eloquent available to us on each and every instance of its Model class (this means we create the repository to house the way that the underlying model is queried). For the sake of brevity, I will omit the PHP docblock in the code in Listing 19-2.

Listing 19-2. A Description of a Repository Object Without the Functionality of Eloquentat Is Provided in All Models

```php
<?php

namespace Claim\Submission\Domain\Contracts;

interface Repository
{
    public function all(array $columns = ['*']);
    public function paginate(int $perpage=1, array $columns = ['*']);
    public function find(int $id, array $columns);
    public function findBy(string $field, $value, $columns=["*"]);
    public function findAllBy(string $field, $value, $columns=["*"]);
```

```php
    public function findWhere(string $where, columns=["*"]);
    public function findOrFail(int $id, $columns=["*"];
}
```

This interface is a little lengthy, but it does include all the basic needs regarding a model's data, including such functionality as creating, reading, updating, and deleting (CRUD). If we take the Eloquent ORM out of the equation, we are then left with the need to manage the model's data in a way that can be repeated easily and used anywhere it is needed throughout the rest of the codebase. That's exactly what the interface listed provides within the encapsulation of a repository class.

Also take notice of the way we defined these methods within the interface. It is done so in such a way that makes use of primitive values and doesn't include references to any other classes in the system. This is ideal, because having fewer dependencies equals fewer problems; however, it is not always a feasible solution. Sometimes things can exist only within the context of another defined class or interface and must be included in the new interface's definition. Strive to stick with primitive values as much as possible when defining interfaces, like we've done in Listing 19-3.

Listing 19-3. An Implementation of a Repository as Defined by the Repository and Criteria Interfaces

```php
<?php

namespace Claim\Submission\Domain\Repository;

use Claim\Submission\Domain\Contracts\Repository as
    RepositoryInterface;
use Claim\Submission\Domain\Contracts\CriteriaHandler;

use Illuminate\Http\Request;
use Illuminate\Support\Collection;
use Illuminate\Database\Eloquent\Model;
use Illuminate\Container\Container as App;
use Illuminate\Http\Exception\HttpResponseException;

abstract class BaseRepository implements RepositoryInterface,
                                        CriteriaHandler
{
```

```php
/** Specify the underlying model class */
abstract public function model(): Model;

/** Service Container */
private App $app;

/** The underlying model class name*/
protected string $model;

/** The current stack of criteria */
protected Collection $criteria;

/** Switch to skip criteria */
protected bool $skipCriteria = false;

/** Prevent overwriting same criteria in stack */
protected bool $preventCriteriaOverwriting = true;

public function __construct(App $app, Collection $collection)
{
    $this->app = $app;
    $this->criteria = $collection;
    $this->resetScope();
    $this->makeModel();
}
public function all(array $columns = ["*"])
{
    $this->applyCriteria();
    return $this->model->get($columns);
}

public function query()
{
    return $this->model;
}

public function find($id, $columns=["*"])
{
    $this->applyCriteria();
```

```php
        return $this->model->findOrFail($id, $columns);
    }

    public function findBy($attribute, $value, $columns=["*"])
    {
        $this->applyCriteria();
        return $this->model->where($attribute, '=',
            $value)->first($columns);
    }

    public function (Criteria $criteria)
    {
        $this->model = $criteria->apply($this->model, $this);
        return $this;
    }

    public function applyCriteria()
    {
        if ($this->skipCriteria === true) {
            return $this;
        }

        foreach ($this->getCriteria() as $criteria) {
            if ($criteria instanceof Criteria) {
                $this->model = $criteria->apply(
                    $this->model, $this);
            }
        }
        return $this;
    }
}
```

In Listing 19-3, we have a general implementation of the Repository and Criteria interfaces inside a single abstract class. Let's look at a quick visualization of the structure we've defined thus far by checking out Figure 19-11.

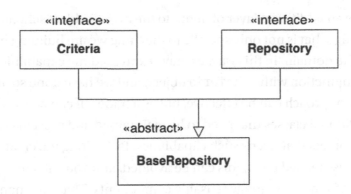

Figure 19-11. *UML of the current implementation*

Figure 19-11 describes a typical scenario of an abstract class implementing multiple contracts (interfaces). The class cannot be instantiated directly but is meant to be extended from in order for the child classes to come "stock" with a default set of functionality you provide in the abstract class. Now, depending on our needs at the time, we could have opted to separate concerns even further by implementing independent child classes for each interface, which would look like Figure 19-12.

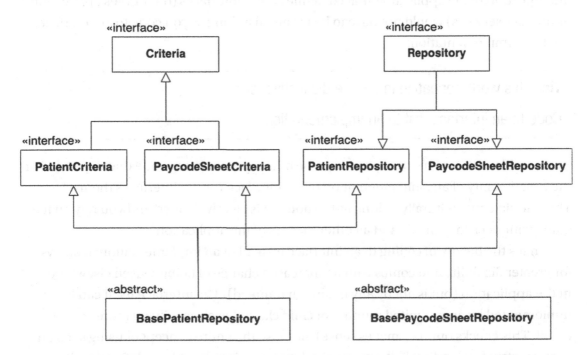

Figure 19-12. *A more sophisticated and flexible version of our Repository and Criteria interfaces*

We now have an additional layer of depth to the overall object schema because it captures knowledge that is not only specific to the thing we are building but, much more importantly, to the domain. In this way, we have expressed the capabilities of a repository when used in conjunction with a `Criteria` object, and we have done so at the level of the domain. This approach can be effective, but as a trade-off can cause a somewhat explosion of additional classes that need to be maintained and most likely replicated for each domain object that needs such capabilities. By limiting the creation of child classes to a strict as-needed basis, this can be avoided, and you can end up with a rich implementation of some potentially reusable components. That's the name of the game! DRY as much as possible, which goes right alongside the concept of reusable code and gets more powerful when you add such strict separation of concerns within the system. Assuming that these capabilities were actually needed for the application to do its job (and you or your team hasn't over-engineered it by defining such hyper-detailed, finely grained micro-objects), make sure that they dont end up a set of long-named interfaces and abstractions that doesn't truly convey the component as a whole or provide any sort of reason for its existence, which is its ability to solve the problem it aims to solve.

The change from Listings 19-1 to 19-2 in terms of code would be minimal, and any other portion of the application that consumes these interfaces (oftentimes application or domain services) would not have to be modified as long as you code to an interface, not to an implementation.

Tip It's worth repeating in a more distinctive form:

Code to an interface, not to an implementation.

To achieve this, you would properly type hint any consuming code that depended on the functionality of any implementation of the interfaces as the interfaces themselves. This should come naturally as long as the domain is clearly defined and you rely on it to guide your decisions in this and all other matters of the application.

That's the beauty of coding to an interface instead of an implementation: it allows for greater flexibility and comes with an increased chance of being reused elsewhere in the application (but is not by any means guaranteed). The interface itself can be implemented by an unlimited number of child classes, each specifying more granular detail. This checks out (i.e., makes sense), because the entire concept of using such an abstract structure and explicit separation of concerns is to be able to define specific instances (aka adapters) of an interface that describe the rules specific in the object's "schema" (if you will), which in turn is what we define inside the interfaces (aka ports). This gives us the ability to create objects in a general to specific way, with the granularity of the object encapsulated within the bounds of the implementing class.

One last thing to note about the diagrams is why they are separated the way they are. What elements go into the calculation that defines the conceptual lines and boundaries around the functionality embodied in the code, splitting it as such via namespaces and physical location within a filesystem?

Tip   The short answer is that when defining the lines separating the concerns of the application, always attempt to model them after the domain and group them by their rate of change. Objects that change at the same frequencies should be kept together.

If we attempt to keep things that change at different rates within the same class, module, or interface as other things that change at that rate, this will pay off later when we are modifying any portion of the component or its structure, because it will have little impact on the code that depends on it (if any at all).

Concluding Thoughts

Domain-driven design is a practical approach to solving modern-day business problems because it keeps the focus on the domain. In the web application world, frameworks are almost always used when the domain code gets to a certain level of complexity. This is for multiple reasons, including the benefit of not being forced to reinvent the wheel for every mechanism the application layer contains. By utilizing Laravel as a means of implementing a domain-driven design, we can craft an application that satisfies the requirements of the project as well as ensures the longevity of the life of our application. When we are keen on following best practices and modern standards in software development, we find that the maintenance of the application becomes simpler, as does refactoring. Extending the capabilities of the application can be achieved relatively easily and can come in the form of domain modules, which make it easy to encapsulate functional logic in terms of the domain itself (i.e., the `Order` module, `Ship` module, etc., from our warehouse application at the start of the chapter).

Keep reading. Keep coding. Keep thinking. Keep it together. Knowledge is power, and lack thereof is ignorance. Don't be the latter.

Index

A

Aggregates
  business invariants, 484
  definition, 483
  design and implementation, 484
  event sourcing, 496
  factories/aggregates (*see* Factories/
    aggregates)
  invariants, 484
  order model
    additional code, 493–495
    addOrderLine() method, 489
    client code, 493
    invariant protection, 490
    online e-commerce order, 485
    OrderLine model, 486, 488
    startCheckout() method, 492
  repositories
    blog application, 466
    ClaimRepository, 464
    Eloquent methods, 465
    Eloquent representation, 468
    features, 468
    operations, 465
    scopes, 466
    web and nonweb applications, 467
  smaller aggregates, 484
Anti-corruption layer(ACL), 47
app/Providers/RouteServiceProvider.php
    file, 268–272

B

boot() method, 163, 165, 167, 168
Bounded context identification, 393
  entities, 394
  identity and group context, 395
  role concept, 398
  roles object, 399–401
  updated group entity, 402
  user entity, 396–398
Broken window theory, 36

C

Claim processing system
  building blocks, 194
  concepts, 193
  core concepts (tools), 195
  development efforts, 193
  domains, subdomains/bounded
    contexts
    abstract core definition, 211
    AUTH bounded context, 207, 208
    central entity, 210
    central forces, 209
    CLAIM SUBMIT and AUTH, 205
    core domains, 204, 206, 207
    feature requirements, 210
    Medi-Cal domain model, 211, 213
    modules, 214–216
    organization/structure, 214

605

F, G

T, U

V

W, X, Y, Z

Printed in the United States
By Bookmasters